America

A Repair Manual

How to End
Special Interest
Corruption

Roo Davison

clear light
press

Clear Light Press
Frankfort, Michigan

Published by:

Clear Light Press
P.O. Box 1087
Frankfort MI 49635

1st edition 2023

Cataloging Information

Library of Congress Control Number: 2020932387
ISBN (Paperback): 978-1931268004
ISBN (Kindle): 978-1931268059

Davison, Roo
     America: A Repair Manual / Roo Davison —1st ed.
     Includes bibliographical references.

Cover Design: Meredith McNabb
instagram.com/meredithmcnabb_design/

.

To Ellie

Table of Contents

Preface

Well, we are in a mess, aren't we? The last few years have seen a global pandemic, economic shutdowns, soaring unemployment, and (at the same time) staff shortages in many businesses. There have been protests over racial justice, riots, looting, and curfews. Supply chain problems continue post-pandemic. Inflation has ramped up. Free speech, abortions, and trans-rights are hot topics.

Beyond these immediate problems, the US has longer-term issues with immigration, offshoring, and financial booms and busts. Long-term inflation plagues education and medicine. Innovation is slowing, government debt keeps climbing with no end in sight.

Politically, there's endless campaigning to fix an ever-expanding roster of issues, accompanied by pushback, political fighting, and extremism—much of it conducted through personal attacks and cancel culture.

How did our country come to this? What's causing so much discord? How can we get out of this mess?

For me, trying to understand what's going on began when I moved to the United States. I was born and raised in the UK. I studied engineering and computer science at university. After graduating, I lived and worked in London, writing software.

In 1996 I met my wife who, at the time, was living in Atlanta, GA. We transatlantic-dated for a couple of years. Then, in 1998, I moved to the US, and we got married.

Until I met my wife, I had no interest in moving to the US and I was relatively ignorant about how things worked here. However, upon arriving, I found myself in an alien environment. I faced new practicalities: banks, real estate, and driving on the right. I had to navigate a new bureaucracy: immigration, the IRS, and Social Security. I wanted to understand a new political system: the Constitution, federalism, democrats, republicans.

Driven by the newness of it all, I was motivated to understand my new country, and I set off on a long journey of informal study. Over the last 25 years, I've learned a lot about law, politics, and economics. However, as my studies proceeded, I started to notice a recurring theme: a difference between the *Idea of America* and *America in Practice*.

Around the world, America markets itself—successfully—as the Land of the Free. The ideals of freedom and individual liberty are compelling; something I want to be a part of. I became a citizen in 2009.

However, America in practice is as bogged down in bureaucracy and regulation as anywhere in Europe. In many ways, the US is worse. Local governments are active. American bureaucrats are efficient. And the police are armed.

The more I investigated, the more I came to see a disconnect between the vision laid out in the Constitution and how the US has evolved in practice. The entire system has become corrupted. America has lost its way. This book is my attempt to map a path back to the American dream.

As someone born in a foreign country, I'll admit to a degree of hubris offering a repair for American politics. What could I possibly bring to the table that home-grown experts in political science could not do better?

It's a fair question. However, I believe my apparent weaknesses are in fact my strengths.

Firstly, as a newcomer, I don't necessarily share assumptions with my American friends or accept "that's just how it is." I've had to consciously learn for myself about America, about the political and legal system. I'm willing to question anything and everything about how it all works.

Secondly, I have lived in the UK under a different political system. I can compare and contrast the two regimes. I can ask why they do things differently and what might be the pros and cons of each system.

Finally, I have no allegiance to any political party. I have no family history with US politics. I have no long-held opinions about controversial issues in American politics.

Instead, I have the mindset of an engineer. I tend to think about things from a systems perspective. I am curious about the forces at play and how they affect outcomes. Applied to our country, that mindset translates into thinking about the Constitution and the design of the legal system. The forces at play are the economic and political incentives that drive political actors.

I do share one thing though with many of my fellow Americans. I have come to loathe politics!

I am tired of endless campaigning. I've had enough of politicians, administrators, and activists telling me what's best for me, what I should think, and what I should value. Most of all, I am fed up with other people's opinions being cast into law and forced upon me.

The ideas in *America: A Repair Manual* are designed to move us firmly in the direction of less government, less politics, and less meddling in our day-to-day lives. Let me find my own way to life, liberty, and the pursuit of happiness. I would like to be left in peace to live my life as I see fit.

Introduction—A Nation in Crisis?

This book is about how to fix the political system in the United States of America.

The sky is not falling. The world is not about to end. Things for us humans are steadily improving by most measures. People are getting richer and living longer, healthier, more comfortable lives. The world is steadily turning middle class.[1] Levels of almost every pollutant have been falling for decades.[2] Worldwide, forest cover has increased by about 7% since 1982.[3] After hundreds of years of humans depleting mother nature's resources, we collectively turned a corner in the last few years and are now starting to use less—not just less per capita, but less overall.[4]

Notwithstanding post-Covid problems, the US is hugely wealthy by historical standards.[5] Stuff is cheaper and more available. Racism, sexism, and other "isms" are steadily declining.[6] And the middle class is indeed shrinking, but mostly because people are moving into the upper middle class.[7]

However, good news is not the message broadcast by the media, politicians, or popular culture. You're more likely to hear that the world is about to end in a new and horrible way. In the last 50 years, life on Earth has nearly ended many times due to pesticides, nuclear wars, toxic chemicals, overpopulation, and mass starvation. Humans have narrowly missed extinction from HIV, Ebola, and Corona. We're encouraged to worry about deforestation, water shortages, and global warming. Economic disaster is always imminent due to running out of oil, offshoring, or AI.

In the US, dozens of issues have plagued us in the last few decades: jobs, healthcare costs, financial meltdowns, housing booms and busts, recessions, trade tariffs, ongoing wars, and immigration. Our universities may be declining,[8] and free speech may be at risk.[9] Economic fallout continues from the Coronavirus pandemic. Racism and police violence have recently come to the forefront of cultural battles.

Politically, congressional approval ratings hit an all-time low of 9% in November 2013[10] and have rarely risen out of the teens in the last decade. Politics are bitter and divisive. Personal attacks have reached new levels of nastiness. Candidates and their platforms become more extreme with each election cycle, especially in presidential elections. The political system is stuck—perhaps even broken. It's reached the point of rioting, culminating (so far) in the Capitol riots of January 2021. A OnePoll survey found that 78% of respondents identified politics as the primary source of stress and anxiety in their lives.[11]

One way to make sense of these contradictory messages is that the US is experiencing two broad, long-term trends: technological improvement, accompanied by political decline.

The trend in technological improvement—innovation and advancing scientific knowledge—has been in place for about 250 years since the start of the Industrial Revolution. Innovation creates new products and services. Free trade spreads them around the world. This has produced today's incredibly wealthy world.

The start of the political decline is subjective, but for the purposes of this book can be dated from the Civil War onwards. The Civil War marked a definitive assertion of federal power over the states. This began breaking down the checks and balances that the Founders had designed into the legal system.

Fast forward 150 years, and the political decline is clear from the sheer size of government—far beyond anything the Founders would have recognized as limited government—as well as the level of public discord. Arguments abound, and scapegoats can be found everywhere: the Left, the Right, voters, non-voters, illegals, Wall Street, the unions, the corporations, terrorists, religious extremists, atheists, capitalism, socialism, the United Nations, the WEF, the 1%, Trump, Biden, Congress, misogynist white guys, the NSA, the NRA. Add your most hated group to the list, whoever they are.

Technological advancement and politics are related in that innovation requires a political climate favoring individual freedom and free trade to flourish. However, the political decline in the US has reached a point where it is interfering with technological improvement. There's too much government. It's hindering progress, draining resources, and increasing social unrest. To revitalize innovation and economic growth, we need solutions to free us from political turmoil.

To fix the problems our country faces, it's important to start by correctly identifying the causes of the problems. However, finding causes is problematic, prompting endless debate. The arguments often sink into well-worn cliché solutions from left and right, spiced with personal insults about how your political opponents are crazy, evil people, denying obvious causes and impeding obvious solutions.

These opinionated arguments have little to do with the real issues. Despite the number, complexity, and diversity of the problems facing us, there's an underlying theme to most of our problems. Albeit a theme with so many facets and disguises that it appears as multiple unrelated issues. That theme is *special interest manipulation.*

Peel back the surface of almost any societal problem, and someone, somewhere, is making a profit and is incentivized to maintain the problem or non-solutions. They do this by hijacking and corrupting government power to give themselves legal advantages over the rest of us.

The entire US political system has become corrupted by special interests. This is a long-term trend that goes back almost to the founding of America. It has ramped up in the last 150 years and grown like crazy since

WWII. It is an accelerating rot in the political fabric of our country. Left unchecked, there's a risk the system could collapse.

Since this is a systemic flaw in our system of government, it requires a systemic solution. *America: A Repair Manual* offers such a solution, a reset to reduce the influence of special interests and to repair the damage they have caused to our country.

How This Book is Organized

America: A Repair Manual is divided into three parts.

Part 1—The Problem is an overview of our political situation: what's gone wrong, why it's gone wrong, and why it can't continue. This section will define special interests, what manipulation is, and how manipulation corrupts our country.

Wrong, as used here, means *departed from the ideal.* In the US, those ideals are mostly defined in the Constitution. This section will therefore contrast the state of the nation with the Founders' intentions. In particular, their understanding of the correct role of government.

Part 2—A Bill of Protections lays out a set of proposed constitutional amendments to fix our problems and move things back towards an ideal system of government, a government that performs correctly.

I call this a **Bill of Protections** because, in the Founders' vision of America, citizens already have all the rights they need. Instead, citizens need protection from the government taking away those rights.

The *Bill of Protections* details exactly what the bill should say: the actual text of each proposal. It's important to be specific because the devil, aka special interest manipulation, is hidden in the details.

Part 3— Implementation looks at some issues involved in getting changes made. I won't describe the legal process of changing the Constitution; that information can be found elsewhere. Nor will I lay out a detailed political plan of action as I don't have the expertise! However, I will discuss some possible first steps. I will also discuss the *transition problem*: how changes can be made with minimum disruption.

Government and Politics

This book focuses on repairing our system of government. Words like *government* and *politics* will appear often. Unless otherwise specified, you should understand these words in their broadest, most generic sense. *Government* means every government (federal, state, local), every agency, all representatives, employees, and contractors. *Politics* means how governments are organized, the legal framework of our country, how laws come into being, how they are enforced, and the political economy—the incentives acting on everyone involved in and around government.

Another word that will appear often is *we*. *We* is a problematic word when discussing politics, because there is no *we* in many contexts, especially when it comes to collective agreements. Unfortunately, avoiding all use of *we* makes for some remarkably clunky prose. So, I've settled for using *we* as sparingly as I can. And where I do use it, I don't mean to imply that we all agree ... because we often don't!

Although the focus here is politics, politics is not everything or even the most important thing. Problems can be viewed through philosophical, sociological, economic, religious, technological, historical, or other lenses.[12]

All that said, politics is important. In fact, *politics has become too important in contemporary society*. The political/legal system acts as a kind of operating system for society. If your operating system is corrupted your computer will run badly. You'll spend your time fighting the computer instead of getting work done.

Similarly, in today's America, politics has become so intrusive in our everyday affairs that it's getting in the way of the good life. It's time to upgrade our politics!

A Note to Non-American Readers

This book is about how to fix politics in the USA. I have little knowledge of how things are done in other countries (except for the UK).

However, governments and special interests face similar incentives in every country. Manipulation is therefore likely to be a universal problem, even though the specific forms it takes will vary widely.

The issues discussed in this book will apply to other countries as much as they do to the US. The solutions I propose apply specifically to the US since they involve repairing the US Constitution, and there will of course be cultural differences between the US and your country. Nonetheless, the principles behind the proposals are likely to be helpful for citizens of any country.

If you agree that special interest manipulation is a problem in your country, and if you agree that individual liberty is a vital contributor to both individual and collective thriving, then you will find much of value in *America: A Repair Manual*.

I wish you success in adapting the ideas here and finding ways to improve your country as much as I would like to improve the US.

Part 1—The Problem

Things fall apart; the centre cannot hold;
Mere anarchy is loosed upon the world,
The blood-dimmed tide is loosed, and everywhere
The ceremony of innocence is drowned;
The best lack all conviction, while the worst
Are full of passionate intensity.

—William Butler Yates, The Second Coming

Chapter 1—Special Interest Manipulation

Politics n. A strife of interests masquerading as a contest of principles. The conduct of public affairs for private advantage.
—Ambrose Bierce, The Devils Dictionary

A *special interest* is any person or group with an agenda they are trying to achieve. Corporations want to make money, unions want to help their members, charities want to help their beneficiaries, churches want to promote their religion, politicians want to get elected, pressure groups want to achieve their goals, and bureaucrats want to keep their jobs. Every individual, and every group, is a special interest.

Being a special interest per se is not a problem. Special interests only become a problem when they engage in manipulation. *Manipulation*, as used here, means *to harness government power to benefit one group at the expense of others.* It means using government power to give someone *a legal advantage* over other citizens.

Every instance of manipulation is a subversion of government's fundamental role—promoting liberty and *legal* equality for all. Each manipulation also builds upon the earlier ones to create ongoing negative feedback loops encouraging further manipulation. In overview, the process looks like this:

1. Special interests manipulate the government to give them a legal advantage at the expense of others.

2. Successful manipulation incentivizes more manipulation and growth in government.

3. More government creates an increased dependency on government, incentivizing calls for yet more government.

4. Economic manipulation creates a long-term drag on the economy, slows innovation, and incentivizes monopolies.

5. Economic problems slowly become moral problems and psychological problems.

6. Individual legal freedoms decline as government power and interference in civil life increase.

7. Attempting to solve problems with politics rather than innovation incentivizes political conflict. Arguments spring up whenever private decisions become public decisions.

8. Each fix to the problems created by manipulation is yet more manipulation, and the cycle repeats, ad nauseum. Things steadily get worse.

The Manipulation Process

The process begins with an individual special interest manipulating the government. Typically, that involves getting legislation or regulations written benefiting that group at the expense of everyone else. Over the years, dozens of variations of manipulation have evolved.

Manipulation includes tax breaks, welfare benefits, cheap loans, rent assistance, subsidies, and occupational licenses. Manipulation includes environmental regulations, quality standards, zoning and land use regulations, labeling requirements, bans or restrictions on sales of some items, and tariffs. And hundreds of variations on these themes.

Economic gain (profit, shutting out competition) motivates most manipulation. However, sometimes manipulation is done for moral reasons (prohibition, bans on homosexuality).

Every manipulation has both public (stated) and private (hidden) motivations, a phenomenon known as *Bootleggers and Baptists*.[1] Pre-prohibition, Baptists campaigned to ban Sunday alcohol sales because of the evils of alcohol. Behind the scenes, Bootleggers supported the bans because they made bigger profits selling illegal alcohol. Politicians publicly took the moral high ground with the Baptists and privately took payoffs from the Bootleggers. Everyone won—except the public.

There always have been and always will be special interests. Long before our country was born, Barons, Merchant Guilds, and Churches were all seeking influence. All special interests face incentives to harness government power to achieve their ends. The Founders were aware of the dangers of special interests—known as *factions* in the language of their day. They designed the Constitution to minimize those dangers.

However, the Founders also made changing the Constitution difficult, while special interests have been working to subvert it from the moment it was adopted. As a result, manipulation has grown steadily over the last 150 years and has accelerated strongly in the last 70.

Manipulation Breeds Manipulation

Whenever a special interest succeeds at manipulation, the incentives increase for further manipulation:

- Successful interests want to maintain and strengthen their position.
- Competitors want to reverse the manipulation or engage in their own manipulation, so they also benefit.
- Unrelated parties see how manipulation has worked for others, so they also try.
- Government employees get jobs, benefits, and increased power whenever their agency gets new things to regulate.

- Politicians get payoffs from special interests and are reelected for "doing something" about problems, even if nothing needs doing.

Each successful manipulation also makes the next one easier:

- Many citizens benefit from and support manipulation in their favor.
- Increased complexity makes it easier to create and hide loopholes.
- Manipulation gets easier to sell. It's seen as necessary, normal, and eventually even desirable to micro-manage everything.
- Moral objections decrease: if you did it for them, why shouldn't you do it for us?
- As constitutional checks and balances erode, it gets easier to pervert the legal system.

After decades of manipulation, the incentives are now so strong that even those who don't want to be involved are forced to get on board. Join in, else your competitors, or the government itself, will shut you down.[2]

Manipulation Means More Government

Different parts of our governments are also special interests. Politicians favor solving problems with legislation because they are elected to legislate. Government agencies favor action by their agency because that is their purpose. Individual government employees are in favor of their jobs.

Any politician or government employee may agree that "there's too much government," but they will still favor their little bit of government. They are paid to favor it, and they will support policies that enhance it.

The more government meddles, the more citizens are forced to engage with it. We're forced to ask permission (permits, licenses), get inspected, meet standards, sign disclosures, and provide information. Government meddling creates forced dependency on government, resulting in more calls for government action to fix problems, and so on.

Government adds to the dependency with anti-competitive behavior. It regulates businesses to reduce competition (licensing). It gives itself legal monopolies (the USPS, the lottery, and water providers). It offers free or subsidized services (education, housing), discouraging market or charitable solutions. It even pays some people (welfare benefits, tax breaks) who then come to feel they need the government.

Regulations create further dependency due to their sheer volume and complexity. We need experts to help us navigate the bureaucracy: lawyers, accountants, tax specialists, engineers, architects, and other professionals. Those professionals are motivated to keep the system complex.

As government gets ever bigger, its tentacles reach further into our lives, and the manipulation grows.

Consequences of Manipulation

The first victim of manipulation is economic growth. Trade, competition, and innovation are all inhibited by import bans, tariffs, permits, occupational licenses, and regulations.

Absent coercion, any time two people agree on a deal, they do it because both gain something. Therefore, each voluntary trade produces a net gain, a slight increase in wealth. Public policy should therefore encourage dealmaking to maximize economic growth, raising the standard of living for everyone.

Instead, regulation causes pervasive interference in free trade and a long-term drag on growth. Any individual rule may have only a tiny effect, but the cumulative impact is enormous. If, for example, regulation had stayed at the same levels as in 1949, then GDP in 2011 would have reached $53.9 trillion instead of $15.1 trillion.[3] In other words, we'd be 3-4 times richer today if the government had not imposed those regulations.

Think about a version of the US where everyone has three times their current income and has had it their entire lives. Even poor people would be three times richer—able to afford more health care, safety, and environmental protection. We'd all have much greater resilience in an emergency, be it a terrorist attack, a financial crash, or a pandemic.

Eliminating Competition Enables Misconduct

As well as promoting economic growth, public policy should also try to minimize misconduct: theft, fraud, pollution, dangerous products, unsafe workplaces, exploitation of workers, discrimination, and so on.

Regulation is one way to curb these excesses. But in practice, regulation is often manipulated to keep competition down. When that happens, regulation now protects misconduct instead of reducing it. A company with a legal monopoly *legally* exploits customers.

Public policy should instead encourage a free market because competition incentivizes honesty. If a company over-charges, competitors can profit by offering a cheaper product. Safe products will out-compete dangerous ones. Workers will have a greater choice of job offers.

Customers also want value for money, safe products, and to feel good about the companies they do business with. They are incentivized to buy cheaper safer stuff from reputable companies.

Competition thus incentivizes both producers and customers towards better, safer products and improved working conditions. Competition increases good behavior by everyone in the marketplace.

When government curbs competition to "protect customers," it has the opposite effect: it enables exploitation. Publicity about exploitation then leads to calls for increased protection, resulting in more regulation and even less competition. Whenever competition is curbed, special interest incentives push things to get steadily worse.

Economic Problems Become Moral Problems

Manipulation starts as a legal strategy that creates economic problems. Then, over time, it becomes a moral problem. Manipulation creates moral hazards.[4] *Moral hazards* are situations involving malincentives or conflicts of interest—situations where you want people to do the right thing but where you are effectively paying them to do the wrong thing. *If you keep paying people to do the wrong thing, the wrong thing eventually seems like the right thing or even a "right."*

Moral hazards also include situations where the government wants one thing and citizens want another, or where short-term government actions (lockdowns) conflict with foundational principles (freedom of movement).

Another moral issue is that manipulation encourages selfishness. If everyone else is getting theirs, why shouldn't you get yours? This thinking permeates society from the top (Wall Street bailouts) to the bottom (welfare benefits) and everyone in between (tax breaks for my peeps, licensing to protect our jobs, zoning to keep out businesses we don't like).

When manipulation addresses moral issues (drugs, kinky sex, hate speech), there's a different problem: regulation encourages moral apathy and negligence. Fundamentally, y*ou cannot make people moral by legislation.* True ethical behavior emerges when individuals actively and consciously decide on the best thing to do. Government diktats about right and wrong short-circuit the self-questioning necessary for moral maturity.

Big Government Encourages Dependency

As well as encouraging moral rot, government intervention also creates psychological dependency. Regulations, for example, are premised on "We know what's best for you" and "We'll keep you safe."

If you keep telling adults they need other (wiser?) adults to look after them, then over the long term, you create infantile and narcissistic adults. Citizens gradually adopt a victim mentality and campaign for others to fix problems instead of taking responsibility for themselves. Everyone feels they are a special case, and that society owes them something. They feel justified in making demands and claiming rights.

Manipulation Fuels Anger

As government and special interests get stronger, citizens get weaker. People sense an ongoing loss of freedom, which fuels anger in political debates. Yet it's often difficult to articulate precisely why people are so angry. Each rule change may be reasonable, judged on its own merits, and getting angry seems irrational. In reality, it is the cumulative effect of thousands of restrictions introduced over decades that fuels the anger.

Eventually, a threshold is crossed. One new rule becomes, for someone, one too many. It's not necessarily that the rule itself is problematic (though it may be), it's just the one that tips the scales. Finally, someone reaches a point of "I've had enough, no more." Anger becomes arguments, becomes law-breaking, and eventually, violence.

Additionally, when the causes are nebulous, people can be persuaded to vent their anger at easy-to-blame but incorrect sources of their problems: immigrants, foreign trade, terrorists, the 1%, the corporations, the unions, the Russians, the President. Or anyone politicians want to blame.

The confusion of morals and laws often creates resentment, as in "Who are you to tell me what to do." The police are supposed to *protect and serve*. Instead, they are often *moral enforcers*—enforcing moral positions that many citizens disagree with. Police violence may be the proximate cause of 2020's riots—the spark—but there was plenty of built-up resentment acting as fuel.

Polarization Is Encouraged

Manipulation incentivizes polarization: left vs. right, rich vs. poor, black vs. white, rural vs. urban, men vs. women, straight vs. gay, and government vs. citizen. The best way to get ahead is to be part of a special interest group and fight for your cause *at the expense of* everyone else.

The political fighting has become increasingly vicious as the stakes have grown higher. Citizens are incentivized to ask politicians to solve their problems for them. Politicians are incentivized to promise they can.

Just watch presidential candidates on the campaign trail. At every stop, they explain how they will help the folks there: inner-city poor, laid-off rust belt workers, farmers, miners, or fishermen. This rhetoric is so common, this thinking so ingrained in the zeitgeist, that we rarely stop to consider that politicians are campaigning to create legal inequality. They are offering political help for some *at the expense of everyone else.* Our politicians are deliberately creating and marketing divisions. Is it any wonder society feels so divided?

Behind the scenes, corporations, unions, charities, and other pressure groups are all donating money, buying favors, and getting rules written to help them or take down rivals. Again, this increases polarization.

Manipulation further encourages arguments by pushing private decisions into the public domain. When private choices become public, or if citizens are paying for private choices through their taxes, then everyone starts to feel entitled to have a say. So we end up arguing, publicly, about contraception costs under Obamacare, school curriculums, zoning, and many other issues.

Things Don't Get Fixed

Another source of frustration is that government is ineffective at solving problems. Government can never be an effective problem solver because the incentives work against it:

- There's no consensus on what the problems are, let alone solutions. When a government defines both, many citizens disagree.

- At the extreme, government policy creates civil war. The War on Drugs, for example, is a real war taking place in the US, with armed forces fighting each other, and real people dying.

- We will never collectively agree on some issues, such as abortion, or gun control. Unless compromises are found, there will be political arguments forever.

- Government solutions typically prioritize special interest benefits rather than solving problems.

- Regulation (you must do it this way) cuts off innovation (let's find a better way to do this).

- Government solutions are imposed by force, and persist for a long time, regardless of how badly they fail.

There is No Conspiracy

Special interest manipulation is not a grand conspiracy. It is not the fault of the corporations or the unions. It is not the 1%, not Wall Street, not the NRA, not the NSA. It is not the Democrats or the Republicans. No cabal of bankers, no secret society of powerful men, and no group of foreign interests are conspiring to bring America down.

Rather, manipulation is an evolved and evolving political economy. Thousands of individual special interests, large and small, each with their own selfish motivations, are competing to manipulate governments and gain legal advantage. The result is like a swarm of termites nibbling away at the legal foundations of our country.

Of course, some termites are much more powerful and greedy than others. Nonetheless, no evil mastermind is pulling strings behind the scenes to achieve some master plan. There are just thousands of hungry termites. They will keep nibbling, one bite at a time, until the whole structure collapses.

Pointing the finger at specific politicians, parties, policies, or special interests won't solve anything. *They are all doing it.* We are seeing the death of America by a thousand cuts, administered by thousands of petty selfish manipulations.

The US has been heading in this direction for the last 150 years, accelerating strongly since WWII. The incentives point to ever more manipulation and government action to correct problems. Every correction makes things worse because the solution is yet another manipulation.

Politicians and political activists have little incentive to support fundamental changes. All activists want to control aspects of moral behavior or the economy, and all control means more government. Once a bureaucracy is in place, it becomes yet another special interest fighting for advantage. Politicians give lip service to repealing the other side's programs, but rarely act on it because of bureaucratic resistance. Meanwhile, both sides actively pursue implementing their programs when in power. Government keeps growing no matter who is in power.

Our governments were designed as a system of checks and balances, but these have gradually been eroded. Over the last 150 years, power has shifted from the states to the feds and from Congress to the President. The courts have steadily allowed increasing breaches of the Constitution in deference to legislative and executive privilege. Administrative law, largely unsupervised by the courts or by Congress, has gradually come to dominate our interactions with the government.

Politically, Republicans and Democrats no longer balance each other out or seek compromise. Both parties are in hock to special interests, though they often favor different special interests. Seen from the perspective of special interest manipulation as the dominant force in politics, there is no significant difference between Trump and Biden: they just have different friends.

Creeping corruption of the political system has reached a point where government spends most of its time tilting the playing field in favor of one special interest or another. Whoever controls the government controls how the field is tilted. As the stakes get higher, the political in-fighting gets more intense.

It's as if there were two rival mafia gangs, fighting for turf. Sometimes the Reds have the upper hand, sometimes the Blues. But for average citizens little changes. Either way, the mafia are in charge.

Manipulation has been going on for decades, with no end in sight. The incentives continue to point in the direction of more manipulation, causing more fighting, increased polarization, and anger. Something fundamental needs to change.

If special interest termites are eating our house, then we need to get the exterminator in before the house collapses around our ears. We need to repair the framework of our country—the constitution.

Chapter 2—Unsustainable Trends

A small leak will sink a great ship.

—Benjamin Franklin

Special interest manipulation is not new. There always have been and always will be special interests trying to achieve their goals by manipulating the legal system. Given the ubiquity of special interests, you could argue that manipulation is business as usual and nothing to worry about. This would be a mistake.

Firstly, manipulation should be curbed because it is morally wrong. Economic manipulation is legalized theft. Moral manipulation is legalized bullying. Claiming that manipulation benefits the public is fraud. And the more manipulation succeeds, the more public morality is undermined.

Secondly, manipulation should be curbed because it goes against everything that the US stands for: freedom, individual rights, equality before the law, and limited government.

Thirdly, pragmatically, manipulation needs to be curbed because there's a real risk of a threshold event—reaching a point where a systemic collapse occurs. To use Franklin's example, a leaky ship may float for a long time, but eventually, it will sink. Once it starts sinking, it's too late to fix the leak.

For the US, a systemic collapse would probably start with economic breakdown (hyperinflation). Economic chaos could easily lead to civil unrest, perhaps even civil war. I hope this never happens, but countries and empires have risen and fallen throughout history. It would be hubris to think the US is immune from the forces of history.

It's impossible to predict if or when there might be a threshold event. However, looking at the bigger picture, many trends encouraged by government policy in recent decades cannot continue, no matter how popular they are. Something *must* change.

Examples of some important trends are illustrated below. Most of them have been in existence since 1900, or longer. However, to keep things on a human scale I have graphed the data from 1950 and projected another 50 years into the future— the lifetimes of most readers. (See Appendix 1 for a fuller discussion of data sources and assumptions).

These graphs are simply illustrations of the data—historical numbers from a spreadsheet, displayed as a basic chart. I am not making predictions, but if nothing changes things will continue in the same direction.

Note that the economic fallout from the response to the Coronavirus will cause blips on most of these graphs when the data is fully available. Nonetheless, the overall trends are unlikely to be affected, other than being accelerated in the wrong direction.

Government Spending

In 1900 total US government spending (federal, state, and local) was about $37 billion. In 1950 it was about $537 billion. By 2017 it reached $6.45 trillion. (All figures throughout the book are in constant, inflation-adjusted, 2012 dollars).

These numbers are so big that they are practically meaningless. No one can imagine spending $200,000,000,000,000 (200 trillion). So, to understand them better, let's recalculate them as dollars per citizen. In 1900 government spending was $487/citizen. In 1950 it was $3,549/citizen. By 2017 it reached $19,840/citizen. The trend in $/citizens, projecting both population growth and government spending growth, is shown in Figure 1.

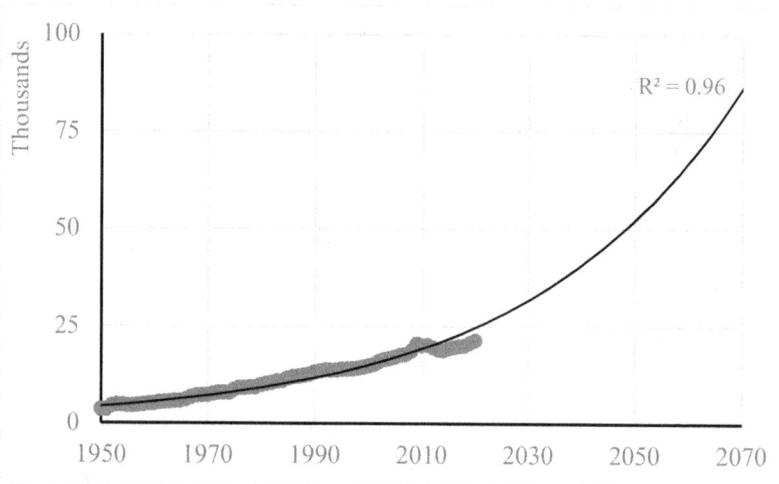

Figure 1—Government Spending Per Citizen

If the trend continues, by 2050 government spending will be about $65,000/citizen, and by 2100 it will exceed $342,000/citizen in inflation-adjusted dollars. Consider:

- Do you get $19,840 worth of government services each year?
- Is your family paying $19,840/year in taxes per person? If not, where is the money coming from?
- Is this a trend that can continue?

This trend is unchanged in any recent administration. Spending and debt reached new records under both Trump and Biden. The only differences between Republicans and Democrats are the excuses for overspending.

Government's Share of the Economy

Another way to look at government spending is as a proportion of the economy. In 1900 spending was about 8% of the Gross Domestic Product (GDP). In 1950 it was 24%. By 2017 it had grown to about 36%. Figure 2 shows the trend (extrapolating both GDP and spending).

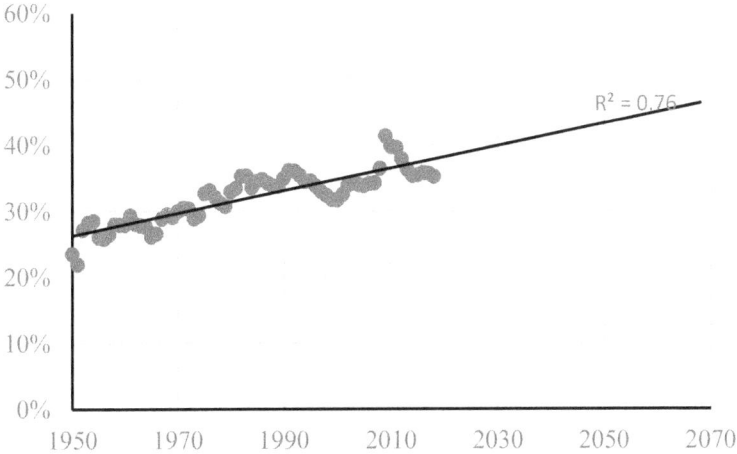

Figure 2—Government Spending as a Percentage of GDP

If the trend continues, government spending will consume an ever-greater proportion of the economy. It will be about 42% of GDP by 2050, 52% by 2100, and approaching 100% by around 2180.

Imagine a world where all spending is government spending. A world where every business is owned, staffed, and run by government employees, one of whom will be you! A world where government standards of efficiency, responsiveness, and customer service are seen everywhere.

You don't even have to imagine that world: Soviet Russia, Maoist China, and North Korea are recent examples. These countries are not appealing visions for the future of the US.

Government Debt

Government spends more than it collects in taxes. With rare exceptions, it has done so consistently over the last century. To cover the shortfall, it borrows or engages in creative bookkeeping. As a result, debt is hidden in multiple categories at federal, state, and local levels. The following figures are estimates.

In 1900 total government debt was about $93 billion. By 1950 it was about $2.1 trillion, and by 2018 around $21.5 trillion. If those trends continue, debt will be $68 trillion by 2050 and $494 trillion by 2100.

Expressed as debt/citizen.: in 1900 debt was about $1,222/citizen. By 1950 it was $14,000/citizen, and by 2017 it reached $66,000/citizen. If those trends continue, debt will be about $176,000/citizen by 2050, and $1.1 million/citizen by 2100. The trend is shown in Figure 3.

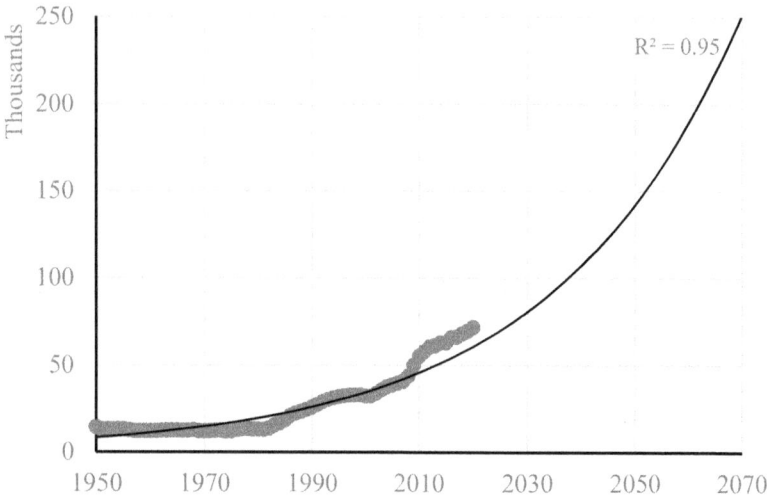

Figure 3—Government Debt Per Citizen

Consider some implications of the trend:

- If the government needed money from citizens to repay its debts, do you currently have $66,000 spare for you and for each member of your family to repay those debts?
- Are you a parent? Each of your children today owes about $66,000, and by 2050 will owe about $176,000. How do you feel about saddling your children with that debt?
- Is this a trend that can continue?

Bailouts

Governments have long tried to save us from economic problems. In the modern era, they have done this by pouring money into the system, starting with the Penn Central Railroad bailout in 1970 to the tune of $3.4 billion, and increasing over time. The 2008 bailouts peaked at about $1.76 trillion.[1]

The trend is shown in Figure 4, which plots spending for each bailout that hits a new peak. The resulting trend is an exponential curve so steep that beyond 2010 the full graph would be several pages high. For 2020, the graph would have predicted a crisis might require a bailout of $15 trillion, or about 2/3 of GDP.

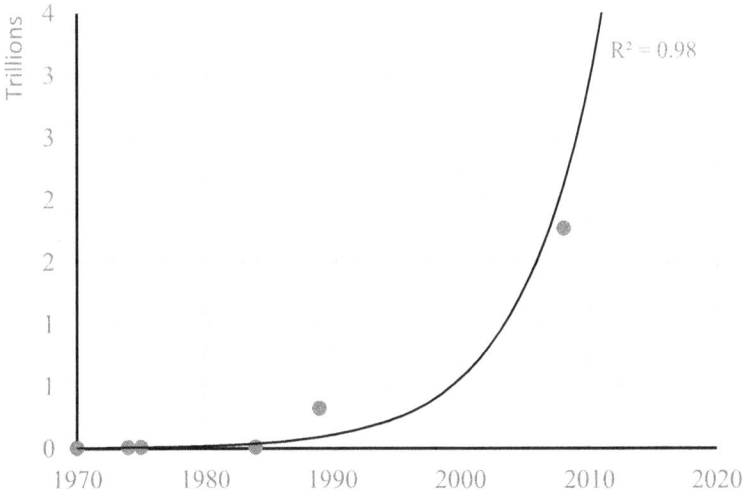

Figure 4—Peak Government Bailout Costs pre-2020

As this book was being published, our country is just coming out of the next crisis bailout—the pandemic. As of Feb 2023, federal spending so far was about $4.6 trillion.[2] This total is likely inaccurate, not yet finalized, and does not include state spending. Even so, this is already about 25% of GDP! And, as usual, the distribution of those funds has been a frenzy of special interest payoffs.[3]

The economic hit of the virus will be much larger than just government borrowing. Estimated costs are already about $16 trillion,[4] in bailouts, continuing economic drag, healthcare issues etc. That number is close to the $15 trillion predicted by Figure 4.

In essence, this damage has been caused by politicians taking a medical problem and turning it into an economic problem, which they then in turn try to solve by spending borrowed money. Yet the feds never pay down debt between emergencies, so each emergency makes us more vulnerable. The US economy cannot take many more emergencies like this!

Bailouts should end because they are an expensive special interest payout. They also subsidize errors made by corporations. If a corporation has taken on too much risk or debt, or otherwise misread the market, then they should fail. If they don't fail, what's to stop the directors who made poor decisions from making them again in the future? It is removing the error part of "trial and error," destroying learning, and creating longer-term economic problems.

Growth of Regulation

Aside from direct costs, governments cost us money in other ways, of which regulation is probably the most expensive. Regulation has direct costs (administrative agencies and employees), but much bigger than that are compliance costs, opportunity costs (money that could have been spent on other things), and unknowable costs due to loss of innovation.

How much does regulation cost? It's incredibly difficult to say because the costs are hidden, widely dispersed throughout the economy, and do not appear on any budget. Nonetheless, they are real costs. A US Chamber of Commerce study estimated about $5,590/citizen in 2016 for federal regulations alone.[5] And it's getting worse.

A commonly used measure of regulation is to count pages in the Code of Federal Regulations (CFR). In 1950 there were 9,745 pages in the CFR. By 2018 there were 185,434 pages. If the trend continues, by 2050 there'll be 271,000 pages, and by 2100 about 403,000. Figure 5 shows the trend.

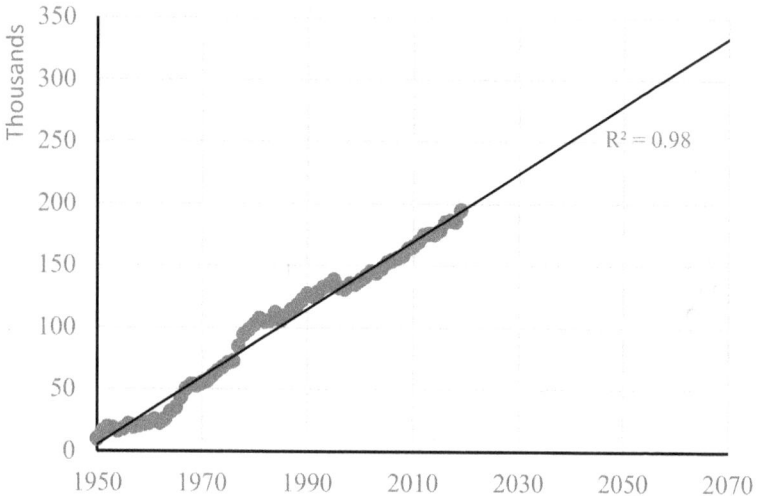

Figure 5—Pages of Federal Regulations

If you read 100 pages/day, five days/week, fifty weeks/ year (a full-time job), it would have taken you 19 weeks to read the rules in 1950. Today it would take about six years, and by 2050 it will take ten years.

The CFR covers federal regulations only. If you add up legislation, regulation, and court decisions at all levels, you'd need at least 40 years to read it (see *Proposal 12— Legislation*). And there's nothing to stop US governments from producing more regulations forever, drowning us in paperwork, and bleeding us dry with compliance costs.

Trump tried to reverse the trend by introducing a rule that federal agencies should lose two federal regulations for each new one created.[6] But it's a temporary reprieve. The Biden administration has reverted to business as usual. The trend is always for more regulation because special interests always want more control.

Trust

As a final indicator that something is wrong, trust in the government has been in decline for over fifty years. In the mid-'60s about 75% of citizens said they "trust government in Washington all or most of the time." Today the figure is about 20%.[7] A 2015 Gallup Poll[8] had 69% of citizens thinking "big government" is the greatest threat to the future (compared to "big business" 25%, and "big labor" 8%). In 1965 only 35% of citizens thought the government was a threat. About 75% of Americans believe there's "widespread corruption" in the government. Americans think there is too much regulation,[9] and that government has too much power.[10]

Polls show citizens' faith in almost all institutions is in steady decline.[11] Small business does best (68% approve), the military a close second (64%). Government institutions overall do poorly (25%).

Many citizens also worry about political partisanship. Polls over the last 15 years show 40-60% of Americans think a credible 3rd party is needed.[12] However, overall, most Americans would like less politics, period. One 2014 poll[13] had 59% of Americans saying the message they would most like to send to the government is "Leave me alone."

Most recently, the Coronavirus pandemic has been a huge wake-up call for many. Historically, nations have often quarantined people with deadly diseases. But, for the first time ever, US citizens were ordered to imprison themselves in their homes, even if healthy, causing simmering anger. Was it any wonder people were ready to riot? American's trust in government institutions has been in decline for over 50 years, but the Coronavirus response has surely accelerated that distrust.

Along with declining trust in government, the trend in citizens' trust in each other has also been declining. The long-term trend for "most people can be trusted" is down from about 45% in 1972 to close to 30% today.[14]

Declining trust is a problem because trust—generalized trust of our fellow citizens—is the glue that holds society together. We expect each other to adhere to the norms and customs of our country. We expect that people will honor their word, that checks will clear, and that the vegetables we buy are edible. We want to trust that our rights will be respected by other citizens and by our government.

This decline in trust is a symptom of government growth. Government power has been hijacked by special interests and used to manipulate us. Why should I trust a government that acts on behalf of special interests? And why should I trust fellow citizens who are part of those special interests, out to take advantage of me?

How Bad Does It Need to Get?

Many other trends in society are going in similar directions to the above: defense spending, militarized police, welfare spending, occupational licensing, education spending, healthcare, and others. All heading in the wrong direction.

For almost every issue mentioned here, graphed or not, the underlying trends have been in place since 1900 or earlier with only minor ups and downs. They are independent of who's in power, republican or democrat. Minor variations occur from administration to administration, but the overall trends persist.

However, people have been issuing dire warnings about government growth, spending, debt, etc. for decades. But the sky has not yet fallen! Why should anyone take notice now?

I don't know when, or even if, it will all come tumbling down. No one does. But I do not want to find out! If you have any sense that things are off course, wouldn't you be interested in changing course now? Does anyone want economic depression, collapse, hyperinflation, or, in the worst case, civil war?

Many citizens assume that a collapse of the US is impossible. But history is full of examples of the rise and fall of great nations. Our neighbor Venezuela has gone from being the richest country in South America to economic collapse in the last 20 years.[15] There's already been one civil war in the US, and it could easily have gone the other way and led to splitting the country in two.

In the last couple of years, we've seen riots in US cities, culminating in an invasion of the Capitol in January 2021. To think disaster could never happen to the US is hubris, dangerous hubris.

How bad do things need to get before there's support for real change?

Chapter 3—Thinking About Solutions

It's not what you look at that matters, it's what you see.
—Henry David Thoreau

Many citizens believe that America is in deep political and economic trouble. A time may come when a reset is needed, a genuine change of direction. When that point comes, what can be done to improve things?

The argument presented in this book is that the fundamental problem in the US is special interest corruption of our political and legal system. Therefore, what's needed, first and foremost, is to remove the influence of special interests on government.

However, it's important to be clear exactly where the problem lies, else we risk attempting to fix the wrong things. The dilemma is that special interests per se are not a problem. Special interests are just groups of people who are passionate about a particular issue. The issue might be anything: corporate profits, welfare, charitable works, a field of study, preservation of the environment, etc.

Society benefits from multiple interests and perspectives, from discussion of differences, from ideas bouncing off each other and producing new ideas. We all benefit when people and groups get specialized at addressing different issues, experimenting, and building expertise in that area.

The problem is not the special interests, it is the manipulation. Special interests are only a problem when their specialness gets written into law, when they succeed at legal manipulation. At that point, they have co-opted government power to *force* their opinion on society.

Which brings us to the real root of the problem: Only government creates legislation, and only government can legally force us to comply. *Thus, government is not the counterweight to the undue influence of special interests; it is the source of that undue influence.* The problem is not that special interests try to manipulate government. The problem is that government is manipulatable.

All US governments need to be made manipulation-proof. No individual, group, corporation, union, charity, profession, or even political party should be able to use government power to help any group *at the expense of the rest of society.* All legal manipulation by anyone, anywhere, must be prevented.

Solutions That Won't Work

Ending manipulation is easier said than done. All special interests want to protect their advantages or expand them. They are incentivized to continue investing time, money, and legal resources into continuing the status quo. They will keep pushing solutions that work for them, even as the country falls apart around them.

As a result, most proposed solutions to society's problems are simply more manipulation and won't fix anything. Our governments have been over-spending, over-borrowing, and over-regulating for more than a century. If today's problems are part of a trend going back more than 120 years, then those problems *cannot be the fault of today's administration, or of any recent administration.* Today's administration is perpetuating the problems, but it is not the cause of them.

Likewise, neither today's administration, nor the next one, will fix 120-year-old problems by carrying on business as usual. Long-term systemic problems won't be fixed by squabbles over today's policies.

It's clear the usual solutions won't work because there are decades of evidence of them not working! Still, it's worth briefly examining why the current policies don't work, to avoid making similar mistakes with the new proposals here. Several common strategies are examined below, along with an explanation of how they are typically flawed, politically, economically, or psychologically.

Regulate The Special Interests

One apparently obvious solution to manipulation is to regulate special interests better.

This may fix some minor problems but won't work as a fundamental solution because the bulk of regulations are written by the regulated. It cannot be otherwise—the regulated are the ones who know their industry. Banks know about banking, pharmaceutical companies know about drugs, and so on. Therefore, regulation itself gets manipulated. Typically, big business gets rules written that appear to curb their activities but act to exclude smaller competitors.

Even if increased regulation was a workable solution, the incentives work against government curbing special interests. Special interests, especially corporations, have better lawyers, better PR, and more money to bribe politicians and influence regulatory agencies.

More subtly, we fundamentally do not want to curb special interests. We want to curb the *manipulation,* the corruption of government and the legal system. It is government that needs to be fixed.

Get Our Side in Power

Many political activists think that the solution to all our problems is to get their side in power.

This won't work because activists don't want to end manipulation at all—they just want their side to win! At the extremes, both the left and right wings in politics want to implement their version of paradise. But one side winning, once and for all, is neither possible nor desirable.

Practically, it's unlikely you could design a system where one side consistently wins, and the other side consistently loses.

It is also not desirable that one side wins every time. If your favorite group always wins, that might work for you, but what about everyone else? Thinking that your side should always win is like trying to win every argument with your spouse. If that's your attitude to marriage, well, good luck! Similarly, if your favorites win every political battle, the more perfect union will eventually end in divorce.

At a basic level, our country needs both left-wing and right-wing perspectives. Neither side is "right," and both sides need the other as a counterbalance. We all need to get along with each other, no matter what our favored political views.

Electing the Right President

Electing the right president is another solution that won't work. It's a version of "get our side in power" with additional problems. Individual presidents have only a small effect, and the differences are often more about style than substance. Candidates make optimistic promises about what they will do: "No more taxes," "Close Guantanamo," or "Drain the swamp." But once in office, they have little power to affect change.

Some might argue that if the President cannot change things, then the President needs more power. But this is to head precisely in the wrong direction. The American system was designed so that Congress makes the laws, and the President executes them and oversees the administration. Ideally, presidents should have *less* power than they do now. It is not the job of presidents to set policy.

There's also an unhelpful psychological dynamic apparent in discourse about presidents. Presidents are often spoken of as if they were our parents, our saviors, or the devil incarnate! People project their hopes, dreams, and fears onto the President. Individual presidents and wannabes are incentivized to play into this to get elected i.e.: "I will do this for you." However, America does not need a savior or a new parent. America needs a government *system* that functions correctly.

A Return to Constitutional Purity

Right-leaning and libertarian citizens will often say things like "If only the government would obey the Constitution all will be well."

They have a point, but the incentives are against a return to constitutional purity. The history of the last 150 years is of steadily increasing manipulation, accompanied by an increased size, reach, and complexity of government. There does not appear to be anything on the horizon that would realistically change the trajectory of manipulation.

Elect the Libertarians

Another often proposed solution is to vote the libertarians (or some other third party) into power. This might produce short-term improvements but would not be a long-term solution.

Firstly, electing a libertarian president would be a version of "if only we had the right person in power." Any individual president is powerless to fundamentally change things.

Secondly, unless the fundamental incentives are changed, libertarians will find themselves in the same position as Republicans and Democrats. Enormous financial, social, and political forces bear down on all politicians. Libertarians might be able to hold for a while, but the forces are so powerful that they are likely to eventually corrupt anyone who stays in power too long.

Tear It All Down

An underlying theme of many cultural protests is to tear down the system in the belief that paradise will rise from the ashes. This shows up in the woke movement, BLM, Antifa, etc. These movements are modern versions of Marxism, substituting "the oppressed" for "the workers."

Yet even a cursory glance at communist or socialist revolutions in the last century (Russia, China, Cambodia, Vietnam, North Korea, Cuba, Nicaragua, Venezuela, etc.) shows that they universally cause death, destruction, and impoverishment.

The US is one of the most successful countries in the world. Problems exist, but let's resolve them by renaissance rather than revolution. Let's keep what works, repair what's broken, and improve what we can rather than risk tearing everything down and starting over.

Resetting the System

In theory, our political system could reverse direction on its own. Government could shrink, dialing back decades of over-regulation and excessive spending. Politicians could relearn manners, logic, humility, and the arts of negotiation and compromise. Special interests could compete in the market instead of in manipulation.

A spontaneous reversal would be nice, but realistically what are the chances? Political incentives have been pushing our country in its current direction for decades. The forces have only increased as special interests have become ever more powerful and pervasive.

So, what's needed is *a reset of the system to change the incentives at play.* I am proposing constitutional amendments to counter special interest manipulation of government. This will include a general re-leveling of the playing field and correction of past manipulations.

This solution would be like a down-to-the-studs renovation of America. The basic structure should remain in place, but it's time to restore and improve things that have decayed. Special interest termites have been eating away at the framework of the country—the Constitution—for decades. The Founders' vision has been perverted. A few cosmetic changes won't fix it. Our system of government needs a major overhaul.

Another way to put this—forgive me for mixing metaphors—is that our country needs a reboot and upgrade to our operating system. In other words, an upgrade to the Constitution.

It won't be easy to upgrade the Constitution. Special interests will resist, and the politically active—campaigners, activists, and politicians—mostly don't want change unless it is in their preferred policy directions.

But most Americans are not at the extremes. About 70% of us fall into what the "More in Common" group called the "exhausted majority,"[1] folks who are concerned, fed up, angry, and even scared at the trends in American politics. Exhausted certainly describes me, and I believe many of us are ready for a more fundamental change.

A reset, a constitutional upgrade, is our best chance for a change of direction. Despite the difficulties, it would be the best way to give control back to citizens. We the People of America, given the chance, will work things out for ourselves, and things will improve.

As a second choice, most of the proposals could also be implemented as regular legislation. That would have a much more piecemeal effect (depending on the jurisdiction) but would still be an improvement.

No matter if done as constitutional amendments or as legislation, changes can only happen if citizens support them. And that starts with a detailed set of exact proposals.

It is not enough to argue in favor of a policy position—privacy, freedom, or social justice— unless those things are clearly defined. Anything less than a precise definition is open to manipulation.

In this spirit, I am offering what I hope is a clear platform, a precise and detailed set of suggestions to reset our country's direction. A clear plan is at least a starting point for getting changes made.

Our country could be restored by some constitutional upgrades. Still, it's important to be realistic. Perfection is not achievable, and manipulation can't be ended entirely.

Like attracts like. Successful people in every field—businesses, charity, religion, academics, artists, and politicians—are drawn towards each other. The rich and powerful will always have greater access to politicians and decision-makers.

Attempts to tear that structure down (such as in Communist regimes) only result in a different set of successful people, and millions of deaths. One of the great strengths of the US is that success is largely based on merit rather than inheritance or force.

Another barrier to perfection is that the world is constantly changing. As society and technology evolve, government needs to evolve with them. The future cannot be predicted, and it certainly can't be planned out in detail. Rather, what's needed is a set of guiding principles, to be applied as needed as new situations arise.

The Founders laid down a set of principles in the Constitution that have served us well over the last 240+ years. The proposals here are designed to reset and reinforce the Founder's insights, to clean them up, and to strengthen them. Hopefully, they can then continue to serve us well into the future.

Chapter 4—The Proper Role of Government

We hold these truths to be self-evident, that all men are created equal, that they are endowed, by their Creator, with certain unalienable Rights, that among these are Life, Liberty, and the pursuit of Happiness.

That to secure these rights, Governments are instituted among Men, deriving their just powers from the consent of the governed.
—Preamble to Declaration of Independence

We the People of the United States, in Order to form a more perfect Union, establish Justice, insure domestic Tranquility, provide for the common defense, promote the general Welfare, and secure the Blessings of Liberty to ourselves and our Posterity, do ordain and establish this Constitution for the United States of America
—Preamble to the Constitution

To organize a reset, let's start by taking a step back and re-examining the purpose of government, based on the Founders' vision as laid out in the Declaration of Independence and the Constitution.

How can we know when government is acting in its proper role? I propose a series of *Tests of Legitimate Governance* to answer that question. These tests will help us decide where government should and should not be acting, at least in principle.

The Test of Purpose

Let's start with the most basic question: *what is the purpose of government?* The Founders gave their answer in the Declaration of Independence. *The primary purpose of government is to protect our individual rights.*

For the Founders, everything began with individual rights. They believed that citizens have *unalienable rights*—rights that cannot be taken away (inalienable rights in modern English). These rights were seen as inherent natural rights, God-given rights, part of what it means to be human. Individual rights are not granted to citizens by any government. Rather, it is exactly the other way around: citizens are sovereign and delegate responsibilities to governments.

The idea of individual rights was not new. The Founders were well-educated in history and philosophy.[1] Their thinking came out of a long tradition, from the Greeks, the Romans, Judeo-Christian thinkers, and through to Enlightenment thinkers such as John Locke (1632-1704).[2]

What was new was that the Founders had the chance to start over and form a government founded on Enlightenment ideas, codifying them in the Constitution that has served us so well.

The Founders' list of rights starts with *life*. You are a living, sovereign individual being. No other person has a right to take your life from you. Violence and killing cannot be allowed, except in in exceptional circumstances such as self-defense.

After life itself, the next right is *liberty*—the freedom to run your life as you see fit. You need liberty to exercise your other rights.

And finally, the *pursuit of happiness.* This is not a guarantee of happiness, it is the right to pursue happiness. In other words, to use your life and liberty to do whatever you believe will bring you happiness.

The Founders listed several other individual rights in the Bill of Rights. Although not explicitly listed in the Constitution, the right of individuals to use their property as they see fit is also a fundamental right. Theft or "taking" of that of individual property cannot be allowed.

Liberty is perhaps the most important right, practically speaking. Liberty is front and center in the Declaration of Independence. One of the Constitution's purposes is defined as *Securing the Blessings of Liberty.* Most state Constitutions have similar references to securing liberty.[3]

Google defines liberty as *the state of being free within society from oppressive restrictions imposed by authority on one's way of life, behavior, or political views; the state of not being imprisoned or enslaved.*

Most people today use the word freedom as a synonym for liberty. Unfortunately, this creates a problem because "free" has two meanings: (1) liberty and (2) at no cost. If I use the word free as in "free education" or "free healthcare," and claim those things are human rights, then I have struck a blow against liberty. You cannot offer someone free healthcare without making someone else pay for it. Free (or low-cost) health and education are laudable goals, but they cannot be turned into rights without simultaneously taking away rights.

So, freedom, when used in this book, should be taken as a synonym for *liberty*, meaning *the absence of coercion.* Forcing some people to comply with the wishes of others is not freedom. Manipulation—harnessing government power to force compliance—takes away freedom. The proposals here are designed to give Americans back their freedoms.

The idea of liberty brings us to the first Test of Legitimate Governance. If the primary purpose of government is to *secure the blessings of liberty,* then it's possible to test if government is acting in alignment with its purpose. The *Test of Purpose* takes the form of a question.

In the language of the Founders, for any government action, the question is: *Does this government action secure the blessings of liberty?*

In contemporary language, the Test of Purpose is: *Does this government action make me more free or less free?* Alternatively, we could word it as: *Does this government action protect individual liberty?*

Note that the main test is phrased as *Does this government action make **me** more free or less free?* Government's primary purpose is to protect *individual* liberty. My liberty, your liberty, everyone's *individual* liberty.

Government has other purposes, among them to *promote the general welfare.* Sometimes individual freedoms might need to be compromised for the common good. But the *primary* purpose of government is always to secure (keep safe) individual liberty. As Locke put it: *The end of law is not to abolish or restrain, but to preserve and enlarge freedom.*[4]

Any government action that goes against this primary purpose is suspect, even if it fulfills a secondary goal. Wherever possible, government should *find another way.* Only in extreme cases should government's primary purpose be violated to fulfill a secondary purpose.

To secure our liberty, practically speaking, government must do three main things:

1. Protect us from external violence, violence from foreign persons. In other words, a border, and a military to protect it.

2. Protect us from internal violence, the violence of one citizen against another. So, a police force and court system.

3. Agree and enforce rules about how we live together, rules that *ensure domestic tranquility* and *promote the general welfare.*

Even with freedom as a guiding principle, there can't be absolute freedom in any society. Sometimes my actions affect other people—we do need some rules to allow us to get along with each other. Ideally, it should be the minimum set of rules that allow maximum individual freedom within the constraints of living in a society. In the classical liberal or libertarian tradition, the rules can be boiled down to: *You should be allowed to do anything you want so long as you cause no direct harm to other people or their property.*

The Test of Moral Authority

To secure our liberty, we citizens create governments that have the three main purposes listed above: defense, police and courts, and basic rule-making. Governments are created by us and *derive their just powers* from the consent of the governed.

What are just powers? In other words: what is the moral authority behind any government action? What can government do, morally, that individual citizens cannot?

For the Founders, government was an expression of the will and action of individual citizens. In Jefferson's words: *[It is] the people, to whom all authority belongs.*[5] Government authority is the authority of the people. They have simply delegated some of it for convenience.

In other words, *government has exactly the same moral authority as any individual citizen.* In Locke's words: *The people cannot delegate to government the power to do anything which would be unlawful for them to do themselves.*[6]

Applying this principle, we can now create another Test of Legitimate Governance:

The *Test of Moral Authority* is: *For any action X the government proposes taking, do you as an individual citizen have the right to do X?*

The test can be phrased in other ways such as:

Do I have the right to force my neighbor to do X?
Does my neighbor have the right to force me to do X?
Do I have the right to do X to my neighbor?
Does my neighbor have the right to do X to me?

In every case, if you or I as individual citizens do not have the right to do X or force X, neither does the government. For example:

Do I have the right to beat my neighbor up on a whim? No, that's battery, and I do not have the right to do that. Therefore, neither does the government nor any person acting on behalf of the government.

Do I have the right to take my neighbor's car without her permission? No, that's theft, and I do not have the right to do that. Therefore, by extension, neither does the government or any government agent.

Do I have the right to point a gun at my neighbor and threaten to shoot her if she doesn't give me a pint of milk? No, that's assault and coercion, and I do not have the right to do that. By extension, neither does the government nor any government agent.

Most of the time, the Test of Moral Authority will give clear guidelines about allowable action. However, there can be exceptions.

Take the example above: I do not have the right to take my neighbor's car without her permission. Nonetheless, I could envision a scenario where it might be okay to take her car, perhaps if a wildfire is advancing towards my house and I needed to get my family out now (and assuming she does not need the car to get her family out).

Even though I can find exceptions, they are likely to be extreme, involving imminent life or death if no action is taken. Exceptions in extreme circumstances do not invalidate general rules or the general applicability of this test to most government actions.

Government's moral authority includes the right to use violence, exactly as I personally can use violence under the right circumstances. If I am threatened, I have the authority to defend myself, up to and including killing an attacker if my life is at risk. However, my use of violence is constrained to defending myself or others. Similarly, government use of violence should also be constrained to acts of defense.

In practice, few people are willing to use violence, so we delegate law enforcement to use necessary violence on our behalf. We delegate the courts to punish criminals. Nonetheless, we can only delegate powers that we ourselves have. The police and the courts have—in principle— precisely the same powers as any individual citizen, no more and no less.

Delegation is both implicit in the wording of the founding documents and explicitly woven into our interactions with government and the language used to describe those interactions.

In most US counties, for example, citizens explicitly delegate the power of lawful use of violence by electing a sheriff. A sheriff is deputized (stands in place of) citizens to uphold the law. Citizen juries decide if criminals are guilty and apply punishments. These processes are highly formalized today, but they started with citizens choosing volunteers to go get the outlaws and then deciding how to punish them.

Similarly, citizens elect legislatures to produce basic rules. We call the people we elect representatives. Who do they represent? We the People! So, how could our representatives have more authority than us?

In some situations, representatives are also called delegates. We are delegating them to negotiate and decide things on our behalf. Again, how could we delegate to them more authority than we ourselves have?

At higher levels of government, delegation of powers is explicitly laid out in the 10th Amendment: *The powers not delegated to the United States by the Constitution, nor prohibited by it to the States, are reserved to the States respectively, or to the people.*

In principle then, citizens delegate power to government to act on our behalf. The Test of Moral Authority helps us define the limits of government authority, based on the premise that we cannot delegate the government to do things that we couldn't do ourselves.

Which brings us to an important question: Is the Test of Moral Authority valid? Can the government do things, morally, that citizens could not do individually? Does the government have more moral authority than individual citizens?

Let me be clear: our collective governments, currently, often do things for which they have no moral authority. I will argue, for example, that drugs should be legal because neither my neighbor nor any government has the right to stop me from taking drugs.

There are also legitimate grey areas requiring compromise, such as pollution, where I may need to accept some restrictions on my behavior on my property for the common good.

However, here I am discussing the question of what moral authority the government *should* have. Specifically, should it be able to do things that an ordinary citizen cannot do *just because it is the government?*

Politicians, experts, activists, and pundits often act as if the government can impose its wishes on citizens. But if that's the case, where does this right come from? Does the government have any moral right to use force on non-violent citizens?

One common justification for government imposing its wishes is "the government was democratically elected and therefore has the right to force us to do X." However, a little clear thinking will quickly show that this is nonsense.

Outside of a possible life-or-death situation, your neighbor has no right to steal your car. Now, could she take your car if everyone else on your block voted to allow it? No, that would still be theft. It makes no difference that your neighbors okayed it.

Keep following this line of reasoning: It makes no difference how many people vote to steal your car. It does not matter if your town, your county, your state, or even the country voted it was okay to take your car. It would still be theft, and it would still be morally wrong. Government does not suddenly acquire moral authority because representatives are democratically elected.

Leaders throughout the ages have claimed the right to tell citizens what to do, and philosophers could debate forever where that right comes from. There are many variations, but they boil down to three main possibilities:

1. *Divine right.* God gave me the authority to tell you what to do.

2. *Thuggery/violence.* If you don't do what I say, I'll kill you.

3. *Delegated authority.* Government has the same authority as individual citizens. We've simply delegated that authority to a few representatives to decide for the common good.

Divine leaders historically were called things like emperor, king, majesty, lord, tsar, pharaoh, pope, caliph, führer and others. Modern variants call themselves supreme leader, chairman, president for life, general secretary, hardest worker, and so on. Ideologies such as communism may substitute the Communist Manifesto for God, but communist leaders otherwise act as if they have a divine right to rule.

Still, no matter what they call themselves, divine leaders, in reality, are the thugs who won, or descendants of those thugs. They control the state agents of thuggery: police and soldiers. All variants of divine right boil down to thuggery if divine leaders force you to comply.

So, after stripping out fancy language, theology, and philosophy, the first two options collapse into one. That leaves only two real sources for the moral authority of government: 1) Thuggery/violence, or 2) Delegated citizen authority.

Nothing is pure in this world, including this distinction. Nonetheless, which system would you prefer, at least in principle? Which system do you want to live under? Which is more likely to preserve your freedoms?

Now if, despite my arguments, you still believe that government has authority above and beyond the delegated authority of its citizens, then ask yourself: where does that authority come from? What stops government use of force from being arbitrary? How do you decide what is morally justifiable government action, and what is mere thuggery? Who decides?

The Test of Moral Authority does not resolve all issues about what government can and cannot do, but it does align strongly with the principle that individual rights are paramount in the American experiment. It provides a baseline, a place to start trying to sort and understand the ethical and legal issues. If a government action fails the test, then in principle the government should not be doing it.

The Test of Consent

Governments are created by us and *derive their just powers from the consent of the governed.* In other words, rules created to enable peaceful coexistence should, as far as possible, be rules that everyone *consents* to.

Maximizing consent is common sense. If large numbers of people disagree, then the rules will create—progressively—annoyance, simmering discontent, resentment, and scofflaws. If it goes too far, there will be open rule-breaking, anarchy, violence, riots, and ultimately civil war.

Since governments *derive their just powers from the consent of the governed*, this allows us to create a third Test of Legitimate Governance.

Using the original language of the Constitution, the *Test of Consent* is: *If citizens do not consent to a government action, that action is unjust.*

In contemporary language, the Test of Consent is: *If large numbers of citizens disagree with a government policy, then government has no right to impose that policy.*

The Test of Consent is less clear-cut than the Test of Purpose or the Test of Moral Authority. There's always someone who disagrees with even the most enlightened of government policies.

So, when applying the Test of Consent, the definition of *large numbers* of citizens is subjective. There's no hard and fast rule, but if more than, say, 10-20% of the population disagrees with a policy then that policy should be questioned, and probably repealed. This is especially true when citizens disagree strongly enough that they are willing to break the law. Organizing society to maximize consent will be discussed in the next chapter.

The Test of Constitutional Authority

Since the US is a constitutional republic, a fourth Test of Legitimate Governance is to ask if government is working within the Constitution.

The Test of Constitutional Authority is: *For any action X that the government proposes to do, does the Constitution give the government authority to take that action?*

This question is debated whenever controversial decisions are taken by any government. The Test of Constitutional Authority should be powerful, but more than 240 years of special interest subversion have thoroughly corrupted it.

Contemporary legislators, administrators, and judges alike often appear to view the Constitution as an inconvenience to the worked around rather than a principle to be upheld. Over the decades, thousands of clever arguments have been made about why expedient exceptions to the Constitution are justified. Each little exception builds on the last one so that over time the Constitution has been undermined by creeping expediency.

The proposals here aim to reverse this creeping expediency. If a policy can't be implemented because it violates the Constitution, then the policy should change, not the Constitution. Otherwise, before we know it, we'll have no principles left to stand on at all. Indeed, doesn't "no principles left to stand on" already describe much of the political landscape?

The Test of Efficacy

A final Test of Legitimate Governance proposed here is to test if a policy achieves its stated aims. If a policy does not work, the government should stop it!

Before implementation, the *Test of Efficacy* is: *For any action X that the government proposes to take, what is the desired result, and is that action X likely to achieve the desired result?*

After implementation, the question becomes: *For any action X that the government is doing, does it achieve its desired results?*

The Test of Efficacy should be another powerful test, but in practice is rather weak. Policy goals are often unclear, measures of success poorly defined, and the motives of those reporting success or failure are tainted. Success may be a statistical artifact rather than concrete results. Apparent success may be ineffective compared to unexamined private or do-nothing alternatives.

If our government is pouring resources into a policy, and occasionally using force to implement it, then unclear policy objectives or measures of success are not acceptable. If a policy fails the Test of Efficacy because we can't apply the test, then that policy fails the test. We need to *know* when a policy is successful.

Even if a policy does have clear measurable objectives, we may still not know in advance if it is going to work. However, there are often clues that it is likely to fail:

- It creates moral hazard.
- It tries to defy fundamental economic principles (ignoring incentives or the law of diminishing returns).
- It imposes other people's morals on citizens (no alcohol allowed).
- It defines standards by subjective measures (feelings).
- It sets quotas on things rather than thresholds (the first 1000 people, rather than the best 1000 people).
- It defies common sense or proverbial wisdom.

Application of the Tests

I've now outlined five Tests of Legitimate Governance: The Test of Purpose, The Test of Moral Authority, The Test of Consent, The Test of Constitutional Authority, and The Test of Efficacy.

Throughout this book, these tests will be applied to different policy areas that our governments get involved in. The more tests a policy fails, the more suspect that policy is. If the goal of the policy fails several tests, government should *stop doing it*. It is not a valid government function. If the goal of the policy is okay, but the methods fail several tests, the government should *find another way* to achieve that goal.

The Grey Areas

The size, scope, and expense of government would be dramatically reduced by returning it to its core functions: protecting our borders; protecting citizens from fraud, theft, and violence; basic rule-making, and a few basic services. Curbing special interest manipulation in the ways proposed here would turn government back in that direction.

Nonetheless, even if all manipulation were ended, there would still be legitimate debates about how far government should go. The grey areas fall into two main camps: the irresponsible, and externalities.

Irresponsible Citizens

A functional society requires responsible citizens. Most people are responsible, but we still need to deal with the irresponsible. There are three main groups of them: the insane, criminals, and children.

The first group of irresponsible citizens is the insane. In principle, mental illness should be treated like any illness: it's a private issue for the patient, their family, and healthcare providers. Insanity only becomes a public issue if the patient becomes a risk to others. Since this is a state-level issue, it won't be addressed here except in passing when discussing criminal justice and gun control.

A second group of irresponsible citizens is criminals. Protecting responsible citizens from criminals is a legitimate role for government. This will be addressed primarily in *Proposal 17—Criminal Justice.*

The third and by far the largest group of potentially irresponsible citizens is children. Children are not adults and cannot be counted upon to act like adults. Children need to be nurtured and educated to eventually become responsible adults. They need a degree of protection from the adult world. Who should do all this? The correct answer is *the parents.* Issues around adulthood and children—and special interest blurring of the issues—will crop up in several places but primarily in *Proposal 1—Adulthood.*

Externalities

An externality is any situation where I act for my benefit, but where my actions might adversely affect other people. For example, pollution. I do something on my property, and pollutants waft away in the wind, or drain into the sewer, and affect everyone around me.

This is an area where debate is needed, and where government action may be appropriate because *everything I do has externalities.* Every breath I take converts oxygen into carbon dioxide, adding to global warming. This is a problem that can't be solved with a blanket rule of "no externalities allowed," because that's impossible. Rather, the question is how much is too much?

Related to externalities are collective action problems—problems caused by large numbers of people all doing the same thing. My individual home furnace, for example, has negligible effects on the environment. But when millions of us run our furnaces, that's a lot of greenhouse gases.

Externalities and collective action problems can sometimes be solved by environmental standards, but *how* we regulate them is important. This will be discussed in *Proposal 12—Legislation,* as well as *Proposal 13—Regulation.*

Chapter 5—Promoting the General Welfare

Congress has not unlimited powers to provide for the general welfare but only those specifically enumerated.
—Thomas Jefferson

In the American experiment, government is tasked with *securing the Blessings of Liberty,* as well as having a duty to *promote the General Welfare.* What is the best way for government to do *both* tasks?

Individual liberty and the common good are often framed as being in opposition to each other. Manipulated definitions of "good" often trump individual liberty.

However, the best way for government to promote the general welfare is to protect individual liberties! These goals are not in opposition to each other, rather they complement each other.

Individual Liberty vs. Centralized Control

Powerful people have always tried to control things, and other people push back. America was born from a revolution against centralized control when King George III became too authoritarian.

The Founders designed the Constitution to safeguard against the reemergence of authoritarianism in the US. They set up checks and balances designed to prevent too much accumulation of power in any person or branch of government. Individual liberty (along with similar new freedoms in European countries) enabled the Industrial Revolution to flourish and produced the explosion in wealth shown in Figure 7.

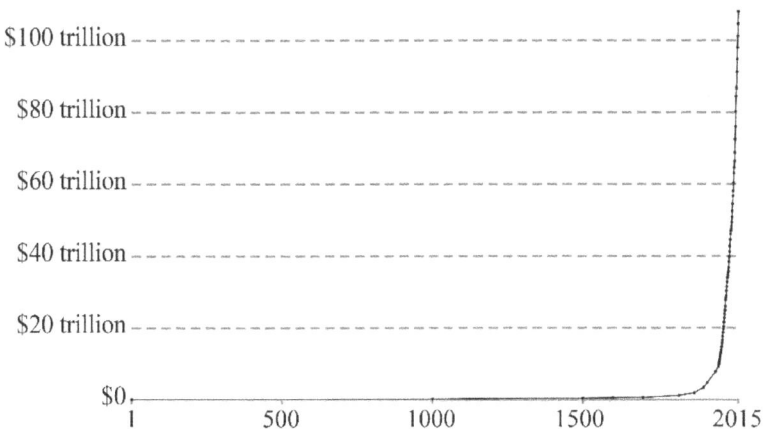

Figure 7—World GDP Growth last 2000 Years[1]

Despite the Founders' intentions, over the last 150 years, the US has been moving back in the direction of authoritarianism. Centralized control has steadily become the norm, and checks and balances have broken down.

This happens because everyone in and around government is incentivized to grow their little bit of government. All government employees are paid to do their jobs. Legislators are paid to legislate. Regulators are paid to regulate. Law enforcement officers are paid to enforce.

Thus, legislation and regulation—centralized control—get created and enforced. Lawsuits produce court decisions—more centralized control—managed by administrators and backed up by law enforcement.

Unhealthy psychological incentives are also at play. Power attracts people who like power. Order attracts people who like order and control. People who are comfortable with violence are more likely to go into law enforcement. Certainly, anyone with an aversion to those things is likely to exclude themselves by not applying for government jobs.

This does not mean that government is staffed by psychopaths, control freaks, and thugs. Most government employees are perfectly normal people who are slightly more likely, on average, to be positively disposed to exercising power, being willing to control others, or using violence.

Over multiple decades, millions of such people have made millions of decisions and taken millions of actions that gradually become baked into government systems and the law. Government itself grows. The growth is imperceptible on a day-to-day basis but clear as a long-term trend in the graphs shown in *Chapter 2—Unsustainable Trends.*

In higher government circles, the incentives get stronger as more power is wielded. Bigger decisions are made, and more money is involved. Reputation management becomes ever more important. Representatives want to get reelected. Heads of agencies want to enhance their status. Presidents and Governors want to leave a legacy.

All these powerful people are incentivized to grow their power and prestige. They may be democratically elected, or legitimately appointed. They may genuinely believe that they are doing good. But their methods—variations on ordering citizens about—are self-serving and antithetical to both individual freedom and the common good.

Peripheral groups also have incentives to grow government. Activists want their preferred policy implemented. Experts think their recommendations should become law. Contractors are pushing for the government to buy their solutions.

These incentives acting on everyone associated with government means we can't depend on getting the right people in government. A systemic fix—restoration and strengthening of checks and balances—is needed to keep government right-sized and on-purpose.

The Evils of Centralized Control

The problem with centralized control—authoritarianism—is that it is anti-thetical to both individual freedom and promoting the common welfare. Centralized control destroys liberty and makes us collectively poorer.[2]

On an individual level, you cannot have freedom if decisions are being made for you by legislators and administrators. Centralized control takes away your *liberty* and your right to the *pursuit of happiness* as you see fit.

On the level of the common welfare, centralized control destroys human intelligence. In the last 250 years, the prime mover of progress has been creativity. Everything about our modern lives (warm dry houses, cars, abundant food, clothes, computers, TVs, etc.) is a human creation. Millions of humans solved millions of problems and invented millions of things. Their solutions were then spread around the world, partly by education, but mostly by free trade of products embodying new ideas.

For this progress to happen, humans had to be free to think, have ideas, create new products, and trade them. But centralized control does the opposite: it slows innovation and blocks free trade. It does this via standardization and regulation that imposes one-size-fits-all solutions. It does it via patents giving special interests control over ideas. It does it through threats of lawsuits making experimentation risky. It puts restrictions on free trade with quotas, import bans, tariffs, and taxes.

One definition of intelligence is *the ability to pursue a single end by different means*. If you legislate to curb different means (by preventing trial and error, or by mandating fixed solutions) then you are cutting off intelligence. Centralization destroys human intelligence.

Another definition of intelligence is *the ability to engage in creative problem-solving*. Again, if you remove the ability to engage by diktat then you destroy human intelligence.

More colloquially, intelligence is often defined as *the ability to think outside the box*. If you restrict who's allowed to play in the box—only experts can solve problems or evaluate solutions—then you destroy human intelligence. You have appointed a few thousand (at most) highly paid government experts to be problem solvers and evaluators and excluded the other 8 billion humans! Or, in the private market, you license your favored experts, again restricting human intelligence.

Centralized government control has other problems and variations on the theme of removing the possibility for intelligent solutions:

- Correcting ineffective solutions is difficult if the solution is man-dated. Error correction has been cut off.

- Centralization suffers from an information problem: bureaucrats in DC cannot know what is going on in your neighborhood and therefore cannot craft effective solutions. If bureaucrats demand more information to solve this problem, now we have privacy issues.

- Bureaucrats also lack the technical knowledge that people working in an industry have.

- Centralization promotes government growth and complexity.

- Government complexity is expensive in both direct costs (government employees) and indirect costs (complying with regulation).

- Freedom is always cheaper in the long run because it lowers the costs of enforcement.

- Control and complexity enable special interest manipulation.

- Government programs often fail one or more Tests of Legitimate Governance, especially the Test of Consent. Many citizens disagree with many government actions, and this is a large part of the political rancor our country is experiencing.

Maximum Freedom and Maximum Consent

As technology and society advance, new problems and variations on problems crop up, some of which are best addressed collectively. There are also genuine grey areas and debate as to how far government should go.

So, some government is needed. But since centralized control is collective stupidity, government should be the last resort for problem-solving. Beyond its most basic functions—basic rules, police and courts, and national defense—government should be minimized.

This does not mean that anarchy or chaos will ensue. We already manage most of our lives and our interactions with each other without government interference. This starts with social convention. Politeness, letting the other guy go first, tipping in restaurants. No one writes rules requiring these things, yet they happen. Social pressure, discussion, and debate are more effective mechanisms for taking care of most problems than government diktat. Problems are always best resolved by the folks who have them. They know the problem intimately and are directly incentivized to find solutions that work for them in real life. And there's no use of force.

After social convention, the next most important mechanism for solving problems is the market—entrepreneurship. Individuals and organizations tackle problems, create solutions, and spread them via education or by selling products and services embodying their ideas.

Everyone on the planet with a particular problem is motivated to solve it. A few will come up with new ideas and offer them to the market where many will evaluate those ideas. A free market maximizes the chances of finding the best solutions to problems through thousands of small experiments. Each of us can choose the best solutions *for us individually,* to maximize our personal freedom. Our collective choices will produce market winners, and failed experiments will fade away.

The free market also maximizes consent without the need for a one-size-fits-all government solution. In a market, I don't know what choices you make. I don't have to know, and *I don't care* because it's none of my business and doesn't affect me. We each choose whatever we want. Collective choices are not needed, and therefore there's no need to argue about them. Certainly, there's rarely a need for *legal* arguments.

Another benefit of markets is that we must pay for our choices. If someone is willing to pay for a solution, then they must *value* that solution. They have skin in the game. Market action is a much clearer signal about what people want than, say, voting, which is (apparently) cost-free.

Over time, market action, competition, and prices guide the market to give people more of what they want. If folks like SUVs, they buy them, and over time we have more SUVs! If Boomers want to move back to the inner cities, lofts and new apartments get built. We have pizzerias because people like pizza.

There are rarely arguments about these things. Each of us individually goes about our lives making the best choices we can with our money. The market works to provide us with whatever we want.

Bottom-Up Government.

Correct use of government starts with minimizing government. Where it is still needed, we should then use it in the best way we can. Broadly, government problem-solving can be top-down or bottom-up.

The top-down approach is epitomized by legislation. Legislators focus on a problem, investigate, consult, discuss, and finally create rules to try and fix the problem. All legislation is top-down. The higher the government, the more top-down it is.

The bottom-up approach starts when individual citizens find themselves in a dispute about something. If it cannot be resolved privately, then the bottom level of government, practically speaking, is the courts. Someone sues someone else. A court hears from both sides, and perhaps from experts or third parties, and then tries to find a good solution to the problem under the circumstances.

Among the things considered is *precedent.* What did other courts in similar situations think was reasonable? Past decisions are considered and argued over. The decision the court makes today sets a precedent for the next court. Over time, a body of law is built up, consisting of thousands of decisions about what makes sense in various situations.

All legal systems are a mix of top-down and bottom-up approaches but may emphasize one over the other. Most of the US legal system is based on English Common Law. For historical reasons, a few parts of the US (Louisiana and Puerto Rico) have legal systems based on the Napoleonic Code inherited from France. In principle, English Common Law is a bottom-up approach, Napoleonic Code is a top-down approach.

Both approaches have advantages and disadvantages, but generally, the bottom-up approach (also known as subsidiarity) should be preferred in a legal system. Courts are preferable to legislation. Local courts are preferable to higher courts. Local legislation is preferable to state or federal legislation:

- Court decisions address real-world problems (when citizens sue) while legislators sometimes address possible problems.
- Local courts and legislators have local knowledge of problems.
- Local court and legislative actions only affect local issues. Since mistakes made only affect locals, errors are less dangerous.
- If a similar problem crops up in multiple jurisdictions, then lots of different solutions will be tried.
- Courts consider precedent but are not bound by it. Questionable decisions might get overthrown by the next court, and there's an appeals process. Error correction is built in and relatively easy.
- By contrast, error correction is difficult when legislation is passed. Repeals are hard politically, and subject to manipulation.
- The local approach is less susceptible to manipulation, and local manipulation does less damage.
- Compliance with local laws (consent) may improve if citizens feel they have a greater say at town hall or in court.

Checks and Balances

A balance of bottom-up/top-down governance was designed into the US system by the Founders. The constitution outlines the principles of the system and the specific roles of the feds, but beyond that, the intention was that government be as local as possible. Cities and counties deal with most day-to-day issues. States deal with issues that are difficult to resolve at a local level (typically roads and other things that cross local boundaries). The feds handle issues that cross state lines (interstate commerce and crime) and protect our borders.

Different levels of government also serve to check and balance each other. If a city is abusing its citizens, the state should step in. If a state is abusing its citizens, the feds should step in.

As a final check, there is democracy. We elect representatives through a democratic process. However, democracy itself also needs to be kept in check, and the US is not a democracy as such—it is a constitutional republic. The Founders thought that unchecked democracy amounted to mob rule. In particular, the majority cannot vote away the rights of individuals. Individual rights are always paramount.

When the Constitution was created, the US had something approximating the above design. It was not ideal, and there were serious flaws such as slavery and women's rights. But the basic framework was sufficiently robust that the flaws could slowly get ironed out.

In the last 150 years though, despite improvements, there has also been corruption. The bottom-up/top-down balance has been reversed and centralism has become the dominant political theme of our times. The federal government has grown out of all proportion and increasingly meddles where it has no moral or constitutional authority. All governments are abusing citizen's rights rather than protecting them.

An overall aim of the proposals in this book is to turn government back towards the original intent: organized from the bottom up, starting with protecting individual citizen rights.

Reasonable Law

Legislation should be the last resort for problem-solving since it removes individual freedom and encourages collective stupidity. Legislation is a moral failure: it is an imposition of a solution against the will of many citizens. This is a primary cause of much of today's political discord.

Most people will obey most laws. But laws need to be reasonable to win the consent of the governed. What is a reasonable law? At the end of the day, it is one that most people agree is reasonable—everyone can see and agree with the reasoning behind the rule.

Some rules are needed—we must agree on some things to avoid chaos. For example, which side of the road we drive on?

It doesn't matter much, from country to country, which side we choose. About 60% of the world drives on the right, the rest on the left. The choices are for historical reasons rather than practical ones.

Within a country though, it matters a lot which side we choose. We must have a collective agreement to avoid mayhem. Even if only 51% of citizens want to drive on the right, everyone needs to comply. The 49% who want to drive on the left will agree to drive on the right because they don't want to die! The logic is clear.

However, the number of things we *must* agree on is small. Almost everyone agrees we need defense, a police force, and courts (though we may argue over details). Almost everyone agrees on the basic rules: no violence, fraud, or theft. No one argues about what side of the road we drive on. Few people take issue with basic services like roads or sewers.

So, what are the arguments about? *Everything else!* Beyond the most basic things, many people disagree with government policy. Is there a need for government education, healthcare, insurance, or welfare? How about minimum wages, occupational licensing, or safety regulations? No matter your opinion on any issue, large numbers of your fellow citizens disagree with you! Most government policies fail the Test of Consent.

Democracy cannot solve these kinds of disagreements. If people see laws as unreasonable, unjust, or immoral, they will fight to keep their freedoms. A law that 51% of citizens like is unenforceable if the other 49% are willing to violate it.

Further, whilst dialog is good, *dialog will not resolve our most intractable arguments.* Some issues, such as abortion, come down to fundamental moral differences. There are no answers everyone can agree on.

How do we solve issues where democratic agreement is impossible? The only practical answer is to agree to disagree. We must collectively learn, or relearn, to live and let live.

Agreeing to disagree sits uncomfortably with many people. We've been sold on the ideas of consensus, the power of democracy, and the will of the people. In practice though, disagreement is rarely a problem. You drive a Ford and I'll drive a Toyota. You support home help for seniors while I support the Red Cross. You like Mozart while I like hip-hop. You go to Church while I go to Temple.

Most complex social and economic issues are managed by millions of individuals making everyday decisions about their own lives. There is no collective will, and *none is needed.* Most of the time, it does not matter what we do, what we say, or what we believe, so long as we do not try and force our opinions on other people. You do your thing, I'll do mine. Live and let live. Do whatever you want to do so long as you don't do any direct harm to me or my property.

This is how most of us behave in our day-to-day lives. But this is not how politics works. In the political arena, politicians decide on our behalf and pass legislation which is then enforced. That's okay where legislation is genuinely needed to avoid chaos. But over the last 150 years, increasing numbers of private issues have become public issues. Instead of deciding for ourselves, politicians (manipulated by special interests) decide for us. Many citizens disagree. The more legislation, the more disagreement.

Bad laws encourage contempt for the law and lawbreaking. When millions of people disobey laws (drug laws, or immigration laws), this is a sign of laws that should be repealed—they fail the Test of Consent.

The more things are decided by politics rather than individual choice, the more people are incentivized to get involved in politics and argue. Politics becomes increasingly heated, the decisions more charged. Behind the scenes, special interests keep getting legislation passed in their favor, unnoticed as the arguments get louder.

A lot of contentious issues can be solved by removing them from the political arena—stop collective decision-making. Decisions are needed, but citizens should decide most issues for themselves. Each of us individually best understands our circumstances. We are our own best deciders.

Ending unnecessary collective decision-making would also end unnecessary public debates. Those who wish to continue debating, privately, can have at it and leave the rest of us out of it! Citizen anger would be lowered: No need to fight over collective decisions, or to obey decisions you don't agree with.

Part 2: A Bill of Protections

That whenever any Form of Government becomes destructive of these ends, it is the Right of the People to alter or abolish it, and to institute new Government, laying its foundation on such principles, and organizing its powers in such form, as to them shall seem most likely to affect their Safety and Happiness.
                    —Preamble to the Declaration of Independence

The *Bill of Protections* is broken down into four broad sections:

- Basic Rights.
- Limits on Government.
- Government and Economy.
- Checks and Balances.

Occasionally overlaps will occur between sections because the real world doesn't divide up into neat categories. In other places, the overlap is deliberate and designed to double up on safeguards by creating extra checks and balances.

Basic Rights

Rightful liberty is unobstructed action, according to our will, within limits drawn around us by the equal rights of others.
—Thomas Jefferson

This section of the *Bill of Protections* describes several rights of individual citizens. They are typically stated in the form "Citizens have the right to..." For example, *Proposal 8—Drugs* starts with "Citizens have the right to take drugs."

I want to be clear: *I am not proposing new rights for citizens, or that government grants these rights to its citizens.* As conscious, sovereign individuals, we already have these rights.

The problem is that governments have been wrongly encroaching on those rights, so they need to be restated explicitly. This is in the same spirit as the original *Bill of Rights* which did not propose new rights for citizens but rather was listing the rights *we hold to be self-evident.*

So, when I say, "Citizens have the right to take drugs," I mean that citizens already have that right, even if it harms them. So read "Citizens have the right to take drugs" as reiterating your natural right i.e.: "Citizens already have the right to take drugs, and we mean it!"

Proposal 1—Adulthood

When I was a child, I spoke as a child, I understood as a child, I thought as a child: but when I became a man, I put away childish things.

—1 Corinthians 13:11

As a grown-up, should you be treated as an adult, or as a child? Government often blurs the distinction, and this is unhealthy for us individually and for society. The idea of government being responsible for us, *in loco parentis,* pervades political thinking and corrupts the relationship between citizens and government.

To reset the legal system, let's start with the issue of adulthood and address head-on the assumption that people cannot look after themselves or decide things for themselves.

Proposed Amendment: Adulthood

1. References to adults in this amendment shall mean real persons aged 18 years or older.

2. Adults have the right to be treated as adults, capable of making decisions of their own free will.

3. Government may not act *in loco parentis* to adults.

4. Government may not forcibly protect adults from their own actions taken of their own free will.

5. Government may not make any behavior by adults illegal unless their actions cause direct harm to other people or their property.

6. Government may not prevent adults from doing stupid, immoral, or dangerous things of their own free will, provided they cause no direct harm to other people or their property.

7. Adults shall be assumed in law to be fully responsible for their behavior and the consequences of their actions.

8. Government may not impose a legal duty on citizens to inform fellow citizens of the risks of their actions, nor a legal duty to listen to any such warnings given.

9. Government may not make citizens or organizations legally responsible or liable for the actions of other citizens.

10. Government may not require citizens or organizations to act in a law enforcement capacity.

11. Government may not require citizens or organizations to violate the Constitutional rights of other citizens.

12. Parents shall be assumed to be legally responsible for the actions of their non-adult children.

13. In guardianship situations, courts shall presume in favor of the wishes of the ward and their rights as an adult. Wards shall have the right to independent legal counsel.

14. Citizens shall have a right of movement and residence anywhere in the US or its Territories, and a right to leave the US, unless incarcerated or under a court-ordered travel restriction.

Responsible Adulthood

For legal purposes, an adult is defined here as anyone 18 years of age or older. 18 is the most common definition of adulthood used around the world and in the US legal system.

Children need to be nurtured, protected, and educated. They are supervised and restricted to guide them and prevent the worst mistakes. Parents (primarily) decide for them to achieve those ends.

Adults, by contrast, decide for themselves. They take actions of their own free will to achieve their ends. This is what it means to be an adult. Unfortunately, there's a downside: Adults sometimes make bad decisions.

So, should society pass laws to control adults and prevent them from doing stupid, foolhardy, or immoral things? If you believe in personal freedom, then the answer must be no.

Applying the Test of Moral Authority, do I have the right to stop my neighbor from doing something I think is stupid or immoral? No, I do not have that right. So long as he does no direct harm to another person or their property, then it's none of anyone else's business. By extension, it is also none of the government's business. My neighbor should be free to do whatever he wants.

This is the essence of the libertarian or classical liberal point of view. It's a fundament viewpoint of most Americans and a core philosophical underpinning of enlightenment thinkers and the Founders.

However, even if you disagree with those political or philosophical viewpoints, the line should still be drawn in favor of legal freedom for pragmatic reasons. If you draw the line anywhere else, you incentivize conflict between citizens.

There's always someone who thinks government force should be used to stop immoral behavior. Many contentious issues fall into this category: drugs, prostitution, guns, abortions, discrimination, hate speech and others.

Each of us has our opinions about what other people are doing. If you see someone making a mistake then say something, if you want. You might even feel a moral duty to speak up if you see others off-track. But a moral duty should not always be a legal duty. You have no legal right to prevent others from making mistakes.

When something is made illegal, then government force is activated. Men with guns and the power to imprison are deployed to stop citizens from doing things they want to do. Taken to an extreme, this becomes civil war.

So how should society deal with adults doing stupid or immoral things? By not interfering. Let adults be adults. Live and let live. The proposal therefore bans government from acting *in loco parentis*, or from requiring other citizens to act *in loco parentis*. Government cannot force any citizen to be responsible for or liable for another's actions, nor require anyone to violate citizens' rights on its behalf.

America The Mollycoddled

Historically, America had a long tradition of self-reliant and independent citizens, in alignment with the classical liberal tradition outlined above. But over the last 150 years or so government policies have increasingly pushed adults towards dependency and incentivized them to play victim. Policies such as:

- Federal regulation of interstate trade—starting in the 1880s, supposedly to prevent big business exploitation, but in the process removing choices from citizens.

- Social Security—starting in 1935, effectively deeming Americans unable to plan for their retirement income.

- Medicare—starting in 1965, deeming Americans unable to plan for their retirement healthcare.

- Occupational Licensing—starting in the early 1800s with medical licenses but accelerating greatly from the 1950s onwards, deeming Americans unable to decide for themselves if a person they wanted to employ was qualified for the job.

- Regulation—growing rapidly from the 1950s onwards, assuming Americans can't decide for themselves what is safe, or what working conditions they would choose.

- Punitive Damages—ballooning from the 1960s onwards, incentivizing attorneys and plaintiffs to find someone else to blame for anything going wrong because they profit greatly from it.

Collectively, these forces have led to thousands of rules and regulations restricting Americans on a day-by-day basis: safety warnings, health notices, cooling-off periods, compulsory healthcare, seat belt laws, requirements to use trustees, licensed contractors, and so on.

All these rules presume adults need protection from their own decisions. They contribute to the pernicious mindset that someone else is to blame whenever citizens feel bad. After a lifetime of government parenting, many of us don't even notice that our freedoms have been taken away.

Specific issues are tackled in other proposals, but the overall legal presumption asserted here is that adults should make their own decisions and accept the consequences of their decisions. If something goes wrong because of a decision you made, the primary responsibility is yours. Children

blame other people. Adults should suck it up and examine their own behavior! That's not to say others are never to blame, but you should start
with an honest examination of your part in the affair first.

Arguments Against Freedom

Individual special interests may not want to control you personally. But
they do want to influence what happens in their area of interest, which
typically involves restricting the choices you can make. Thousands of special interests have each individually manipulated the law, adding up to
(probably) tens of thousands of restrictions on citizens.

On behalf of special interests, armies of attorneys, politicians, and spin
doctors have been arguing for decades about why citizens should give up
their freedoms. The arguments get complex, but for our purposes here,
they are divided into three broad categories:

- Organizing things for the collective good.
- Preventing mistakes.
- Preventing immoral behavior.

The Collective Good

Organizing things for the collective good is a valid government function.
Basic rules are needed: the rules of the road (literally), no fraud, theft, or
violence, organization of police, courts, legislatures, and so on.

The problem is that government goes too far. We can test when government has gone too far with the Tests of Legitimate Governance. The
more tests a policy violates, the more questionable the policy. We should
be especially wary that government doesn't violate its primary function—
protecting individual rights—in pursuit of its secondary function of promoting the public good.

Mistakes

Mistakes happen, and they sometimes have adverse consequences. It
might appear at first glance that preventing mistakes is a worthy goal. But
mistakes have benefits:

- Humans learn by trial and error. Preventing errors thus prevents
  learning—for both physical skills (learning to drive), and social
  skills (learning to drink responsibly).
- On a personal level, making mistakes and learning to cope with
  them emotionally helps us mature.
- At a societal level, the scientific method is formalized trial and error. Technological progress depends on errors!

So, mistakes and errors are necessary, and public policy should allow for them. Government should only have a role when one person's mistakes might harm other people, such as:

- Regulating dangerous factories, nuclear power stations, air traffic control, etc.

- Preventing collateral damage when people do stupid things in public places (no drunk driving).

- Preventing public excess—sex, drugs, and rock and roll are fine in the privacy of your own home, but you should probably keep it down in public.

Even in these situations, the emphasis should be on minimizing and preventing harm to others, rather than preventing self-harm.

Immorality

Another argument for control is to keep citizens' moral behavior in check: X is evil and should be banned. Substitute your favorite synonym for evil: disgusting, unfair, immoral, discriminatory, racist, bigoted, etc.

This fails the Test of Moral Authority. Do I have the right to force my neighbor to see things my way? No, I do not have that right, and neither does the government. Government attempts to control moral behavior also create moral hazards, contradictions, and other drawbacks:

- You doubtless have opinions on contentious issues—drugs, kinky sex, abortions, guns, censorship, racism—but what makes your opinion, or any opinion, the correct one?

- If you think other people should have their moral choices controlled, you should be equally open to having your choices controlled. Do you want other people to decide how you run your life?

- Banning activity does not stop it. Did Prohibition, the War on Drugs, or bans on prostitution prevent any of them?

- Government manipulation of moral behavior is typically at the behest of special interests.

Rather than enhancing morality, bans often encourage law-breaking and societal decay:

- For some people, including almost everyone in the 15-25 age range, the mere fact that something is illegal makes it attractive to try out! Keep it legal, and its glamor is lessened.

- Bans weaken our capacity for moral reasoning. If you tell your kids to avoid drugs because they are illegal, and yet your kids see everyone doing drugs, they are learning contempt for the law.

- Bans have side effects. The War on Drugs, for example, encourages violence.

- Laws requiring the police to act as moral enforcers *of other people's morals* create distrust between police and citizens. They divert resources from real crimes like theft, fraud, and violence.

In short, government has no role in trying to control the moral choices of adult citizens. Do whatever you want, so long as you do no direct harm to other people or their property. Government should not be in the morality business at all—that's the business of the churches. In the US, in principle, we have a separation of church and state.

Young Adults

Legislators have created many laws that violate the rights of young adults, such as banning alcohol sales to those under 21. Typically, these laws are justified on the grounds of protecting people from harm.

Nonetheless, laws to protect young adults from themselves fail every Test of Legitimate Governance. They fail the Test of Purpose by violating young adults' rights. They fail the Test of Moral Authority because I have no right to prevent my young adult neighbor from drinking, and neither does the government. Drunken frat parties are evidence that these laws fail both the Test of Consent and the Test of Efficacy.[1] And nothing in the Constitution allows alcohol bans on 18-year-olds to pass the Test of Constitutional Authority.

Public safety is a valid government concern. However, alcohol bans for young adults are an example of government violating its primary role (protection of individual rights) to fulfill a secondary role (public safety). So, 18-year-olds should be allowed to drink, but drunk driving by adults *of any age* is unacceptable.

Other examples of restricting young adults on safety grounds can be solved without age discrimination. For example, several states require drivers to be 21 to apply for a Commercial Driver's License (CDL) to prevent inexperienced drivers from controlling large vehicles. Fair enough, but how about making it a requirement that CDL applicants have had a regular license for at least five years, or require more training? Many states allow teenage drivers to get a regular driver's license sooner if they take driver's ed. The same idea could work for CDL. Indeed, the Feds are already experimenting with pilot programs.[2] If there must be discrimination, let's at least discriminate based on demonstrable skills.

If you think that an 18-year-old is too young to drive a truck (let alone, drink alcohol), then you must question *all* decisions that 18-year-olds make: voting, enlisting in the military, college choices, marriage, etc.

Rather than micro-manage them, let's let young adults manage themselves. There will be winners and losers, and I guarantee you that stupid decisions will be made, including fatal decisions. But stupid decisions are made every day anyway.

Maybe the education system should teach decision-making skills! That's beyond the scope of this book, but what we can do here is stop the legal system mandating choices for young adults. The law must treat adults as adults.

An alternative solution to the problem of immature adults is licensing. Young adults could take a test to prove they are fit to be treated as adults, or if they were fit to be parents.[3]

Practically, adults do become fully launched by taking on adult responsibilities.[4] They leave school, get a job, leave home, and set up their own families. Still, the idea of licensing adults is probably abhorrent to most. If adulthood became politicized, if we had to take exams to get licensed as an adult, there'd be no end to the nonsense that might arise. Defining adults as anyone 18+ avoids possible manipulation.

Exceptions

There are two potential exceptions to the proposals on adulthood.

First, emancipated children. Legally, children are typically considered to need adult supervision. But a few children can and do act as adults, and sometimes even legally separate themselves from their parents to become emancipated minors. There are mechanisms under state and common law to deal with these rare situations, and they work well enough.

The second exception is the opposite one: unemancipated adults. Some adults cannot act on their own behalf, typically due to mental disabilities or developmental problems. They may still need parents or other trustees to help them. The most extreme cases are Guardianships, where a court appoints a Guardian (typically a family member) to look after the affairs of the person needing help (the Ward).

Guardianship is problematic because adult citizens are being deprived of their rights. Guardians have legal powers over the affairs of the Ward and can abuse that power. The National Council on Disabilities estimates that 1.3 million people are in guardianship arrangements, a number that has tripled in the last 3 decades.[5] Special interests—lawyers, charities, and businesses helping guardians and wards—are profiting.

Guardianship is a concern, but state governments are already trying to curb excesses and find alternatives to guardianship. State experimentation to find the right balance should be encouraged since each case is unique and blanket rules cannot fix everything.

At a constitutional level, the proposal here defines general principles. In disputes, courts should presume in favor of the wishes of the Ward. And wards will also have the right to independent legal counsel, as they always should have done. These are reasonable checks and balances.

Proposal 2—Legal Equality

The ordaining of laws in favor of one part of the nation, to the prejudice and oppression of another, is certainly the most erroneous and mistaken policy.

—Benjamin Franklin

Government can create laws that discriminate between groups. Those laws are a cornerstone of special interest manipulation.

To lessen the grip of special interests, our country needs true legal equality. That means laws that are *written equally* and *applied equally*. The government's role here is to provide a level legal playing field.

Proposed Amendment: Legal Equality

1. Government shall treat all citizens equally in all its operations.
2. All laws shall be written to apply equally to all citizens, except for laws that may regulate the operations of large organizations to better protect individual citizen rights.
3. Government may not discriminate for or against specific individuals, groups, organizations, classes of business, or areas of commerce.
4. Government may not try to make citizens equal by treating some unequally.
5. Government may not create laws treating government agents differently from other citizens, nor create exceptions or exemptions from the law for government agents, except where agents may have their rights restricted to better protect citizen rights.
6. Government may not create special classes of crimes against government agents.
7. Government may not claim sovereign immunity to negate its obligations under the Constitution.
8. All laws regulating the behavior of large organizations shall apply equally to government itself.

Equality Before the Law

When the Constitution was first written, women had no vote and slavery was common. Over the years the law has allowed and at times required discrimination against some racial groups, religions, and people from specific countries. It has taken many decades, many changes in the law, and even a few Constitutional amendments before *We the People* has come to include women and racial minorities. Progress has been made, but there's still work to be done. So, with respect to inequality, what next?

Inequality has been a hot topic in the last few years, mostly focusing on discrimination (prejudice), and economic inequality. Racism, sexism, and economic inequality are important issues we'll address later.

In this section though I would like to address the broader issue of *legal inequality*. Jim Crow laws, laws barring women from voting or holding specific jobs, Japanese internment during WWII. These types of discrimination were forced on us, *by law*.

The US has abolished most forms of legal discrimination over the last 60 years. But it is still there, still causing problems. It's time to stop all forms of legal discrimination, once and for all. Fix that problem, and social pressures will quickly minimize other forms of discrimination.

The discussion is divided broadly into two sections: inequality between citizens, and legal difference between citizens and government employees.

Legal Inequality Between Citizens

Do citizens currently have equality before the law? No, but we're closer than we've ever been from a historical perspective.

At first glance, the Constitution appears to guarantee equality before the law. The 14th Amendment reads *no State shall [...] deny to any person within its jurisdiction the equal protection of the laws*. The 14th was adopted in 1868 to help freed slaves get equal treatment. It was a big step in the right direction but left some ambiguous loopholes.

One ambiguity was that laws were applied equally, but they were not always written equally. This enabled practices such as the "separate but equal" approach to racism that was pursued by southern states before the passage of the 1963 Civil Rights Act. Even today, governments write laws that discriminate. It may be positive discrimination (affirmative action), but it is still discrimination.

Another problem is that the 14th Amendment applies to states, but not to the feds. The feds have felt free to discriminate and not provide equal protection for everyone within their jurisdiction. This opens the door to, for example, no due legal process for suspected terrorists.

The biggest problem though is manipulation: legislation that creates and enforces legal inequalities to benefit special interests. Legislation that dictates who can do what work, sell which products, have access to special loans, get tax breaks or subsidies, or get protected by tariffs.

This legislation is typically framed as providing a benefit for the common good, such as protecting customers. Nonetheless, it gives one group a legal advantage at the expense of the rest of us. This violates the central function of government: protecting our individual rights. *You cannot protect individual rights by giving some groups more rights than others.*

The intent here is to end all laws helping one group of citizens at the expense of others. No citizen should ever have legal advantages. If governments have powers to legally discriminate, that power will be manipulated and abused. The answer is not improved management of government power, but rather removal of that power altogether.

A worrisome trend in recent decades is government attempts to force people to be equal (economically or socially) rather than providing a level legal playing field. Affirmative action is an example.

Even if well-intentioned, the use of legal force to discriminate opens the door to manipulation. Discriminating to fix discrimination also defies common sense: Two wrongs do not make a right. Affirmative action will be banned by the proposals here.

One exception that will be allowed here is the regulation of large corporations. Treating corporations as artificial persons has legal and economic advantages. Nonetheless, they are not real people, and they shouldn't have the same rights as citizens. Since large corporations can have disproportionate impacts on the environment and public safety, let's allow for them to be regulated for those issues.

Further, to avoid potential abuse, let's also give government skin in the game. The definition of large organizations assumes government itself is a large organization, subject to the same rules that it creates for others. (See *Appendix 2—Definitions and Assumptions* for details).

Legal Inequality Between Government Employees and Citizens

Of particular concern when it comes to legal inequality is when government employees are treated, legally, differently from regular citizens.

An example of this is crimes against government employees, such as 18 USC § 11 which makes assault on a federal employee a federal crime. Most post offices display a notice restating this law as it applies to mail carriers.

These laws create problems. For starters, they are unnecessary. Mail carriers don't need a special law protecting them from assault because assault is already a crime everywhere. Further, most government employees are the same as private sector employees. Your mail carrier is no different from the UPS guy.

Over-complexity and extra-criminalization together create a quasi-double jeopardy. Double jeopardy is the legal principle that you should not be convicted twice for the same crime. Assault is assault. If legislators create variations on assault based on incidental details—such as who the victim works for—then you potentially prosecute several crimes when only one was committed.

Additionally, special laws for government employees contribute to an us-and-them mentality that poisons relations between government workers and citizens. The only thing special about government workers is that they work for us!

To avoid these problems, let's create a blanket rule: no special laws protecting government workers. The law should treat all citizens equally, including citizens who happen to work for the government. All legal privileges for government employees should end. Period.

Some government employees (police, prison officers, and the military) need to use force as part of their duties. Legal protections for police officers (in particular) have become controversial. Over several decades, things have swung too far in favor of the police, and the proposals here will end qualified immunity,[1] which has become an abuse allowing cops to commit crimes with impunity.

Nonetheless, as part of their job, police officers use threats, restraints, and sometimes violence. Most police violence is probably justified, especially when individual officers are under threat. Defunding the police is not a practical solution.

What's needed is balance, which largely comes down to clarifying what *necessary* force means. Refining the meaning of *necessary* is an ongoing task for courts and legislators, with no easy answers.

This issue is discussed further in *Proposal 19—Law Enforcement.*

Government Pensions and Taxes

Many government employees can opt out of Social Security in favor of federal and state employee pension plans. However, this is not government-as-employer offering generous pensions. This is government-as-lawmaker offering workers a *legal* advantage. It's an abuse of government power. It is corruption. Legally advantaged pensions will become illegal when government cannot create legal exceptions for its workers.

Tax breaks for government workers are a similar moral hazard. Currently, this mostly crops up as tax breaks for veterans in the federal tax code,[2] and property tax exemptions in some states.

These tax breaks should go. It's not a problem if government-as-employer offers veterans generous pensions. But government-as-lawmaker cannot be allowed to violate its fundamental duty to ensure equal treatment under the law. It is often argued that this is justified because veterans have sacrificed so much. But those veterans made sacrifices to preserve America, and legal inequality is not what America is about.

We cannot allow government workers, of any sort, to get exceptions like tax breaks. It is a violation of government's fundamental duty to provide equality under the law.

Taken to its logical extreme, we'd have government workers, some with tenure, paying no taxes yet supported by taxpayers who have money extracted from them by force. We'd have recreated feudalism.

Proposal 3—Free Speech

If freedom of speech is taken away, then dumb and silent we may be led, like sheep to the slaughter.

—George Washington

Free speech is under attack. There are worrying trends in the suppression of free speech in the media, universities, and Big Tech.

There's also pushback, and things will improve, but we can't allow the government to be the one pushing back. The government's primary role is to protect individual rights, including 1st Amendment rights.

Proposed Amendment: Free Speech

1. Government may not restrict freedom of speech in any form, written, spoken, or via any other form of media or communication.

2. Government may not disallow nor compel any form of speech or choice of words, nor require warnings about speech.

3. Government may not engage in censorship or require citizens to engage in censorship.

4. Large organizations offering any public notice board, forum, or media platform may not engage in censorship of those who contribute to that notice board. Tools allowing other users to block content shall be allowable.

5. Hate speech, or any variant thereof, shall not be a crime or grounds for tort actions.

6. Defamation shall not be a crime. Defamation shall be allowable as a civil tort, but plaintiffs must show both an intent to defame and deliberate known falsehoods publicized widely by the defendants.

7. Speech per se may not be construed as violence in any legal proceeding, criminal or civil.

8. Lying to government agents shall not be a crime per se.

9. No government agent may knowingly lie to citizens.

We Need Free Speech

We must have free speech. Thinking and learning is an unending process of thesis, antithesis, and synthesis. This happens in every conversation over the kitchen table, in political debates, in business meetings, and in the formal scientific method. Free speech is necessary for free thought, for a free life, and for human progress.

As is their right, not everyone agrees. The limits of free speech have probably been contested from the moment speech evolved. In the US, the legal limits have been argued about since the Constitution was written. In recent years the arguments have intensified.

Many are concerned about social media creating echo chambers where radicals talk to each other and reinforce their views. People are losing their jobs for their opinions, getting canceled, and having social media accounts suspended, most notably Trump himself while still president! On campuses, attacks on free speech have become more extreme.[1] In politics, accusations of lying or disinformation have become the norm from both sides.

Despite the heat of the arguments, there is plenty of pushback. With Elon Musk's purchase of Twitter in 2022, free speech is arguably getting a revival, and recent attempts at censorship are coming to light. Alternative social media platforms are springing up. New podcasts and news outlets are pushing back against media bias or supplying counterbalancing bias. On campuses, a few academics are starting to speak out against censorship and compelled speech[2]. Chicago University issued the "Chicago Principles," reaffirming their commitment to free speech.[3]

Reaffirming the Right to Free Speech

All this pushback is positive. All will be well, provided that the government does not try to control free speech. However, the government has already been meddling in free speech in several ways. There are calls for legislation to curb lies or even a rethink of the 1st Amendment. [4]

However, activists who argue for censorship are playing with fire. When the government defines truth, then truth becomes political and open to manipulation. Censorship tools wielded against your enemies today will be used against you tomorrow. This way lies madness, let's not go there!

Rather than more control, let's instead reaffirm America's commitment to free speech. The proposals here will roll back several laws which go too far in the wrong direction. There's also a fix for the contemporary problems with Big Tech censorship.

In the US, free speech is a protected individual right under the 1st Amendment (1A). Attempts to curb free speech fail the Test of Constitutional Authority and further fail the Test of Purpose because government's primary responsibility is to protect those individual rights.

Curbing free speech fails the Test of Moral Authority: do I have the right to stop my neighbor from speaking her mind? No, I do not, and by extension neither does the government. I can disagree with her, question her, and find evidence to dispute her point of view. But I have no right to prevent her from speaking. Neither does the government.

Although survey data varies depending on what questions you ask, most Americans are in favor of free speech, [5] so censorship fails the Test of Consent. And curbing speech is such a nebulous goal that it's difficult to see how any restrictions would pass the Test of Efficacy.

Attempts to curb free speech thus fail all the Tests of Legitimate Governance. Nonetheless, there is scope for strengthening these protections to cut out some ill-advised legislation and curb some other legal problems.

There is a need to strengthen the 1A because the original wording has created a problem. The relevant part says: *Congress shall pass no law [...] abridging freedom of speech.* Clearly, Congress cannot create legislation abridging freedom of speech. But what about the states? Or, in the modern era, what about executive or administrative orders, the courts?

Since the passing of the 14th Amendment (1868), the Supreme Court has normally taken the position that rights like free speech are always protected. The proposal here makes this explicit: no government may impinge on free speech. All branches, agents, employees, and representatives of any US government have as their primary duty the protection of individual rights, including free speech.

Another aim of the proposal is to repeal all hate speech laws. Free speech must include the right to say hateful things, even if those things are immoral, wrong, or upsetting. Most Americans agree that hate speech is immoral but should not be illegal.[6] Hate speech laws fail the Test of Consent.

A common argument for hate speech legislation is that speech can hurt people's feelings. At the extreme, this becomes a speech is violence argument, claiming that violence is anything that makes someone feel bad.

This approach cannot work (and thus fails the Test of Efficacy). It's not possible to build a society based on protecting people from their feelings because we don't all have the same feelings. Feelings are subjective and cannot be a basis for a legal system based on objective standards.

If you are insulted, offended, or hurt by other people's speech, then ignore it. Walk away. If you can't do that, then you need help from a therapist, not a lawyer. The reality of adult life is that we can't control the others around us. We must each of us learn and mature to the point where we can function well no matter what others say to us.

In the big picture, if you are worried about hate speech here's the solution: *love speech.* If you think someone else is saying something hateful, then feel free to lovingly persuade them of their errors.

Libel and slander laws, and related court cases, are another area where the law needs to be dialed back. There has always been a distinction between being able to speak freely and being shielded from the consequences of that speech. Libel and slander lawsuits have been allowed under common law for a long time.[7]

Those lawsuits will still be allowable, but with some checks to prevent excessive damages.[8] Firstly, the government should never prosecute defamation cases; defamation is a tort, not a crime. Secondly, the plaintiff in a defamation case should have to prove both an intent to defame and the deliberate use of falsehoods by the defendant. Thirdly, *Proposal 18—Civil Justice* will limit punitive damages, lowering the financial incentives that encourage slander and libel cases.

Another area needing revision is the criminalization of lying to government agents. Government agents often need information from the public to do their jobs, and lying to them is usually illegal. For example, under 18 USC §1001, making false statements to any federal agent or concealing information is a crime.

Lying to government agents might occasionally cause problems, but the criminalization of lying causes worse problems. It's too easy for prosecutors to turn mistakes into offenses. And there's a potential conflict with the 5th Amendment: you have a right not to incriminate yourself, but it may be a crime to withhold information.

To avoid these conflicts let's remove lying to government agents as a crime per se. That does not mean you can lie to the government with impunity. If you lie in court, having sworn to tell the truth, then you are committing perjury. If you affirm in writing that you are telling the truth whilst, in reality, you are lying, then you are committing fraud. Lying may be evidence of a crime but lying per se should not be the crime.

Social Media

In recent years, Big Tech social media platforms have been engaging in censorship, culminating in the removal of President Trump from most social media platforms in late 2020.[9] This has been deeply controversial.

The Founders saw government censorship as the problem and wrote the Constitution accordingly. Individuals, such as publishers, have always been free to decide what they would or wouldn't publish. So, as the Constitution is written, private entities do have the right to censor. However, the world has changed, and this has become a problem.

If most speech takes place on social media, and if social media belongs to private organizations that can censor, then speech has become subject to censorship. It's not government censorship, but it is so wide-ranging that it might as well be. Effectively, Big Tech now owns the town square and can remove you from it if they don't like what you say.

There's a simple fix proposed here. Let's subject big organizations to the same rules as government itself. Big organizations shouldn't be allowed to violate any individual citizen's constitutional rights.

As applied here, big organizations offering a social media platform will not be allowed to censor that platform. It will be allowable for those organizations to supply tools so that individual citizens can block things for themselves, flag things as potentially untrue, or post counterarguments. However, the platforms themselves should not censor users.

Proposal 4—Freedom of Contract

*No State shall...pass any...Law impairing the Obligation of
Contracts...*
—US Constitution, Article I, Section 10, Clause 1

US governments have found a multitude of ways to interfere with contracts between citizens, defying both the unusually clear wording of the Constitution and the moral authority of government. It's time to reassert our freedoms, including freedom of contract.

Note that Freedom of Contract is closely related to Freedom of Trade, and the issues may overlap. Broadly, domestic issues are addressed here, and foreign issues in the next chapter.

Proposed Amendment: Freedom of Contract

1. Government may not interfere with contracts made between citizens.
2. All contracts between citizens shall be legal provided that:
   a. All parties are willing participants in the contract.
   b. No direct damage is caused to third parties or their property.
   c. The contract does not violate the Constitution.
   d. No contract may indemnify any person from breaking the law, nor punish them for reporting lawbreaking.
3. All parties to a contract shall have a duty of care to:
   a. Be honest in the transaction.
   b. Disclose any information known to them that they believe to be relevant to the contract.
   c. State relevant qualifications and experience to perform any service if asked.
4. Other than requirements they may have internally for government employees, government may not restrict employment or service contracts between citizens, including:
   a. Setting wage or payment rates, or minimum or maximum rates.
   b. Requiring occupational licensing or registration.
   c. Specifying education, training, or experience requirements.
   d. Requiring posting of qualifications.
   e. Requiring compulsory insurance or bond.
5. Government may not impose employment or service contract restrictions indirectly via conditions attached to government funding, grants, or contracts.
6. Large organizations may not enter agreements with the intent of:
   a. Creating cartels or monopolies.

    b. Restricting the rights of third parties to compete.

    c. Evading any law.

7. Courts shall presume that a contract is valid and enforceable unless proven otherwise, and may not void contracts unless there is fraud, coercion, or contract terms that violate the Constitution.

8. Nothing in this amendment nor any clause of the Constitution may be used to restrict fair competition or protect businesses from competition.

9. Government may not presume contracts where none explicitly exists between the parties.

10. Gambling shall be legal without government restriction.

Why Freedom of Contract is Important

If you and I are both free citizens of a free country, shouldn't we be free to agree to any deal between the two of us that we wish? The Founders thought so and barred governments from interfering in contracts. All legislation restricting contacts violates the Test of Constitutional Authority.

Restrictions on contracts also fail the Test of Moral Authority: do I have any right to tell my neighbor what deals he can do? No, I do not. So long as he does no direct harm to me or my property it's none of my business. By extension, it is also none of the government's business.

Left to themselves, citizens do mutually beneficial deals. Why would you agree to a deal that didn't work for you? Why would the person you're making a deal with do it if it did not work for them?

Individual deals benefit the people making the deal. They also benefit the rest of us. If every deal creates a small gain, then more deals, faster, maximizes economic growth.

Growth creates choices and improves the chances of everyone getting exactly what they want. Over time, the marketplace gets increasingly efficient at meeting the needs of society. Increased choices lessen fraud and coercion: if you don't like an offer, you have a higher chance of finding an option you do like. Dishonest actors will get squeezed out.

Overall, freedom of contract is a win-win for everyone, supplying both individual freedom and simultaneously *promoting the common good.*

Despite the collective benefits of freedom of contract, special interests want you to have less freedom. Unions want you to employ their members. Corporations want a monopoly for their products. Professional associations want you to use their licensed professionals. Religions want you to obey their moral ideals. Every government agency wants you to get their permission before you act.

Most special interests only want to restrict freedom in their area. They may even favor freedom of choice in principle, just not as it applies to them. But collectively special interests have persuaded legislators, over many decades, to impose thousands of rules about what kinds of deals citizens can make. Rules about wages, hours, overtime, working conditions. Requirements to use union labor. Occupational licensing restrictions. Things we're allowed to buy and sell, quality standards, safety standards, required disclosures and warnings, required permits, studies, reports, and public consultations.

No matter how well-intentioned, government controls remove freedom of choice from citizens. We don't need the government to tell us what our interests are, or how to achieve them. Everyone is already motivated to act in their own best interests.

Many Americans agree with freedom of contract in principle but worry in practice about the power of large corporations. There's a perception that freedom of contract might allow the strong to exploit the weak.

So, how can things be arranged to maximize freedom of contract but keep potential exploitation in check? Simple: let citizens and small organizations negotiate any deals they want between themselves. And let the government create rules (if needed) to ensure big corporations—and the government itself—play fair. A distinction between small and large dealmakers allows for maximum personal choice. It keeps the government off the backs of citizens and small businesses but provides a safety net against exploitation by big business.

Additionally, this would prevent large organizations from using the government to shut down competition. Practically speaking, regulations are written by the regulated (see *Proposal 13—Regulation*) so they write rules to shut down the little guys. If only large corporations are regulated, small businesses can compete.

Competition also constrains the regulators. If big business is over-regulated it will fall back compared to small business. If it goes too far, big business will push back. There will be a balance of forces.

Over time, these provisions will create an increasingly diverse marketplace. Competition will produce the best mix of innovation, customer choice, lower prices, and good corporate practices. There will be less chance of monopoly abuse. If you don't like an organization, shop elsewhere. Vote with your wallet and don't give them your business. This will become easier when large organizations have no power to shut down small organizations.

Consequences

A fully restored right to freedom of contract will end a lot of legislation and regulatory oversight (except for the regulation of big corporations). Some of the most important changes are discussed below.

Employment Law

Over the decades, governments have created many restrictions on employment contracts. These range from the very definition of who is an employee or a contractor (typically for tax reasons) through restrictions on pay (minimum wages), benefits, working hours, overtime rates, working conditions, health and safety rules, and so on.

The intent here is that employment laws violating freedom of contract should go. If regulation is needed, it can be reapplied, but only to large organizations. Small firms and individuals will be exempt.

Note that safety standards are unlikely to slip. Both employers and employees want safe working conditions to avoid accidents and lawsuits. Incentives are already aligned to keep everyone healthy and safe.

Minimum wage legislation started in the US with the Fair Labor Standards Act of 1938, part of Roosevelt's New Deal. Minimum wage laws are well intended; enabling workers to earn a decent living is a noble goal.

Despite good intentions, minimum wage legislation fails every Test of Legitimate Governance. It is a violation of freedom of contract and thus fails the Test of Constitutional Authority. It violates the government's primary role of protecting individual rights, failing the Test of Purpose.

As regards the Test of Moral Authority, I have no right to tell my neighbor who he can employ or for how much, and I have no right to stop his employee from agreeing to work for $1/hour. So long as the two of them agree voluntarily, then it is none of my business, and it is none of the government's either.

Minimum wages also (arguably) fail the Test of Consent. This is difficult to be clear about because most surveys on the matter address the rate of any minimum wage and not the wage itself. Still, it's fairly easy to find people on both sides of the minimum wage argument.

Lastly, minimum wages fail the Test of Efficacy. Minimum wages are supposed to help the poor, but decades of evidence show these laws don't work.[1] They hurt most the people they are intended to help.[2]

This is because minimum wage legislation violates the lessons of Economics 101. The higher the cost of employing someone, the less employers will employ them. Thus, for young and unskilled workers, minimum wages cause unemployment. They do not have a skill worth paying minimum wage for, but they cannot gain skills without working. They are prevented from getting on the employment ladder.

Bureau of Labor statistics show that most minimum wage workers are inexperienced. They are predominantly young, unmarried, or working part-time.[3] They are a tiny proportion of the workforce, 2.5% and falling. Even if you would like higher wages for the poor, is it reasonable that kids fresh out of high school earn a living wage on their first job?

Another reason to abolish minimum wages is that they are deeply racist.[4] In industry after industry, over the last 80 years, the introduction of minimum wage laws decimated black employment rates.[5] Given a choice between a black guy and a white guy with the same skills and the same minimum wage, a bigoted employer may prefer the white guy. If the black guy was willing to work for $1/hour less, the employer is now paying for his bigotry if he employs the white guy. Minimum wage laws thus subsidize racism by removing economic penalties on employers who discriminate.

Now, would it be better if the black guy didn't have to work for less to get the job? Yes, but if that's what it takes for him to get the job, shouldn't he have the choice? And once he's working, maybe his bigoted employer will get to know him and trust him. He'll gain experience. He can work his way past discrimination.

Minimum wages should go. But there will be resistance. Minimum wage policies have survived decades of evidence that they are ineffective. They persist due to pressure from special interests such as:

- Unions, working to keep competition down for their members.
- (Ironically) minimum wage earners who don't want competition from someone willing to work for less.
- Manufacturers of equipment to automate minimum wage jobs.
- Politicians seeking votes from the well-meaning, whilst cynically ignoring the evidence that the policy is ineffective.

If you want to see everyone earning a living wage, I appreciate your good intent. But minimum wage legislation is not a solution. It causes chronic unemployment among the young, especially young African-American men. And it is a violation of our freedoms as citizens. Please, *find another way*. Let's free people to find their own way out of poverty.

Occupational Licenses

In 1950 about 5% of occupations required a license. Today it's closer to 30%, varying by state. A 2015 White House study[6] found that Ohio imposes licenses on 33.3% of workers; in Florida, it's 28.7%; in California, 20.7%; and in Nevada, 30.7%. Sixty occupations are regulated in all states. 1,110 occupations are regulated in at least one state.

Despite their ubiquity, occupational license laws violate every test of Legitimate Governance: The Test of Moral Authority (I have no right to tell my neighbor who he should use an electrician), The Test of Purpose (my rights cannot be protected by giving other individuals more rights), The Test of Consent (few would argue about doctors, but licensed hairdressers are obvious nonsense), and The Test of Constitutional Authority (nothing in the constitution about licensing).

As regards the Test of Efficacy, occupational licenses are usually justified on grounds of protecting customers. We need licensed electricians because electricity is dangerous, we need licensed lawyers because the law is complex, and so on. However, the degree of protection consumers get is questionable.

Occupational licenses are a classic Bootleggers and Baptists situation. Publicly, consumer protection is lauded. But behind the scenes, occupational licenses are about special interests gaming the system. Professions have become cartels: a small group of people who legally keep others out, restrict competition, and keep their profits high. Occupational licenses are government-created economic inequality!

Occupational licenses also restrict innovation. Monopolists have little incentive to innovate—they are happy with the system as it is. If improved products or methods come along, the licensed people can keep them out, or control them.

As an example of licensing slowing innovation, take flu shots. Nowadays these are often available at pharmacies. It's quick, easy, local, and frees up doctors and nurses to focus on other things. It's a win for everyone, but it wasn't enough to just have the idea and try it out. The law had to be changed in most states. That happened in the 1990s, but why was the extra step of changing the law needed?[7]

Furthermore, pharmacists are still over-qualified. Why not a person trained to do nothing except flu shots? Or what about citizens injecting their own flu shots? Diabetics often self-administer insulin shots, so why not flu shots?

Let me be clear: I am in favor of well-trained professionals. The higher the stakes, the higher my motivation to find the right person. If I needed heart surgery, I'd look for a surgeon who went to a reputable school, specializes in heart surgery, and is board-certified to the Nth degree.

When looking for a professional, qualifications help find the right person. They are so helpful that they don't need to be a legal requirement. Customers are *already* incentivized to ask for qualifications. Vendors are *already* incentivized to get meaningful qualifications and market them to customers. Let's encourage qualifications but avoid problems that arise when qualifications become licenses.

Gay Marriage

From a legal perspective, marriage is a contract. If two (or more) adults of any sex want to get married, there should be no legal obstacle. That's what freedom of contract means!

Opinions vary widely among US citizens about gay marriage and its effects on society and child-rearing. If a church declines to sanctify gay marriages, that's their right as a private institution. If you think every child should have a mother and a father raising them, feel free to campaign for traditional marriages.

Citizens can have any opinion they want, but since the US has a separation of church and state, no government should take any position on the morality of gay marriage. The state's role is not to decide how adult citizens arrange their lives. The state's role is to protect our rights, including the right to freedom of contract.

If a government worker disagrees with gay marriage and is unwilling to uphold the law, they should quit or be fired. Government workers are paid to do their jobs, and if that clashes with their moral convictions then they should quit. No one is forced to work for the government.

In December 2022, Congress passed a "Respect for Marriage" bill making gay marriages legal everywhere in the USA. It is good to correct past mistakes, but such legislation should not be necessary. We already have freedom of contract under the Constitution.

Divorce and Family Law

Many men complain that family law and the divorce courts are biased in favor of women.[8] Historically, women were at a big disadvantage under traditional gender roles, and a legal rebalancing was needed. [9] However, finding the correct balance is difficult. Every situation is different, especially when children are involved. The proposals here do not address marriage or divorce explicitly. However, there will be implicit changes:

- Legislation should never override freely made contracts, including prenups. The law should assume both parties are consenting adults. If one of them later changes their mind, it is up to them to renegotiate. The law should be neutral.

- Legislation should not presume contracts not explicitly agreed upon by both parties, including common law marriages. Adults can enter into informal agreements, oral or written, and if something goes wrong the courts may need to resolve disputes. However, legislation should not presume, for example, that if a couple lives in the same house for six months they suddenly have the same legal obligations as a formal marriage.

- *Proposal 30—Children* stipulates that both parents should have equal rights and responsibilities concerning the children in cases of divorce or dispute.

Family law and the divorce courts are rife with manipulation. Lawyers, child protection agencies, and psychological providers all profit when people divorce and fight over the kids.

Even though divorce implies conflict between the parties, the law itself must be neutral. Legal neutrality starts with an assumption that both parties have equal agency, equal rights, and equal responsibilities. Existing agreements between them should be honored.

Price Gouging

During the Coronavirus scare, price gouging was once again headline news, with complaints about prices for hand sanitizer and facemasks.[10] Amazon, eBay, and other retailers got letters from state prosecutors urging them to crack down on excessive prices—and many complied.

About 40 states had price gouging laws as of 2020.[11] They are supposed to protect the public from excessive prices after natural disasters. Anecdotally, these laws are popular, though there's little hard data on that.

Nonetheless, price gouging laws should be repealed because they violate every Test of Legitimate Goverance. They fail the Test of Constitutional Authority because nothing in the Constitution allows price fixing. They fail the Test of Purpose because they make me less free. They fail the Test of Moral Authority because my neighbor does not have the right to tell me how much I should pay for something, and neither does the government. When citizens buy high-priced stuff despite price gouging laws, then those laws fail the Test of Consent.

Worst of all, price gouging laws fail the Test of Efficacy because they make things worse when disaster strikes. This happens because they ignore a central lesson of economics: *To ensure low prices for customers, you must allow sellers to charge high prices.*

Understanding this apparent paradox requires an understanding of prices. Prices are not a moral issue, and they are not all about profit. Prices are primarily information that allows the market to respond to the needs of buyers. Let's use facemasks as an example.

Suppose there's a pandemic. Buyers want facemasks and can't find them. Since the buyers compete with each other, they start bidding up the price. High prices signal a shortage of facemasks.

Sellers see the price signal, and since they want to make money, they are motivated to find or produce more facemasks to sell. The higher the price, the higher the motivation and the more sellers will try and join in.

Prices also enable sellers to make economic calculations about how to get facemasks to buyers. They may incur extra shipping costs to get masks from factories to users quickly. If prices are high enough, manufacturers will stop making other things and start making facemasks instead. It takes time, money, and effort to convert a factory from making (say) auto parts into a facemask factory. And it takes time, money, and effort to convert it back to auto parts production later. Only if prices get high enough is this effort worth it.

Eventually, if prices are allowed to go up enough to motivate enough sellers, there comes a point when there's a surplus. The higher the price in the early stages of the shortage, the quicker this point is reached. Now, instead of buyers competing and driving prices up, sellers are competing and driving prices down. Competition quickly forces prices down until they are close to the sellers' costs, or even go below costs while the market finds a new equilibrium. Anyone who wants a mask can get one cheaply.

For all this market magic to happen, prices must be able to move freely so that everyone in the market—buyers, sellers, manufacturers, wholesalers, shippers, and retailers—has clear information about what the market wants. At the end of the day, *the market is citizens freely making decisions about what they want and are willing to pay for.* Prices are a summation of the decisions made by individual citizens. No government agency can predict this, control this, or manage it. Prices are simply the best way to collect information about what people want.

Further, for government to override prices is profoundly undemocratic. Citizens bid prices up when they want things and are willing to pay for them. When the government says, "You're not allowed to buy that item at that price," they are effectively saying, "We don't care what you want." It is a violation of our rights to freedom of contract and freedom of trade. It violates our free will and the pursuit of happiness as we each see fit.

High prices in this context are often described as gouging or exploiting customers. And no doubt a few lucky people happened to have a box of facemasks and saw an opportunity to sell them at a huge profit.

However, rather than hurting consumers, these early sellers are performing a valuable service. If a seller takes her $1 facemasks and puts them on eBay asking $20 each, *and gets her asking price.* now everyone knows what facemasks are worth today. The price signal is strong and clear, especially as an average of thousands of sales.

Further, there is no gouging, and no buyers are exploited. All transactions are voluntary. *No one is forced to buy.* Instead, high prices encourage buyers to think, prioritize, and only buy if sufficiently motivated. If you are at home with a well-stocked freezer, do you need an expensive facemask? No, you can probably wait a few weeks and let doctors and nurses get them first.

The benefits of the price system are especially stark compared to the alternatives. Firstly, if the government imposes a low price, manufacturers are disincentivized from producing facemasks. Price controls cause shortages. Secondly, a fixed price distorts how masks are distributed. Absent a market price, allocation takes place in one of three ways:

1. First come, first served. This will prioritize the young and healthy who can move faster, rather than old, infirm, or poor people who can't get to the store quickly.

2. Random, such as a lottery. This offers zero guarantee that people who *need* facemasks will get them.

3. Government management of supply. This is government officials guessing what people need since only individuals know what they actually need. It's also subject to manipulation.

A further economic consequence of price gouging laws is that they subsidize selfishness in the form of *hoarding.*

Suppose you had a box of 20 facemasks, and a pandemic starts. If the government capped prices at $1 each, you might keep them, just in case, even if you had no use for them, and it only costs you $20 to keep them. If instead facemasks are selling for $20 each on eBay, you'd lose $400 by hoarding them.

Now, is it selfish of you to hang onto your masks? Sure. It might be nice of you to give your surplus masks to a hospital. But they are your masks, and it is your choice what you do with them.

Nonetheless, public policy should not encourage hoarding. Rather, it should encourage the circulation of masks to maximize the chances of them ending up where they are most needed. Price caps encourage hoarding, rising prices encourage circulation.

And there are many other problems with price gouging laws:

- The laws themselves are typically badly written. What price is excessive? When does it become gouging? Legislation often uses ambiguous terms: "excessive prices," "unconscionable prices" and so on.

- When there's a disaster, government resources should be focused on helping victims rather than prosecuting sellers who are also helping, even if at a high price. To maximize help after a disaster, let those who see a profit opportunity pile in!

- These laws are unnecessary. People *already* dislike being taken advantage of. If my supermarket doubled prices after a tornado, I might buy food from them today because I need it, but I'll punish them tomorrow by buying it elsewhere. They know it and I know it, so we are both motivated to be reasonable.

- State prosecutors urging retailers to curb price gouging are asking retailers to deliberately distort market pricing and thus market feedback on what consumers want. Government has no right to set prices let alone urge commercial organizations to do it for them.

Words like gouging imply blood-splattered nastiness. But no one is being gouged, no one is being forced to do anything against their will. Rather, this is a moral crusade, with state prosecutors acting as moral authorities. How is asking retailers to charge reasonable prices different from (say) asking them to cover their female models in burkas because they are being immodest?

Price gouging laws are government acting as a theocracy, with prosecutors as the priests of high moral virtue. But this is not how things should be done in the US. Separation of church and state means it is not the job of any government to act as a moral arbiter of citizen behavior beyond the basic protections of no violence, theft, or fraud.

Enforcement of Contracts

It is the job of the courts to protect and enforce all our rights, including our rights to freely enter contracts. It is vitally important that the courts enforce contracts.

Enforcement is important for the individuals who agreed to the contract. If you employ someone to fix your roof, and it's still leaking, then you want it repaired. If you buy something and don't receive it, then you want your money returned.

In the big picture though, it's also important for society that contracts are upheld. If contracts are difficult to enforce, then everyone becomes increasingly cautious about making deals. They might do extra due diligence or buy extra insurance, which costs time and money. Poor enforcement of contracts thus slows down the rate of deal-making, lowering economic growth.

Poor enforcement also results in experiments not being done because they are too legally risky. Suppose, for example, that a terminally ill patient agrees to take an experimental drug, and two weeks later he's dead. Even though he'd probably have died anyway, and even though everyone relevant (i.e.: the patient) knew he was taking an experimental drug, someone may think they have a suit against the medical researchers and will sue them for killing their relative! Unless the medical researchers feel safe entering these contracts, they won't! No experiments, less chance of a cure. Everyone loses.

The legal system and courts are an operating system within which deals take place, and poorly functioning courts are a drag on economic growth. So, for the benefit of those making contracts, and for the benefit of society, the rule should be that courts assume a contract is valid and enforceable unless proven otherwise.

In theory, courts already treat contacts this way. Restating the obvious will help the courts to resist manipulation. Defense lawyers will no doubt remind the courts of their duties if necessary.

Proposal 5—Free Trade

The exercise of a free trade with all parts of the world [is]
possessed by [a people] as of natural right.

—Thomas Jefferson

As free citizens of a free country, we should be free to trade as we see fit, with anyone, anywhere, anytime. As well as being an individual right, free trade is also good public policy—it makes us all richer.

The US reluctantly recognizes the benefits of free trade and has made agreements with most of our major trading partners. However, those agreements are riddled with exceptions and rules that benefit special interests. And every president wants to meddle, one way or the other.

Let's cut to the chase and free up free trade.

Proposed Amendment: Free Trade

1. Citizens have the right to trade goods or services with anyone anywhere.
2. All goods and services legally traded within the US shall be legally tradable across US borders.
3. Citizens may conduct trade in any currency, keep financial accounts in any country, and move any amount of money across US borders. Citizens shall not be required to report these accounts or transactions except in summary form for tax returns, or by court order where there is probable cause of a felony.
4. Government may not place trade embargoes or restrictions on foreign countries, persons, or goods, nor enter into international agreements that restrict citizens from free trade, except as allowed for below.
5. Government may create regulations to ensure public health and safety when trading:
   a. Weapons of mass destruction.
   b. Items where accidental release might cause mass harm.
   c. Biological organisms where accidental release may cause ecological damage.
6. Government may place temporary restrictions on the passage of persons or goods arriving in the US from countries where a disease epidemic is in progress and where there is potential for contagion.
7. Government may regulate imports by large organizations to ensure US environmental and safety standards are met. Individual citizens and small organizations shall not be subject to these regulations.

8. Citizens may cross US borders without being subject to search or seizure of their person or property, except for reasonable screening to ensure transportation safety.

9. Government may not collect taxes or fees, nor place controls on persons, goods, information, services, or currencies crossing US borders.

10. Government may not require citizens to declare or disclose cross-border activity, except when needed to regulate public health and safety as allowed for in this amendment.

Free Trade Makes Us Wealthy

Interference in free trade has some constitutional justification. Congress has the authority to *regulate commerce with foreign nations,* and to *lay and collect taxes, duties, imposts, and excises.* Despite this, the power to regulate trade should be severely curbed because interference in free trade violates all the other Tests of Legitimate Governance.

Trade restrictions fail the Test of Moral Authority. Do I have the right to tell my neighbor who (or where) she can buy stuff from? No, I do not, and by extension neither does the government.

Trade restrictions fail the Test of Purpose by restricting citizen rights, most notably the constitutional right to freedom of contract.

Trade restrictions fail the Test of Consent. Approval ratings for free trade have varied in the 30-60% range in the last 20 years.[1] No matter if you are for or against free trade, half of your fellow citizens disagree.

Finally, free trade restrictions fail the Test of Efficacy. They lead to a less efficient economy, impoverishing us individually and as a nation.

Stop for a moment and look around you. Your house is probably insulated, with glass in the windows, central heating, hot water, and lights. You probably have a car, and maybe you fly on occasion for business or pleasure. You have this book or your e-device.

It's easy to take these things for granted, yet most of them didn't even exist 150 years ago. The modern world was created by innovation—the invention of new things. That innovation was in turn motivated and spread by free trade—millions, now billions of people trading with each other.

Trade motivates everyone to innovate, search for better ways to do things, and find new services and goods to sell. Trade alleviates poverty. Trade encourages honesty and trust between trading partners. Trade lowers the chances of war by improving international relations, and by making the costs of war (trade disruption) too expensive.

These are all valuable benefits that public policy should encourage. The aim of the proposals here is to restore free trade to be fully free, with only some limited exceptions for extremely dangerous stuff.

Arguments Against Free Trade

Despite the benefits of free trade, our politicians want to control imports. In public, they argue that restricting imports is for the collective good. In private, they get campaign contributions from special interests.

As a result, although the US has trade agreements with about 20 countries, those agreements have all been manipulated. The manipulation benefits CEOs and favored corporations[2] at the expense of ordinary citizens. Trade restrictions are government-sponsored economic inequality.

Aided by special interest lobbies, politicians have been honing the arguments justifying their interference since the beginning of the republic. The most common arguments fall into three categories: *Protectionism, Standards,* and *Embargos.*

Protectionism

Protectionism starts when a US industry feels threatened by imports. They pressure politicians to save them from "unfair" competition by putting in tariffs or import restrictions.

Industries are indeed subject to competition from abroad, and sometimes the foreigners will win. The question is what, if anything, should be done about that? The correct answer, here in the US, is *to do nothing at all.* Let it happen.

In a free market, consumers have no moral responsibility to buy anything from anyone. US producers have no moral claim that US citizens should buy from them rather than a foreigner. It's called a free market because everyone is free to buy and sell as they see fit.

The US produces millions of fine products and services and Americans willingly buy them. Producers advertise Made in the USA because citizens want to support American businesses.

However, when a producer persuades the government to ban or tax foreign goods they've gone too far. Our government, instead of protecting equal rights, is now giving preferential legal treatment to favored citizens (corporations) at the expense of the rest of us. This should never be allowed. It is a government-backed protection racket.

Economically, protectionism does not work. In the short term, it protects the few at the expense of the many. In the long term, it tends to cause a collapse of the protected industry. To understand this, think about the incentives when tariffs are imposed.

For the foreigners, they have an extra hurdle to jump: The price of their product just went up. But since they still want US customers, their incentives now are to try harder. They find ways to cut costs, improve quality, and add features.

For the domestic company, the incentives are the opposite. They are protected, so they don't have to compete. They can keep churning out the same stuff at the same price forever.s

As time goes on, the foreign products get better, the domestic products stagnate. The home industry sells less and less. Maybe they'll hang on for a few years, or a decade or two. But eventually, they will go bust. If this story sounds familiar, how about 1980's Chrysler vs. Toyota is an example.

Competition from foreigners causes US job losses. But jobs are lost and created every day. Industries grow, shrink, and close due to innovation and competition from both domestic and foreign producers. There's nothing special about foreigners that justifies extra protection.

Losing a job is a hardship. It's tough to be out of work, especially when a whole town is affected by a factory closure. Nonetheless, those who lose jobs have no moral claim to force others to buy stuff from them, or their company, even if it would save their jobs.

In the big picture, for human progress, obsolete industries should change or die. Collectively, we get richer through innovation, increased efficiency, making things cheaper, and doing things we couldn't do before. Saving obsolete jobs makes us poorer.

Defense

Defense, in the minds of many, is a valid justification for tariffs. Trump, for example, raised tariffs on foreign steel supposedly to protect domestic steel supply lines for our military.

This is a questionable argument. Certainly, the military was not demanding protection of their supply lines from Trump. The administration used them as an excuse to line the pockets of special interest friends.[3] Who benefits? The domestic steel industry. Who pays? Anyone who buys anything with steel in it: autos, kitchen appliances, lawnmowers, bridges, and skyscrapers.

If the military needs things made in the US, then let them secure their supply lines accordingly, and leave the rest of us out of it. When the government takes our rights away to defend us, it has done exactly the opposite of its proper function.

Besides, in the big picture, trade with other countries, with positive results for all, makes it increasingly unlikely either side wants to start a war. More trade, less war. Free trade is a strong defense.

Now, having domestic manufacturing capability is important. Covid disruptions to supply lines highlighted the drawbacks of depending on any one source for vital goods. But US corporations are already moving away from China. They are motivated to diversify to protect their profits and don't need to be forced by government diktat.

In any case, some of those US corporations went to China in the first place because the US became over-regulated. If we want to encourage domestic manufacturing, let's do it by making the US an easier place to do business.

Standards

Trade restrictions due to standards are usually justified on the basis that goods from abroad might be unsafe (diseased foods, dangerous toys), or don't meet US environmental regulations (auto emissions standards).

No one wants to be hurt by dangerous stuff, and basic consumer protection measures may be useful. However, standards are not needed to protect us because the incentives are already aligned to keep us safe.

Suppose a toy was found to be dangerous. US retailers would immediately take it off the shelves and issue recalls. Selling dangerous stuff damages their reputation, damages sales, and opens them up to potential lawsuits. They are motivated to avoid danger and correct mistakes.

The source of the toy is irrelevant to retailers since they are only concerned about their reputation. Nonetheless, producers are also incentivized towards safety. Both foreign and domestic producers want to sell popular and safe toys to maximize their profits.

Since everyone is highly motivated towards safety, regulation that encourages safety is superfluous. The real reason for the regulation is a manipulation of imports to benefit special interests.

Standards have another downside: they curb innovation. US regulations, for example, require catalytic converters on gas-powered cars. What if someone invented a less polluting gas engine that didn't need a converter? What if the converter prevented other solutions from working properly? This happened with lean-burn gas engines, which are potentially less polluting than current technology.

Legal barriers both discourage experimentation and make new products difficult to market. Yet, it is innovation that improves our lives the most over the long run. Public policy should encourage innovation.

Embargos

The third major government barrier to free trade is embargos, which try to force foreigners to behave in a way that Uncle Sam finds pleasing by punishing them for misbehaving. As of 2022, about half a dozen countries were fully embargoed, including Cuba, Iran, and North Korea. Further embargos exist for specific items.[4]

Take Cuba as an example. Most US-Cuba trade has been embargoed since 1960 by acts of Congress, such as the Cuban Democracy Act (1992) which aims to move the Cuban government toward "democratization and greater respect for human rights." Along with trade restrictions, travel to Cuba is also made difficult.

Now, individual legislators or officials might have opinions about Cuba like anyone else. Other than hubris, there's no problem with the US government having an official position on the desirability of the Cuban regime. But when our leaders impose embargoes, they have stepped over a line. Their actions violate every Test of Legitimate Governance.

As free citizens of a free country, it is for us each individually to decide how we feel about Cuba and act accordingly. The government has no right to tell me what to think about Cuba.

Embargos are our government infringing on our rights to free trade, our rights to freedom of movement, and our rights to freedom of association. This is a violation of government's primary role: the protection of our rights. It is American citizens who are being prevented from exercising their freedoms, by their own government.

Embargos also fail the Test of Efficacy. If embargos were undermining the stability of the Castro regime, they have been doing a piss-poor job of it for over 60 years! The Castros are not living in poverty, it is ordinary Cubans and Americans who are hurt. Citizens of both countries are prevented from trading, vacationing, or visiting family.

It's not even clear how Cuba could respond, even if their government had a mind to. How would they show "democratization and greater respect for human rights?" The legislation does go into greater detail but, still, this is an arbitrary standard with ill-defined measures of success. Legislation of this sort is political grandstanding; it serves no useful purpose.

Maybe there's a better way to do things. In 1996, New York Times columnist Thomas Friedman noted that no two countries with McDonald's restaurants had ever gone to war with each other. Counter examples (Russia and Georgia) have occurred since 1996, but the premise still makes sense. When two countries have wealthy middle classes who trade with each other through things like McDonald's, then they risk losing it all if there's a war. Trade disincentivizes war.

So, if the US wants peace with Cuba, let's trade with them! Both sides could then compare Cuba's socialist paradise with our capitalist paradise. Maybe the Cubans would move towards democracy faster if they had greater contact with the US. Even if they decided to keep their system, both sides would benefit through trade and cultural exchange.

These same arguments apply to all embargoed countries. Embargoes punish ordinary citizens while having little effect on the leadership. Other than for things like arms sales (where a country might use those arms against us), the proposal here is to end embargos.

Price, Currency, and Capital Controls

As well as embargoes and tariffs, the feds impose restrictions on free trade through price, capital, and currency controls. A price control is where the government fixes the prices of something. Capital controls are things like taxes on money flowing in and out of the country. Currency controls (a subset of capital controls) are things like reporting on cash transactions within the US and across borders.

Price controls are set within the US since our government has not yet worked out how to get other countries to do as they are told! For example, during the 1973 OPEC oil crisis, Nixon tried to curb rocketing oil prices by putting a maximum price on gasoline. The result: no gasoline and long lines at the gas pumps.[5] Gasoline sellers (oil companies and importers) sold it to other countries where they could get a better price.

Price controls create shortages and lower quality. If sellers can't make money, they move elsewhere, cut quality, or quit. Price controls result in the opposite of their advertised goals. In any case, it is for citizens to decide how much they are willing to pay, not the government. Price controls were banned in *Proposal 4—Freedom of Contract.*

Both capital and currency controls interfere with free trade and restrict citizen freedoms. The proposal here clarifies our rights to trade in any currency, as well as keep accounts in foreign currencies and foreign countries. It also bans reporting of currency movements. It will be difficult to recreate capital or currency controls.

Safeguards

In general, the government's only role in trade is to ensure public safety and honest dealing. Only a few basic safeguards are needed.

One safeguard allowed here is that goods imported for commercial resale by large corporations should meet US safety and environmental standards.

This exception is not strictly necessary. If customers want goods that meet safety and environmental standards, that's what they'll buy! Goods that don't meet those standards to the customers' satisfaction will fail in the marketplace.

However, many citizens don't entirely trust this process. So, let's allow regulation of imports by large corporations. Large corporations do most of the commercial importing, so most imported goods will have to follow US standards. This will then leave individuals and small businesses free to import whatever they want.

Unregulated small-scale imports potentially have health or safety risks to the public. However, the risks are likely minimal compared to the benefits of free trade. Private imports will be a tiny proportion of imports. Anything unsafe will only be used by a few citizens. It's their choice and their responsibility to use that stuff safely, and they'll be sued if they endanger others. It's also quite possible those private imports still meet US standards or similar foreign standards, though we won't be checking.

If a private import becomes popular, then the importer will grow into a large firm, or a large firm will start competing. Either way, a big firm is now importing, subject to regulation if necessary.

Organizing things in this way balances freedom and safety. Individuals will be free to do as they want without interference. Yet health and safety standards will still apply to most imports. And it will be difficult for special interests to resurrect protectionism. If a large organization manages to restrict imports by a rival, or if regulation proves over-burdensome, then small firms and individuals can bypass the restrictions.

A final benefit of this arrangement is that it opens the market to new and experimental products. These might arrive initially in small numbers by private imports. But if they work and become popular, standards can be applied later, if needed.

A second safeguard proposed here is the regulation of biological agents, in particular foreign plants and animals that might escape.

About 50,000 foreign plants and animals are known to be in the US. About 4,300 are considered invasive since they have no natural predators.[6] Once loose in the ecosystem they run rampant. Asian Carp, Fire Ants, Boa Constrictors, and Kudzu are examples.

It makes sense to try and keep invasive species out, because even well-intended private actions may cause havoc if there's an accident. A citizen may import a couple of cute animals intending to keep them locked in a private zoo. But if the animals escape and start breeding, we all pay the price, so it's reasonable that we, via our government, should have a say.

A final safeguard is that if there's an outbreak of disease abroad, the rules here will allow for restrictions to ensure domestic safety. Those could be bans on foods, or bans on movements of diseased individuals until the risks are over.

Proposal 6—Privacy

*The right of the people to be secure in their persons, houses,
papers, and effects, against unreasonable searches and seizures,
shall not be violated, and no Warrants shall issue, but upon
probable cause, supported by Oath or affirmation, and particularly
describing the place to be searched, and the persons or things to be
seized.*

—4th Amendment of the Constitution

The Constitution has little to say about privacy. The closest it comes is the
4th Amendment's provisions against unreasonable search and seizure, and
the 5th Amendment's right for citizens to remain silent and avoid incrimi-
nating themselves.

Even those scant protections have steadily eroded as exceptions to
searches and seizures have grown over the years. With the advance of
technology, Big Brother, aka Uncle Sam, really is watching you. It is time
to correct this trend and affirm a specific constitutional right to privacy.

Proposed Amendment: Privacy

1. Citizens have a right to privacy. Citizen activity and citizen communications are private unless they occur in a public forum.
2. Citizens have a right to privacy in their interactions with commercial service providers. Service providers may not release data on
   individual citizens to any 3rd parties without the express permission
   of the citizen.
3. Government may not engage in surveillance of citizens on private
   property or in private places without a court order, except for government agents physically watching from an adjacent property.
4. Court permission for surveillance shall be known as a surveillance
   warrant, and may only be granted under the following conditions:
   a. The requestor shows probable cause of felony criminal activity.
   b. Warrants shall be for named individuals only.
   c. Warrants shall list specific methods and technologies to be used
      for surveillance.
   d. Warrants shall be valid for a maximum of 90 days.
5. The requestor may apply for extensions of a surveillance warrant,
   in 90-day increments. Extensions must meet the same conditions as
   the original warrant and be issued by a judge not party to the original warrant or previous extensions.
6. Details of surveillance warrants issued shall become public
   knowledge no later than ten years after the first warrant expires.

7. Citizens have the right to record their communications with any other party and shall have no obligation to inform other parties they are recording. These recordings shall be admissible in a court of law in disputes between the recorded parties but shall otherwise be private unless all recorded parties agree to their release.

8. Providers of communication, data storage, and data processing services shall have a duty of care to keep their services private and to use the best reasonable technologies to ensure privacy.

9. No citizen shall be obligated to release private information about themselves or another citizen unless by court order.

10. Citizens have the right to encrypt their data on computing or storage devices. They may not be required to decrypt their data.

11. No manufacturer or vendor of security, privacy, or encryption technology may be required by law to bypass their technology.

12. Communications between government and citizens shall be private unless taking place in a public forum or unless the citizen specifically waives their right to privacy.

13. Government may not force citizens to reveal details on their financial affairs except for:
    a. Summary income figures needed to complete tax returns.
    b. Court orders as part of a criminal investigation.
    c. Court orders after a guilty verdict where restitution is required.
    d. Bankruptcy proceedings.

14. Surveillance data collected in public places may be kept for 30 days, after which time information identifying individuals must be destroyed. Destruction may be delayed by court order if required as evidence in an ongoing criminal investigation or civil lawsuit.

15. Surveillance data may not be the sole evidence cited in any criminal or civil prosecution.

16. Government agents in public places shall have no expectation of privacy. Citizens shall have the right to record them at work.

17. Government agents may not prevent the operation of recording devices on private property or interfere with said devices or recorded materials.

Privacy Vs. Protection

When the constitution was being written, specifying a right to privacy was unnecessary because the government had little ability to spy. If the Founders wanted to spy on a citizen, they had to send a man on horseback to find him and physically watch him. Those days are long gone. Privacy has been overwhelmed by technology—cameras, computers, drones and phones, GPS trackers, and black boxes in cars.

Once upon a time, no one knew if you were jaywalking, burning US flags, or running naked down Main Street in the middle of the night. Unless you were unlucky enough to run into a cop, or unless someone complained, no one knew or cared about your petty misdemeanors.

In the modern age, Big Brother is watching you. Add in some AI, and the government will be able to fine you every single time you commit an infraction, no matter how small.

However, just because the government can spy does not mean they should spy. Surveys show about 60-80% of citizens are concerned about privacy violations by government and big business alike.[1] Privacy violations therefore fail the Test of Consent

Privacy violations also fail the Test of Moral Authority. Do I have the right to spy on my neighbor? No, I do not. If he's doing something in plain view in his yard, then I will see it. But that does not give me the right to trespass, hide cameras in his house, or bug his phones. By extension, the government also has no right to invade his privacy.

And, if you agree that privacy is a fundamental right, then snooping also fails the Test of Purpose. Government sying makes you less free.

Although citizens might have ways to push back, such as encryption, government (and big business) will always be able to afford better technology. It's unlikely any individual can fully protect themselves from a government agency determined to watch them. So, instead, they need greater legal protection.

The proposal here therefore makes privacy a constitutionally protected right. Although both government and businesses alike need to collect data to operate, what they collect should be kept to a minimum, be under citizen control, and never be shared without our permission. Government demands for over-reporting (especially of our finances) will be curbed. Organizations will have a blanket duty-of-care to keep citizen communications and data private.

Law Enforcement

Most privacy invasions are justified by arguments that the government needs to intrude to fight crime and enforce the law. Citizens do want protection from criminals and terrorists who would harm us, have us living in fear, or otherwise take away our freedoms.

On the other hand, privacy intrusions also take away our freedom. The government could, for example, mandate that our phones record us and report on us at all times. There'd be less crime but also less freedom.

In the big picture, both law enforcement and privacy protections exist to maximize citizen freedoms. Therefore, when privacy and law enforcement potentially conflict, law enforcement does not trump privacy. Rather, the question is about balance. How can privacy and law enforcement be balanced to maximize freedom?

Currently, the government has tilted too far in favor of law enforcement—incentivized by the drug war, enabled by technology, and allowed by the Supreme Court. It's time to rebalance, strongly, in favor of privacy. This is not to say that law enforcement can never violate privacy. There do need to be reasonable exceptions to fight crime. The problem, as always, is the definition of reasonable.

Searches

For most of our nation's history, the courts' definition of reasonable searches followed the 4th Amendment which required law enforcement to get a warrant to invade your privacy, a warrant justified by evidence of a possible crime. Over the years the courts—in their efforts to resolve ambiguities—have carved out various exceptions to the need to obtain a warrant, such as:

- *Consent:* if a person consents to a search, then no warrant is needed!

- *Plain view:* something illegal is happening on private property but easily visible from neighboring property.

- *Hot pursuit:* officers chasing someone have broad leeway to keep chasing them over private property.

- *Incident to a lawful arrest:* if officers arrest a suspect, they can search them, their car, or their house if they enter it to do the arrest.

- *Exigent circumstances:* officers have probable cause but no time to get a warrant, such as if someone is shooting at them, if they see a crime in progress, or if someone's life is at immediate risk.

- *Borders:* border patrol agents have broad powers to search for illegal goods crossing borders and to ensure travel safety.

These exceptions are reasonable. But starting in the early seventies, the Supreme Court started making more dubious exceptions. A recent one is community caretaking.[2]

This exception arose because, sometimes, the police act as Good Samaritans rather than merely as law enforcers. Suppose that you cut your arm badly, and you dial 911. A police officer gets there before the EMTs. Whilst holding a towel on your arm and waiting for the EMT, the officer notices your stash of pot.

Is it reasonable that you are then prosecuted for something a police officer found on your property while not acting in a law enforcement capacity? The courts say yes, but for many citizens this is questionable. If the officer came across bomb-making equipment he should act. But victimless crimes, such as smoking pot?

As usual, the idea of community caretaking started with something small and expanded. The original case involved a damaged car that was towed after an accident. It was then searched to remove a gun that "might be a danger to the public" if stolen.[3] Over several decades, the courts expanded acceptable searches from impounded cars, to arrested people at booking, sick motorists, warning homeowners about hazardous materials, 911 calls, and on and on.

Law enforcement officers should help people in emergencies. They have a moral duty to help as fellow citizens, and usually a contractual duty as part of their job. But a duty to help is not a reason to invade our privacy and use it against us.

Left unrestrained, this steady increase of police powers to invade our privacy affects attitudes to law enforcement. If a good cop (rescuer) can turn into a bad cop (persecutor) for the slightest offense, people start to distrust the police. An "Us vs. Them" mentality begins to develop. Over decades, that eventually fuels riots and "defund the police" campaigns.

Surveillance

Law enforcement has always been able to watch potential criminal activity from neighboring properties (the classic stake-out). In the modern era, this has steadily expanded with mail intercepts, phone taps, audio and video bugs, computer hacks, and doubtless other technologies to come.

Technology has reached a point where blanket surveillance is possible—monitoring phone calls, emails, tracking GPS—of all citizens, all the time. Most US citizens think the government should not be allowed to do this,[4] and the NSA's blanket surveillance of US citizens has yielded little in the way of concrete anti-terror results[5]. Blanket surveillance fails every Test of Legitimate Governance and should be banned. Privacy has been taken away for no reason and at a high cost.[6]

When it comes to individual suspects, some people do need to be watched, and the rules here will allow for that. But let's watch them within our system of checks and balances.

The proposal here is for a new surveillance warrant. There will be strict guidelines about how those are used to prevent their scope from expanding over time, and strict reporting requirements so citizens know who, why, and how the government is snooping.

Governments will also be banned from requiring organizations to put backdoors into their technology. Backdoors are an invitation to government abuse and hackers. We'll be safer overall to do the opposite—require companies to protect client data. Apple Computer, for example, encrypts data on their devices using a key that only the owner knows. Even under court order, Apple cannot hand over data to the government. This is the way things should be.

The Effect on Law Enforcement.

Taken together, the provisions in this amendment will create much stronger privacy rights for citizens.

That will in turn create some difficulties for law enforcement. Nonetheless, law enforcement works for us, and not vice versa. Making life convenient for law enforcement at our expense has things backward.

It's not even clear that high-tech surveillance is effective for catching criminals compared to old-fashioned police work. Responding to tips, following leads, collecting evidence, and getting search warrants if needed is often slow, painstaking, and low-tech. But it works! Public policy should encourage what works, rather than what looks sexy and exciting to politicians and government hackers.

Citizen Recordings

As a final part of the checks and balances, the proposal also addresses issues arising when citizens make recordings of each other and government agents at work.

When it comes to citizens recording conversations, citizens should have a right to record themselves, so long as they do not harm others.

Recording devices are becoming so common it's probably safer for everyone to assume they are being recorded. However, there do need to be legal protections when recordings take place in private. The rule proposed is that you can record interactions, but those recordings must be kept private unless they become part of a court case. Public releases of private conversations should not be allowed, without the permission of all the persons recorded.

However, when government agents are at work, they should not have the same expectations of privacy as ordinary citizens. Government agents work for us. We want to know what they are doing and that they obey the law. This is part of the system of checks and balances.

The proposal is that citizens should have a blanket right to record any government agent at work *in public places.* Private property owners will also have the right to record anything happening on their property.

This leaves some grey areas: inside non-public-access parts of police buildings, courts, prisons, and so on. There are too many possibilities to mandate rules here. Let's leave the courts to decide what is reasonable under various circumstances.

Proposal 7—Sex

Most unenforced criminal laws survive to satisfy moral objections to our established modes of conduct. They are unenforced because we want to continue our conduct, and unrepealed because we want to preserve our morals.

—Thurmond Arnold

There have always been people who want to control what others do in their bedrooms. A few have managed to get their moral positions made into the law of the land.

In recent decades, this trend has eased. Laws on deviant sex have slowly been disappearing. This proposal is largely designed to accelerate this trend and get the government out of our bedrooms altogether.

Proposed Amendment: Sex

1. Government may not interfere with or legislate sexual activity between consenting adults on private property or in private places.

2. Sex for hire between consenting adults shall be legal.

3. Adultery shall be legal.

4. It is the responsibility of citizens to clearly say No if they do not consent to sexual activity, and to clearly state what constitutes unacceptable sexual activity to them. Government may not require affirmative consent to sexual activity.

5. The age of consent to sexual activity shall be 16. If one or both parties are less than 16 years old, consensual sex between them shall be legal so long as they are within three years of age of each other.

6. In prosecutions for sex with a minor where the minor appears to be at least 16, prosecutors must prove both knowledge and intent to commit an illegal act by the accused.

7. Legislation criminalizing sex with minors shall be written to protect minors from predatory adults but may not criminalize adolescent experimentation.

8. A register of sex offenders shall not be allowable.

Stay Out of Our Bedrooms

The intersection of sex and the law is a prime example of special interests trying to force their moral codes on others.

If you believe in personal freedom, and that private means private, then what consenting adults do in the bedroom is none of your business. Certainly, the law has no business here, so long as the sex is consensual, and so long as no harm is done to other people or their property.

Applying the Test of Moral Authority: do I have the right to tell my neighbor what she's allowed to do in her bedroom? No, none of my business. By extension, it is also none of the government's business.

We'll get into some specific areas of concern below. But generally, most laws about sex also violate the Test of Purpose, the Test of Consent, and the Test of Constitutional Authority. Therefore, the aim of the proposals here is to banish the government from our bedrooms once and for all. So long as any sexual activity is between consenting adults, it is none of anyone else's business.

Note that these provisions are about private sexual activity. Most citizens would not want to see public sex. It offends many, and children shouldn't be exposed to it. Reasonable public decency laws are okay.

Adultery

The proposal on adultery is likely to be uncontroversial to most readers.

About 80% of Americans think that adultery is morally wrong, but similar numbers think it should be legal and that it should not disqualify people from holding elective posts or running public corporations. So, let's just remove adultery as a crime (which it still is in 21 states.)[1] Other than in divorce proceedings, it's none of anyone else's business.

Prostitution

There has been prostitution throughout recorded human history. Currently, it is illegal everywhere in the US except in parts of Nevada, yet it goes on.

Prostitution is an estimated $14.6 billion/year industry in the US.[2] Perhaps 15% of men have paid for sex and maybe 30% of single men over age 30. Since prostitution is a crime and carries a social stigma, it's safe to assume that US surveys underestimate its prevalence.

What might the real figure be? Well, in Germany prostitution is a legal $18 billion/year industry. Germany's population is about a quarter of the US, implying the figure for US prostitution is closer to $70 billion/year.

Once you start to dig into it, accurate information on prostitution is difficult to find. Most research in the field is badly done by poorly qualified researchers with a built-in bias against prostitution, reported by a media looking for sensationalism rather than the truth.[3]

Prostitution laws are the result of special interests getting their moral code implemented as law. Yet these laws violate our existing constitutional rights to freedom of contract and thus fail the Test of Purpose. They violate the Test of Moral Authority: I have no right to tell my neighbor who she has sex with and under what conditions, including sex for hire. Prostitution laws violate the Test of Consent when many citizens engage in prostitution, and when polls show about 50% of the population think it should be legal.[4]

So, all laws against prostitution should go. This will solve several related problems:

- It stops the war against sex-workers and customers.
- It lowers the chances of violence.[5] Prostitutes can come under the protection of the law, and disputes can be solved in court.
- Pimping and prostitution rackets are less likely if prostitutes have legal protection.
- It removes a moral hazard of police involved in sting operations, pretending (aka lying) that they are willing to pay for sex.
- It will remove most prostitution from the street. If prostitution is legal, you can advertise and have customers come to you.
- Social and medical issues will be easier to solve in an atmosphere free of legal intimidation.

If you believe that prostitution is wrong, feel free to persuade prostitutes and customers alike of your moral superiority. If you think that prostitutes become prostitutes because of poverty, feel free to help them find other work. If you think prostitution causes social and health problems, feel free to find solutions. Any way you want to help, it will be easier if prostitutes aren't hiding from the law.

One justification for making prostitution illegal is to combat sexual slavery, trafficking, and child prostitution. These crimes should be pursued and prosecuted vigorously, and legalizing prostitution will complicate law enforcement's efforts. That's unfortunate, but citizen rights come before an easy life for law enforcement.

Moreover, experience in Germany, New Zealand, and Australia—places where they have legalized prostitution—shows we're likely to see less slavery and underage prostitutes. Admittedly, confusion and poor research are common in this area, and the results are debatable.[6] Still, when prostitution is legal, prostitutes are incentivized to report slavery and child prostitution— they don't like the illegal competition.

Adolescent Sex

Sex with children should never be allowed. Parents have the primary responsibility of protecting their children, but the government also has a role in finding and prosecuting people who commit sex crimes against children.

However, your children will eventually become adolescents, and now you have a problem. Adolescents will engage in sexual experimentation. This is what adolescents do.

Adolescent sex is a concern for parents who want to help their children through this period. But it makes no sense to involve the law. What possible public good comes from locking up horny teenagers?

We could debate at what age children become adults for purposes of being able to consent to sex, but let's not bother. We'll use 16 since this appears to be the most commonly used age in jurisdictions worldwide.

Sex between adults and minors is typically considered a crime even if the minor consented, and even if the perpetrator did not know that the minor was a minor. Defendants with neither intent nor knowledge of criminal behavior can be convicted of this crime.

Normally this would be too dangerous a moral hazard to be allowed in a justice system. Statutory rape is considered a justifiable exception because children are unable to understand what consent is and therefore are unable to give meaningfully give consent.

When a child looks like a child and acts like a child, then adults should not be having sex with them, no matter what. But what about minors who look and behave like adults?

Over the last 150 years, the age of puberty has fallen steadily across the western world. In 1860 the average age of puberty for girls was 16.6, by 2010 it was 10.5.[7] The trend for boys is similar, though boys tend to reach puberty about a year later than girls. During the same 150 years, the age of consent has risen from as low as 8 to as high as 18, varying by state.

In short, biology and the law are in conflict here! Mother nature is getting adolescents interested in sex earlier and earlier, whilst the law is going in the opposite direction. This produces absurd results.

Nearly half of US high school students have had sex,[8] yet in many jurisdictions, this is a crime! Perhaps as many as seven million unprosecuted statutory rapes take place a year. Where prosecutions do take place, they sometimes result in absurdly cruel punishments for teenage lovers.[9]

Situations of murky morality and legality arise. Suppose that a grown-up-looking 15-year-old lies about her age to a 19-year-old—perhaps even producing a fake ID showing she is 16—and they end up in bed. Should this be a crime? I have difficulty thinking that it should.

And what about sexting—teens sending nude photos of themselves to each other—falling afoul of child pornography laws? Sexting is stupid adolescent behavior, but how is it useful to criminalize it?

What's needed are rules that protect adolescents from predatory adults but still allow them to be adolescents without the involvement of the legal system.

Firstly, a general provision that legislation concerning sex with minors should not be used to criminalize adolescent experimentation. The courts can sort out details within the general principle.

Secondly, a three-year age window would provide a straightforward mechanism to protect adolescents from undue legal duress. If the consorting adolescents are within three years of age of each other, even if one is legally an adult, then no crime.

Thirdly, if illegal sex occurs where the minor looks old enough to be 16, then prosecutors must prove the knowledge and intent of the defendant. The "statutory "part disappears if the minor looks like an adult.

Taken together, these three measures will keep most adolescent experiments legal but protect children and adolescents from predatory adults.

Bad Legal Solutions

Until recently the long-term trend has been for liberalization in sex laws, but forces are at work to reverse this trend. Moral unease about sex, and rightful disgust about sexual assault, rape, and child abuse, have started the US down some dangerous legal paths that need to be curbed.

The Sex Offenders Register

Sex offenders' registers first came into being in the '40s in California but took off nationally in the '90s with the Jacob Wetterling Act (1994) and Megan's Law (1996).

Sex offenders' registers are popular with both parents and politicians, but evidence for their effectiveness is nonexistent. They do not protect children, because pedophiles rarely prey on random children. Over 90% of sex abuse cases involve relatives or family friends.[10] Sex offenders' registers fail the Test of Efficacy. And there are many other downsides.[11]

Registers empower vigilante groups. They often lead to social ostracism for offenders and their families. Yet some people on the register have close to zero chance of repeat offending and are not a danger to the public.

Take, for example, the teacher who slept with an adult-looking 17-year-old student. They should not be employed in teaching, but are they a risk to the public? What about urinating in public? Consensual sex between teenagers? Teenage sexting?[12] Involvement in prostitution? Some states allow inclusion on the register for these reasons.[13]

Sometimes innocent bystanders are hurt by the register. Innocent property owners can be punished for the sins of a neighbor,[14] unable to sell their houses because a registered offender lives nearby.

Registers often violate the principle that laws should not be applied retrospectively. States have been trying to get people registered even though they were convicted and served their time before the register came into existence. This violates several state constitutions and the US Constitution's ban on *ex post facto* laws.[15]

Public policy ideally should encourage the reintegration of offenders— have them working and contributing rather than draining charitable and welfare resources. Instead, many jurisdictions restrict where registered offenders can live, if they can come near a school, and so on. The restrictions are so severe that Miami and other places have tent cities under interstate bridges where offenders have gathered.[16] They continue to be punished for the rest of their lives by inclusion on a register.

To resolve the issues outlined above, and to repair the damage to many core principles of our legal system, the proposal is that sex offenders' registers should be banned.

Now, although registers should be illegal, tracking may still be useful for a few very dangerous people. *Proposal 17—Criminal Justice* allows for tracking of repeat offenders, including sex offenders. Technology can give us the benefits of the sex offenders' register, without the drawbacks.

Other legal protections against sex offenders will also remain. In most jurisdictions, an employer (such as a school) can request a criminal background check as a condition of employment. Even without a register, potential employees' crimes will show up.

Sex on Campus

One recent force driving the over-legalization of sex has come from universities. Administrators are incentivized by government regulation to try and control sexual activity to keep students safe.

As some feminists have pointed out, female students having sex with professors used to be seen (by them) as a sign of their liberation.[17] You could, literally, fuck the administration. Fast forward to today, and almost any potential sexual contact between a professor and a student is seen as a criminal abuse of power. The gains of women over the last 50 years are in danger of being reversed.

Administrative meddling and activist spin about rape culture is blatantly sexist. It assumes women are victimized children who need protection from predatory professors and male students. But women are not children.

Most university students are legally adults who are attending university to *learn*. Along with their academic studies, they are honing their social skills, their awareness of power hierarchies, and decision-making skills, including decisions about who they have sex with. There will be mistakes and regrets, but that's life. Humans learn by trial and error.

If genuine coercion or abuse happens, it should be investigated and prosecuted. But a blanket ban on adult students consorting with professors of their own free will goes too far. Adults need to be treated as adults.

In making this argument, let's acknowledge that some universities have been complicit in crimes. Prized male athletes have gotten away with rape and assault.[18] This is wrong. If a star athlete commits a crime, they should be prosecuted for it. Period!

However, a conflict of interest arises when a university wants the prestige and income a star athlete generates but is also responsible for policing on campus.

A first solution to this conflict of interest is that possible felonies should be investigated and prosecuted by an outside police force, even if the campus has its own police. That would typically be the county sheriff or municipal police. This idea is included as a general principle in *Proposal 38—Interaction Between Governments.*

A big university can dominate a small town or county and could still influence law enforcement. But sheriffs are usually elected, and police chiefs are answerable to elected city officials, so a check is in place. If a university wanted to further ensure impartiality, they could take it another step and have sex crimes investigated at a state level.

Other problems arise when university administrations investigate accusations of sex crimes, often violating due process.[19] These issues are discussed further in *Proposal 15—Administrative Law.*

Affirmative Consent

Another recent trend inviting the government back into the bedroom is the issue of consent. Did you want to have sex or not?

Rape, or any forcing someone to have sex against their will is wrong. Rape is a crime, but it is often difficult to prosecute. Victims may feel threatened, embarrassed, ashamed, or fear being accused of having led on the rapist. Witnesses or physical evidence are rare. All too often, it comes down to a he-said-she-said situation.

How can society deal with crimes that come down to the word of one person against another? The best solution we've found so far is a jury. Juries may not be perfect, and perhaps some sexual predators get away with crimes because of imperfections in the justice system. But juries are still the best means yet discovered.

If better ways to handle these cases arise then they should be considered. But some current suggestions would completely undermine the basic principles of our entire legal system.

One suggested solution is affirmative consent. Over the last few decades, anti-rape campaigners made "no means no" a cornerstone of their efforts. No does mean no, and a large majority of citizens would agree. However, campaigners are now pushing further: [20] "No means no" has become "only yes means yes." Initiatives are underway in about 2/3 of the states to get these affirmative consent laws on the books.

These are bad laws. Some are so vague that almost any physical contact between a man and a woman could be classified as sexual abuse.[21] They are often ambiguous about how you would prove affirmative consent. Is it enough to *say* yes, or do you need it in writing? There's no end to the nonsense that could evolve if legally safe sex starts to require consent forms and court mediation.

Sex is not simply a mechanical process that can be governed by written rules. Yes, sometimes sex is just sex, and sometimes sex is a commercial transaction. But for most people most of the time sex is romance, love, poetry, emotion, passion, and lust on both sides. Sex is a dance, a courtship, sometimes even a battle that both sides willingly engage in. Sex is an interplay of active (typically masculine) and receptive (typically feminine) energies. It is often profoundly emotionally and physically ambiguous, and difficult to talk about.

If you don't want to have sex, that's your right. But given the nature of sex and courtship, you have the responsibility to clearly say no. If you are psychologically or emotionally unable to say no, then you need help from a therapist, not a lawyer. The proposal here is to keep the law (in the form of affirmative consent) out of the arena of sexual relations.

To be clear: I am not talking about the use of force or violence here; I am talking about the much more frequent situations of confusion, regret, or remorse. Everyone makes mistakes, everyone has done things they later regret. This applies to everything we do, including our sex lives.

Citizens shouldn't be able to turn personal regrets into legal revenge on the other(s) involved. Well-intended compassion should not lead to the overthrow of long-proven legal principles.

Guilty Until Proven Innocent

Another possible legal solution proposed in sexual assault cases is to reverse the presumption of *innocent until proven guilty*. This isn't the case in the US yet, but it is under discussion.[22]

Some argue that a reversal of assumptions would be a rebalancing, a correction of the power that men have had and continue to have over women in many contexts. It is wrong for men to abuse power over women, anywhere, anytime, anyplace. Abuse should be corrected, but reversing legal defaults is not a solution.

Innocent until proven guilty is a cornerstone principle of our justice system. Reversing it invites abuse of citizens by other citizens, and by government. Likewise, juries must continue to consider *the preponderance of the evidence* in deciding cases.

These legal principles arise from centuries of experience. We mess with them at our peril. Sticking to principles makes it difficult to prosecute some cases. That's a problem, and sometimes a personal tragedy, but it is still the best way known to preserve justice overall.

Proposal 8—Drugs

There'd never been a more advantageous time to be a criminal in America than during the 13 years of Prohibition. At a stroke, the American government closed down the fifth largest industry in the United States—alcohol production—and just handed it to criminals—a pretty remarkable thing to do.

—Bill Bryson

The War on Drugs is Prohibition all over again. Did our politicians learn nothing the first time?

Drugs cause social and health problems, but those problems are not solved by making drugs illegal. Instead, illegality has created drug cartels, incentivized violence, jailed millions of people, and eroded citizen freedoms. All in the name of winning an unwinnable war.

It is time to end this nonsense. Let's legalize drugs. Period. Solutions to the other problems will be easier to find if government violence is removed from the equation.

Proposed Amendment: Drugs

1. Citizens have the right to take drugs.

2. Drugs shall be defined here as any substance that a person may take into their body by any means and for any reason.

3. Citizens may take drugs of their own free will, so long as they pose no immediate risk of damage to other people or their property.

4. Citizens have a right to assist others in taking drugs. Provided that all parties are acting of their own free will, assistants shall not be liable for damages caused to the drug taker by the drugs.

5. Citizens have the right to possess, transport, mail, manufacture, grow, trade, import, and export drugs.

6. Any citizen manufacturing or trading drugs shall have a duty of care to label their drugs with a list of contents and make available all information on the provenance of the drug that they possess.

7. Impure drugs or drugs of uncertain provenance may be sold legally so long as they are labeled as such.

8. Government may regulate large organizations involved in the manufacture or trading of drugs to ensure accurate labeling and purity standards.

9. Citizens committing crimes or torts under the influence of drugs shall be presumed in law to be fully competent and responsible for their actions.

The War on Drugs

Constitutionally, the government has no authority to ban drugs, and drug laws therefore fail the Test of Constitutional Authority. If the government did have constitutional authority, why was there a need to pass the 18th Amendment to prohibit alcohol?

For those who want to, taking drugs, be it alcohol or cocaine, is a liberty they have as part of their pursuit of happiness. Since government's primary purpose is to protect our liberty, drug bans fail the Test of Purpose.

Further, do I have the right to stop my neighbor from taking drugs? No, I do not have that right. So long as he does not harm me or my property, it's none of my business. By extension, it is none of the government's business. Neither I nor the government have any right to stop anyone from making, growing, buying, selling, transporting, or taking any drugs. The War on Drugs thus fails the Test of Moral Authority.

Since about 30% of adults have taken illegal drugs in the last year, the War on Drugs manifestly fails the Test of Consent. That same statistic shows that the war has failed to defeat drugs and thus fails the Test of Efficacy.

The War on Drugs fails every Test of Legitimate Governance. The solution: legalize drugs. The War on Drugs is a prime example of government intervention making things worse in almost every imaginable way.

Civil War

The Fed's annual "Household Survey on Drug Abuse," suggests about 12.7 million people use illegal drugs a month, and maybe 30-40 million people in a year. Since the survey involves the government asking citizens about illegal activities, these numbers probably underestimate the problem. Some private surveys put drug usage at twice the Fed's rates, maybe 60-80 million people. That's about 25% of the population or about 30% of adults. Add in those who tried it once or twice back in the day, and polls show that about 40% of adults have taken illegal drugs.

Let's call this what it is: this is a civil war. *Our government is at war with 40% of the adult population.* The War on Drugs is a real war, with real guns, and real people dying, right here on US soil.

The civil war has lasted about five decades now. Thousands of people have died. Billions of dollars have been spent. There's been enormous collateral damage to the legal system and our constitutional rights. Millions of police, court officials, and prison staff are employed to wage war on citizens. Millions of citizens have been held in prisoner-of-war camps, aka jail.

How could this possibly meet the Founders' vision of governments *deriving their just powers from the consent of the governed?* There is no consent here, and there never will be. The only possible solution here is to agree to disagree about drugs, to live and let live.

The Wages of War

People have been arguing about drugs, both for and against them, for centuries; especially when alcohol is included as a drug.

Let's agree, for our purposes here, that drugs cause health and addiction problems, and lower productivity even among functional drug users. Drugs are a motivating factor for some criminals. Drug users also affect the wider community, particularly close family members, but also the victims of drug crime, or via social service and healthcare costs.

In short, drugs cause problems. But that's no justification for civil war. Rather, the war itself creates worse problems. Illegality and fear of prosecution damage the health of US citizens:

- Addicts have fewer treatment options and research on treatments is hampered.
- Hiding drug usage causes drug takers to take drugs in unsanitary places and reuse needles.
- Health risks are increased by a lack of purity standards or labels.
- Violence associated with the war has killed and wounded many: drug dealers, police, and innocent bystanders alike.

The civil war has done profound economic damage to the US:

- Non-violent drug users are in jail: not working, not contributing, not paying taxes. Upon release, they have difficulty finding work.
- Families of jailed drug users are on welfare or draining charitable resources; their children are being raised in one-parent families with increased odds of doing badly at school and in the workplace.
- Property values are lowered where drug violence breaks out.
- Drugs are more expensive because resources are wasted on violence and evading the law.
- No taxes are collected on illegal drugs.
- Citizens are paying for increased law enforcement, courts, and prisons.
- The financial system is burdened with regulation and reporting to try and find illegal money and prevent laundering.
- Drug policy makes other kinds of crime more likely (theft and violence in particular), costing society dearly in actual losses plus increased insurance and policing costs.

The civil war has fueled unhealthy trends in government growth and perversions of the legal system:

- As of June 2021 (the 50th anniversary of the "War on Drugs ") the US government had spent about a trillion dollars on drug policy.

- Drug enforcement agencies and drug prevention programs have ballooned.
- Drug policy has incentivized anti-money laundering laws, regulations, and hassle for innocent banks and citizens.
- Drug policy has incentivized the militarization of law enforcement.
- Drug policy has incentivized abuse of our privacy.
- Drug policy has incentivized the perversion of civil asset forfeiture.
- Drug policy has fueled breakdowns in the *separation of powers* principle.
- Drug policy is racist. Whites are slightly more likely to take drugs than blacks, but blacks are arrested 2.7 times more often for drug-related offenses, and typically get longer sentences.[1]
- Collectively, the abuses of the legal system outlined above have incentivized public distrust of the police. The police have become enforcers of other people's morals and abusers of our rights,
- Drug policy has soured international relations with military interventions in South America and other places.
- From an economic perspective, government drug bans created the cartels. The Feds have created and fueled organized crime in the US and especially in Mexico.

End the War

The War on Drugs is a civil war. The US government is waging war on about 40% of the population that has taken drugs. It has been a 50-year rolling disaster. It is a cancer on our country, our legal system, and our constitutional principles. The war simply has to stop.

Solutions to many problems caused or incentivized by drug policy will appear throughout this book. The damage is so extensive that it may take the country a long time to heal.

As for the drugs themselves, no one knows how to fully solve society's problems with drugs. But the way to find solutions is to free American citizens to innovate. Let's give Americans back their freedoms.

Proposal 9—Guns

Guard with jealous attention the public liberty. Suspect everyone who approaches that jewel. Unfortunately, nothing will preserve it but downright force. Whenever you give up that force, you are inevitably ruined.

—Patrick Henry

Gun control is another issue on which we will never collectively agree. Those who believe Americans have an absolute right to bear arms will never agree with those who think guns should be controlled. Reasonable gun control is impossible when we cannot agree on what reasonable is.

Every gun-assisted suicide, murder, mass shooting, or accident is a tragedy. I wish I had a solution to these problems, but I do not. *Nobody* has a realistic solution. As a society, we need to start looking in other places than the usual ban-guns/more-guns dichotomy.

Practically speaking, banning guns is a fantasy that won't ever work. Trying to remove guns from America would likely cause a civil war, and most of the folks who feel strongly about it are already armed!

Since we won't ever ban guns, let's reassert that they are clearly and forever legal and roll back the petty restrictions on gun ownership that have grown in the last 100 years. Let's move the argument elsewhere: how can gun safety be improved, both for the owners and for society?

Proposed Amendment: Guns

1. Citizens have the right to own and carry arms.
2. Arms shall be defined here as any weapon that an individual can physically carry, excluding weapons having explosive warheads or other technologies of mass destruction.
3. Any weapon legally used by law enforcement officers shall also be legal for citizens to own, carry, and use without restriction.
4. Citizens may carry arms openly or in a concealed fashion in public places, on public lands, in government-owned places with public access, and on public transport.
5. Citizens shall lose the right to carry arms:
   a. During their sentence if convicted of a felony.
   b. For ten years after the end of their sentence if convicted of a felony involving violence.
   c. During and for ten years after discharge, if admitted by court order to a psychiatric facility.
6. Citizens who lose the right to carry arms:
   a. Shall surrender their arms to law enforcement.

b. Shall have a right of appeal and may regain their rights if they can demonstrate they are not a danger to other citizens.

7. Citizens may not be disarmed for any reason other than as allowed for in this amendment. Red flag laws shall be unconstitutional.

8. Exceptions to the right to bear arms may be made in places where the accidental discharge of a weapon has a high probability of catastrophic damage or harm to large numbers of people.

9. During transfers of ownership of arms:
   a. The parties shall have a duty of care to present and make copies of each other's ID documents and record a description of the arms being transferred including photos and serial numbers.
   b. Citizens may not knowingly transfer arms to persons who have lost the right to carry arms.
   c. Arms transfer records are private, their disclosure may only be required by court order where there is probable cause a felony has been committed involving a specific firearm.

10. Government may not require citizens to declare arms they own or transfer, nor create de jure or de facto registration, licensing, or permitting of firearms or gun owners.

11. Citizens shall have no obligation to declare to law enforcement that they are carrying arms.

12. Children may carry arms on private property under adult supervision. The supervising adult shall have a duty of care to ensure the safe use of the arms.

13. Gun owners and users shall have a duty of care to secure their arms against accidental discharge, theft, and usage by unauthorized persons.

14. Government may impose no other restrictions on ownership, on carrying of arms, on the trading of arms between adults, on ammunition sales, or sales of firearm accessories.

15. Government may impose no restrictions on weapon design features, accessories, or modifications.

16. Private citizens have the right to bar visitors on their property from carrying arms.

17. Citizens believing themselves to be temporarily at risk from their own arms may voluntarily surrender their arms to law enforcement.

18. Law enforcement agencies shall be required to accept and hold arms for citizens who lose the right to bear arms or who hand them over for safekeeping, free of charge to those citizens. Surrendered arms must be returned to the citizen if they regain their rights or may be sold or destroyed with the citizen's permission.

A Right to Bear Arms

The right to bear arms as written in the 2ⁿᵈ Amendment (2A) is ambiguous, causing many arguments over the years. The relevant part reads: *A well regulated Militia being necessary to the security of a free state, the right of the people to keep and bear arms shall not be infringed.*

Although the first part of that statement is difficult to parse, the second part is explicit: *the right of the people to keep and bear arms shall not be infringed.* Constitutionally, the right to bear arms is a protected individual right, no matter what the Founders' reasoning. The Supreme Court agrees that this right applies to individuals,[1] and about 38 state constitutions also guarantee a right to bear arms. Government infringement of that right fails both the Test of Constitutional Authority and the Test of Purpose.

Even if it were not an explicit constitutional right, do I have the right to prevent my neighbor from having a gun in her house? No, I do not! Do I have a right to prevent her from defending herself? No, I do not! Do I have any right to stop her from carrying a gun down the street? No, I do not!

So long as my neighbor does not harm me or my property, it's none of my business what guns she owns or carries, what they look like, what the magazine size is, or how fast they fire. It is none of my business, and none of the government's either. I have no moral authority to prevent my neighbor from bearing arms, and neither does the government. Attempts at gun control fail the Test of Moral Authority.

Gun control, and especially the removal of guns, also fails the Test of Consent. Whichever side of the argument you are on, large numbers of your fellow citizens disagree. On an individual level, gun ownership is at all-time highs—about 120 guns per 100 citizens. Concealed carry has become popular and is legal in most states.[2] About 30% of citizens own guns, and about 40% of households have a gun in them.[3]

Politically, increasing numbers of local authorities are pushing back against unconstitutional federal and state laws. Towns, counties, and states are declaring themselves 2A sanctuaries—places where the 2ⁿᵈ Amendment is safe. Virginia, in early 2020, had a pro-gun-control governor and state assembly, and 91/96 counties declaring themselves 2A sanctuaries.[4]

The 2A sanctuary movement may be largely symbolic, but it symbolizes a disagreement deep enough to inspire action. It is evidence, yet again, that gun control does not have the consent of the governed.

The Test of Efficacy

Gun control laws should go because they have failed, so far, every Test of Legitimate Governance. Despite this, the feds, states, and cities have passed, collectively, hundreds of laws restricting guns. The courts have done little to stop this river of legislation.

In the modern era, gun control took off at the federal level with Roosevelt's 1934 National Gun Act. Controls have steadily become increasingly restrictive since then. Legislators have gotten away with this abuse by categorizing gun control as an attempt to curb violence, be it by criminals, terrorists, or crazies.

All reasonable people want to reduce gun violence. But there's no agreement on how to do this. There's plenty of disagreement about how effective gun control measures have been, but in the big picture, the number of guns in the US has approximately doubled since the early 1990s while the number of gun deaths per capita has halved in the same period.[5] Violence overall has been declining for centuries.[6]

Violent gun death is statistically so rare that when it does happen it is shocking. There's an immediate and understandable uproar about preventing gun deaths. Typically, the cry is for a ban on guns, or types of guns. Yet there's little evidence that these measures lower violence.

Arguments for gun control almost always mistake the tool (the gun) for the user (the human). Or they mistake the tool (the gun) for the issue (suicide, drug crime, insanity, terrorism). And, whilst the data is arguable, guns seem to be used more often for self-defense than for crimes.[7]

As a further blow to the Test of Efficacy, does anyone realistically think that guns could be taken away from Americans who want guns? Many gun owners would probably be willing to fight to retain their rights.

Moreover, no one even knows how many guns there are. The Global Small Arms Survey puts the number at 393 million guns in 2018.[8] That survey is considered reliable but might still underestimate the numbers.[9]

Imports and manufacturing of guns have been climbing steeply for years.[10] Even if government succeeded in banning the commercial manufacture and import of guns, you could make your own. Guns are relatively simple and can be made by a competent machinist. 3D printers have already been used to produce guns, and the technology is improving.[11]

So, no matter what, guns are not going away. Any time disaster strikes, people rush to buy guns. Gun stores sold out as the Coronavirus scare took hold in March 2020.[12] There was a second spike in gun sales during protests in the wake of the George Floyd killing in May 2020.[13] And a third spike after the Capitol Hill Riots in January 2021.[14] Both Democrats and Republicans are buying guns, this isn't a partisan issue.

If there were practical steps that could lower gun-related deaths, most people would probably be in favor of them. *But we do not agree on what those steps are.*

The one thing that I can guarantee won't work is trying to take guns away from citizens who want their guns. The government has tried banning things in the past: alcohol, drugs, prostitution, and gambling. It doesn't work, never has done, never will. When large numbers of people want something, they will find ways to get it.

Experience in other countries bears this out. Australia banned many guns following mass shootings in 1996. Yet the statistics say only 20% of gun owners complied. The Australian government estimates about

260,000 illegal weapons remain in Australia[15]. Private estimates suggest 2-5 million illegal weapons (In a country of 25 million people). New Zealand's 2019 weapons ban has also had low compliance rates.[16]

Restating the Right to Bear Arms

Since arms restrictions violate every Test of Legitimate Governance, most gun control measures should disappear. Let's agree to disagree and reset things to the default position of individual freedom and respect for the Constitution. The proposals here are designed to do that.

Currently, the Constitution has no definition of *arms*, so they are defined here as *any weapon that someone can physically carry, excluding explosive warheads*. That includes guns, blades, non-lethal weapons (tasers, pepper spray), and any future weapon technologies yet to be invented (phasers, disruptors).

This definition is deliberately broad and is designed to do away with petty and useless restrictions on arms. Assault weapons, machine guns, magazines that carry 37 rounds, short barrel shotguns, silencers, bump stocks, and any type of ammunition should be legal without question, restriction, licensing, or registration. All of it should be legal. Period.

For many 2A advocates, the 2A is a bulwark against tyranny—government violence against citizens. To strengthen this, the proposal here is that any weapon that law enforcement can legally use will also be legal for citizens to use. If, for example, the police are allowed to use grenade launchers, then so can citizens. (Some states already allow grenades, tanks, or whatever. If those states want to continue allowing that anyway, even if law enforcement is not using them, they can have at it.)

Gun Registration

For those who believe that gun ownership is a safeguard against government tyranny, gun registration is a no-no. It's telling the tyrant where the guns are. On the other hand, there may be times when it's useful for law enforcement to trace the provenance of a gun used in a crime.

To balance these two needs the proposal here bans registries but instead gives gun owners a duty of care to keep records of gun deals. Faced with law enforcement actively investigating a crime, most gun owners will probably hand over their records if asked politely. If not, law enforcement can request the records via a court order if they have probable cause. Meanwhile, the proposed transfer process is designed to prevent the general tracking of arms.

Criminals don't care what the rules are and won't follow them. A basic, easy-to-use, reasonably comprehensive safety net will solve 99% of problems. Beyond that, increasing controls harass law-abiding gun owners with little effect on criminals.

Other Restrictions

The principles here are designed to remove all restrictions on bearing arms, with a few reasonable exceptions:

- In places where accidental discharge has a high probability of causing mass harm to others, like airplanes, or gas refineries.
- Felons convicted of violent crimes should not have guns.
- People with mental health problems should not have guns.

The proposal puts rules in place to allow for those issues, as well as allowing for appeals of those rules in individual cases, mediated by the courts. In other words, checks and balances.

How to Lower Gun Violence in Society

No one has solutions to the gun violence issues in our society. Anyone who says they do has either an untested theory or an agenda.

One of the most obviously false arguments in the gun debate is the notion that making guns illegal will remove them from the hands of criminals and terrorists. Criminals will break any law you pass, and your average terrorist could give a rats-ass about Congress banning assault-style weapons. Gun restrictions appear virtuous but don't stop gun violence.

So, if the easy but false solution of banning guns was taken off the table, how else might gun violence be lowered? The proposals on guns outlined here, whilst not offering specific solutions, will help by correcting incentives. Gun violence is likely to go down because:

- If the false solution of banning guns is taken away, people might start looking for other solutions. Experimentation will eventually produce some new ideas that work.
- The NRA (and similar organizations) can focus on safety and training, and away from political campaigns to protect the 2A.
- Technological solutions to gun safety (such as guns that only fire for their owners) might become more popular if they are voluntary. Gun owners want their guns to be safe but don't want to be forced into specific (special interest) solutions.
- The proposals on dealing with the mentally unstable and those at risk of suicide might help with keeping guns out of their hands while they are at peak risk.
- Law enforcement can spend their time chasing actual criminals rather than enforcing arbitrary regulations on innocent gun owners.

Other proposals in this book will also lower crime. Of those, the most important is to end the War on Drugs. If drugs were legalized, street dealing would disappear because it would be cheaper and safer for customers to buy over the internet. Territorial disputes between drug dealers would become irrelevant. Gang warfare would fade away.

Finally, collectively, the proposals in this book would boost the economy, which in turn would lower crime.

Poverty per se does not cause crime, and to suggest so is an insult to millions of relatively poor people who are decent law-abiding citizens. Nonetheless, poverty and crime are correlated. It's plausible that if you are desperately poor *and see no way out of it* then you might be more likely to do something illegal.

Boosting the economy is likely to lower crime because if potential criminals can do well by legal means, they will have less of an incentive to turn to crime. Special interests have been slowing the economy for decades, helped by misguided government programs such as welfare, minimum wages, and the destruction of the education system. Those issues are addressed in several proposals here.

Technology is also lowering crime. Crimes against physical property are becoming increasingly difficult because of GPS trackers, security cameras, toughened glass, improved locks, and other innovations. Those technologies are not specific to gun violence, but as crime goes down, violent crime should go down with it. Less crime → fewer criminals carrying guns → lowered chances of gun violence.

Proposal 10—Abortion

The problem comes because life is not our only moral value.
Another value we all, liberal and conservative alike, find precious
is freedom. In most cases, as a matter of fact, when these two
values clash, we opt for freedom over life.

—Cristine Robinson, Unitarian Minister

Abortion is one of the most deeply contentious issues in American politics. In the last 50 years, Roe v. Wade (RvW) has been the legal backdrop, accompanied by some states trying to find legal ways around RvW, and other states making abortions even easier. Following the 2022 Supreme Court overturn of RvW the political fights go on.

Yet abortion is a problem that politics can never solve. Abortion is a fundamental moral disagreement, not a factual or legal problem. A legal solution that will satisfy everyone is not possible.

Since we will never collectively agree, the only long-term solution is to agree to disagree. RvW worked for about 80% of the population. Let's write a version of RvW into the constitution and be done with it as a legal issue. The moral and social arguments will continue. But let's take this off the table as a legal and political issue.

Proposed Amendment: Abortion

1. Women have the right to an abortion.
2. It is the pregnant woman's choice alone to have an abortion or not. No other person shall have legal standing in the decision.
3. There shall be no legal duty for the mother to inform the father of her pregnancy or her decision to abort.
4. In any situation where the woman has a child without the consent of the father, she shall have no legal right to support from the father for herself or the child.
5. Abortions shall be fully legal for any reason up to 20 weeks of the pregnancy.
6. Abortions after 20 weeks shall be legal when a medical doctor believes complications of the pregnancy are a significant risk to the life of the mother.
7. Government may not impose restrictions on a woman's choice to have an abortion, nor on any medical professional's provision of abortion services.
8. Government may not impose regulations that apply in a de jure or de facto manner to abortions only.

9. In disputes about where the 20-week cut-off point is, or about the medical risks of pregnancy to the mother, the consulting doctor's opinion at the time of consultation shall take precedence.
10. Except in cases of fraud, courts may not overturn doctors' decisions, nor punish them for decisions taken.

We Will Never, Ever Agree

Both sides in the abortion debate have strongly held values. If you think that abortion is immoral, then a woman's right to choose can never take precedence, and vice versa. *These two positions can never be reconciled.*

A default assumption behind the proposals in this book is that adults should be able to do anything they want, so long as it causes no direct harm to other people or their property. Abortion is one of the few places where this rule breaks down. The life of the mother and the life of the unborn child are in conflict.

Applying the Test of Moral Authority: do I have the right to prevent my neighbor from killing a child? Well, yes! Under most circumstances, I think have both a right and a moral duty to save the child. On the other hand, do I have the right to force a woman to carry a child for nine months, and look after it for the next 18 years? No, I don't think I do have that right. Further, do I have any right to even know that she is pregnant? No, again, none of my business.

Thus, the Test of Moral Authority itself fails here. This is a fundamental moral conflict that cannot be solved by reason, facts, or debate. Of course, we should seek to understand each other and have compassion for opposing viewpoints. But debate cannot resolve strongly held but contradictory moral viewpoints.

Let's Agree to Disagree

Since abortion is irresolvable as a moral argument, I propose a compromise based on pragmatically agreeing to disagree.

Abortion has long been an issue, but the recent legal landscape was defined by RvW which, from 1973 up until its overturn in 2022, effectively legalized abortions, with conditions. Political and legal arguments have raged throughout that time, for and against.

Despite the political wrangling, there has been essentially no change in public opinion. Gallup has run polls since the mid-70s, with consistent results throughout.[1] About 20% of citizens think that abortions should never be legal. About 25% think they should always be legal. The majority, about 50%, think they should be legal with restrictions.

In other words, after decades of arguments, no one has changed their minds. And no one is likely to change their minds in the future. So, my proposal is we agree to disagree and run with rules close to RvW.

RvW attempted to balance the rights of women to control their bodies with the rights of prenatal life. The court decided that up to the point that a fetus was viable—able to live on its own outside the womb—it should be the woman's choice. After that point, the fetus had the potential to become a person without its mother's help, and the rights of the fetus became paramount.

RvW will never satisfy those who believe that abortion should never be legal, or those who think it should always be legal. It will work for most people who fall somewhere in the middle. About 80% of the population can live with RvW, even if it is not their preference. It's unlikely we could do better, so let's compromise there.

Those who want to continue the debate are welcome to do so—as a debate. For both sides: you have the right to your opinion, and you have the right to keep persuading through discussion, publications, education, and the media. By all means, offer counseling and services to pregnant women. Meanwhile, please, stop trying to force women to follow your moral code. *Find another way.*

Fathers and Mothers

The proposal here makes it clear that any decision to abort should be up to the mother. Her body, her choice. However, what about the father? Shouldn't he have a say? The correct answer is morally yes, but legally no.

If you give the father a veto, you have taken away the mother's right to do what she wants with her body. You have given the man a right at the expense of the woman and effectively made the woman into a slave of the man. This cannot be allowed in our legal system.

I'd hope that any woman considering an abortion would discuss it with the father, especially if she is in a long-term relationship with him. But that's her decision to make, and hers alone. None of my business, none of yours, and certainly none of the government's.

Now, similarly, if men have no say in abortion decisions because that makes the woman a slave of the man, the opposite is also true.[2] If a woman decides to have a child without the father's consent or knowledge, then she should have no legal expectation of him supporting her or the child. That would give her a right at his expense and effectively make the man into the slave of the woman. This cannot be allowed in our legal system.

Again, I hope any woman considering having a child secures the support of the father. But if she decides to go ahead without his support, the consequences of her decision are her responsibility alone.

It takes two people to produce a baby. Pregnancy may require difficult decisions, made in the face of strong feelings, strong opinions, and the dynamics of the relationship. Meanwhile, the law must remain neutral. Both parties have agency over their choices. Neither party should have any legal right to impose obligations on the other against their will.

Backdoor Legal Activity

If a version of RvW is reinstated via constitutional amendment, pro-life activists are likely to start repeating RvW-era back-door legal strategies to curb abortions. Strategies such as making licensing of abortion clinics difficult, waiting periods imposed on women, shaming legislation (requiring women to look at ultrasound images of the fetus), or legislation forcing doctors to send copies of ultrasounds to state officials in violation of medical privacy.[3]

On the pro-choice side, campaigners veered (and continue to veer) too far in the other direction, arguing for legislation allowing abortions at any time.[4] This is also crazy. Few people support third-trimester abortions, let alone post-natal abortions, aka murder.

The proposal above is designed to stop this sneaky strategic legislation in either direction, by specifically banning de jure or de facto legislation that applies to abortions only. There will no doubt be arguments and court cases about what that means in practice. However, let's at least lay it down as a principle. The legal system should leave women and their doctors alone.

Why Is This Still an Issue?

Abortion is a contentious issue and people disagree. But it's also obvious that we'll never reach a collective agreement. So why have our politicians not been content with a compromise that most citizens can live with?

Might the fights continue because politicians are paid to keep fighting? Morally, this is an unwinnable fight. Politically (and financially) it is highly profitable for politicians to keep fighting forever, funded by extremists on both sides who believe that they can one day "win" once and for all.

Meanwhile, most ordinary citizens, the 80% of us who can live with RvW, are probably fed up with the fighting and wish it would stop. Hopefully, the proposals here will take abortion off the public stage. Those who want to keep fighting can take it private. Leave the rest of us in peace to get on with our lives.

Proposal 11—Discrimination

Our constitution is color-blind, and neither knows nor tolerates classes among citizens.

—John Harlan, Supreme Court Justice

Discrimination is considered morally wrong by most Americans, and it is usually economically stupid. Things are not perfect and can still be improved, but our government's approach to discrimination is problematic.

Discrimination is rife with moral hazards and tensions, starting with the awkward fact that discrimination has benefits. Further, a right to free speech must include a right to speak discriminatory views. In short: individuals should in principle have the right to discriminate. And in practice, individual discrimination is a minor problem.

So where is discrimination a problem? When it is forced upon us by law. In other words, government discrimination. This is the issue that needs to be tackled.

Proposed Amendment: Discrimination

1. Discrimination shall be defined here as the unjust or prejudicial treatment of people on any arbitrary grounds, including their opinions, beliefs, race, gender, sexual orientation, religious affiliation, ethnic origin, or handicap.

2. Citizens have the right to discriminate, so long as they do no direct physical harm to other persons or their property, nor allow harm through gross negligence.

3. Government may not discriminate, affirmatively or negatively.

4. Government may not:
   a. Create laws that discriminate between citizens.
   b. Create laws criminalizing discrimination.
   c. Create laws that require discrimination.
   d. Apply or enforce laws in a discriminatory manner.

5. Disparities may not be used as prima facie evidence of discrimination in any legal process. Disparate impact laws shall be illegal.

Discrimination Serves a Purpose

The US has had a long, troubled history of discrimination, both legal and illegal. A history that includes the displacement of Native Americans, slavery and abolition, the women's rights movement, the civil rights movement, the gay rights movement, and most recently Black Lives Matter.

Tremendous strides have been made. By historical standards, racism, sexism, and other forms of discrimination are much reduced. Nonetheless, things are not perfect, discrimination still exists. So, jumping to the heart of the matter: where to next? The essence of the proposals here are:

- Let individuals discriminate as they see fit, legally speaking, so long as they do no direct harm to other people or their property, nor allow harm through gross negligence.

- Stop the government (and large organizations) from discriminating in any way whatsoever, positively, negatively, for or against any individuals or groups.

This is close to the opposite of the current system. Bear with me, there is method to my madness.

Let's start by clarifying the meaning of discrimination. Discrimination is a word with different meanings, meanings that have blurred and morphed over time, and which have both positive and negative aspects.

Discrimination in its original meaning—the ability to see and make distinctions—is beneficial. Our sense-making organs make distinctions. It is the new noise, the new sight, the new smell that gets our attention. Humans are sensitive to differences in our environment, because new and different might kill us.

We are programed by evolution to react with caution to people who are different. We are wary of strangers, of people who look different or dress differently. Any clue that a person is not one of us, of our family or tribe, is a reason to be cautious. They may be a danger to us.

Didn't your mother tell you never to talk to strangers? The is folk wisdom for a reason: discrimination based on first impressions keeps us safe. No matter how enlightened you may feel you are, your nervous system is pre-programed (i.e.: has prejudices) to react to potential danger.

Suppose you are alone on a dark street, and someone approaches wearing a hoodie. Is it a monk, a mugger, or an innocent passer-by? Do you cross the street, or keep going? Or perhaps you meet someone covered in red spots. Do they have unusual taste in makeup or a disease? Do you keep your distance, or offer your hand in friendship? Personally, if in doubt, I'd act on my prejudice until I have more information. Better safe than sorry.

The other main meaning of discrimination describes something longer term or systemic, after first impressions and reactions. Not offering a job, or not promoting someone purely because they are black or a woman. This systemic discrimination—prejudice—is potentially a problem, particularly when it becomes legalized discrimination.

Government and Discrimination

Our biological programming makes us wary of differences, of folks outside our tribe. It's a triumph of modern society that so many people of disparate backgrounds live together in comparative harmony.

So long as our interactions are harmonious, difference and diversity are highly beneficial. Difference brings new skills, perspectives, ideas, strengths, and foods to society. America is often described as a melting pot. The melding of people and cultures from around the world is one of our great strengths as a country.

Let's assume that a large majority of citizens are in favor of the melting pot and want to minimize systemic discrimination. What then should the government's role be in that?

Let's first acknowledge that there has been plenty of discrimination in the past, that some of it continues today, and that it can be painful to those on the receiving end of it. And let's also assume that government attempts to end discrimination are well intended. Nonetheless, something must change because the approach taken is deeply flawed.

Most recent government attempts to combat discrimination focus broadly on affirmative action—trying to correct past wrongs by tilting the playing field, legally, in favor of the previously discriminated against group. This approach fails every Test of Legitimate Governance.

Starting with the Test of Moral Authority: do I have the right to stop my neighbor from discriminating? I think the answer is no. So long as she does no direct physical harm to any person or their property, then I have no right to stop her. By extension, neither does the government.

Now, you may disagree with that conclusion, so I'll unpack it a bit. First, do I have the right to stop my neighbor from having discriminatory thoughts? No, I do not. I cannot know what she thinks, and it's none of my business. Do I have the right to stop my neighbor from expressing her opinions? Again, no I do not. I may disagree with her, but she has the right to free speech. Do I have the right to stop my neighbor from acting on her opinions, so long as she does no direct harm to another person or their property? Again, I don't think I do.

The notion of direct harm here is important. Hurt feelings on the part of the person being discriminated against cannot be considered direct harm from a legal standpoint, they are subjective. Subjective feelings have no place in a legal system based on objective standards, and any attempt to measure the success or failure of a policy based on feelings must necessarily fail the Test of Efficacy.

Affirmative action also fails the Test of Purpose. You fundamentally cannot have both "equality before the law" and "protected classes."

Affirmative action fails the Test of Consent. Although almost everyone things discrimination is bad, most Americans think that race (for example) should not be a factor in college admissions.[1]

And finally, if *all men are created equal*, then legal discrimination cannot pass the Test of Constitutional Authority.

Part of the problem with discrimination is that it has both moral and legal dimensions. Affirmative action—a legal solution to a moral problem—is rife with moral hazards. Affirmative action is not correcting discrimination, it is reversing it. It is a version of punishing us all for the sins of our fathers. It is trying to enforce morality.

However, you can't force people to be moral—you can only encourage them. People should do the right thing because they see it is the right thing, not because they are told to do it. When you try and force people to be moral, you get push back and resentment. At the end of the day, each of us individually must face our discrimination and wrestle with it.

So, to come back to the question being considered here, what should the government's role here be? With respect to the moral struggle, the correct answer is *nothing at all*. It is not the job of the government to dictate morality to citizens. Government should protect individual rights, and prevent violence, theft, and fraud. But moral decisions are up to individuals.

Nonetheless, government does have a role. Since everyone agrees that discrimination is wrong, the correct course of action is to *require our government to be a model of non-discrimination, held to the highest standards*. That means equal laws. Laws that treat everyone the same and are applied to everyone the same. This approach offers several advantages:

- It aligns government action with its primary purpose, protecting individual rights.

- Giving governments a legal obligation to be non-discriminatory will ensure a backstop of legal protection for minorities. Alongside that, society is already moving towards less discrimination because that's how most people want it.

- This approach will lower a great deal of simmering anger among citizens. Anti-discrimination laws fuel anger, as in "who are you tell me how to behave."

- Removing anti-discrimination laws removes layers of bureaucracy, government agents acting as self-righteous moral bullies, most court cases about discrimination, and other moral hazards.

- Getting government out of the discrimination business, once and for all as a constitutional fix, will ensure that things like the Jim Crow laws can never again arise. Legal discrimination enables more discrimination, rather than curbing it.

Legal Loose Ends

This proposal requires governments to be non-discriminatory, and as a result, most anti-discrimination laws will disappear. Some of the important implications are discussed below.

Commerce

Many jurisdictions require businesses open to the public to be non-discriminatory. The argument is that if you are open to the public, then you must serve all members of the public.

This fails the Test of Moral Authority. Do I have the right to tell my local corner store owner who she must serve in her store? No, I do not have that right. By extension, neither does the government.

In a legal system based on private property, free speech, freedom of association, freedom of contract, and free trade, *both sides must be free to say yes or no.* I can't force her to serve anyone, and I can't force anyone to buy from her.

Luckily, no force is necessary. Stores want to sell stuff. Usually, they only exclude people when forced to, as happened under Jim Crow.[2] If a store does discriminate, they are losing money in the process and punishing themselves already! The incentives are to serve everyone.

There is no need for regulation here, and the proposal will do away with it, with a possible exception for big business if necessary.

Employment Discrimination

Employers have choices about who to employ and a degree of power over their employees. Employers can discriminate, and possibly do in a few individual cases. Still, it's difficult to see how this continues to be a systemic problem in the modern era since discrimination is unprofitable.

Take the oft-quoted statistic that women earn 79¢ for every dollar made by a man. This statistic is nonsense when you normalize for relevant factors, such as hours worked, type of work done, work experience, etc.[3]

However, let's assume for a moment it was true that women made 79¢ on the dollar. And suppose that you are, say, an underpaid female accountant. If you want to earn more, then start your own firm staffed with female colleges. You could charge 90% of what the men are charging, and you'd get lots of customers because of your lower prices. Money talks, even to misogynists. You'd increase your wages and wipe the smiles off those good-ole-boy's faces. There's nothing (other than anti-discrimination laws) to stop entrepreneurial women in any industry doing this. This rarely happens because the pay gap does not actually exist.

Since free market competition already incentivizes commercial organizations toward non-discrimination, regulation is unnecessary, not to mention expensive, legally ambiguous, and tempting for manipulators. The proposal here will end all anti-discrimination laws applying to individual citizens and small businesses.

Proof of Discrimination

Although this proposal bans anti-discrimination laws applying to individuals and small businesses, regulation of big businesses and government will still be allowed. Which then raises another problem. If a discrimination case comes to court, how do you *prove* discrimination?

Discrimination is often subjective, and statistics are often misleading. As a result, proving discrimination can be difficult. The courts have tried to solve this by using disparities as proof of discrimination. In legalese, this is known as disparate impact.[4] For example, a measure of discrimination in employment law is the 4/5 rule. If a workforce has proportionally less than 4/5 of a minority than the general population living nearby, then the employer can be charged with discrimination. Racial disparities are taken as proof of racial discrimination, and the employer must now prove they are innocent. This approach is problematic for several reasons.

Legally, disparate impact is a violation of the principle of *innocent until proven guilty*. Citizens, including corporations, should never have to prove their innocence. It is for prosecutors to prove their guilt.

Disparate impact also removes intent from the legal equation. Corporations can be guilty of discrimination even if they did not intend to be. Intent is not always necessary in a criminal prosecution, there can be crimes of gross negligence as well as "strict liability" crimes which are usually regulatory (like this one). However, whenever intent is removed from the equations the risks of manipulation and injustice go shooting up. Intent should be in the equation whenever possible.

Worst of all, disparities are simply not evidence of discrimination. As Thomas Sowell pointed out in *Disparities and Discrimination,*[5] disparities arise naturally in human societies and activities. Attempts to remove disparities, on the mistaken assumption that they are evidence of discrimination, are a fool's errand.

This proposal specifies that disparities may not be taken as prima facia evidence of discrimination. Additionally, *Proposal 17—Criminal Justice* puts intent firmly back into legal processes. For something to be a crime, the perpetrator must intend to commit a crime. Anything else is an accident or ignorance.

Hate Crimes

Another class of discrimination crimes that must go is hate crimes. Hate crime laws are a prima facie violation of the 1st Amendment. Citizens have a right to their opinions, no matter how stupid, and the legal system should judge people for what they do, not what they think.

So, although determining intent is important in criminal trials, courts should focus primarily on *whether* defendants intended criminal action, not *why*. Determining intent is already difficult enough, figuring out why is superfluous level of complexity. If Bill assaults Joe, it does not matter if he did it because he didn't like Joe's skin color, the color of his shirt, or because he was desperate for money. Assault is assault, and Bill should pay for his actions, not for his reasons.

Courts already find some crimes abhorrent and give longer sentences, so adding hate charges is useless and unnecessary legislation.

Title IX

A major part of federal antidiscrimination efforts in education over the last fifty years has been Title IX.

The relevant part of title IX reads: *No person in the United States shall, on the basis of sex, be excluded from participation in, be denied the benefits of, or be subjected to discrimination under any education program or activity receiving federal financial assistance.*

Firstly, note that federal financial aid will go away under the various proposals here, and *Proposal 30—Children* specifically removes the feds from education. However, since many states have something like Title IX in their legislation, we'll still address Title IX here.

Title IX introduces a moral hazard: government shouldn't bribe organizations to be good because morality is not government business. Also (ironically) government should not engage in bribery because bribery is immoral! That part of Title IX should go under this proposal.

Government schools will still need to be non-discriminatory. That accounts for about 90% of K-12 students[6] and about 75% of university students.[7] For those institutions, nothing much will change. If you want your child protected by title IX, send them to a government school.

Non-discrimination has become woven into the fabric of our education system. Title IX came into existence in 1972. Two generations of women have been raised under it, mothers, and grandmothers of the current generation. Sex-based discrimination is unlikely to return to the education system anytime soon.

Limits on Government

It will not be denied that power is of an encroaching nature and that it ought to be effectually restrained from passing the limits assigned to it.

—James Madison

Our country was founded on the vision of limited government, but over 240 years, those limits have been broken time and again. This section of the proposals focuses on dialing back government over-reach.

Government has overstepped its bounds in many and varied ways and increasingly so over the decades. The Founders recognized that governments tend to expand, and they designed checks and balances to keep government right-sized.

In particular, the principle of *separation of powers* has steadily been eroded. The foundation of that principle is the federal/state/local split of government responsibilities. Yet, over the last 150 years, the feds have steadily been encroaching on former state issues.

At the federal level, the system was further designed to split responsibilities between the different parts of government. Congress writes laws, the President administers them, and the courts resolve disputes or ambiguities. But here too power has moved from Congress to the President and the administration. Unelected and unaccountable bureaucracies have steadily come to rule over most of our interactions with government.

Our governments produce a never-ending river of rules for us citizens to follow—legislation, regulations, ordinances, executive orders, administrative orders, and so on. Their scope and power also vary by source, from Congress to City Council.

Backing up the rule makers are courts. In the process of resolving disputes and cleaning up ambiguities, the courts produce yet more orders that affect citizens. Law enforcement agencies enforce it all. And the military, who in theory keep our borders safe, seems to have expanded to become a kind of global police force, often executing questionable missions around the world.

In short, we have overwhelming and excessive complexity and a government that has grown out of all proportion to anything intended by the Founders.

Many things need repair here. As a first pass, the proposals will apply the Tests of Legitimate Governance to cut out unjustified government activity and complexity. We'll try to minimize moral hazards and manipulation opportunities.

And we'll try to reapply and take seriously many long-held principles of good governance such as:

- *Separation of powers.*
- Equality before the law.
- Checks and balances.
- Due process.
- Innocent until proven guilty.
- That intent is important in criminal proceedings.
- Subsidiarity (the principle that government actions and decisions should be as local as possible).

The discussions that follow will mostly refer to lawmaking at the federal level. However, similar problems exist in all governments, and the solutions are likewise intended to apply to all levels of government.

Proposal 12—Legislation

The more corrupt the state, the more numerous the laws.

—Tacticus

The volume of legislation and regulations that apply to you would take over forty years of full-time study to read and understand. That's an entire working lifetime. And the compliance costs are enormous.

There have to be meaningful limits on government rule-making.

Proposed Amendment: Legislation

1. Government has a duty to produce clear, simple, and effective legislation.
2. Legislation shall be defined here as any government rule that has the force of law on citizens.
3. Regulations required by, implied by, or written to clarify legislation and which have the force of law on citizens shall be known here as the supporting regulations. All rules defined here for the creation of legislation shall also apply to supporting regulations.
4. Legislatures may not delegate legislative authority. No other parts of government may create legislation.
5. Legislatures may not delegate discretionary authority to administrative bodies for any matter having force of law on citizens.
6. No legislative act may have more than 10,000 words. The sum of all supporting regulations for that legislation may be no more than an additional 10,000 words.
7. All legislation must have a Flesch Reading Ease score of 50 or more.
8. All legislation shall be posted in a public place for at least 30 days in its final version before legislators vote on it.
9. Legislators shall be required to certify that they have read all legislation in its entirety before voting on it. Any legislator unable or unwilling to do so shall not have their vote counted.
10. If more than 10% of legislators demand it, there shall be a line-by-line vote on the legislation.
11. Legislation shall become law no sooner than one year after it has been passed.
12. Legislative bodies may override the one-year requirement by a 2/3 majority vote. Legislation so passed will expire six months after the next general election unless renewed by a 2/3 majority of the new legislature.

13. Legislative votes on internal government affairs may be implemented immediately but must otherwise meet all other stipulations contained in this amendment.

14. Legislation may never be applied retrospectively except that if a crime is abolished anyone convicted of that crime shall be released from punishment and have that crime expunged from their record.

15. A government's jurisdiction ends at the physical border of that government. No US government may:
    a. Assume, require, or try to coerce compliance with its legislation outside of its physical borders.
    b. Write legislation with the intent of influencing the laws of foreign countries.
    c. Enter into any treaty with foreign countries that supersedes US law or the US constitution.
    d. Enter into any treaty with foreign countries violating the rights of foreign citizens that would be protected rights for US citizens.
    e. Enforce or prosecute another jurisdiction's laws.
    f. Include foreign laws by reference within US laws.

16. All legislation shall be effective for an initial period of ten years, or for a lesser time if decided by the legislature. At the end of that time, the legislation will expire unless reenacted.

17. Where legislatures decide on a lesser time before renewing legislation, they may only renew legislation within six months after a general election.

18. A public review of the efficacy of any legislation shall be required before reenactment.

19. Any amendments to legislation shall become effective no sooner than one year after they are signed into law unless passed under the emergency legislation rule above.

20. If legislation is passed in violation of the rules outlined here, citizens may enter a defense of "ignorance of the legislation" against prosecution under that legislation.

21. *Transition*: All existing legislation at the time of passing of this amendment shall be reworked over time to meet its conditions.
    a. Each legislative act and supporting regulations shall be taken one by one, in reverse chronological order by date of enactment, and amended or abolished to meet the rules defined here.
    b. New laws may be created while old laws are reviewed, but there must be at least one review for every new law passed. Once all old laws have been reviewed, the process shall start over in perpetuity.

Rules and Rule Makers

In theory, legislators write legislation that has general applicability, and regulators write regulations focused on an industry or issue. In practice, in modern times, there's little distinction between the two. But there should be because (usually) regulation is more about inspections and ensuring compliance, whereas legislation is enforced.

This proposal focuses on the creation of legislation and regulation. *Proposal 13—Regulation,* focuses on how regulation is applied and enforced.

At the federal level, writing legislation is Congress's job. Article 1 of the Constitution says *All legislative Powers herein granted shall be vested in a Congress of the United States.*

Then, in 1928 the Supreme Court decided that Congress had an *implied* power to delegate legislation.[1] This small expedient exception to the clear wording of the Constitution has grown, over nearly a century, into a travesty of the original intent.

Congress no longer writes legislation—they have delegated it to the administration. This is one cause of the ever-expanding administrative state. Unelected and unaccountable bureaucrats have created an explosion in the volume of rules, accompanied by an explosion of manipulation. Regulation is the motherload of manipulation opportunities.

We need to start cutting back because it would take over 40 years to study the rules that apply to you. Here's how that's calculated:

The current combined federal legislation and regulations cover about 277,000 pages. That consists of the legislation, the United States Code (USC), 88,436 pages (as of 2023)[2], and the regulations, the Code of Federal Regulations (CFR), about 188,343 pages (as of 2021)[3].

If you read 100 pages/day, 5 days/week, 50 weeks/year (a full-time job), it would take you about 11 years to read them. By the time you were done, you'd then need another couple of years to read the changes made since you started. So, 13 years total.

Those reading rates are about what an average medical or law student reads when studying.[4] Most people can read faster than 100 pages/day,[5] but reading legal code is not like reading a thriller. The code is full of legal jargon, cross-references, numbers, grandfathered exceptions, and so on. Careful study is needed to understand it.

The numbers above are for federal regulations. States, counties, and municipalities also produce legislation, regulations, codes, and ordinances. Probably no one has an exact count, but let's assume that the average volume of state/county/municipal rules combined is in the same ballpark as the federal regulations. That's another 13 years of study.

Also coming from the federal administration are presidential executive orders, about 2 years to read. (and separate from the CFR cited above).

Next are court decisions. The US legal system is based on English Common Law, with an overlay of civil law (legislation). However, common law principles—courts finding law— still apply. So, to fully understand the law as it applies to you, you would have to study all court cases that set precedents—legally binding rules about what constitutes reasonable behavior under various circumstances.

It's probably impossible to work out the total number of words handed down by courts in the last 250 years. To take one example, the Supreme Court's decisions are published in the United States Reports, estimated (end 2022) at about 600 volumes of about 1000 pages/volume[6]. The US Reports contain administrative and statistical information, party invites, and other court business as well as actual legal decisions. Let's assume that half of the US reports are about actual case decisions.

That's 300,000 pages, or about 12 years of study for the Supreme Court alone, plus a year to catch up with the decisions made while you were studying. Lower court decisions in your jurisdiction are binding on you as well unless there has been a higher-level case that overturns them. Thousands of lower courts are making decisions every day.

So, putting it all together the total so far is:

Federal laws & regulations	13 years
Estimated State/local laws & regulations	13 years
Presidential executive orders	2 years
Supreme Court decisions	13 years
Total	**41 years**

This total leaves out lower court and administrative decisions, so 41 years of study is conservative, and may even underestimate the problem by decades.

How much rule-making is too much? There's no answer to that, but surely, we are way, way past the point of too much. And it's getting worse. Federal regulations alone have doubled in size since 1974 and have grown 20% in the last ten years. The feds even publish a legal newspaper, the Federal Register, to help keep on top of federal business. The 2022 edition was 80,765 pages long—another 3 years of reading.

The sheer volume of legislation is such that each of us is probably unknowingly committing several crimes a day.[7] If a prosecutor wanted to get you, they could find something to charge you with. And behind it all, is special interest manipulation.

Putting Limits on Legislation

Currently, there are no meaningful limits on legislation, either in volume or complexity. Legislators can and will keep producing legislation forever.

The proposals here are designed to cut the volume dramatically and simplify things. We'll also take steps to minimize manipulation.

Drafting and Passing Legislation

To restore proper *separation of powers*, we'll start by requiring that legislators write both legislation and regulations and can't delegate the task. In practice, it may still be the case that staffers and regulators do much of the drafting. But the *responsibility* must lie with elected legislators, who will explicitly vote to enact every bit of it, legislation and regulation alike.

Next, bills themselves will be limited to a maximum of 10,000 words (about 40 pages) for legislation and the same for all supporting regulations. That may mean there are more bills passed (doubtful given the other measures enacted here). However, even if that happens small bills break issues down into digestible chunks. It will be harder to hide special rules for special people.

Legislation should be readable, achieved by mandating a readability requirement in the form of the Flesch Reading Ease Score. The Flesch ranks how complex a piece of language is on a score from 0—100. The higher the score, the easier it is to understand. 90+ means a 5th-grade student should understand it. 50-60 is high school graduate level. Scores below 50 are university student levels of complexity.

Flesch and similar metrics have flaws. Nonetheless, some measure of readability is desirable. Florida, for example, requires insurance policies to have a Flesch of at least 45. We'll apply a similar standard to legislation.

Legislation should be complete before it is voted into law. Currently, Congress passes incomplete legislation as a byproduct of delegating legislation to the administration.

Take, for example, the Dodd-Frank Wall Street Reform and Consumer Protection Act (2010). It would take a couple of weeks to study the 848 pages of Dodd-Frank.[8] (For comparison: this book has about 360 pages in total). But a bigger problem is that the bill is unfinished. Rather than lay down rules for citizens to follow, the bill instead instructs the bureaucrats to create those rules. As a result, Dodd-Frank may never be fully finished—the regulations are still being written! By 2016 estimates were that the bill had spawned 28,000 pages of regulation to describe 274 rules. It was maybe 70% done.[9]

Unfinished bills promote legal uncertainty and manipulation. No one knows what the law is. It changes and evolves as the bureaucrats work away at it in dark corners of DC, aided by special interests "consulting" and getting things written the way they want. It discourages innovation and trade because any new product may fall foul of rules that have not yet been written.

To solve these problems let's require the posting of draft legislation *and supporting regulations* 30 days before any vote. Citizens will have a chance to digest the rules and give feedback before the vote. This will have the added benefit of slowing down the production of new rules.

Once legislation is written, legislators next need to read it! It's astonishing that this needs to be made a requirement, but legislators frequently pass bills that they have not read.[10] The politics are such that legislators often bitch about the other side not giving them enough time. A 30-day posting rule will give them that time. Further, if they are unable or unwilling to certify that they have read the legislation, then they don't get to vote. Legislators will be highly motivated to read.

Advance reading (by both legislators and citizens) raises the chances that manipulation will be spotted and removed. Additionally, if more than 10% of legislators request it, voting on bills will proceed line-by-line. If a few legislators suspect something untoward is hidden in a bill, they can force a line vote as an extra check against corruption.

Emergency and Short-Term Legislation

In principle, the law should be as stable as possible. The law does evolve with society, but it should change slowly because the law acts as a container within which citizens can innovate, but where the boundaries are clear.

Wars and other disasters might sometimes require emergency legislation, and the rules here allow for that but will also require any such legislation to be reenacted immediately after the next election. This is a check against temporary emergency rules becoming permanent.

There's also a need to safeguard against the opposite problem: excessively short-term legislation, such as legislation that expires annually. Short-term legislation undermines legal stability—it is deliberate legal uncertainty. It enables politicians to exact regular bribes from special interests who want to get those rules kept or removed.

The proposal here tries to balance stability and change. Legislation will normally last ten years and then get reviewed and renewed. Short-term legislation is allowed but may only be renewed once per election cycle, after the election of new legislators.

Reviewing and Changing Legislation

Once passed, all legislation will need to be renewed every ten years and will expire unless specifically re-enacted. The renewal process will require a review of the effectiveness of the law including cost-benefit analysis.

Take Dodd-Frank again. Between 2010 and 2016, republicans made over 150 attempts to modify or repeal the bill. No matter if you are for or against any specific attempted amendment, legislation is difficult to repeal or change.

Even if Congress might like to repeal an act, they face pressures to leave things as-is. Bureaucrats won't support repeals that cause job losses. And special interests will fight any repeal of their benefits. Starting over may be less attractive than living with the devil you know.

So, rather than stumbling on with poor legislation by default, inertia, or fear, let's reverse the assumptions and require legislators to vote for the status quo! That, or design something better. Further, *Proposal 35—Term Limits,* will ensure that most of the representatives voting will be new faces, with fresh perspectives and no personal attachment to the old legislation.

The intent here is to force legislators to review if the rules are working and change them if they don't work. Regular reviews of old legislation will also slow down the production of new legislation. Hopefully, the system will tilt towards ensuring the simplicity and efficiency of the existing rules, instead of constantly producing greater complexity.

Jurisdiction

US governments should stay within their geographic bounds. Despite this, Congress (in particular) sometimes passes legislation designed to affect foreign jurisdictions. For example, the *Hong Kong Human Rights and Democracy Act of 2019.*

China's Ministry of Foreign Affairs responded to this bill by saying the US had "sinister intentions" and that its "plot" was "doomed to fail."[11] In other words, *fuck off,* written in diplomatic language. If China passed a *US Human Rights and Democracy Act*, you might have a similar response.

Insofar as this bill affects Americans, what moral authority does the US government have to tell us how to think or act towards Hong Kong? It is up to individual citizens to decide how they feel about Hong Kong and act accordingly.

Overall, these bills are a violation of American citizens' rights. They waste representatives' time and sour international relations. This is bad political theatre. The proposal here will ban legislation designed to affect foreign governments.

Now, on the flip side, other governments should also not be able to dictate what happens within the US. The proposal includes a general provision that our governments may not enter foreign treaties that override the constitutional freedoms of US citizens.

Ignorance of the Legislation

With these new checks and balances, legislation and regulation produced by US governments should be rolled back and dramatically simplified. However, what if legislators break the rules? As a catch-all check, let's give citizens a court defense of "ignorance of the legislation."

The US legal system broadly adheres to the common law principle that ignorance of the law is no excuse. In the context in which this arose, this made sense because the law was found by the courts and could be defined as "what everyone thinks is reasonable under these circumstances."

The law in this sense is the evolving consensus of what citizens think is reasonable, discovered, and written down by the courts. Legislation, by contrast, is a set of rules thought up and written down by a legislature. Law evolves, legislation is created.

Nonetheless, the ignorance of the law principle has been applied by the courts to legislation, with limited exceptions.[12] Is this reasonable when it takes over 40 years to read that legislation?

It would not make sense to overturn the presumption that ignorance of the law is no excuse, but a limited version of it would be useful. The proposal gives citizens a defense of *ignorance of the legislation* which will apply in situations where legislation is created in defiance of the rules for creating legislation. This will give citizens a push-back mechanism against misbehaving legislatures.

Proposal 13—Regulation

The real point of audits is to instill fear, not to extract revenue; the IRS aims at winning through intimidation and (thereby) getting maximum voluntary compliance.

—Paul Strassel[1] (former IRS Agent)

There's a place for reasonable regulation, but reasonable is subjective. In practice, it's often defined by special interests using regulation to shut down their competitors.

The previous amendment addressed the volume and complexity of legislation and associated regulation. This section focuses more on who and what is regulated and how regulation is applied.

Proposed Amendment: Regulations

1. Organizations subject to regulation shall be known here as the regulatee. Any government agent or agency administering or enforcing regulation shall be known as the regulator.
2. All legislation or regulation designed to regulate business, commerce, or trade:
   a. Shall apply only to large organizations and government itself.
   b. May specify performance standards but not specific methods or technologies used to attain those standards.
   c. May not ban, prevent, or require permission for innovations.
3. Certificate-of-need and scope-of-practice requirements or any equivalents shall be illegal.
4. Disputes about regulatory matters shall be treated as civil torts. Regulatory infractions shall only rise to the level of criminal matters where violations are intentional and result in actual harm to customers or the public at large.
5. In disputes about the interpretation of legislation or regulation courts shall presume in favor of citizens.
6. Regulators shall have a duty of care to ensure that regulatory actions minimize inconvenience and lost business to the regulatee.
7. If a regulator finds a violation of regulations, they shall give the regulatee formal notice of the violation. The regulatee shall have 30 days to come into compliance.
8. Regulators shall have the right to post notice of a violation at the regulatee's place of business, giving details of the violation, the potential risks to customers, and the regulators' best estimate of the probably of those risks being actualized. The regulatee shall have the right to post a counter argument to the regulators' notice.

9. Regulators may not require regulatees to cease operations. Customers shall decide if they wish to continue doing business with the regulatee despite notice of violations.

10. If a regulator believes that the violation of regulations is so dangerous to the public that further action must be taken, then they shall have the right to sue in civil court for the regulatee to suspend business until a resolution is found.

11. All court cases involving regulators filing suit against a regulatee must heard by a jury.

12. Courts shall have the right to cause regulatees to come into compliance with regulations.

13. Courts may only cause a regulatee to suspend operations by a majority vote of a jury.

14. Only the courts shall have the right to punish regulatees for violation of regulations, and only if the regulatee has shown willful intent to violate regulations or a reckless disregard for public safety.

15. If regulators lose a suit filed against regulatees, they shall be responsible for the regulatees' reasonable court costs.

16. In cases where regulators sue a regulatee, the jury may find against individual agents who have exceeded their authority or failed to act reasonably.

17. Regulators may not carry weapons in the course of their duties.

18. If regulators find evidence of crimes being committed by regulatees, they shall report those crimes to a law enforcement agency for investigation.

Regulations

Regulations are typically sold as necessary to solve problems and ensure public safety. However, as discussed in *Chapter 5—Promoting the General Welfare,* individual freedom is the best way to solve society's problems.

Regulation should be minimized because it is the opposite of innovation. Not only that, but its very existence slows the adoption of new ideas. In a market, if an improved product turns up, customers will prefer the new. The old ones will fade away. But regulations are enforced, even when everyone agrees they are bad. Getting them changed is a political process that has little to do with helping citizens.

It's sometimes argued that more regulation is needed because the world has become more complex. That's true, but fundamentally technological complexity is the opposite of government complexity. To understand this, let's breakdown the idea of complexity into a couple of subcomponents.

Let's call one *number of choices* and the other *level of detail you need to know.*

In the commercial/technological world, new products and services keep coming on the market. Products may be brand new (personal computers), or more minor variations on old themes (new flavors of breakfast cereal). Either way, there are more choices.

At the same time, technology attempts to hide the level of detail you need to know. This process is imperfect because we're simultaneously offered more choices, but the trend is for technology to get easier to use. Think of the progress of computers: starting with punch cards, then magnetic tapes, keyboards, the mouse, graphical user interfaces, and most recently touch screens and the beginnings of voice control. Eventually, you'll be able to tell your computer, house, or car what you want in plain English—or plain any language—and it will do it for you.

Compare that to increasing government complexity. Government creates regulations, which are designed to restrict our choices—you must do it this way. At the same time, since ignorance of the law is no excuse, citizens are presumed to know an ever-increasing amount of detail. Detail such as the 188,343 pages worth of federal regulations as of 2022.[2]

So, to summarize:

Technology = more choices + less detail you need to know.
Regulation = less choices + more detail you need to know.

Over time, technology gets more efficient, cheaper, and reliable. Regulation makes things slower and less efficient (paperwork, reviews, inspections), more expensive (costs of compliance), and less reliable (arbitrary rules, bureaucratic error). Government itself is creating much of the excess complexity we experience in the modern world, and it is unproductive complexity.

Manipulation

Despite the problems, the volume of regulation keeps growing. Regulation is the motherload of manipulation opportunities, and special interests are hard at work producing more of it. Politicians, bureaucrats, and industry insiders are all profiting mighty and highly incentivized to keep the administrative-regulatory state growing.

Regulations are easy to hijack because the regulations in every industry are written by those who work in that industry. How could it be otherwise—the people who understand an industry are the people who work there, so they are the ones consulted when regulations are written.

After decades of the regulatory state, dozens of variations of manipulation have evolved, spawning thousands of rules and restrictions such as licensing requirements, manipulation of standards, certificate-of-need requirements, and scope-of-practice requirements.

Licensing requirements are government-imposed cartels. Ask an expert in any field how to protect the consumer. Is it any surprise they recommend having an expert, like them, take care of it for you? Only us doctors, attorneys, real estate agents, master electricians, etc. know how to keep the customer safe, so you'd best give us a monopoly.

Standards (health and safety, or performance) can be written so that they are expensive to achieve or need specialist skills or tools that (surprise!) the industry experts already have. So, for example, even though big pharma complains about the expense of FDA drug approval, the same process keeps small pharma out of the market. When a small company or research team has an idea for a new drug, it gets bought out by a big company. The small group can't afford to bring the product to market. Big pharma keeps its monopoly!

Certificate-of-need requirements are situations where a supplier must justify the need to start a business. For example, a medical chain might want to build a new hospital in a city but must first prove that the hospital is needed. As part of the approval process, regulators ask the current hospital owners what they think. Certificate-of-need requirements thus amount to getting permission from your rivals to compete with them.

Scope-of-practice requirements are rules about what professionals can and can't do at work. Professionals should follow good practices, but they should also be legally free to innovate and experiment. Their training and experience will keep us safer than manipulated government rules.

Another problem with regulation is cultural capture. This is where regulators start to think like the regulated, seeing the rules as an unnecessary bother. They get lax about enforcement—especially with friends. This ranges from the feds granting oil drilling leases without full environmental assessments,[3] down to your local building inspector telling the electrician, who he went to high school with, that he should fix a problem to meet code, without coming back to check he did!

Overall, regulation is so riddled with flaws, moral hazards, and manipulation that it has, over time, become the opposite of what it purports to be. Regulation hurts those it is intended to help and benefits those it is intended to curb. Regulation is a terrible cost to our society. It is time to roll back regulation to a minimum set of rules needed for us to live peaceably together.

Fixing Regulation

Earlier proposals will eliminate most regulations that impinge on individual rights. *Proposal 12—Legislation* will minimize the volume of any remaining regulation. In this proposal, we'll introduce further checks and balances to minimize manipulation and address some enforcement abuses.

Preventing Manipulation

The first step in minimizing regulation is to restrict it to big business only. Big business produces most of the goods and services in the economy, so if regulation is needed this is the place to apply it.

Applying regulation to big businesses only prevents those businesses from manipulating the rules to shut down small businesses. It keeps government off the backs of individuals and small businesses and leaves them free to innovate. It balances safety and individual freedom. Government's role is to maximize freedom, not to maximize safety.

Next, let's stop anti-competitive regulatory practices. Standards must specify the results required, not how to achieve those results. Certificate-of-need and scope-of-practice requirements will be banned.

Finally, as a general catch-all, let's stipulate that permission should never be needed to innovate. Citizens should always be free to innovate and find new ways to solve problems.

Enforcement

If regulation is intended to keep everyone safe, then the mindset of a regulator should be that of a safety inspector, not that of an enforcer. To ensure this is the default mindset, let's incentivize it.

Firstly, all regulatory processes should be treated as civil matters. Disputes should be resolved in civil courts. A regulatory infraction is a tort (a wrong to be righted) and not a crime (criminal activity to be punished). Only if regulatees willfully and persistently refuse to correct wrongs should matters become criminal.

Secondly, let's end the abuse of regulators having the power to shut down businesses unilaterally, in defiance of *separation of powers*. Let's instead have a system where regulators post notice of possible violations at the regulatee's place of business, and the regulatee has 30 days to fix the problem. Regulatees will be able to post a counter argument and continue doing business if they see fit. It will be for customers to decide if they feel safe.

If a regulator thinks violations are creating a danger to the public, and the regulatee does not agree, they should sue. This would introduce a check on the arbitrary exercise of power *before* a business is shut down. The courts can arrange expedited hearings if fast action is needed.

Next, let's end the threat of gun violence against peace-loving businesses by requiring regulators to be unarmed. Armed regulators reinforce the "us and them" mentality that both government agents and citizens often hold. If individual regulators don't feel safe at work, they are free to find other employment.

If regulators suspect genuine criminal activity, they will need to call on a law enforcement agency to investigate. This provides a check on regulators by splitting responsibilities between inspectors and enforcers.

As a final check against enforcement overreach by regulators, let's give them skin in the game. If a regulator sues a regulatee and loses, then the regulatee will be entitled to costs. Pressure will come to bear on regulators if they cost their agency money. That pressure will ensure that decisions to take regulatees to court are not made lightly.

Collectively these rules should enable us to keep the major benefits of regulation in place whilst cutting out the worst abuses. Big businesses will be regulated and inspected, and violations will be corrected. But only in the most dangerous situations will organizations get shut down. Checks and balances will apply.

These measures are unlikely to affect public safety in any material fashion because everyone is already motivated towards safety. Customers want to be safe. Businesses don't want to harm customers, risk lawsuits, or risk loss of insurance cover.

Taking the force out of regulation will keep things civil, balanced, and cooperative.

Proposal 14—Executive Orders

When the President does it, that means that it's not illegal.
— Richard M. Nixon

Executive orders issued by the President of the United States have been deemed by the courts to have the "full force and effect of law." Typically, governors' executive orders are also considered law in their state.[1]

Nonetheless, executive orders having the force of law on citizens are a breach of the *separation of powers* principle. This is an especially dangerous breach because it enables one person to make the law. There's a name for this form of government: it is called a *dictatorship*.

Proposed Amendment: Executive Orders

1. Government has a duty to maintain the *separation of powers* doctrine in all its operations.

2. Executive orders shall be defined here as any order or proclamation issued by the President of the United States, by State Governors, by heads of lesser US governments, or by an administrative agency.

3. Executive orders are intended for the efficient management of government operations and shall apply only to government employees in the execution of their duties.

4. Executive orders shall not have the force of law on citizens.

5. Executive orders may not suspend, nullify, or modify legislation or the constitution.

6. Executive orders issued in secret shall only apply to government agents who are privy to the secret.

7. Legislators shall have the power to rescind any executive order issued within their jurisdiction by a simple majority vote. In legislatures with two chambers, an executive order may be rescinded by either chamber.

8. In the event of extreme civil unrest, legislators may institute temporary curfews and closures of public spaces. Such actions may last no more than 24 hours and shall require a 3/5 majority of legislators to agree. Actions may be repeated, in 24-hour increments, by 3/5 majority.

9. Persons in violation of a legislative curfew may be detained by law enforcement until the end of the current 24-hour curfew period but shall not be considered to have committed a crime.

Flirting With Dictatorship

For our purposes here, executive orders will mean any public order issued by any part of an executive/administrative branch of government, though we'll focus mainly on presidential executive orders.[2]

By the end of the Trump administration, we'd reached order #13,976. Executive orders don't automatically expire when a president leaves office but may have a built-in expiration or get rescinded. Assuming 4 pages per order (eyeball estimate from Obama's orders), the orders would take up about two years of reading at 100 pages/day.

Executive orders come in four broad categories:

1. Orders affecting internal operations of the relevant administration.

2. Orders triggered by pre-determined legislative criteria.

3. Orders triggered by emergencies.

4. National Security Orders.

The first case is internal government operations. The President runs the federal administration, governors run state administrations, and so on. They issue orders to their respective administrations to get the job done. These orders might affect citizens but usually only as a side effect.

The second case is situations where a legislature has decided in advance about action needed under specific circumstances, but the executive pulls the trigger. For example, if repairs are needed, then roads may need to be closed, even if this hinders freedom of movement.

The third case is emergencies. Presidents, Governors, Majors, and even administrative agencies will issue orders in emergencies. Often legislation grants these powers, but since emergencies are difficult to predict, the powers granted are often vaguely worded.

The final, fourth category of executive orders are those about national security issues. These will be addressed briefly at the end of this proposal.

Most executive orders are non-controversial and fall into the first two categories: internal government operations, and actions needed in pre-defined circumstances. The real problems start in the third case, executive orders triggered by emergencies.

Examples of emergency orders are the lockdown of Boston after the Boston Marathon bombing in April 2013; the January 2015 travel bans in New York threatened by winter storm Juno, and curfews following riots after the death of George Floyd. And multiple orders in response to the Coronavirus: stay-at-home orders, business closures, bans on rights of assembly, mask mandates, and so on.

Should Executive Orders Be Law?

Executive orders having the full force of law have no place in our legal system. They are a breach of *separation of powers* and often violate all the Tests of Legitimate Governance.

Executive orders that violate individual rights fail the Test of Purpose. Government's first duty is always to protect individual rights—individual liberty trumps administrative opinions about the common good.

The Test of Moral Authority applies even in emergencies. Do I have any right to stop my neighbor heading downtown tonight, even if riots are possible? No, I do not have that right, and neither does the government, including presidents, governors, or majors. No official suddenly gains powers to be a dictator just because they were elected.

Executive orders often violate the Test of Consent. There were many instances of citizens disobeying mask mandates during Covid. They disobeyed because they disagreed. There was no consent of the governed.

At the federal level, executive orders as law violate the Test of Constitutional Authority. Article II, section 1, says *executive power shall be vested in a president of the United States of America.* Article II, section 3 says *The President shall take care that the laws be faithfully executed.* In other words, the President is head of the executive and must ensure laws are carefully implemented. Nowhere does the constitution empower presidents to create new laws!

A common argument in support of executive orders is that the President should act if Congress will not. But here in America, Congress makes laws. If Congress can't decide what to do, then maybe no clear course of action is available, or maybe no action is needed. Either way, let's do nothing, rather than have a dictator decide.

If you like the current president, you may think that their actions are justified because you agree with them. But the perceived correctness (to some) of any president's plan is irrelevant. It is simply not their place to impose a plan. Even if presidents had the legal right (which they do not), top-down rule-making should be a last resort. *Legislative deadlock is a feature, not a bug.* The longer the delay, the higher the chances of citizens finding their own solutions— unmanipulated solutions.

Re-Separation of Powers

To restore a *separation of powers,* the proposal is that executive orders should never have the power of law on citizens. Laws that affect citizens should be enacted by legislatures only. And no executive order can ever suspend citizen rights, legislation, or any constitution (state or federal). No travel bans, no forced evaluations, no lockdowns, no forced closings of businesses, no curfews.

It's easy to ban executive orders as law, but the political forces causing their growth will still exist. Every president pushes for their policies while the other side complains like crazy. Then there's a change of administration and the roles reverse! But no matter which side is pushing or complaining, presidents keep gaining power.

Tension between presidents and Congress has been present since the beginning of the republic. The tension is deliberate, part of the checks and balances. Over time though, things have gotten out of balance. Presidents have become too strong.

To rebalance these power dynamics, let's allow legislatures to override executive orders by majority vote. At the federal level, Congress can already override an executive order, but it is a long process.[3] Congress must pass a bill overriding the order, which the President can veto, which Congress can overturn the veto etc. The proposal here would shorten this process to a straight vote. In any bi-cameral legislature (the feds and every state except Nebraska), either chamber can overturn the executive order.

Effectively, this would result in deadlocks favoring the legislature's position, including doing nothing if the legislature cannot agree. *Primum non nocere*—first do no harm—should be the default. This is the safer default position when Congress and the President disagree.

Some states and local jurisdictions may already have similar rules in place; this proposal aims to make them universal.

Emergencies

Executive orders have appropriate uses in emergencies. Mobilizing police, national guards, and emergency workers. Temporarily closing government facilities. Coordination of transport and communications, and so on.

What happens though when the government wants citizens to act? What if a hurricane is coming, and your governor thinks people should leave the coast?

The basic answer is persuasion, not force. Rather than ordering people to leave as the hurricane approaches, the governor might advise everyone near the shore to shut up their houses and leave. There will be high compliance because citizens are already motivated to leave. They don't need to be ordered. They'd be even more motivated if the governor announced that anyone staying had no guarantee of help from emergency services. A few citizens will make poor decisions, but that's their responsibility as adults in a free society.

Further, there's no guarantee that politicians will get it right. And when a leader makes a wrong call, it affects everyone at a high collective cost. For example, when Winter Storm Juno approached New York in January 2015, a travel ban shut the city down, costing millions of dollars. Yet the storm missed! The travel ban was both a violation of individual liberty and a wrong call.

Civil Unrest

What is a proper government response to civil unrest, demonstrations, or riots? Demonstrations per se are a reasonable exercise of 1st Amendment rights and freedom of assembly. But problems arise when demonstrations go too far. Riots are a genuine risk to public safety, and grounds for government intervention. Even so, that does not justify the removal of citizens' rights.

If the authorities want to clear out downtown, they should again use persuasion rather than force. They will likely find this easy because people are already motivated to stay safe. Most citizens would voluntarily follow stay-at-home requests to avoid riots.

Additionally, absent the power to force compliance, officials would be incentivized to find other solutions to potential problems: negotiate with protestors rather than order them around, offer alternate venues, and so on.

All that said, it's possible that civil unrest can get so extreme that temporary curfews, etc. may be justified. Nonetheless, it is still an invitation to dictatorship if one person has the power to employ that force.

So, as a last resort, the proposal allows legislatures to implement curfews and travel bans, under strict conditions. Bans will be in 24-hour increments, with a 3/5 majority of the legislature needing to agree/reconfirm their decisions every day. This aims to balance public safety and the risks of a dictatorship.

Coronavirus

The basic advice with Coronavirus was to self-isolate to slow down the spread of the virus. This seemed like good advice at the time, but the quality of the advice was not the issue. The important question is should the government have the power to force people into self-isolation? The correct answer must be no. Free citizens of a free country should be free to choose how they want to respond to any health emergency.

I have every right to protect myself as I see fit, including self-isolation, or denying people access to my property. But do I have any right to order my neighbor to self-isolate? Do I have the right to imprison her in her own house? No, I do not have that right. And neither does the government. This fails the Test of Moral Authority.

In New York City though, the major ordered restaurants to do take-out only, closed night clubs, theatres, and cinemas, and ordered hospitals to cancel elective surgery.[4] Other states and cities took similar actions.[5]

Citizens obeyed because the situation seemed urgent. But this is police state action on the slippery road to a dictatorship. Several states had discussions about how to hold primaries safely.[6] Imagine if Trump had tried to suspend the presidential election. Would this ever be acceptable, even in a health crisis?

Once again, no orders were necessary. It would have been enough to advise people to stay home and give them reasons why.

National Security and Secret Executive Orders

The fourth type of executive orders outlined above are national security orders, known (currently) as Presidential Decision Directives (PDDs).

The National Security Council (NSC) advises the President on foreign policy and national security and recommends actions if needed. The President's decision is then announced in a PDD.

What is disturbing about PDDs is that some of them are classified yet still have the full force and effect of law. These are secret laws! And while some national security issues require secrecy, in general secrets are anathema to an open society. Secret laws are a violation of everything American stands for, another step down the slippery road to a dictatorship. Sooner or later, someone will find themselves in a Kafkaesque nightmare: accused of a crime but not told what the crime is.

As a safeguard against secret laws, let's stipulate that PPDs will only apply to government employees who are privy to the secret.

Government secrets are addressed more fully in *Proposal 33—Open Government.*

Proposal 15—Administrative Law

Every revolution evaporates and leaves behind only the slime of a new bureaucracy.

—Franz Kafka

Everyone hates bureaucracy, even the bureaucrats! And yet there's a never-ending river of forms, procedures, licenses, inspections, permits, and postings as the administration grinds on. These bureaucratic processes often violate *separation of powers* when the administration acts as all three branches of government in one.

This section proposes general rules for administrative actions, reinstating *separation of powers*, and addressing issues such as permits, licenses, and general paperwork. Other specific issues (taxation, Social Security, policing, healthcare) are dealt with in later proposals.

Proposed Amendment: Administrative Law

1. Government has a duty of care to ensure that administrative processes are as simple, efficient, and cost-effective as possible.

2. Government agents shall presume in favor of citizens whenever any administrative process is ambiguous.

3. Citizens subject to administrative processes shall always retain their full constitutional rights. No process may disadvantage citizens who choose to exercise their rights.

4. Government may not trade services or benefits for a citizen's waiver of their constitutional rights. Citizens who voluntarily waive their rights may reassert them at any time.

5. Government may not charge fees for expedited processing of administrative issues.

6. Government may not require citizens to have permits or licenses for any activity unless there are proven public health issues or proven tragedy of the commons issues irresolvable by other means.

7. Government may not require citizens to register, tag or label their possessions unless there is a proven public health issue involved or unless that possession is often left unattended in public places.

8. Government may not require citizens to post a notice on any property they own or of any activity they wish to undertake unless there is a proven public health issue involved.

9. Government may not charge citizens for permits, licenses, registrations, tags, identity or travel documents, or equivalents thereof.

10. The right of private citizens to use their property as they see fit is a fundamental individual right. Government may not restrict citizens

from using their property as they fit unless said use does direct physical harm to neighbors.

11. Government may not require structures built on private lands to meet building standards unless the building is intended for public access or is within 100 yards of a building on another property.

12. If zoning restrictions are placed on private property that creates a difference in the property value of more than 20%, the owner shall be entitled to compensation for their loss.

13. Forms that any government requires citizens to complete may be no longer than five letter pages of 12-point text. No accompanying explanation of a form may be longer than the form itself.

14. For issues where large sums of money are involved, forms may have an additional page per $1,000,000 value.

15. Where forms are needed on a repetitive basis, government shall have a duty of care to prefill them based on the previous filing.

16. It is the responsibility of government to check forms for errors and request corrections. Penalties for mistakes, errors, or late filing of forms shall not be allowed except where a citizen is found guilty of criminal charges by a court.

17. Administrative subpoenas shall be illegal.

18. Administrative courts and tribunals shall be illegal. Disputes between citizens and the administration that cannot be settled by negotiation must be decided in regular court by the judicial branch of government.

19. No administrative agency may fine or punish citizens. Fines and punishments shall be the sole prerogative of the courts.

20. Where a citizen owes the government money the amount due shall be the original amount plus interest at the rate of the consumer price index from the due date. If a citizen has overpaid, they shall be owed a refund plus interest calculated in the same manner.

21. If a government or citizen believes they are owed money by the other party, then they should give notice in writing. If agreement and payment of the sums owed are not reached within 60 days of notice, then either side shall have the right to sue in civil court for the sums due. The suit shall be filed in the lowest level of court that state law allows.

22. Criminal charges may apply in cases where over $1,000,000 is owed and there is intent to defraud or deny payment.

The Rise of the Administrative State

With the shift of power in the federal government over the last 150 years, Congress has delegated its powers to the President and an alphabet of federal agencies, giving them increasingly free reign to write the regulations that rule our lives. This has created the administrative state, a vast, unelected, and unaccountable bureaucracy. Similar processes have taken place at state levels.

Scholars differ about the constitutionality of the administrative state. One argument is that it began in the late 19th century with the need to regulate new trans-national industries such as railroads. The Constitution has nothing to say about this because the issue arose after it was written.

An alternate view sees the administrative state as the King's prerogative in a new form,[1] i.e.: the government can tell you what to do because it is the government! From this point of view, the Constitution was designed to prevent the administrative state, even if the Founders did not use that term.

Let's leave those arguments to the scholars. If the administrative state came after the Constitution, then the Constitution is out of date. If the Constitution was designed to prevent the administrative state, then it has failed. Either way, let's update the Constitution!

We need a correction because the administrative state has gone too far. The rules, the costs of compliance, the number of government workers, and the abuses of power are out of control. And as the administrative state gets bigger, so does the amount of manipulation.

Governments administer things, so some administration is needed, but there needs to be a correction of the over-reach. The corrections fall into two main categories: restoring *separation of powers* and changing incentives to have the administration right-size itself.

Separation of Powers

The administrative state often violates *separation of powers*. For many day-to-day aspects of life, the administration writes the laws (regulations), polices them (inspections), judges them (administrative courts/decisions), and punishes them (administrative fines/seizures).

In theory, you can appeal administrative actions through the regular courts. In practice, appeals are expensive and time-consuming, creating a de facto abuse of *innocent until proven guilty*. The IRS, for example, fines you first, and then tells you how you can appeal!

Sometimes administrative investigations can turn into inquisitions where you don't know who your accuser is, or even what you are accused of, let alone the right to face your accuser.[2]

As a first step to fixing abuses, the proposal bans administrative courts and administrative fines. If laws have been broken, and if citizens and administration cannot negotiate it out between themselves, then they should appeal to the courts for adjudication.

Citizens are *innocent until proven guilty* in a regular court of law! Anything else is a violation of *separation of powers*, and a recipe for abuse.

Changing Incentives on Administrative Growth

The proposals in the *Basic Rights* section above will curb government by reasserting citizen rights. The measures outlined below supply an additional check by changing the incentives on administrative growth. Administration should only ever occur where citizens need it.

Zoning

Private property rights are implicit in the Constitution but have nonetheless been routinely abused, especially in the last 100 years or so.

Zoning laws are a modern invention in the US. The earliest comprehensive zoning code arose in New York City in 1916. Zoning took off primarily through the 1920s and 1930s. The Supreme Court decided zoning was constitutional in Euclid v. Ambler Realty Co. (1926).

Should your neighbors, or the government, be able to tell you what you can and cannot do on your property? If you are doing something harmful (pollution or putting up a dangerous structure), then the neighbors should have some say. On the other hand, zoning often goes too far. Should your neighbors have a say in things like how tall your building is, what it looks like, or what business you do inside? Zoning leads to conflict and resentment among neighbors as they dispute each other's use of private property.

The proposals here set the standard back in favor of individual owners being able to do what they want, so long as they do no direct harm to neighbors. This is not an outright ban on zoning, but there will be a right to sue for damages if zoning causes more than a 20% degradation in the value of your property.

Licenses and Permits

In a free country, citizens should be free to do anything they want so long as they cause no direct harm to other people or their property. So, in principle, citizens should never need to ask government permission for anything. Permits are a violation of citizens' freedom to decide for themselves.

Governments, though, are incentivized to create permitting requirements. Politicians and administrators like to control things, and it gives the appearance of "doing something" about problems. Permitting can even be a profit center for government.

Permitting also enables manipulation. If, for example, you needed a permit to park a food truck on your lot, those who turn up to complain at city hearings are likely to be existing restaurant owners. At the local level, friendships (of business owners and city councilors) may also affect permitting decisions.

The proposals here are designed to do away with most permits. The are only two situations where permits might be reasonable:

1. Genuine public health risks, such as factories.
2. Tragedy of the commons issues.

"Tragedy of the commons" refers to situations where a public resource may be overused if too many people use it. For example, limited fish stocks in fisheries, or limited camping spaces in parks. Sometimes these situations can be handled privately, but often permits are a good solution.

Even where permits are still required, it's likely to be corporations who will need most of them—they do most of the large-scale dangerous stuff. Ideally, this arrangement will allow a balance of freedom for individual citizens and regulation of big business.

Another way to stop growth in permitting is to disallow government from charging for permits.

The standard argument is that if you need a permit you should pay for it like you pay for any service. However, there's a difference between a service that you *want* and a service that you *must* take. Permits should serve the public interest, but if the government profits from permits, then they are incentivized to demand permits, needed or not. Permits become a protection racket.

If charging for permits is disallowed, then the incentives are correctly aligned. If permits are a cost rather than a profit center, governments will then try to minimize them. Citizens will only support them if they see a genuine need.

This will also reduce corruption. Special interests manipulate permitting to keep rivals out (like in the food truck example above). Governments are incentivized to along with manipulation when they profit. No profits from permits means fewer permits means less corruption.

Defunding permitting also lowers government incentives to ask for unnecessary information or action. For example, annual vehicle registrations are an excuse to collect taxes and fees. If those were disallowed, we'd probably quickly evolve to a system where you registered your car when you bought it and deregistered it when you sold it—which is what governments do with their own vehicles.

Government Paperwork

As regulation has grown so has the volume of information governments demand from us. Everyone is unhappy with the situation, but there's always an administrator somewhere who thinks "If only we had this extra bit of information, we'd solve this problem."

For example, the IRS requires you to supply information about your finances. And they require almost everyone else who does business with you to supply a different version of the same information. Basically, the IRS does not trust us. Their solution: have us spy on each other!

When citizens complained about the burden of paperwork, Congress had a solution: create a new bureaucracy to track paperwork. Producers of federal forms must apply to the Office of Management and Budget and get a control number for the form. Each form must include an estimate of how long it will take to fill out, including the time taken to collect information.

Well, great! The solution to the paperwork problem is that now we know how big it is. There's a vague requirement that paperwork should be justified, but no actual provision for a reduction. It's simply a cruel joke that knowing how long it takes to fill out a form is a meaningful check.

For an actual reduction in paperwork, let's directly limit the size of forms. The proposal here limits government forms to five pages, with accompanying instructions no longer than the form itself. That's a severe restriction, intended to force government agencies to simplify forms and only ask for the most necessary information.

Larger regulated projects could reasonably require extra paperwork. To allow for this, large projects can have an extra page of forms per million dollars. A $300 million project to tear down a polluted factory and clean the site up might be accompanied by larger environmental reports. A $2 billion nuclear power plant may need lots of paperwork. But ordinary citizens involved in everyday business will be spared most paperwork.

In addition to this proposal, *Proposal 1—Adulthood* will ban government from requiring citizens to act in a law enforcement capacity, and *Proposal 6—Privacy* will ban requirements to release private information about other citizens (except by court order). Together this should stop governments from making us spy on each other. No more IRS forms telling on your neighbors or people you do business with.

Suppose you make an error filling out a government form. Now what? Currently, it's up to you to get it right, and you might be punished if you get it wrong with administrative fines and penalties.

However, the administration typically fines you first and allows you to appeal after, reversing *innocent until proven guilty*. Administrative fines also breach the principle of *separation of powers*—guilt is for the courts to prove and punish.

Fines also create perverse incentives. If the administration makes money from errors, then they are incentivized to create complex forms where errors are common. Perhaps not deliberately, but there's little incentive to keep things simple. Form designers can ask for any information they feel like, and fine you if you don't provide it.

Compare the government approach of fining you to, say, the cable company. Suppose you apply for cable service but made a mistake on your application—perhaps you misplaced a digit in your social, and they can't pull credit. The cable company makes money by serving you, you get their services by cooperating. Both sides are incentivized to get any problems resolved ASAP. Additionally, if they tried to fine you for the mistake, you'd tell them to go to hell and get a satellite dish instead.

Incentives are rarely aligned so well with government services. Often, the service is imposed on you. And government jobs rarely depend on keeping customers happy.

To correct this, the proposal reverses the usual assumptions. It will give the administration a duty of care to check forms for accuracy and disallow them from fining you for errors. And it will require them to pre-fill recurring forms. You can correct those forms as necessary, but meanwhile, there's less work for you and less chance of errors.

Trading Constitutional Rights

Negotiation, creating win-win deals, is a cornerstone of our personal and commercial lives and public policy should encourage it. However, sometimes power is so imbalanced between the parties involved that deals between them might be unfair. Deals between government and citizens are one of those situations. The question here is: should citizens be allowed to trade their Constitutional rights in return for government services?

In principle, adult citizens can trade their rights if they see fit. On the other hand, if government's job is to protect constitutional rights, why would any government ever need to ask citizens to give up those rights?

Despite this clear principle, citizens are often asked to trade rights for services. For example, the 4th Amendment protects us against unreasonable searches. But many states deem issuance of a driver's license as implied consent that you'll allow the police to search you and your vehicle, even in the absence of reasonable cause. You may have given implied consent to take a drug or alcohol test if stopped while driving.

States are arguing that a driver's license is a privilege, and it has a price: your 4th Amendment rights. This is a dubious argument and the start of a slippery slope. The point of a license is to prove that you are a safe driver. Public safety is reasonable, but why do you need to give up your rights? Further, is a driver's license a privilege when most adults need one to function in modern society?

So, for example, it's reasonable that police stop drunk drivers and check for alcohol. But there's no need to violate the Constitution to do it. If the police believe a driver is drunk, they can ask for their consent to a breath test. If the driver refuses, the police can get a search warrant over the phone within 15-20 minutes.

Since 2014, this is a solution Nevada has been testing since the Supreme Court of Nevada ruled implied consent unconstitutional. The court decided consent is only consent if you have the right to withdraw it![3]

This may seem like a small thing, but why allow the government to violate the Constitution at all? Its primary job is to uphold the Constitution and protect our rights. Each small chip taken out of our Constitutional protections may be insignificant by itself: hardly worth arguing about. But those small chips add up. It's like a beaver taking down a big tree, nibbling away one bite at a time until the tree collapses under its own weight.

So, the proposal here insists on the Constitution. Governments may not ask citizens to trade constitutional rights for government services. Citizens may waive and un-waive their rights as they see fit, but it must be citizens who control their rights, not the government.

In the Nevada example: by requiring a warrant, police officers must justify their actions and a judge must agree. This is how the Constitution is supposed to work—checks and balances. Let's let it do its job, as it has done for centuries. The alternatives—arbitrary stops, searches, and drug tests—are the route to a police state.

Reports so far indicate that Nevada police have not found this a burden because drivers normally say yes when asked to take the test. The few who don't agree have not bogged down the system.

Proposal 16—Judicial Review

The powers not delegated to the United States by the Constitution, nor prohibited by it to the States, are reserved to the States respectively, or to the people.

—10th Amendment of the US Constitution

One of those checks built into our system of government is that the court system should be independent of the executive and the legislature.

Despite this, the courts, in particular the Supreme Court, have slowly been corrupted over the last 100 or so years. They no longer properly perform their function of keeping the other branches of government in check.

It is time to restore the independence of the courts.

Proposed Amendment—Judicial Review

1. In any dispute between citizens and government, the courts' primary responsibility is to protect citizens' rights.
2. Where government action imposes restrictions upon a citizen, government must affirmatively prove they have the right to impose said restrictions.
3. Courts shall always presume in favor of citizens should there be any ambiguity or doubt.
4. Courts shall presume in favor of a citizen's agency in any decision that a citizen makes.
5. Every court at any level of government, and any jury in any type of court case shall have a right of judicial review.
6. Where any court finds an executive or legislative action to be unconstitutional, they shall have a duty of care to issue a judicial stay of that action. The judicial stay shall remain in place until all appeals are exhausted.
7. Executive privilege, legislative privilege, or equivalents shall not be a valid defense of any order issued that infringes upon a citizen's rights or freedoms.
8. In any court case, it shall be for the courts alone to decide proper punishment or restitution. Statutory punishments, damages, restitutions, or equivalents shall be illegal.
9. The Supreme Court shall have a maximum of nine justices.
10. Where a justice for any court is nominated by the President, the Senate shall hold a confirmation vote within 30 calendar days of the President's nomination. If the Senate fails to hold said vote, then the nominee shall be deemed approved.

Functions of the Court System

For our purposes here, the functions of the courts can be divided into three sections:

1. Checks and Balances—preventing the intrusion of government upon citizens and protecting rights—are covered in this chapter.
2. Criminal Justice—punishing criminals and redressing criminal wrongs—will be addressed in *Proposal 17—Criminal Justice.*
3. Civil Justice—resolution of disputes between citizens (and sometimes between government and citizens)—will be addressed in *Proposal 18—Civil Justice.*

The first role of the courts, covered in this chapter, is their role as part of the checks and balances of government. In legal terminology, this is called "judicial review." The courts, especially the Supreme Court, can review laws, rulings, and orders handed out by legislatures and the executive and overturn them if they believe them to be unconstitutional. They have been failing in this role.

The courts are meant to be independent but have come to be part of the government apparatus suppressing citizens' rights instead of protecting them. When there are disputes, subtle pressures push judges towards agreeing with the government. Judges are, after all, government employees. Additionally, judges are under pressure to fix the problems in front of them today and don't always have the big picture in mind.

As a result, thousands of small expedient decisions have been made over the last 150+ years that add up, in total, to the courts tilting towards the government rather than towards citizens. Decisions may have solved small immediate problems, but they started trends that created larger problems. You start by prosecuting an anti-war speech as sedition,[1] and you end up criminalizing hate speech in violation of the 1st Amendment. Or you deem it reasonable to regulate sawn-off shotguns beloved by criminals and you end up with hundreds of laws about firearms in violation of the 2nd Amendment. And so on.

Other proposals address some topic-specific court decisions and how to correct them. This proposal addresses general principles of how to handle disputes between citizens and government.

Independence of the Courts

To restore checks and balances, let's start by reasserting the independence of the courts. Judges should be independent, but presidents and congress have been trying to subvert judicial independence over the last 100 years. Two main issues will be addressed here: appointments of judges—and especially threats to pack the Supreme Court—and statutory punishments.

Judicial Appointments

On September 18th, 2020, Justice Ruth Bader Ginsberg died, and President Trump nominated Amy Coney Barrett to take her place. The political uproar started immediately! Ginsberg was seen as a left-leaning moderate. Supposedly, the appointment of Barret in Ginsberg's place gave the court a 6-3 conservative bias. An alt-right dystopia was looming.

Further, since an election was pending, there were immediate cries for the appointment of the next justice to be delayed to "give the people a say." Speculation started that Biden would pack the court with a slew of left-wing justices to achieve DNC goals.[2] Talk of packing the court erupted again in June 2022 after the overturn of Roe vs. Wade.

Both parties are equally guilty of partisan politics at different times. Rather than apportion blame, let's instead immunize the system against political fights. Supreme Court appointments have become too important because Congress has abdicated its responsibilities to legislate difficult issues. Instead, Congress has delegated rulemaking to the administration and leaves difficult decisions to the courts. If Congress did their job the courts would be less important, and fights about who sits in the courts would be less partisan.[3]

On court packing specifically: packing the court is a bad faith idea, no matter who proposes it. The court is meant to be above politics, which is why justices are appointed for life. Packing the court, or threats thereof, are deliberate attempts to introduce partisanship.

Suppose that Biden decides the court leans too far right and appoints extra left-leaning justices to balance it. Will the next Republican president leave things like that? No, if one side packs the court, now the incentives are for the other side to pack it further in the opposite direction. Since justices are appointed for life, the Supreme Court would get bigger and bigger. This cannot work.

In any case, worries about court biases are overblown. Justices swear to uphold the Constitution, not their political views. It's their job to keep their personal biases out of the equation, and the record indicates that they do it well, especially in modern times.

Since 2000, most Supreme Court cases have had a large majority. In 36% of cases, the justices reached a unanimous decision. Only 19% of the of the time did the court decide something on a 5-4 split.[4] And the court is trending toward greater consensus. Polls show most citizens value how apolitical the court appears to be,[5] though the recent overturning of Roe vs. Wade may be an exception.

Nonetheless, let's remove the moral hazard of court packing. Since nine justices have become the norm, the proposal here formalizes that constitutionally. This would prevent political games with court packing.

Next, there's the issue of appointments to the federal courts, which have become bitter partisan fights in the last decades, especially at the Supreme Court level.

Presidents are highly motivated to appoint judges as part of their legacy, so no changes are needed there. On the other hand, a change is needed in the confirmation process because the Senate has been playing games. In 2016 Republicans obstructed Obama's nominees to replace Justice Scalia, arguing that the next president should decide. Democrats tried to return the favor in 2020 with Trump's nominee to replace Justice Ginsberg.

Despite this, all arguments that judicial appointments be delayed in an election year so that the people can decide are nonsense. The people did decide, and their decision remains valid until a new administration is sworn in. If we took this argument seriously, then in an election year *all* presidential decisions should halt, and all legislators up for reelection should be barred from voting. This is obvious nonsense that would bring government to a halt every election year.

Let's instead short-circuit this nonsense by *requiring* the Senate to vote within 30 days of a presidential nomination. If they do not vote, the nominee is deemed accepted. If the Senate votes against it, then the President can nominate a new candidate, and the 30-day clock starts over. The entire process will be much less prone to politics and political delay.

Statutory Punishments

After court appointments, a second area of judicial independence that needs attention is statutory punishment. The basic question is this: if someone breaks the law, who decides what the punishment should be?

Under English Common Law there were sometimes statutory punishments—punishments decided by Parliament, or the King. This was then inherited in the US system, though arguably under the design of the US system, this already violated the *separation of powers* principle.

In recent decades legislatures have become increasingly prescriptive—mandating fixed fines or jail sentences, or mandatory sequential sentencing. The result is arbitrary justice—the courts have no choice about punishments and cannot consider extenuating circumstances.

Clinton's 1994 three-strikes rule, for example, required judges to hand out bigger punishments to people who had committed three or more crimes. This resulted in absurd punishments for petty drug offenders. Even Clinton, in retrospect, thinks it was a mistake.[6]

So, to restore judicial independence, the proposal is that judges and/or juries always have the final say on punishment, even if legislatures are recommending sentences.

Note that perfection is not possible here. A judge might well impose a questionable punishment, too lenient or too tough. Even so, bad judgments are preferable to bad legislation. Appealing judgments is much easier than repealing legislation.

Individual Rights First

The primary purpose of government is to protect individual rights. Therefore, in any dispute that involves government infringement of citizen rights, then the courts should presume in favor of citizens.

This is not to say that government can never violate any citizen's rights. Grey areas exist about how far government should go. Sometimes a citizen's rights need to be curtailed for the protection of other citizens. However, if citizen rights are ever to be violated, the bar for allowing this should be high. The reasons should be clear, provable, and constitutional.

Our government has increasingly been violating our rights over the last 150 years. The courts have allowed abuses, rather than prevented them. To resolve this creeping abuse, the proposals here reassert that courts, like all parts of government, have a primary goal of protecting individual rights. If citizens and government conflict over rights, the courts should presume strongly in favor of the citizens. If legislation is ambiguous, presume in favor of citizens. If a government tries to take away citizen rights', require them to prove constitutional authority to do so. If a government decides something for a citizen against their will, presume in favor of the agency of the citizen.

Grinding Citizens Down

One problem that citizens have when fighting unconstitutional government action is that the government has a huge amount of legal and financial resources to pour into legal disputes.

Suppose a government takes some action (via legislation, regulations, or executive orders) that citizens think is unconstitutional. Suppose someone sues the government and wins. Typically, one of two things might happen:

1. Although the court finds the government action to be unconstitutional, it also finds a reason to leave the unconstitutional law in place until the issue is resolved. (Usually, because government lawyers argue about how "urgent" the problem is that the government is trying to solve).

2. The court issues a stay of the government order, temporarily suspending it, but the government then immediately appeals, and (mustering its mighty legal firepower), gets the lower court's decision overturned.

Either way, the unconstitutional law is still in place, and citizens are still fighting it, putting in time and money, as well as having to keep complying with a law that at least one court has found unconstitutional.

The government, and government lawyers, can keep this up for years. If they ultimately lose, they can then introduce a similar but not quite the same law and start the process over again.

When governments do this, they are effectively using their legal and financial resources to grind down citizens and grind away citizen rights. Governments will always have more resources than citizens. To counterbalance this somewhat, the proposal here clarifies, firstly, that all courts and all juries have a right of judicial review. In other words: any court can find any government action unconstitutional.

When a court does find an action to be unconstitutional, the courts shall have a duty of care to issue a judicial stay—the government action will be suspended, and any legislation, regulations, or orders will be temporarily put on hold.

The action will then remain suspended until all appeals are exhausted. This is deliberately designed to tip the scales of justice firmly in the direction of citizen rights. Even if the government ultimately wins, the law will have been on hold for the interim.

Executive and Legislative Privilege

Over the decades government prosecutors have invented many novel legal theories to justify government abuses of citizens. Among the most galling are *executive privilege* and *legislative privilege*.

These legal terms are a cover allowing the courts to sanction government abuses on the premise that the executive or legislators have a right to abuse citizens. These privileges are nonsense. Government has exactly the same moral authority as any individual citizen. Government privilege therefore cannot exist.

The President cannot order me to do something *just because he is the President.* Congress cannot legislate me to do something, *just because it is Congress.* In both cases, if their orders violate my freedoms, my freedom comes first. Here in the US, citizens are sovereign, and citizen rights come first.

The proposal here therefore makes these privilege arguments illegal.

Proposal 17—Criminal Justice

*In all criminal prosecutions, the accused shall enjoy the right to a
speedy and public trial, by an impartial jury ...*
—Bill of Rights, Article VI

The United States has the highest per capita prison population of any
country in the world. About 2.2 million people are imprisoned as of 2015.

Things are getting worse! The number of crimes keeps rising, and convictions rise with them. Buried in the figures are other disturbing facts,
primarily that the government is a racist institution. The Land of the Free
has become the Land of the Imprisoned.

Proposed Amendment: Criminal Justice

1. Government has a duty to provide an efficient and just criminal jus-
    tice system.
2. All persons are *innocent until proven guilty* in a court of law.
3. No person shall ever have to prove a negative in any court.
4. Private right-of-action prosecutions or lawsuits shall be illegal un-
    der all circumstances.
5. Prosecutors shall be required to show intent in criminal prosecu-
    tions.
6. Prosecutors shall be required to cite named individual victim(s) in
    criminal prosecutions wherever possible.
7. Possession of information shall not be a crime per se nor the sole
    evidence of intent to commit a crime.
8. Conspiracy shall not be a crime per se. Persons peripherally in-
    volved in a crime may only be charged for their direct involvement.
9. Persons arrested on suspicion of a crime shall be charged within 24
    hours or released without prejudice.
10. Plea bargaining shall be illegal. Persons charged with a crime must
    be tried in a court of law.
11. Government and organizations may not offer rewards for reporting
    law-breaking or supplying information to catch law breakers.
12. Prosecutors may offer witnesses immunity in return for testimony.
13. Persons charged with a crime shall then be released immediately
    from custody without bail. The accused shall be required to attend
    their trial and any other court-ordered hearings but otherwise will
    remain free until a court finds them guilty and sentences them.
14. In felony cases, if prosecutors believe that the accused is a flight
    risk or a threat to other people or their property, they may apply to

the court for further restrictions on the accused's pretrial freedoms. Courts shall have the power to require accused citizens to:

a. Surrender their passports.

b. Wear tracking devices.

c. Refrain from approaching specified persons or places.

d. Remain in custody until their trial.

15. Accused citizens shall be brought to trial within 100 days if they are in pretrial custody, and otherwise within one year. Cases not brought to trial within the time limits shall be dismissed without prejudice. Courts may make reasonable exceptions for delays requested by the defense.

16. Government shall not seize, hold, or otherwise prevent an accused citizen from having free and full use of their property, unless by court order following a conviction. Courts may make reasonable exceptions for:

a. Materials required for forensic testing.

b. Evidence that could be destroyed by a defendant pretrial.

c. Ongoing searches of property for evidence.

d. Alleged contraband that is potentially dangerous to the public.

17. No person shall be held in violation of a court order or other legal process when they are unable to complete that process due to another court order or legal process.

18. Courts may take previous convictions into account when deciding punishment, but not previous arrests.

19. Criminal acts or omissions punishable under multiple provisions of the law may only be punished under one provision.

20. Where multiple crimes have been committed, it shall be for courts to decide if sentences shall be concurrent or consecutive.

21. Punishment for crimes shall consist firstly of making whole the victims. The perpetrator shall pay reasonable costs incurred by the victims. Courts shall have discretion to require the perpetrator to pay:

a. Up to an additional 20% of damages to the victim for difficult-to-quantify costs.

b. Punitive fines of up to three times the actual damages.

c. Reasonable costs incurred by the court for collection of damages and fines.

22. The collection of money from the perpetrator and its distribution to the victims shall be the sole responsibility of the court.

23. Punitive fines shall be distributed to charity as defined in the Constitution.

24. Where costs of restitution exceed the assets of the perpetrator, the perpetrator shall be required to make reasonable payments over

time, with interest at prevailing rates, until restitution is complete. Restitution payments may not be discharged in bankruptcy.

25. Courts may sentence the perpetrator to incarceration if they believe the perpetrator continues to be a danger to society, or for repeat offenses.

26. Incarceration shall not be used as punishment for non-violent crime unless the proceeds of the crime exceed one million dollars, or for repeat convictions.

27. Death penalties shall not be allowed.

28. If the victims request it, non-monetary restitution shall be allowable at the courts' discretion.

29. Where children are prosecuted in the criminal justice system:
    a. Children may not be tried as adults.
    b. Incarcerated children must be segregated from adults.
    c. Children incarcerated for violent crimes must be segregated from other children.
    d. Incarcerated children shall have the right to a judicial review of their case at ages 18 and 21, aiming to release them if they are no longer a risk to the public.
    e. Government shall have a duty of care to educate incarcerated children to become responsible adult citizens.

30. Courts may mandate tracking devices for felons likely to repeat offend under the following conditions:
    a. The offender has a felony conviction for a crime involving violence or is a repeat offender of any felony.
    b. The offender is an ongoing risk to the public.
    c. Tracking devices shall use the best reasonable technology so that only the offender knows they are being tracked/
    d. Tracking information shall be available to law enforcement but shall otherwise be private.
    e. All costs of tracking shall be borne by the state.
    f. Offenders shall have a right to appeal their risk assessment.

Criminal Injustice

Protecting citizens from criminals and crimes is an important government function, but something seems to be seriously out of whack. The criminal justice has become an expensive and racist system putting increasing numbers of citizens in jail for victimless crimes.

Let's start with some facts and figures. Using 2015 data:[1]

- About 2.2 million Americans are in prison.

- 6.7 million Americans were in the criminal justice system (prisoners, probationers, parolees, and those awaiting trial).

- Prison populations have gone up 400% since 1980 compared to a 35% growth in the US population. (There's been a slight decrease since 2010, but only time will tell if this is a change in the trend).

- The US has the highest per capital imprisonment rate in the world, with 5% of the world's population and 25% of prisoners.

- African Americans are 45% of the prison population.

- Chances of spending time in jail at some point in their lives: black men 33%, Hispanic men 17%, white men 6%.

- If African Americans and Hispanics were sentenced at the same rate as whites, the prison population would halve!

- 46% of state prisoners are there for non-violent drug, property, or public order offenses.

- Drug offenses accounted for 16% of state prisoners and 50% of federal prisoners.

- Prisons cost the country $70 billion a year in direct costs, as well as huge indirect costs.

- Private prisons (starting in the mid-80s) give private corporations a financial incentive to get more people in jail!

- Correction of social problems by incarceration does not appear to work—most offenders re-offend, and our problems go on unabated.

There needs to be a correction. Three main areas are addressed here: punishment and incarceration, administration of the justice system, and children.

Punishment and Incarceration

There are too many people in jail. This is mainly due to the inappropriate criminalization of victimless crimes, and to an over-emphasis on punishment of perpetrators, rather than on making the victims whole.

How many crimes are there? No one knows! In 1982 the Justice Department tried to count the number of federal crimes. They gave up after two years. The official in charge of the count, Mr. Ronald Gainer, said that you "will have died and resurrected three times" and still be trying to figure out how many crimes exist.[2]

This alone should give you pause for thought. If the government themselves cannot count the number of crimes, how is it reasonable that citizens are held to a standard where "ignorance of the law is no excuse?"

Punishment is necessary to deter some criminals and prevent breakdowns in the social order. Dangerous and persistent repeat offenders should be in jail to protect the rest of us, and left unchecked, crime breeds crime.

However, for other offenders, especially non-violent offenders, jail should not be the default choice. The costs of jail to society outweigh the benefits:

- There are the direct costs to taxpayers of maintaining and staffing jails and paying for housing, health care, and in some cases education costs of inmates.

- Prisoners are unable to work or be customers for businesses.

- Some families are on welfare because a breadwinner is in jail.

- The system breeds sociopaths, it brutalizes some prisoners to the point where they no longer care how they affect others.

- Former convicts have difficulty finding work. [3]

For most prisoners, their contribution would be average. They'd have an average job at average wages and be an average consumer. Locking up one average citizen has little effect. But if you lock up 2.2 million citizens, and add in everyone on parole and probation, we've now handicapped some 6.7 million customers, producers, taxpayers, and innovators. Now the loss to society adds up quickly. This is a huge drain on the economy in both direct and hidden costs.

Additionally, a few of those folks are potential outliers—people who could have a big impact. Perhaps there's a version of the next Steve Jobs in jail right now for some minor drug infraction or other victimless crime.[4]

Maybe it's time to think again. The proposals here aim to change the emphasis of punishment for non-violent crime.

Most *non-violent* offenders should be treated as owing a debt to the victim to be repaid under court supervision. This would be similar to how bankrupts repay their debts under court supervision, though backed up with the threat of jail if the offender fails to comply.

By treating minor criminals as owing a debt, most of them would stay out of jail and hopefully be working, supporting their families, and paying taxes. Society gains workers and customers, and simultaneously lowers welfare, charity, and jail costs.

Treating criminals as owing a debt to victims also clarifies who the victims are. Combined with the provision that prosecutors must cite a named victim in any prosecution, it removes spurious "crimes against society." Drug laws, for example, are often justified on the premise that drugs are a danger to society. This is ambiguous from a legal perspective. Absent a victim claiming they have been personally hurt, almost anything could be construed as dangerous to society. It's someone's opinion, motivated by special interest agendas. Putting named victims back in the frame would remove much of this moral hazard.

An Alternative Way to Keep the Public Safe

Dangerous people should be in jail. At the other end of the spectrum, those who commit victimless crimes (taking drugs) should probably not be considered criminals at all. And then there is everyone else in the middle, where it will be up to the courts to decide if a person is dangerous or persistent criminal enough to be in jail.

Locking people up punishes criminals and keeps the rest of us safe, but it is also expensive. However, we now have a technology—tracking devices—that offers us a way to keep people out of jail and yet still protect the public. The proposal here gives the courts the option to require repeat or dangerous offenders to wear a tracker.

Trackers are a deterrent for the trackee (the person wearing the tracker)—their chances of being caught are high if law enforcement knows where they are when a crime is committed. Law enforcement can more easily find trackees if needed or eliminate them as suspects if they are nowhere near a crime scene.

Safeguards are needed if the courts are allowed to track people. Firstly, we only want to allow tracking of violent or persistent offenders. There needs to be evidence that they are an ongoing risk to the public, and the trackee should have the right to appeal their tracking, in case of errors.

Secondly, only law enforcement (and the trackee) should have tracking information. If it's public there's a potential vigilante problem. Technology will help here: trackers will eventually be implantable—both difficult to remove and invisible.

This tacking protocol would also apply to sex offenders. The sex offenders register needs to go, but technology enables us to have the benefits of the register, without the drawbacks. Let's apply our technology!

The Death Penalty

The US has had a death penalty—and an abolitionist movement—since its founding.[5]

Constitutionally, the death penalty is an ongoing debate. Most states and the Supreme Court have increasingly restricted the use of the death penalty over the decades.

Morally, there's no clear argument. Perhaps some crimes are so heinous that death is justified. Nonetheless, most people would not be comfortable making that decision, let alone carrying it out. This shows up in polls. Americans tend to be slightly in favor of the death penalty (about 56% for them in 2018).[6] This leaves many against it.

Worldwide, most countries have either banned the death penalty or don't use it in practice.[7] The US ranks 8th worldwide in executions, after China, Iran, Saudi Arabia, Iraq, Pakistan, Egypt, and Somalia. These are not countries we want to compete with on human rights!

In the absence of clear moral or Constitutional arguments about the death penalty, it should instead be abolished for pragmatic reasons:

- Abolition of the death penalty is the trend. About 20 US states have already stopped using it.
- Executions cannot be undone. As forensic science advances, a few people on death row might prove to be innocent.
- Jailing someone for life is much cheaper than executing them, mainly due to legal costs.[8]

The number of people on death row is tiny (about 2700), and the number of executions has averaged about 30/year for the last 45 years. Is it worth spending so much time, energy, money, and legal arguments over such a small number of people? The proposal is to end the death penalty.

Administration of Injustice

Excessive prison populations are not the only problems with the justice system. The entire system needs an overhaul to reinstate due process.

About 60% of the people in jail are awaiting trial[9]. Typically, they've been charged but cannot afford bail. Often, they present no risk to the public, they are just poor.

Keeping those folks in jail costs about $9 billion/year in direct costs alone. That's $9 billion/year spent in violation of *innocent until proven guilty*. $9 billion/year spent keeping the poor poor, preventing them from working and supporting their families. There are also indirect costs, which are unknown but surely of a similar magnitude if you add up lost jobs, lost customers, welfare, and charity.

Meanwhile, the bail bond industry writes about $14 billion a year in bonds and employs about 15,000 bail bond agents. Writing bail bonds for profit is illegal in most of the rest of the world. [10]

In the days of the Wild West bail made sense—anyone accused of a crime could easily disappear. Today, anyone skipping out will be tracked through driver's licenses, credit cards, and cell phones. They will be found and shipped home. In any case, most defendants don't even want to skip town because it is where they live, work, and have family.

An even worse problem with pretrial incarceration is that many jail inmates have not even been charged. In most states, prosecutors have 72 hours to decide whether to charge you or not. That's easily enough time to lose half a week's income or get fired for not turning up for work. It looks bad to employers if you need to explain that you were in jail, even if uncharged. Pretrial incarceration is public shaming, no matter how innocent or guilty you are. And, as usual, it hits the poor the hardest.

The proposal here aims to stop these abuses by requiring that anyone arrested is charged within 24 hours and then released by default. If that's not enough time, prosecutors can always file charges later when they have sufficient evidence. Courts should only impose greater restrictions if the defendant is a genuine flight risk or dangerous to others.

Is there a risk of pre-trial defendants committing crimes? Yes, and the courts will need to manage risk. Still, incarceration should be a last resort rather than the default. Hopefully, tracking devices can also become commonplace risk management tools.

Still, there will be crimes committed by pretrial defendants, some of them heinous. These crimes are likely to be rare but highly visible. Victims will understandably complain that the perpetrators should have been in jail. But if defendants are free until proven guilty, then for every new crime, thousands of other defendants will go back to work. Their families will remain intact, fewer people will depend on welfare or charity.

Defendants who continue their normal lives while awaiting trial are unseen and uncounted compared to the few high-profile crimes committed by a tiny minority of other defendants. Yet surely, they are equally as important. For society as a whole, all sides must balance.

Legalized Double Jeopardy: Charge Stacking

The penal code is huge, complex, and growing. By some estimates, every citizen commits at least three felonies a day[11]. Once accused of a crime, ambitious prosecutors can easily find variations on the theme and come up with a dozen extra charges to add to the list, a process known as charge stacking,[12] a form of legalized double jeopardy.

The proposal here aims to ensure that criminals are only punished once for a crime. Additionally, courts will have the final say on punishments. If a defendant has had several charges stacked against them, courts will have the discretion to decide what is the right punishment.

Legal Gotchas

There are anecdotal stories of persons convicted of a crime who fail to carry out their sentence because they are arrested on another matter, and who are then in further trouble for not completing the first sentence.

Suppose you had a DUI and were ordered to attend driver's ed. classes. Suppose you are later arrested and held on an unrelated matter but released without charge, which caused you to miss a class. You have now failed to complete your DUI sentence and potentially you'll face further charges.

This is unfair, and a good attorney could probably get someone in this situation out of it. However, attorneys are expensive. So, as a safety measure, let's have a general rule that you cannot be found guilty of failure to complete a legal process because another legal process prevented you from being there.

Plea Bargaining

This brings us to the big granddaddy of problems in the justice system: plea bargaining.

The 6th Amendment gives citizens the right to trial by jury. Despite this, about 95% of prosecutions don't come to trial.[13] Prosecutors and defendants instead plea bargain (negotiate). Typically, the defendant pleads guilty to a lesser crime in return for not exercising their rights.

Plea bargaining is often justified as an efficient way to deal with criminal prosecutions. It eases the workload on the justice system. But it also creates perversions of justice.

Suppose a poor defendant is arrested for a minor crime they didn't commit. That defendant has children at home and a job they need to keep. They are already in jail, pretrial, and unable to afford bail, and now the prosecutor stacks on new charges, some of them with statutory minimum sentences. The minor crime the defendant was originally accused of might now result in a 20-year jail term if they are found guilty.

The prosecutor then offers a deal: plead guilty to a minor offense, pay a fine, and get a suspended sentence. Alternatively, spend the next six months in jail until your trial comes up, then risk losing and spending the next 20 years in jail! Faced with no real choice, and because they are already in jail, the defendant pleads guilty even though they are innocent.

The prosecutor chalks up a win and adds it to his resume. The judge signs off on it because his docket is full months into the future. The public defender is overwhelmed and glad to clear a case off his books.

Everyone wins, except the defendant who pled guilty to a charge even though he was innocent because he was too poor to exercise his rights, and because the risks were so stacked against him. Although he may have gotten out of jail, he now has a criminal record, with negative effects on his job prospects and his ability to claim welfare benefits.

How is this justice? In any other context, we'd call this blackmail. You have a constitutional right to a trial by jury, but if you choose to exercise it then the system will punish you.

It gets worse! Suppose two people are falsely accused of a crime, based on the evidence of a snitch. One takes a plea; the second is convicted at trial. A few months later the snitch owns up that they falsified evidence. The person who went to trial has their conviction overturned and their record cleared. But the person who took a plea "admitted" to the crime and is still held guilty. They must serve out the agreed punishment and will be left with a criminal record.

Plea bargaining has too many moral hazards and potential perversions of justice to allow it to remain. The proposal here makes plea bargaining illegal.

Some will object that the criminal justice system is in danger of collapsing if every defendant goes to trial. However, it's hard to see that as a justification for plea bargaining. Maybe the criminal justice system should collapse—everyone would then be highly motivated to fix it!

Possession of Information

We live in an information age. Almost anything can be found online, yet the average user has little idea where the stuff they read comes from, if crimes were committed in its acquisition, or even if it's true! It's also easy for information to end up on our computers without our knowledge.

The potential for abuse here is too great, so the proposal is to disallow possession of information as a crime. Possession of information might be evidence of a crime, but possession alone should never be a crime.

Conspiracy

Conspiracy is when two or more people agree to commit a crime. In theory, it makes sense that conspiracy is a crime. In practice, it causes so many problems that it should be abolished.[14]

The main problem here is that conspiracy laws clash with 1st Amendment rights. Suppose two people get together over a latte and chat about how they could rob a bank. They might be shooting the breeze, arguing over last night's news, or writing a novel together. Or, possibly, they may be intending to do it. But unless and until they rob the bank, no crime has taken place. And it is often not obvious where the boundary lies between fantasy and reality, between talk and action. When does mere knowledge and proximity to crime become participation in it?

Over many decades, conspiracy laws have morphed into another way for prosecutors to "get" people, often people with minor connections to crime. An example of this is the girlfriend problem.

Suppose a drug dealer is caught and prosecuted. His girlfriend, who lives in the same house, can be charged with conspiracy. Under those laws, she is effectively considered a full partner in crime and charged with the same crimes.[15] She could be charged with crimes she had no knowledge of or crimes committed by other criminal partners she has never even met.

Yes, the girlfriend may have known something. Maybe she answered the phone, banked money, or had other minor parts to play. But conspiracy laws treat her as a full partner in crime *by default*. This is unjust: she should be charged for what she did, not what her partner did.

This has been a known problem for over 30 years,[16] and thousands of women are in federal prison because of it. Legislators on both sides of the political spectrum acknowledge the problem, yet nothing gets done. It's long past time to fix this problem.

The fix is to abolish conspiracy as a crime. Criminals should be charged for their actions, not what they might have known about or thought of doing, or who they know. This does mean that a few genuine plotters and supporters of crimes will get away with it. That's an unfortunate cost of preserving 1st Amendment rights.

Rewards for Reporting Crime

It might seem on the surface that rewarding citizens for reporting crime would result in less crime. If you reward reporting, you'll probably get more reporting. But crimes will likely be reported in proportion to visibility rather than seriousness.

Suppose that you offered $100/crime reported. You'd get lots of reports of dogs pooping on sidewalks—which takes place in public. You'll get far fewer reports of wife-beating—which takes place in private.

Similar distorted incentives already occur where police departments appear to prioritize catching drivers violating traffic rules over catching burglars. Catching and fining drivers is easier and more profitable for the police, even though burglaries are arguably a more serious problem.

If you try to correct the incentives by paying citizens in proportion to the severity of the crimes, you potentially have citizens reporting ambiguous situations in hopes of a reward. Deciding which crimes get what rewards is also open to manipulation and political abuse. Is drunkenness a crime? Flag burning? How about smoking in public, having communist views, or being greedy?

Finally, if you pay people to report crime, you introduce a level of distrust into social relations. Taken too far, you get situations like East Germany before the fall of the Berlin wall where hundreds of thousands of people were reporting their fellow citizens to the Stasi (secret police). This is not how things should be in America.

So, the proposal here is to disallow government (and large corporations) from offering rewards for reporting crimes. If a citizen reports a crime, they should report it because they believe it's the right thing to do, or because they are being hurt by that crime, not because they get paid.

An explicit moral position is being made here: serious crime should be reported and dealt with. But not-serious crimes: that's a judgment call. The definition of not-serious crime: *no one cares*. If no one cares, it probably shouldn't even be a crime. Who makes that judgment? We do, we the people.

Criminal Snitches and Immunity

Rewarding criminals for reporting crime is yet another moral hazard in the justice system. Prosecutors can sometimes catch a criminal because a snitch gives evidence. But there's a price: the snitch is incentivized to lie, leading to perversions of justice. Hardened criminals can get away with crimes or gain sentence reductions for snitching.

The inherent moral hazards are too large to bear. The proposal is that prosecutors won't be allowed to offer rewards to snitches. There will no doubt be grey areas here, but the principle should be clear, and the courts can resolve any issues that arise.

That said, one situation where prosecutors may need an exception to the no-rewarding-criminal-reporting rule is offering immunity in return for testimony. An exception is needed because the 5th Amendment gives us the right to silence. To motivate criminals to testify about other criminals, state and federal laws allow for conferring immunity in return for testimony. This does create new potential moral hazards, especially when courts offer blanket immunity. Nonetheless, offering constitutional protection in return for giving up a constitutional right is balanced. Let's leave it up to the courts to sort out the details.

Private Rewards

Private rewards for crime reporting have the same moral hazards as government rewards: they incentivize people to focus on one crime to the exclusion of others.

In contrast to government rewards though, there's a balancing force to keep the hazard in check: private citizens are spending their own money. They will only spend it on important-to-them issues. Typically, private rewards are offered to help solve specific crimes, such as witnesses to an assault, or to help find a missing person.

Spending money is a form of the right for you to control your property as you see fit. And, arguably, spending money is also a form of self-expression protected under the 1st Amendment. So, the proposal allows private citizens to still offer private rewards as they see fit. It is the spending of other people's money (especially taxpayer money) that will be curbed.

Private Right of Action

Private criminal prosecutions (private right of action) are illegal under federal law, but legal in some states. This has started, in the last few years, a disturbing trend.

In September 2021, after the Supreme Court overturned Roe v. Wade, Texas passed an anti-abortion law.[17] Among other things, this law created a private right of action. Citizens could sue other citizens for "aiding and abetting" abortions, and profit to the tune of $10,000. Florida then proposed a bill against Critical Race Theory, using a similar approach.[18]

Regardless of what you think of those issues, this is unleashing a trend of legal madness. Imagine if every time either political party had enough power, they implemented an extreme policy backed up with a private right of action. They would effectively deputize citizens, *and pay them,* to find other citizens breaking this law.

This can only end in a totalitarian state where every citizen is a vigilante, being paid to spy on and sue each other. This would destroy all trust that citizens may have in each other. It would be a legislated end to "live and let live" and "agree to disagree."

This is madness, and it needs to be stopped before it gets out of control. *Proposal 1—Adulthood* already bans government from requiring citizens to act in a law enforcement capacity. To reinforce this, the proposal here outright bans private right of action.

If someone is personally wronged by another, they will still be able to sue in civil court to correct the wrong. This proposal is purely about having a private right to prosecute someone for breaking the law.

Children and Crime

Some children commit crimes, and the justice system must deal with them. When this happens though, is important to remember they are children.

It is unreasonable to apply adult standards to children until they are adults. Despite this, the law freely exercises a double standard here. On the one hand, adults are often treated as irresponsible children who, for example, can't drink until they are 21. On the other hand, it treats children as responsible adults who can be charged with adult crimes.

It's reasonable to extend adult privileges to children in return for responsible behavior, but the other way round does not work. Children should not be prosecuted and punished as if they were adults. To ensure this, the proposal here is that children should never be tried as adults.

When children commit crimes, punishment may include incarceration. If children are removed from society, the government should have a duty of care to try and educate them to become responsible adults. Child criminals should also be kept separate from adult criminals to avoid criminal mentoring or abuse.

Finally, in the hopes that even criminal children can mature into responsible adults, the proposal requires that anyone incarcerated as a child has an automatic right to a review of their case at ages 18 and 21. Where possible, these young adults should be integrated back into society.

Parents of children who are incarcerated or fostered under court order will still have a duty to provide child support, basically under the same rules that absent parents are normally required to follow. Parents should continue to support their children even if they are criminals.

Racism

The criminal justice system is racist. On average, racial minorities are arrested and convicted more often, and serve longer sentences.[19] If current trends continue, 1 in 3 black males can expect to spend time in jail in his lifetime, and 1 in 6 Hispanic males, compared to 1 in 17 white males.

Statistically, blacks do commit more crimes, and black-on-black homicides account for most homicides in the US.[20] This may account for the higher rates of police stops and arrests. Having arrests on your record then translates into longer sentences.

However, even though black-on-black homicide rates are high, the system is still racist.[21] Further, if blacks are investigated more often, then more crimes will be found. The more law enforcement looks for crimes the more they will find, irrespective of skin color.

There's no easy solution to fixing institutional racism in the justice system. American has a long and ignoble history of locking up people seen as a threat or a problem: American Indians on reservations; Japanese Americans in WWII internment camps; blacks and Hispanics in jail.

Much of the debate about how to fix these problems is marred by poor statistics, misinformation, posturing, and sometimes (still) outright racism. Let's avoid that here and focus on practicalities.

The single most important step needed to reduce racism is legalizing drugs as described in *Proposal 8—Drugs*. The civil war on drug takers is a major plank of institutional discrimination and injustice. Legalization will remove possession and dealing as crimes. It will take drug dealing off the streets and lower violence rates.

Other steps outlined here in this proposal will reduce the size and scope of the criminal justice system. There's too much crime in our country because the definition of crime has become too broad. Banning plea bargaining and giving courts more control over charge stacking will help end unnecessary prosecutions and convictions.

Next, let's eliminate arrests as a factor in sentencing decisions. People are *innocent until proven guilty.* An arrest is a police officer's opinion that someone may have committed a crime. But only the courts should have the power to decide if they are guilty. Removing arrests as a sentencing factor would ease resulting sentencing disparities.

The bail system is also biased against blacks,[22] who are frequently denied bail or required to pay more. Poor blacks end up in pretrial detention, locked up despite being *innocent until proven guilty.* Yet another reason to do away with bail altogether.

Finally, let's also acknowledge that many racial problems are, at root, poverty problems. Those problems have been worsened by decades of a welfare state that discouraged marriage and stable families, education policies making it difficult for poor inner-city kids to get out of the ghetto, and minimum-wage laws making it difficult for poorly educated kids to find work. Those issues are addressed in other proposals.

Mental Health

Estimates suggest about 20% of jail inmates have mental health issues,[23] and treatment might be a better option than punishment. However, this is a complex problem that can't be fixed with a simple constitutional rule. States and local governments will have to continue experimenting to find solutions.

Proposal 18—Civil Justice

That excessive bail ought not to be required, nor excessive fines imposed, nor cruel and unusual punishments inflicted.
—George Mason, Virginia Declaration of Rights

The civil justice system exists primarily to resolve disputes between citizens. Of particular concern are torts—lawsuits to correct wrongs. If you wrong me, then I can sue and ask the courts to correct the situation. However, correction has become overcorrection—especially when punitive damages are assessed.

Attorneys, legislators, and pundits have been arguing about tort reform for decades, for[1] and against it.[2] Nothing fundamental has changed. Perhaps this has something to do with attorneys profiting from the current system and donating to politicians of both parties.

Maybe it's time to rebalance the system in favor of justice.

Proposed Amendment: Civil Justice

Note: some legal terms used here are explained below. Lawyers love their jargon, but we citizens say *lupus non timet canem latrantem*!

1. Champerty, Maintenance, Barratry, and attorneys working on contingency agreements shall be illegal.

2. Attorneys may work pro bono, and plaintiffs may sue large organizations and governments to correct public wrongs, provided that the plaintiffs do not profit financially from those lawsuits.

3. Outside of small claims courts, successful defendants shall have a right to reimbursement of reasonable costs of their defense.

4. Juries shall make their best estimate of actual damages and, in cases with multiple defendants, apportion fault between them. Damages shall be apportioned in proportion to fault.

5. The ability of the parties to pay damages shall not be a criterion in the apportionment of blame or damages.

6. Where a plaintiff seeks punitive damages, criminal justice standards of proof, including intent, shall apply to that trial.

7. Punitive damages may not exceed three times the actual damages.

8. Punitive damages shall be distributed to charity as defined in the Constitution.

9. Courts may not order actions that result in the punishment of 3rd parties not involved in a trial.

10. Courts shall have the right to find a plaintiff's suit to be malicious in intent and to fine the plaintiff.

Civil Injustice

Modern society is a remarkable example of cooperation. By and large, people keep their word, honor their deals, and get along with each other. If problems arise, they are mostly resolved by negotiation, or by agreeing to disagree. Only as a last resort do people sue each other to correct wrongs.

This is as it should be. Wrongs should be corrected. Individuals hurt by accidents and errors not of their own volition should be able to seek compensation. But beyond this, lawsuits should be minimized. Lawsuits are a drain on society in direct and indirect costs.

The up-front costs of lawsuits are obvious for those directly involved. Lawsuits cost time, money, and energy for lawyers, courts and court staff, juries, plaintiffs, witnesses, and defendants.

The indirect costs are hidden but even bigger. Lawsuits result in wasted time and energy for 3rd parties, either to comply with legal decisions or to avoid being sued. Everyone is subject to extra safety warnings, checks, legal disclosures, and paperwork. Professionals become cautious, often over-cautious. Products and services cost more to pay for the extra work. Insurance costs rise to pay for potential lawsuits and punitive damages.

Beyond the money spent on wasted activity, there's an even bigger hidden cost: the cost of experiments not done. The costs of drugs not tried, lives not saved, new ideas not brought to market. Science and technology progress through trial-and-error experiments. *Errors must occur for progress to be made.* But who will risk making errors if they might be punished for them? Punitive damages (in particular) punish everyone by clamping down on innovation.

And finally, in the big picture, an excessively litigious society is also a low-trust society. Imbalances in the justice system are one cause of the decline in the public's trust in government and each other, discussed in *Chapter 2—Unsustainable Trends*.

For-Profit Lawsuits

There are too many lawsuits because the incentives in the civil justice system have become distorted. Civil justice has evolved into an out-of-control for-profit legal industry, grinding down defendants by funding lawsuits against them, and taxing the rest of us through the side-effects.

For-profit law has enabled and been enabled by a host of creeping legal reforms, most of them since WWII: pain and suffering damages (sometimes in absurd sums), strict product liability, federal class actions, no-fault insurance, attorney advertising, ever-expanding intellectual property protections, and others.[3]

The proposals here aim to reassert fundamental legal principles and change the incentives at play by lowering profits. The emphasis should be on a for-justice legal system, rather than a for-profit legal system. Courts and legislatures can sort out the details within the reset framework.

Restoring Legal Principles: Champerty, Maintenance and Barratry

Champerty is a legal term for third-party funding of litigation. It is where Andy pays Bill to sue Clare. Andy gets a share of the profits if Bill wins but is not named in the suit. Andy would not be punished if the court decided the lawsuit was frivolous or malicious. In plain language, champerty is buying into someone else's lawsuit.

Maintenance is like champerty except that the funder of the lawsuit doesn't share the profits. Andy pays Bill to sue Clare, but Bill keeps the profits if he wins.

Barratry is where someone persistently and maliciously uses the courts to harass someone. Bill sues Clare over and over for petty reasons – her dog ran into his yard; she parked in the wrong place; she had noisy parties—or whatever. Barratry is using the legal system as a bullying tactic.

Champerty, maintenance, and barratry were illegal under English law dating back to the 13th century. The US inherited those bans and kept them until the 1960s when states started to repeal them under special interest pressure (trial attorneys).

However, our ancestors were not stupid. Champerty became illegal in the first place because in medieval times unscrupulous barons and royalty would fund weak lawsuits hoping their support would strengthen it. If successful, they shared the damages awarded.

Champerty, maintenance, and barratry are all versions of allowing power and money to buy the legal system and use it for profit, revenge, or harassment. This is legalized bullying. It is a corruption of a for-justice legal system.

The proposals here aim to restore these legal principles. Several states are already at work trying to restore a version of barratry in the form of anti-SLAPP laws (Strategic Lawsuit Against Public Participation). This proposal will cut to the chase and ban barratry and its friends.

Contingency Fees

Contingency fees have long been controversial in legal circles because they are arguably a form of Champerty where trial attorneys are profiting from someone else's lawsuit. Contingency fees combined with punitive damages have created financial bonanzas for them, distorting incentives and the justice system itself.

The proposal here aims to end this perversion of justice. It will ban attorneys from working on contingency. Plaintiffs will need to pay upfront legal costs, and risk losing those costs. This is a benefit; plaintiffs should have skin in the game to prevent frivolous lawsuits.

Lawyers will argue against this, and they are skilled at arguing! However, if the lawyers feel strongly enough about an issue, they can work pro bono. And nothing here is intended to stop the ACLU or other charities from suing the government or corporations to correct wrongs. The proposal explicitly allows public interest trials, so long as they are brought to correct wrongs, not to profit trial attorneys.

Changing Incentives: Punitive Damages

At the root of problems with the for-profit legal industry are punitive damages, which fund most of the excessive legal activity. There needs to be limits on punitive damages, who pays, and who benefits.

Civil courts are meant to solve disputes and correct wrongs, whilst criminal courts are meant to punish people who deliberately break the law. Sometimes though, civil cases blur into the criminal. Punitive damages were allowed under English Common Law, and the US legal system inherited them. They took off in a big way after WWII, and by the early 1990's they had become controversial.[4]

Punitive damages are meant to deter others from willful malicious conduct.[5] However, they also introduce moral hazard and malincentives. How is justice served if one person profits from suing another? The legal system should correct injustices and make-whole any financial losses. But if awards for damages are so high that the plaintiff profits from bringing a lawsuit, then the wrong has not been corrected, it has been reversed. This is not justice.

Suppose I key your car and you sue me. Justice demands that I pay you the costs of repairing your car and for your time. Things should be restored to how they were before I vandalized your car. But if I also end up buying you a new house, then something has gone wrong.

Punitive damages may send a message to other potential wrongdoers. But that does not mean individual plaintiffs should get lottery-style payouts for bringing a lawsuit. If you reward victims (and attorneys) for bringing lawsuits, then you incentivize lawsuits, no matter how weak the case or how trivial the harm is.

The proposal here is designed to correct this imbalance. If a court decides punishment is needed then so be it, but any punitive damages awarded will go to charity. Punitive damages should not benefit victims, courts, governments, or attorneys. Paying any of those groups will encourage lawsuits. Giving money to charity benefits society but does not directly incentivize lawsuits. See *Proposal 32—Misuse of Force* for details.

As a further safeguard, if punitive damages are requested, then the lawsuit is veering towards the criminal. At that point, criminal justice standards of evidence, and intent, should then come into play. This will protect both the defendant and justice itself. Let's keep the lines between civil and criminal cases as clear as possible.

Deep Pockets

A related problem with punitive damages is the issue of who pays. An injustice has crept into the system in the form of a legal strategy known as "deep pockets." This is a legal theory of joint-and-several liability. It involves situations where several parties might share some responsibility for wrongdoing, but the one with the most financial resources is often the primary target of the lawsuit, rather than the one who bears the most responsibility.

For example, a doctor fails to follow instructions when using a drug, and a patient is hurt, but the drug company is sued because they have a lot of money. Or someone gets shot, and the gun manufacturer is sued rather than the shooter. Or a driver does something stupid, but the auto company is sued instead of the driver.

Deep pockets can be thought of as a civil law equivalent of a criminal conspiracy. In a conspiracy, persons with only a peripheral connection to a crime are considered as full partners in crime. Deep pockets functions similarly, construing people with only a distant connection to an event to be fully liable.

Arguments for deep pockets typically focus on how it is only fair that defendants, the victims, get compensated. However, while defendants who are wronged should be made whole— if possible—how is it fair that people with no connection to an event are made to pay? This is an abuse.

Typically, the people paying are shareholders of a large company. When a company pays out $100 million, the costs are spread out among millions of shareholders. The loss per shareholder is small but real. Often you, dear reader, are among those hurt, though your pension.

The moral hazards here are too great to allow. Let's reset the system to where it should always have been. The people most responsible for wrongs should be the people who pay.

Will this result in a few victims who are not made whole because the people who hurt them are unable to pay? Yes, it will. Sometimes, this is the price of justice. Justice for some cannot be created by perpetrating injustice on others.

Profits Vs. Justice

The changes proposed here will be unpopular with some trial attorneys— attorneys who are well-practiced at arguing. There will be plausible arguments against these proposals. However, as novelist Upton Sinclair once remarked: *It is difficult to get a man to understand something when his salary depends upon his not understanding it.*

Lawyers are one of the most powerful special interest groups since they understand the system so well, but this does not give them any right to manipulate the system for profit. Rather, lawyers should ideally be held to higher ethical and legal standards than the rest of us in their professional lives.

Through no fault of any specific individual, the financial incentives in the legal system have become so distorted that the justice system is harming society rather than helping. Many arguments made for the legal changes in the last 70 years have been couched in terms of Victim Vs. Persecutor. In the big picture Profits Vs. Justice is a bigger problem.

The big profits go to attorneys who are profiting from punitive damages and contingency fees.[6] They are incentivized to keep suing, despite the distortions in the economy, and unfair losses to shareholders. In the process, they contribute to the moral rot in society because anytime something goes wrong the first reaction is to blame someone else in hopes of being able to use government force to extract money from them.

Let's take steps to tip the balance back towards Justice. Overall, the rule changes proposed should result in fewer lawsuits. Plaintiffs will have to feel aggrieved enough to pay to sue—so there should be fewer frivolous lawsuits. Attorneys will get paid but won't have the bonanza of sharing in punitive damages. The workload for the courts should go down, and the remaining lawsuits can be processed faster. Excessive punitive damages should fade away.

Hopefully, in the big picture, rebalancing the legal system can also go some way to restoring public trust in each other and our institutions.

Proposal 19—Law Enforcement

The means of defense against foreign danger historically have become the instruments of tyranny at home.

—James Madison

Over the last 150 years federal law enforcement has steadily expanded in scope and size. From the mid-60s, we've seen an increasing militarization of police forces in the form of SWAT teams.

There's a place for federal law enforcement, and there's a place for SWAT teams, but it's gone too far. The US is heading in the direction of a militarized police state. Time to reverse this trend.

Proposed Amendment: Law Enforcement

1. Law enforcement officers (LEOs) shall have a duty of care to respect and protect citizens' constitutional rights.

2. LEOs shall have a duty of care never to lie to or otherwise deceive citizens unless they have probable cause that the citizen is a suspect in a criminal investigation.

3. LEOs may never receive immunity for crimes they commit, on or off duty. There shall be no statute of limitations on felonies committed by LEOs.

4. LEOs convicted of felonies shall be released from government employment and may never again be employed by any government.

5. LEOs may not use excessive force on citizens.

6. Any law enforcement action where officers carry automatic weapons, explosives, stun grenades, tear gas, or other military-grade weapons shall be known here as a SWAT Action. The officers involved shall be known here as the SWAT Team.

7. Only state governments may create SWAT Teams. No federal or local agency may have SWAT Teams.

8. SWAT Actions may only take place with a court's permission in the form of a SWAT Warrant, which in addition to the usual requirements for a warrant, may only be issued for felonies and where LEOs are at credible risk of being fired upon.

9. No-Knock warrants shall be illegal.

10. Anonymous tips alone, unsupported by other evidence, shall be insufficient cause for search or SWAT warrants.

11. SWAT Teams may not be used for regulatory or administrative inspections or enforcement, crowd control, security patrols, or monitoring of public protests.

12. SWAT Teams shall have a duty of care to co-operate with local law enforcement, follow local laws, and ensure all required warrants are served correctly.

13. SWAT Teams may not shoot pets unless they are likely to cause permeant or life-threatening injuries to a team member.

14. SWAT Team members shall be equipped with recording equipment during SWAT actions. Recordings made shall be admissible in court hearings.

15. Law enforcement agencies shall keep a public database detailing SWAT Actions performed. Congress shall define standards for the collection and collation of said data.

16. Tenants and property owners subject to a SWAT Action shall have the right to see copies of relevant court orders immediately upon demand after the SWAT team has secured the premises.

17. SWAT Teams shall be liable for property damage caused by their action. They must secure the property immediately after the action and return it to its original state within one week, or alternatively agree and pay costs to the owner within one week.

18. Government may not delegate police powers of arrest or use of force to any persons who are not sworn-in LEOs.

Blaming the Wrong People

Law enforcement officers (LEOs) are the sharp end of government action. They are armed and ready to use necessary force in the course of their duties. As such, some tension between police and citizens is almost inevitable. In an era of "defund the police" it's easy to think that US law enforcement is a major problem.

Law enforcement does require some repair, and this section will address issues like federal overreach, bad cops, and excessive militarization of the police.

However, in the big picture blaming the police is often blaming the wrong people. Think about the phrase "law enforcement." It has two parts: law and enforcement. Discontent is often about the enforcement when the problem is the law itself. If police are enforcing bad laws, it is the laws that need to be fixed, not the police.

There are examples throughout this book of government acting without moral or constitutional authority—violating constitutional rights, protecting special interests, moralizing, and treating adults like children. Much of this overreach does not have the consent of the governed. So, when the police are tasked with enforcing these bad laws, it incentivizes resentment, simmering discontent, scofflaws, and, occasionally, violence.

Lowering tension between law enforcement and citizens will require fixing both the law and the enforcement.

Federal Law Enforcement

Federal law enforcement agencies have existed since 1789 when the Marshals Service[1] and the Customs Service[2] were formed. The constitution has little to say about this, for or against. Practically thought, it makes sense that federal agents protect US borders. Federal enforcement of federal laws also seems reasonable, especially for multi-state crimes.

Constitutional or not, federal law enforcement has been growing out of control in the scope of activities, number of agents, and costs. Over 40% of current federal crimes have been enacted since 1970.[3] Former state issues have been taken over by the feds. And the trend may be accelerating, arrests for federal crimes doubled between 1994 and 2010 alone.[4]

Again, the problem is often not the enforcement, it is the laws themselves—laws in violation of the 10th Amendment: *The powers not delegated to the United States by the Constitution, nor prohibited by it to the States, are **reserved** to the States respectively, or to the people.*

Numerous proposals in this book will curtail federal law, but ending the War on Drugs is probably the single most important step to take. Once federal laws are reigned back, federal law enforcement will naturally recede with it.

Bad Cops

Crime rates for LEOs are difficult to track, though they do seem to be much lower than for the general population.[5] This maybe because the system shields cops, though that's difficult to prove. It seems more likely that most cops are decent people trying to do a professional job under difficult circumstances.

Nonetheless, there are a few bad cops and even bad police departments.[6] In those rare cases, the main problem is that cops are almost impossible to fire, even if they have criminal convictions. This cannot be allowed to continue.

LEOs have special legal powers over citizens. As such they need to be held to a higher standard of behavior. The proposal here is that if an officer commits a crime, then they should no longer be trusted to work in law enforcement or hold any government post. Bad cops should never be allowed. Period.

If a cop commits a felony, then they should be prosecuted for it. No matter if they were on or off duty. It is a gross breach of the public trust when police officers commit crimes. To restore that trust, let's remove statute-of-limitations provisions for crimes committed by LEOs.

The War on Citizens

Perhaps the biggest problem with on-the-ground policing is the increasing militarization of the police, and the attendant problems of police coming to see citizens as the enemy.

In 1971 Nixon started the War on Drugs, and after 9/11 Bush announced a War on Terror. Drugs and terrorist acts were already illegal but
declaring war on them worsened trends of government over-reach and
erosion of civil liberties. The War on Drugs, in particular, is a civil war, a
War on Citizens.

The most visible form of the War on Citizens has been SWAT teams.
In all but name, SWAT teams are military strike units, armed with military
weapons, using military tactics against US citizens. SWAT teams first
appeared in the mid-60s when the LA police realized they were being out-
gunned by drug dealers. Their response: more and bigger guns!

There's no central source of information on SWAT teams[7], and most
police departments oppose transparency. Still, it's believed that every major city now has a SWAT team as well as about 80% of small towns (25-
50,000 people).

In 2015 there were an estimated 50-80 thousand SWAT raids.[8] The
tactics are what you would expect: breaking down doors, tear gas, and
machine guns. But you might be surprised at the targets. SWAT teams are
routinely deployed against illegal poker games, businesses employing illegal immigrants, and barbershops with unlicensed hair stylists.

In Prince George's County, MD, SWAT teams were deployed about
once a day in 2009, overwhelmingly to serve search or arrest warrants.
Half of those were for "misdemeanors and non-serious felonies." Maryland is one of the few states providing data on SWAT team usage. In 2008
the mayor of Berwyn Heights, MD was mistakenly attacked and terrorized
in his home by a SWAT team. Maryland later passed a law requiring police to disclose statistics on their use of SWAT teams.

SWAT teams have become popular because the incentives encourage
them:

- Politicians and police chiefs look good by being tough on crime.

- The wars on terror and drugs provide money for the equipment.

- Surplus military equipment is abundant due to ongoing US wars
  abroad; manufacturers encourage a second-hand market (so they
  can sell new stuff to the military), and the feds subsidize it.

- Police officers want to serve on SWAT teams because it is sexy
  and exciting, and many officers are ex-military who have been
  trained to see citizens as potential insurgents.

- Once created, SWAT teams tend to be deployed for increasingly
  routine police work to justify their existence and maintain training.

Whilst the police have been equipping themselves as a military force, the
courts have been making it easier for them to come get you. The worst
abuse is the no-knock warrant.

English Common Law required law enforcement to announce themselves since at least the early 1600s. As late as 1958 the Supreme Court explicitly upheld this principle.

However, in 1995 they created an exception to prevent the destruction of evidence.[9] The Court decided that it was okay—under the right circumstances—for the police to bust through your door unannounced in a military-style raid. With that small exception made, the incentives changed. By 2015 there were an estimated 20,000 no-knock warrants/year.[10]

Should law enforcement be allowed to smash through your door, throw in a stun grenade, and then rush in with machine guns? Isn't this a recipe for disasters, accidents, and deaths? Is this how things are done in a civilized country?

After 400 years of legal precedent, has our government suddenly found a better way to do things? I think not. No-knock warrants are a gross violation of the 4th Amendment: *The right of the people to be secure in their persons, houses, papers, and effects, against unreasonable searches and seizures, shall not be violated.* No-knock warrants are an open invitation to a police state, and they should never, ever, be legal.

So, how can things be arranged so that SWAT teams are available for the rare situations they are needed yet still have checks and balances in place to prevent mission creep?

To start with, let's set a higher bar for initiating SWAT actions by requiring SWAT warrants before deployment. Law enforcement should convince a judge there's probable cause of a felony and a high chance of meeting armed resistance. Currently, about 80% of SWAT actions are to execute search warrants, usually for drugs, often for misdemeanors. This is an abuse. SWAT teams are the wrong tool for petty crimes and searches.

Requiring SWAT warrants will result in far fewer SWAT actions and less need for SWAT teams. However, the remaining SWAT teams still need to be readily available and well-trained. This can be done by allowing only state-level SWAT teams.

This arrangement meets the criteria of far fewer SWAT teams, thus lowering costs. At the same time, each team will be used relatively more often for relevant work, so they will quickly accumulate experience and skill. They should be effective when needed.

Allowing only states to have SWAT teams creates prudent checks and balances. Local or federal law enforcement wanting to use a SWAT team will have to request it and justify its legality in state court. We'd get state oversight of SWAT usage. We'd have the possibility of federal oversight of the states, which is preferable to having the feds oversee themselves.

Checks and balances will be further strengthened by the other provisions. Requiring public records of SWAT deployment will give us press and citizen oversight. Individual team members will need to wear bodycams so that if anything goes wrong there's a record. And, finally, the

SWAT teams will have a duty of care to liaise with local law enforcement. Input from local LEOs who know the locations and often the people involved should minimize SWAT raids on the wrong addresses.

Liability

Under current law, if a SWAT team raids your house and damages it, you'll have to repair it yourself. The governing legal principle is *ex turpi causa non oritur actio*. (Don't you love it when lawyers go all Latin on you!)

In plain English: if you are doing something illegal you can't sue for resultant damages arising from law enforcement. So, for example, if you've kidnapped someone and the police break the door down to rescue them, you can't sue for damage to your door.

Despite the legal precedents, SWAT actions need to be an exception. About 80% of SWAT actions are to execute search warrants. 35-65% of those searches find nothing illegal! About 10% of SWAT raids are on the wrong address.[11]

In theory, if you're innocent and the police harm your property, you can sue for damages. However, that involves you in new costs with no guarantee you'll win. The proposals will instead reverse the assumptions—SWAT teams will be liable for damages they cause. If a SWAT team breaks down your door, then they must fix it.

Making the police liable for any damage caused in a SWAT raid will incentivize them to consider the least damaging methods of catching suspects and question if SWAT is needed. Checks and balances!

This will occasionally mean that *ex turpi causa non oritur actio* is not applied. However, even if police do catch a criminal by breaking down a door, the criminal is still presumed innocent until the court agrees they are guilty, and that may come months or years later. Both the courts *and* associated law enforcement practices should maintain the presumption of innocence until proven guilty.

Proposal 20—Defense

Peace and friendship with all mankind is our wisest policy, and I wish we may be permitted to pursue it.

—Thomas Jefferson

We need a military, and the defense of the country is something that almost everyone agrees on. However, the US has a habit of flexing its military muscles and is almost permanently engaged in war around the world.

Many people, irrespective of political party, would like to see military action and military expenses cut by a lot.

Proposed Amendment: Defense

1. The federal government has a duty to provide a strong defense of the country but also a duty to pursue peace and friendship with all mankind as the fundamental principle of US foreign policy.

2. The US shall not interfere in civil wars in foreign countries nor aid either side unless there is a direct and credible threat of that war leading to an invasion of the US or its territories.

3. The US shall not interfere in elections or changes of regime in foreign countries.

4. Except in self-defense, the US military may not fire upon foreign countries without explicit congressional approval for that military action.

5. The US military may be used in foreign peacekeeping missions in co-operation with other countries so long as:
   a. There is an international agreement providing justification.
   b. The US provides less than 50% of the personnel involved.
   c. The US bears less than 50% of the total costs.

6. Congressional approval is required whenever more than 1000 US military personnel (including support staff and contactors) are deployed in a foreign country. Congress must:
   a. Approve the deployment by majority vote.
   b. Take a separate vote for each country involved.
   c. Define the terms and conditions of deployment.
   d. Renew their approval every six months.

7. Congressional approval for war shall consist of a 3/5 super majority vote in both houses, renewed every six months.

8. Congress may withdraw approval or order withdrawal from any military deployment or war at any time by majority vote.

9. Congress may not delegate any approval or vote about military action.

10. If approval for a military deployment has lapsed or is withdrawn, Congress shall define the terms and timetable for withdrawal. In the absence of a plan, personnel and equipment in that country shall be withdrawn as quickly as can be safely achieved.

11. If the US or US military are attacked the President may order all necessary defensive steps for up to 30 days from the first attack. Beyond 30 days the President must receive congressional approval for continued military action.

12. State governors shall have absolute authority over their National Guards except when Congress has made a formal declaration of war and authorized military deployment pursuant to that war. Any federal law or executive order concerning National Guards may be vetoed by a 2/3 majority of State Governors.

13. The military shall never be deployed in a military role within the US or a US territory unless there is an imminent or active invasion by foreign powers. This shall include any situation where military personnel are authorized to use force against civilians.

14. The military may be deployed within the US for emergency, disaster, and humanitarian relief purposes. During such deployments, the military may carry arms for personal protection. Those arms may not be used to coerce citizens.

15. US military personnel shall have no powers of arrest of US citizens on US soil except to arrest trespassers on military property.

16. US civilians arrested or detained by the US military must be handed over to civilian authorities on US soil within 24 hours, or within one week if the civilian is arrested abroad.

17. The US military shall keep a publicly accessible database of civilians arrested or detained, including records of when and where they were handed over to civilian authorities.

Defense

The preamble to the Constitution states that government should *provide for the common defense*. Congress and the President are granted constitutional powers to enable that.[1] Defense therefore passes the Test of Constitutional Authority.

Defense also passes the Test of Consent—when it is defense! If the US was under attack or being invaded almost no one would object to our military defending us. In practice, things are rarely so clear-cut. The line between defense and offense is blurred, and this has resulted in ambivalence among US citizens over military actions taken in our name.

Perpetual War and Perpetual Risk

War is a terrible thing, to be avoided if possible. Despite this, there have been about 245 armed conflicts worldwide since WWII, with the US starting 201 of them. About 30 million people have died in US started conflicts, about 90% of them civilians.[2]

Those figures are estimates, and exact data may never be available. It's difficult to get at the truth when "armed combat" and "war" appear to be ambiguous when uttered by politicians. And military operations are often cloaked in secrecy.

Nonetheless, even if it's difficult to be precise, the US military has been involved in an awful lot of conflicts over the years. If foreign troops were landing in the US few would quibble about unleashing the military to protect us. But that is rarely why the US goes to war.

Instead, our leaders sent troops off to bomb and invade other countries half-way round the world and meddle in other people's conflicts. There are many people in the higher reaches of government (the neocons) who think war is the answer. Their typical justification—preventing bad things from happening—has a terrible moral hazard: It is impossible to predict the future!

No matter how good our intelligence, no matter how many WMDs are stashed, and no matter which side is obviously the good guys, we can't know what is best. It is not our war. Even if the foreign country has invited us in, the US is meddling in other people's disputes.

Every foreign intervention comes with terrible risks. The US is risking our troops' lives as well as foreign casualties, military and civilian. Military action messes up foreign countries in unknown and unforeseeable ways, causing the collapse of civil society and economic ruin.

Worst of all, US intervention abroad risks civilian lives on US soil. Whenever the US meddles abroad, someone could decide to return the favor. Rightly or wrongly, those who committed the 9/11 terrorist acts were motivated in part by, as they saw it, bringing the war back to the US.

Why are our leaders putting us at such terrible risk?

Perpetual Bills

The military is expensive. The 2017 federal budget allocated $853.6 billion to defense, divided between the military ($617 billion), veterans' affairs ($180.8 billion), and foreign aid ($55.8 billion).[3] Defense costs about 21% of the federal budget, the third biggest spending item after Medicare/Medicaid and Social Security.

Hidden in those numbers are what amount to a slush fund, controlled by the pentagon and largely unaccountable to Congress.[4] Congress keeps approving these funds, ignoring their oversight duties.[5]

Costs add up especially quickly for multi-year operations. War on Terror operations in the middle east had cost about $6 trillion,[6] by 2018.

Perpetual Ambivalence

Attitudes among US citizens to military action abroad are mixed.[7] Most Americans support the US playing a role on the world stage and engaging in interventions that have multinational support. They are broadly in support of action when the US is directly threatened. They are skeptical about long-term engagements in places like Afghanistan. They are against unilateral military action.

On spending, attitudes vary depending on world affairs. But on average citizens are split about 1/3 each on spending "too much," "too little," or "about the right amount."[8]

Historically, the military is one of the most trusted branches of government. However, it's easy to confuse supporting the military with supporting interventionist policy. Special interests are eager to exploit that confusion—interests such as supporters of one side in foreign civil wars, policy hawks, defense contractors, and big businesses wanting military protection of foreign assets. These special interests influence all political decisions, making it difficult to get clear answers to questions that need to be asked about any military deployment.

Constitutional Mission Creep

Some people, groups, and countries dislike the US. Even if the US never intervened on the world stage, there would still be those who wish us harm and who fundamentally disagree with the American way of life. It would be naïve to think that war or foreign intervention is never necessary. Nonetheless, war is a terrible thing with terrible risks.

So, what's the best way to balance a strong defense and a desire for peace? Obviously, the military must defend our borders. But almost always the debate is about sending troops abroad. Should the US be involved in other people's conflicts? Is military action a justified defensive move? Will it make us safer? How much will it cost, and is it worth it?

Every situation is different, but these are always difficult questions to answer, and special interests are highly incentivized to meddle. The best antidote to this is lots of people involved in the decision, but the opposite is happening.

Under the Constitution, only Congress can declare war, but presidents have been slowly granting themselves more authority over the years. Most presidents since WWII have stepped up to and probably over the line. Obama's 2007 missile attacks on Libya,[9] and Trump's 2018 missile attacks on Syria[10] both set off intense debates, again, about the Constitutional authority for their actions.

The National Guard

State militias were formed in the earliest days of the colonies and formalized in the Constitution *to execute the Laws of the Union, suppress Insurrections and repel Invasion.*[11] The President could use them for federal purposes under rules set by Congress. However, there was enough ambiguity that during the 1812 war, several governors refused to mobilize state militias to invade Canada.

The 1904 Militia Act formalized state militias under the name National Guards, and in 1908 Congress designated the National Guard as the first line of reserve. In so doing, Congress found a way around the Constitution, allowing the President to draft entire National Guard units no matter what governors said. In 2004, about 37,000 National Guards were drafted to fight in Iraq, unavailable to help at home if needed.

In 2006, Congress gave the President powers to federalize National Guards during natural disasters. They did it by defining natural disasters as insurrections, bypassing the legal precedent that US troops should never be deployed on US soil.[12] All 50 governors objected to this change in the law.

Redeploying Checks and Balances

The proposals here are designed to reverse the trends of the last century or so. Let's reinstate checks and balances to ensure US military deployments only take place when genuinely necessary.

As a first step, let's raise the bar for US military engagements. The primary criteria will be no sending in troops without a formal declaration of war, and no bombing without congressional approval. We'll also bar Congress from delegating that authority.

Now, are there times when the US military should intervene without being formally at war? Maybe, but it's too tempting for presidents and policy hawks to get involved unilaterally. So, let's allow for intervention if the US is part of a multinational peace keeping force, where multinational means US involvement is less than 50% of the troops and costs.

Next, Congress must do its job. Congress has abdicated its responsibilities, allowing presidents to act unilaterally.[13] The proposed rules will force Congress to explicitly vote and approve foreign military deployments (over 1000 personnel per country) every six months.

At home let's reverse the federalization of National Guards. They will remain under state control unless Congress makes an actual declaration of war. Presidents will have no power to federalize National Guards for ambiguous foreign skirmishes, natural disasters, or domestic border patrols. As a further check, state governors will have the collective power to veto any federal law or executive order concerning their National Guards by a 2/3 majority.

And finally, to protect against possible abuse, let's limit military powers to arrest citizens. Where an arrest does happen, the citizen must be handed over to civil authorities on US soil asap! No holding US citizens abroad in limbo or extraordinary renditions.

Will there still be covert military actions in foreign countries? Extraordinary renditions, secret prisons? Possibly under extraordinary conditions, but the provisions here will increase the probability they are uncovered. Even if we can't eliminate illegal actions, we can at least minimize them.

Reducing Costs

To reduce costs, two questions need to be answered. Firstly, does the US need such a big military? Secondly, could we get a better bang for our buck?

Every military excursion costs money, and even in peacetime contractors and suppliers want the military to buy the latest equipment. Military budgets could probably be trimmed, but spending levels are for Congress to decide.

Nonetheless, spending will likely go down as a result of the proposals here. It will be explicit US policy to pursue peace with other nations. Banning interference in foreign countries will lessen costly military action.

Other amendments to the tax code and a ban on government borrowing will force Congress to set spending priorities. That might result in reductions in military spending. However, since the military is one of the legitimate roles of the federal government, the military should remain a high priority for spending during budget deliberations.

Government and Economy

The more the state "plans" the more difficult planning becomes for the individual.

—Friedrich A. Hayek

This section deals broadly with issues where our governments try to meddle with the economy and civil life. Issues such as:

- Taxation.
- Social Security and Welfare.
- Money, debt, loans, and subsidies.
- Monopoly.
- Intellectual property.
- Healthcare & Education.
- Immigration.

The Cost of Living

Why is the cost of living so high? Why is housing so expensive? Why do you need two incomes to raise a family these days? How did education and healthcare (in particular) get so expensive?

The economy is complex, and detailed answers to any of the above questions quickly get bogged down in multiple possible causes, difficult-to-prove theories, and impossible-to-collect data. We'll get into the weeds of some of those issues below.

In the big picture though, the answer is obvious. *As a country, we keep pouring resources into the most economically inefficient part of the economy: the government itself.*

Put more accurately, the government keeps taking resources, by force, from the private sector. At the same time, governments keep imposing inefficiencies, by force, on the private sector in the form of regulation.

You may have seen a version of the "Chart of the Century" shown in Figure 8 below. Although this chart only goes back 25 years, you can see clearly that the more a sector of the economy is interfered with by government, the higher the inflation rate. Education and medical care in particular have experienced rampant government control and rampant inflation.

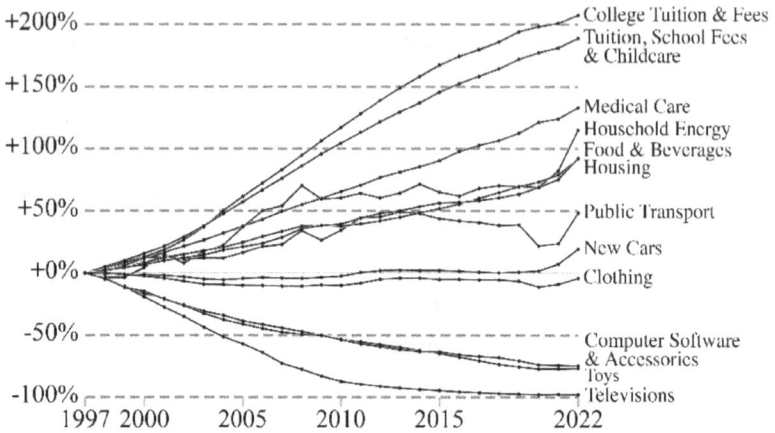

Figure 8—Relative Inflation in US Economy[1]

All the proposals in this book aim to scale back the size and scale of government, and the amount of regulation. This section focuses on some of the most important aspects of government operations that directly affect the economy.

Proposal 21—Taxation

A wise and frugal government, which shall leave men free to regulate their own pursuits of industry and improvement, and shall not take from the mouth of labor the bread it has earned—this is the sum of good government.

—Thomas Jefferson

We need to pay taxes to pay for the government and the services that it offers us all. Right?

Well, maybe. It's possible to design a society with no government and no taxes. Every service that governments offer could be done privately, and probably more effectively. However, that's not the world we live in, and many Americans don't believe that such a system is possible without a descent into chaos and violence.

So, let's assume most of us agree that some government is needed. And if we have a government, then we must pay for it. and we will have taxes. The question then is how much government, and how much tax? Many citizens think there's already too much of both!

Proposed Amendment: Taxation

This proposal is the single largest amendment here. Social Security, which is closely related, is dealt with in the next amendment. Personal Saving Accounts are defined in the Social Security proposal.

1. Government shall have a duty to ensure a clear, simple, and stable tax system.
2. Corporations shall be defined here as any organization, partnership, artificial person, or entity that is not a real person. Except as specified below, real people and corporations shall be treated the same for tax purposes.
3. States shall be defined here as including any US possession or Territory where the citizens are considered to be US citizens.
4. There shall be an individual income tax of 10% on taxable income. All income from any source shall be treated the same for income tax purposes except:
   a. No taxes shall be due on sales of a personal primary residence.
   b. Capital gains shall be indexed for inflation.
   c. Gifts and bequeaths between spouses shall be tax-free.
5. There shall be no personal exemptions or deductions except that citizens may deduct from pre-tax income:
   a. All monies placed in a Personal Savings Account.
   b. All monies donated to a charitable organization.
   c. Up to $1,000,000 of any bequeath or gift in any tax year.

6. States may collect a retail sales tax on goods and services that are both sold and delivered within that state if state citizens vote for said tax. Where sales taxes are charged, there shall be one tax rate for the entire state and for goods on which taxes are due.

7. There shall never be sales taxes on the following:
   a. Services that consist primarily of labor.
   b. Leases or rental agreements of residential property.
   c. Food and drink bought for consumption off the premises,
   d. Medical products and services.
   e. Educational products and services.
   f. Sales of real estate.
   g. Sales of personal used property in non-business contexts.

8. States may create other sales tax exemptions on selected classes of goods if citizens vote for that exemption. States may not create sales tax exemptions for classes of buyers.

9. States may not impose any taxes on goods crossing state or national lines.

10. No business shall be required to collect sales taxes until the tax year after their gross sales first exceed $20,000.

11. Corporations shall pay taxes on profits at the same rates as real citizens. There shall be no corporate exemptions or deductions except that corporations may deduct from pre-tax income:
    a. Reasonable business expenses.
    b. Reasonable research and development expenditures.
    c. Reasonable capital investment expenditures.
    d. Dividends paid to shareholders.
    e. Business losses carried over from previous years.

12. Tax returns of publicly listed corporations shall be public.

13. Organizations may apply for charitable status in their state of organization. Rules for charities shall be:
    a. Organizations spending more than 10% of their income on political campaigning shall not be eligible for charitable status.
    b. Charitable status shall apply for tax purposes in all states.
    c. All donations and income must be retained within the charity or used for charitable purposes.
    d. Charities shall file an annual informational tax return detailing income and expenditure. These returns shall be public.

14. Organizations may apply for political organization status in their state of organization. Rules for political organizations shall be:
    a. Political organizations may engage in political campaigning.
    b. Political organizations may not engage in commercial activity except for fundraising pursuant to their political aims.

   c. Political organization status shall apply for tax purposes in all states.

   d. Political organizations shall not have any tax-exempt status, and donations to them shall not be tax-deductible.

   e. Political organizations shall submit tax returns detailing income and expenditures, including individual itemization of any donation or expenditure greater than $10,000. Those returns shall be public.

15. There shall be no other taxes of any sort or by any other name.

16. No government agency or body other than state governments shall have taxing authority.

17. All taxes shall be collected by the states, with a single tax collection agency per state. It shall be the responsibility of that agency to forward sums collected to the appropriate recipients.

18. All taxes received from whatever source shall be split 1/3 federal, 1/3 state, and 1/3 local.

19. Apportionment of local taxes between municipalities and counties shall be a 50/50 split of taxes received in that jurisdiction.

20. Persons and organizations required to file an income tax return shall file one tax return only. Families may file a joint tax return.

21. Persons with multiple residences shall file in the state where they spend most of their time. They shall declare an approximate time (defined as +/- 10%) spent at each residence. The filing state shall prorate and forward the taxes accordingly to the other states.

22. Corporations with multi-state operations shall file income taxes in the state where their principal US place of business is located, and file sales taxes in every state they do retail business in. Income taxes shall be prorated between states by the average number of employees per jurisdiction.

23. US citizens living abroad shall pay US taxes on US income only and may choose any state to file their taxes.

24. Where states have different tax rates, taxpayers and tax collectors shall prorate amounts of taxes paid according to the formulae above and to tax rates for each state.

25. Citizens receiving income from abroad may deduct any foreign taxes paid from their US income taxes, up to the US tax rates.

26. No tax returns need be filed unless taxes are due.

27. Citizens shall pay their own income taxes. Government may not require withholding of taxes on behalf of other citizens.

28. Government may not require any citizen to report financial or other tax-related information on another citizen except by court order as part of a civil or criminal proceeding.

29. Annual filings and tax payments in full are due on the Tuesday after the first Monday in November (Election Day).

30. Government may not require payment of estimated taxes in advance but may offer discounts for early or estimated payments.

31. States shall publish annual public reports detailing their tax collection procedures and results for the previous tax year.

32. Congress shall have the right to audit any state's tax collection procedures. The results shall be public.

33. Taxpayers, their executors or heirs, or any representative with the taxpayer's permission, shall have the right to an audit of their tax filings and payments.

34. States may change any tax rate if approved by voters in a state-wide referendum under the following conditions:
    a. Referendums may only take place in presidential election years.
    b. There shall be a separate referendum for each tax type.
    c. Each referendum shall offer voters the choice to raise rates by 1%, lower rates by 1%, or leave unchanged,
    d. The choice with the most votes and gaining at least 50% of the votes shall win.

35. States may not introduce other tax brackets or classes of taxpayers.

36. Government may not require citizens to participate in insurance schemes.

37. *Transition:* Upon the passing of this amendment:
    a. The new tax system and rates shall apply from 1st January of the following year—the Changeover Date.
    b. States shall create new tax legislation and supporting regulations by the Changeover Date. There shall be one new tax act per state. No earlier tax legislation may be grandfathered into the new system.
    c. All States shall have a referendum to decide if citizens wish to have a sales tax and the initial rate, which, if charged, must be a round number and no more than 10%.
    d. Federal tax authorities shall be required to cooperate fully with state authorities in the setting up of the new tax system.
    e. Corporations and citizens may carry over tax losses and depreciation from the previous tax system into the new system.
    f. On the Changeover Date, all earlier federal, state, and local tax codes become void. There shall be a general amnesty for issues that arose under the old laws. Previous tax collection agencies and courts shall be dissolved, and their employees released from government employment.

Your Money or Your Life

Taxes are one of the most complex issues we citizens face in our interactions with governments. *The complexity is deliberate.* Governments have been engaged in manipulation by taxation since governments existed.

Every taxing entity keeps thinking of new and creative ways to tax citizens to achieve dubious social or economic goals. Regardless of the pros and cons of any individual tax, the collective result is madness. Taxes have become a cancer, ever metastasizing, invading our lives. Taxes, and fighting about taxes, are draining the vitality out of our country.

Let's start with the government's right to tax us at all. Government collects taxes from us which pay for services that benefit us all. However, there's a moral hazard: paying your taxes is not voluntary. If you don't pay then, ultimately, men with guns will come and take your money.

It rarely comes to that in practice, but if you don't pay your taxes, there will no doubt be a long legal process involving demand letters, serving of papers, courts, and so on. But at the end of the day, if you keep refusing to pay, *you will be forced to comply.*

Thus, taxes fail the Test of Moral Authority. Do I have the right to force my neighbor to pay for services? No, I do not. I don't have the right to force her to pay for anything, even if it's for the public good. By extension, neither does the government.

Despite this, I think most citizens are willing to pay some taxes, so long as they are used for the common good. Except that, we don't all agree on what the common good is. Beyond the most basic services (defense, police, courts, and roads), most government actions fail the Test of Consent—large numbers of citizens disagree.

When policies fail the Test of Consent, then government is acting like a mafia—forcing you to pay for services you don't want under threat of violence. This might be legal, but it is not right.

Another problem with taxes is that their sheer complexity has become a drag on society. The federal tax code is a monster! Even the IRS has difficulty estimating how big it is. The rules are made up of several parts: the code itself, supporting regulations, and administrative or judicial decisions resolving ambiguities. There are also tax guides and journals that are not officially law, but which you need to read to understand it all!

The Taxpayer Advocate Service (TAS)[1] in its 2008 report to congress puts the code itself at about 3.7 million words. At 250/words per page that's about 14,800 pages or 29 weeks of reading at a study rate of 100/pages per working day. The TAS estimates the supporting regulations are about 11,700 pages or 23 weeks of reading. A print-out of the regulations would form a stack of paper a foot high!

Even greater detail can be found in the CCH Standard Federal Tax Reporter. The IRS describes this as "a leading publication for tax professionals that *summarizes* administrative guidance and judicial decisions issued under each section of the Code." That publication takes up 9 feet of shelf space—about 105,000 pages or 4 years of reading[2].

Add that all up, and it comes to at least five years of study to understand the tax code, as well as continuous study to keep up with ongoing changes. Some other estimates provided by the TAS are:

- The size of the code has tripled since 1975, and changes are accelerating, happening almost daily.

- Citizens and businesses spend 7.6 billion hours a year complying with tax rules. That translates into 3.6 million full-time workers!

- Tax compliance costs about $167 billion a year, equivalent to about 14% of tax revenue. If tax compliance were an industry, it would be the single biggest industry in the US.

- About 60% of citizens use a tax preparer to do their returns and about 22% use software. Complexity increases the chances of innocent mistakes.

There are many federal taxes: income taxes, capital gains, estate and gifts taxes, excise taxes (gas tax), payroll taxes (Social Security and Medicare), tariffs (on imports), exit taxes (on those renouncing US citizenship), and miscellaneous fees/charges on utility bills and so on.

Variations on dozens of other taxes exist at state and local levels: property taxes, millages, sales and use taxes, local income/capital gains taxes, luxury taxes, road taxes, windfall taxes, sin taxes, miscellaneous fees on goods and services (such as airport taxes). And so on, ad nauseam

From each individual taxing authority's perspective, each new tax is just an oh-so-reasonable small thing. In the big picture, it is collective madness. Every tax implies money from your pocket as well as legislation, regulation, and court cases. They imply compliance hassle for you, and bureaucrats to manage it all.

Is there a limit to new things that could be taxed, or how complex it could get?[3] I doubt it. We already have too many taxes and too much complexity.

Where did this complexity come from? It comes from special interests manipulating the tax system. It comes from taxing authorities continually tweaking and adjusting things, finding new taxes to raise to support questionable goals, and employing thousands of administrators in the process.

Want less smoking? Tax cigarettes! Less driving? Tax gasoline. Want to encourage whaling, offer a deduction.[4] What to punish rich people? Tax luxury cars. Want less marshmallow consumption, tax it.[5] Want to encourage "exceptional trees," offer a deduction.

Those examples are all real taxes and deductions! There's always somebody, somewhere, who thinks that something can be stopped by taxing it or encouraged by offering a deduction. Typically, these schemes appeal to politicians and the public alike because the taxes are concentrated on a few, and the supposed benefits accumulate to many. Yet they all come with huge moral hazards:

- Different taxes for different citizens fail the Test of Purpose (equal rights) and the Test of Moral Authority (I have no right to force my neighbor to pay more for some services than others).

- All arguments that individual taxes pay for specified services are bunk from a financial point of view because money is fungible. Nonetheless, separating income and spending streams gives politicians an excuse not to exercise financial discipline.

- Many of the categories used to decide what should be taxed are arbitrary. What, for example, is a luxury car?

- It is not the government's job to change our behaviors by taxing some things and exempting others.

- Each of us has individual gains and losses, but society overall gains nothing by shuffling money from one pocket to another.

- Complexity hides the overall tax burden.

- Complexity is expensive, personally, and in bureaucratic overhead.

Another deliberate source of complexity is progressive taxes—making the rich pay more. Many citizens feel that the rich should pay more, but the moral case for this is dubious. How would you feel if stores set prices depending on your salary? In a market, we each pay for what we want and what we use. Why should anyone pay more for services they often don't want just because they earn more?

Activists often claim that increasing taxes on the rich would solve all our problems. But this can never work because the rich don't have enough money! In 2020, the collective *total* income of the top 1% of taxpayers (about 1.4 million people) was about $2.4 trillion.[6] Compare that to the 2020 federal budget of about $4.8 trillion and a close to $1 trillion deficit.[7]

In the big picture, the problem isn't that the rich don't pay their fair share. The rich are already paying most of the taxes (directly, or via corporate, payroll, property, and other taxes). The real issue is that the government is spending much more than its fair share.

Progressive taxes also create moral hazard. At the low end, the hazard is citizens receiving services they don't pay for. About 44% of citizens pay no federal income taxes,[8] yet they receive federal benefits. There's no fairness about this, it's a form of mob rule. And it also creates social conflict when the poor are encouraged to think they are owed benefits.

At the high end, the hazard is that progressive taxes make governments over-dependent on the rich. This can play out in one of two equally unhealthy ways:

One possibility is that the rich have an excessive say in how things are run. They demand their special interest privileges, restrictions on competition, etc.

The second possibility, if they don't get what they want, is they leave and deprive the government of funds. The biggest taxpayers, typically corporations, can deprive government of funds by playing games with offshore subsidiaries in low-tax jurisdictions, either lowering their tax bill or delaying payment.[9]

At the state level, even your average millionaire can get fed-up and leave. For example, from 2007-2010 Maryland imposed a 6.25% tax on persons earning over a million dollars a year. The result: some 31,000 people left Maryland, and tax revenue *fell* by about $1.7 billion![10] Many of those millionaires took their businesses with them when they moved, costing Maryland a bunch of lower-paying jobs as well.

Special interests are forever trying to manipulate the tax code—avoiding taxes or getting subsidies. The result is thousands of pages of IRS rules creating hundreds of tax loopholes. Loopholes encourage resentment between taxpayers and non-taxpayers, between the subsidized and the subsidizers, and between recipients and non-recipients of tax breaks.

If, for example, I buy a new electric car, my neighbors subsidize it through their taxes. No matter how worthy the subsidy or tax break is, other people are paying for it. Why wouldn't they be annoyed?

These resentments rarely cause open conflict, but they nonetheless sour relationships between people. Government policy is fueling dissatisfaction and the feeling something has gone wrong in our country.

Radical Simplification

This madness needs to end. Rather than arguing forever about the pros and cons of every tax, let's go for radical simplification:

- One income tax, 10% on income from any source, capital gains indexed for inflation.

- One sales tax at 10%, with food, housing, healthcare, and education excluded. Startup businesses won't have to charge or collect sales tax until their turnover exceeds $20,000.

- Gifts and bequeaths between spouses would be tax-free.

- No deductions, except charity, Protected Investment Accounts, and a $1 million deduction for gifts/bequeaths.

- Corporations will pay tax on profits at the same rates as individuals, dividends will be tax deductible (ending double taxation).

- No other taxes whatsoever!

- Taxes are to be collected by states, no other government body would have taxing authority. Taxes collected are prorated equally in three ways between federal, state, and local governments.

- Tax rates can change, but only by 1% at a time, by state referendum, one vote per presidential election year.

Here are the advantages:

- It is simple, your annual tax form can be one page long, Simplicity in turn makes manipulation difficult. A constitutional level fix has a high chance of remaining simple, and taxes would be fixed at every level of government in one go.

- The new tax code will be permanent (other than small and rare rate changes), making it much easier for citizens to plan.

- Restricting government income will force them to prioritize spending rather than expand services through additional taxation.

- The only way the government can increase its income is by implementing policies that stimulate the entire economy, which in turn benefits us all. Everyone's interests will be aligned.

- Everyone pays taxes, eliminating the moral hazard of citizens demanding services they don't pay for. Yet it is still progressive, the higher your income or spending, the more you pay.

- Small business startups will be encouraged by keeping them out of the sales tax system until they reach a threshold.

- No more IRS. State tax offices would be more accountable to citizens, and subject to oversight by both states and feds.

- There will be competition between taxing states. If you don't like how your state does it, move next door.

- All income would be taxed at the same rate. The tax system will be neutral about how to earn money.

- Since everyone pays the same tax rates, the tax system will be neutral about marriage and children.

- Citizens will get to vote on tax rates. Governments must persuade rather than impose increases. Citizens could even vote away (in time) all taxes and therefore most government.

How Much Will This Raise?

This system would radically simplify tax collection and have the benefits outlined above. However, the point of taxes is to fund government activity. So, how would all this affect the total taxes raised?

I can't give you a figure for taxes raised under the new system. I'd need an army of economists to even give you a guess. Nonetheless, we can get ballpark figures from the research of the Fair Tax[11] movement, and the Flat Tax[12] movement.

The Fair Tax movement proposes that a universal sales tax of 23% would cover all federal spending, replacing all federal taxes. The Flat Tax movement calculates that a 19% flat income tax would meet all federal spending. (Both are slightly more complex than the headline rates due to provisions to help the poorest citizens).

Both sales taxes and income taxes have pros and cons. Rather than trying to decide which is better, let's take their headline figures: a sales tax of 23%, or an income tax of 19%, and split the difference.

The proposal is one income tax of 10%, one sales tax of 10%, and no thresholds. Simple to administer, easy to remember. Simple, simple, simple! And there's a high probability the total tax take will be about right given the research done by Fair Tax and Flat Tax movements.

If I've got it wrong, if the government needs more, and *if citizens agree*, they can vote to change the tax rates. But the government would need to persuade us rather than impose tax hikes on us. We'd have actual democratic decisions on an issue important to citizens.

Tax receipts are only loosely related to tax rates and are difficult to predict due to incentive effects. If you double tax rates you won't double the take. You might end up with less because taxpayers take rates into account when making financial decisions.[13] A taxpayer might work less overtime because it's not worth it when they shift into a new tax bracket. They might invest in tax-free bonds instead of stocks. They might move to a cheaper state or find ways to move funds offshore.

This works in the other direction as well. If taxes were halved, there's an excellent chance the government would net *more* income. People might work harder if they can earn more. They might declare income they have been hiding because the benefits no longer outweigh the risks of being caught. The Fair Tax campaign estimates that tax evasion already costs something like $2,500 per taxpayer.

With the caveat that estimating income from tax changes is very difficult, here's a guess as to the overall effect of the changes on income:

- Overall revenue may initially go down. Revenue will be about the same for states and counties. The feds will take a hit in income.

- Different states may have different rates (and submit different amounts to the feds). This is a benefit—competition between states will give clues to the optimal rate/take ratio.

- Most poor and middle-income people will pay less overall in taxes. Gas taxes and property taxes especially eat up a disproportionately large part of poor people's incomes.

- Higher-income taxpayers will probably pay something close to what they pay now. Although tax rates for the rich are high, the rich can afford good advisors and rarely pay headline rates.

- The rich, who spend more, will pay more in sales taxes.

Related side effects will be:

- Tax rates will become a direct democratic issue.

- Compliance rates (people paying their taxes) will go up.

- Most federal tax collection employees will lose their jobs, though some will move to the states. Overall, the new system will need fewer people to run it, lowering costs.

- No more IRS. State agencies will be more accountable and can be subject to federal oversight.

- There will be much less tax preparation work and lower costs for taxpayers. Accountants can turn their attention to more productive activities, such as advising clients on how to generate extra income.

Overall, there would be a general and ongoing boost to the economy from lower taxes and lower compliance costs, as well as everyone being incentivized to earn more. In the long run, we'll collectively be much richer, off, though it may take a few years for the wrinkles to even out.

In Conclusion

Keep it simple! The bare bones of a tax system are laid out above in about 1350 words, or about 1150 words if you exclude details about the transition to the new system. There will be details to sort out at the state level, but they will be subject to the limitations laid down in *Proposal 12— Legislation.* State tax codes will have a maximum of 10,000 words of legislation and 10,000 words of supporting regulations. It will remain simple.

Compare that to the current 11.6 million words of federal tax code, plus tens of millions of words in supporting regulations, administrative decisions, court judgments, tax publications, and explanations; as well as state, county, and municipal tax codes.

Does the tax code need to be so complex that tax compliance is the single largest industry in the US? No, it does not. Time to simplify.

Proposal 22—Social Security

If we can but prevent the government from wasting the labours of the people, under the pretence of taking care of them, they must become happy.

—Thomas Jefferson

Social Security is bankrupt. It's also, financially, a bad deal for people saving for their retirement. No amount of tinkering will fix Social Security because it is fundamentally a Ponzi scheme. It needs to go.

Nonetheless, Social Security can't be switched off overnight. Millions of people have planned for it their entire lives. So, let's keep promises made to those who are already invested, but find alternatives for those who are younger. Social Security can wither away over the next 50 years or so.

Proposed Amendment: Social Security

1. Citizens have the responsibility to provide for their own security in case of unemployment, ill health, or old age; and to provide for their children's security until their children reach adulthood.

2. Citizens shall have the right to save income in tax-advantaged accounts to be known as Protected Savings Accounts (PSAs).

3. Citizens may put any amount of pretax income into any PSA belonging to any person.

4. All income and growth within a PSA shall be tax-free. Any funds withdrawn from a PSA for the allowed uses shall be tax-free.

5. Allowed uses of PSA funds shall be:
   a. Medical and health-related expenses.
   b. Unemployment expenses.
   c. Education expenses.
   d. Any expense after the fund owner reaches 65 years of age.

6. PSA funds used for disallowed purposes shall be treated as income taxed at 30% in the year in which the funds are withdrawn.

7. PSAs will be individual accounts intended for the benefit of the owner, or dependents of the owner at the owner's discretion.

8. Citizens moving residence between the US and foreign countries may convert PSAs to and from broadly equivalent foreign schemes without US tax consequences.

9. Upon the death of the owner of a PSA, the contents of the PSA shall pass to the owners' inheritors and the PSA shall be closed.

10. PSAs may be opened at any financial institution and must be designated a PSA. Beyond designation as a PSA and tax reporting these accounts may not be treated by law differently than other fi-

nancial accounts. There shall be no mandatory trustee arrangements required, nor restrictions on allowable investments.

11. Citizens may transfer money between each other's PSAs without tax consequences.

12. Funds invested in PSAs shall be protected from torts, criminal damages, and bankruptcy. PSA funds may not be seized or garnished unless crimes are committed in the creation or funding of the PSA itself.

13. *Transition:* Upon the passing of this amendment the current Social Security system shall become voluntary as follows:

    a. Future payments into the system will be voluntary.

    b. Payments into the system may be made from a PSA.

    c. Citizens may choose to leave Social Security by withdrawing their funds plus accumulated interest, at the rate of inflation, and place them in a PSA.

    d. All currently existing tax-advantaged savings schemes offered by any government will be rolled over into a PSA without tax consequence. The old schemes will end.

Mandated Social Security?

Do I have the right to force my neighbor to save for her retirement? No, I do not. By extension, neither does the government. Social Security fails the Test of Moral Authority.

Social Security fails the Test of Constitutional Authority. The original legislation had to pretend it was a tax to circumvent the federal government's lack of authority to impose the new scheme.[1]

About 30% of people believe that Social Security won't be there when they retire. 39% are unsure, and only 31% believe that it will be there for them[2]. For those aged 18-24, only 11% believe they will get anything. Many people arrange their affairs to minimize Social Security taxes. Overall, it is safe to say that Social Security fails the Test of Consent.

Social Security is a poor investment. One 1999 study compared Social Security to investing in an index fund.[3] A 38-year-old earning $40,000 p.a. would have needed to live to be 143 to do better in Social Security. The same worker earning $68,400 p.a. would have had to live forever. Social Security fails the Test of Efficacy.

Finally, since government employees and clergy can opt out, Social Security fails the Test of Purpose. Some citizens are legally less free than other citizens.

Social Security would be illegal if it were a private scheme because it is a Ponzi scheme: current payers are paying for current recipients. No amount of tinkering will ever fix this—it is fundamentally flawed. The entire system needs to be replaced.

A New System

Social Security needs to go, but millions of people have been raised on Social Security and depend on it. They have planned their whole financial lives and retirements around Social Security. Also, arguably, some form of social safety net does promote the common good.

So, let's keep Social Security for those who use or have planned for it, but offer an alternative for those who no longer believe in it.

What are the issues a social safety net should account for? The big ones are healthcare, unemployment, and retirement. For the sake of simplicity, let's add education to that list. Education is not a safety net issue as such, but it is a major concern of parents, and most people would probably agree it should be a national priority. Ideally, all social safety net issues should come under one system. Easy to understand and use, flexible, and difficult to manipulate.

The proposal here is based on the existing Health Savings Account (HSA) schemes. It would create Personal Savings Accounts (PSAs) incentivizing citizens to save for their security, like HSAs but with improvements.

The first improvement is that HSAs require trustees to administer them. PSAs will not need a trustee. Compulsory trustee arrangements assume you cannot be trusted with your own money and need a special interest to look after it for you—for a small fee.

Next, HSAs have arbitrary restrictions—no short sales, no margin, and various disallowed investments. Legislators have assumed it is their job to keep us safe from our own mistakes, as they see them. PSAs by contrast will be normal banking and brokerage accounts designated as PSAs. You'll need to spend money coming out of them within the rules and account for them at tax time. Other than that, they will be normal accounts. You invest as you see fit, with no restrictions.

Lastly, PSAs will be usable for any major social safety net issue: health, unemployment, retirement, or education. You won't have to decide today between healthcare or your children's college fund. Save today, and spend in the future as needed.

That's it! The proposal outlines a new system in about 450 words. The original 1935 Economic Security Act creating Social Security had 64 pages or about 1600 words. Even though it was a model of brevity by today's standards, it has still spawned thousands of pages of regulations and needs 60,000 employees to run it.[4]

There will be details to sort out in the new system via regulation and/or court cases. Nonetheless, overall, this will be a vast simplification and will end a great deal of meddling in your financial affairs.

Under this proposal, the old system will remain in place but will become voluntary. The feds will need to honor the commitments made to millions of people who planned their retirements around Social Security. If you are fully invested in Social Security or think it's a good deal, then keep investing. Younger people who already believe they won't get any benefits can start investing in PSAs instead.

Those who are partially invested in the old system will have the option to take the monies they have invested in Social Security, plus accrued interest, and move it to a PSA. Where citizens have funds in other protected accounts (IRAs, HSAs, 401Ks, 529 plans, etc.) all those funds will automatically roll over into PSAs, without tax consequence.

PSAs are designed to have every advantage: no taxes, flexibility, minimal rules, and maximum protection from lawsuits and bankruptcy. All the older schemes and associated bureaucracy can disappear.

A major difference between Social Security and the new system is mandates. Currently, you *must* contribute to Social Security (with a few special interest exceptions). The new system will be voluntary. Saving for a rainy day should be encouraged, but it should not be mandatory. Rather than forcing people to save, let's incentivize them. The proposed PSAs are so deliberately tax-advantaged, protected, and flexible that I can't imagine any sane person not using them. Force will not be needed.

Will there be a few people who don't save? Yes. Will there be a few people who invest badly and wipe out their savings? Yes. But no system can protect everyone under all circumstances, and to try to do is to infantilize them. The perfect system does not exist, and certainly, the government should not force its idea of perfection on anyone.

If the government feels that citizens are at risk, they can offer advice. If Wall Street feels that citizens need trustees to look after their pensions, they can persuade us to employ them. But no force should be allowed!

For the unfortunate few who fall through the cracks and have insufficient savings, there will still be the traditional fallbacks: families, friends, and charity. Meanwhile, most people will have greater financial security under the new system.

Many folks might even have a little extra to spare for family members who have fallen on hard times. PSAs are structured so that you can transfer funds to other PSAs belonging to other people if you wish. They can act as a kind of mini charitable foundation if you wish to use them that way.

Proposal 23—Welfare

Charity is no part of the legislative duty of the government.
—James Madison

Social Security was addressed in the previous amendment, but there are other government welfare programs. No matter the specific program, welfare is rife with moral hazards, malincentives, and unintended consequences. Welfare is bankrupting us.

Welfare needs to change, radically, and most citizens want it to change. However, the welfare state has become such a staple of government in the US that it is politically dangerous to mess with it, which makes it almost impossible for legislators to fix anything.

So, the proposal here is to end all federal welfare and start over again at the state level. Anything less than a complete start-over will result in a massive, exhausting, and unwinnable fight about what to keep and what to let go. Let's avoid that.

Proposed Amendment: Welfare

1. The federal government may only create welfare programs where the benefit is payable to all real citizens without qualification.
   a. States may create welfare programs as follows:
   b. Benefits may only be paid to real citizens.
   c. Benefits may last for a maximum of two years.
   d. Recipients may not re-apply for a benefit for a period equivalent to the length of time they last received the benefit.
   e. Voters must approve new programs by state-wide referendum.
   f. Voters must reapprove each welfare program every 10 years.
2. Local governments may not create welfare programs.
3. Funds for welfare programs must come from general revenue. There shall be no additional taxes levied, insurance premiums or pre-payments charged, nor debts created to fund welfare programs.
4. No superior government may require any inferior government to offer, administer, or fund a welfare program.
5. All welfare programs shall be designed to:
   a. Link benefits to work or training for work.
   b. Encourage recipients to come off welfare as soon as possible.
   c. Encourage marriage and stable families.
6. All welfare benefits must take the form of a cash payment directly to the citizen or their PSA.
7. All welfare benefits due to children shall be paid into PSA accounts for those children with their parents acting as trustees.

8. Citizens eligible for any welfare benefit may assign that benefit to any other real citizen, PSA, or charity.

9. Welfare benefits shall be taxable.

10. Upon the passing of this amendment, current welfare programs shall be eliminated except for Social Security, which shall be phased out as described in the Social Security amendment.

Welfare: Not the Government's Business

The typical argument for welfare is that helping the poor and needy promotes the general welfare and is thus a valid government function. Helping is indeed a good thing, but the government cannot be the one to help.

Welfare fails the Test of Constitutional Authority. Welfare is not an enumerated responsibility of the federal government, and the 10th Amendment clearly says *powers not delegated to the United States by the Constitution, nor prohibited by it to the States, are reserved to the States respectively, or to the people.*

Welfare fails the Test of Moral Authority. Do I have the right to force my neighbor to support my favorite charity? No, I do not. I don't have the right to force her to support *any* charity, and neither does the government. Helping is good. *Forcing* people to help is bad.

Welfare fails the Test of Purpose. It makes me less free by forcing me to give some of my money to other citizens.

Welfare fails the Test of Consent. A large majority of citizens don't support welfare in its current form. Multiple polls point in the same direction.[1] For example, Heritage Foundation polls found:

- 94% think that welfare fraud and waste need to be eliminated.

- 92% think benefits should be conditional on work or work training.

- 88% think welfare should pay for outcomes (be in rehab, get a job, complete a training course, etc.) rather than be a direct handout.

- 81% think welfare should not penalize or discourage marriage.[2]

Finally, welfare fails the Test of Efficacy. Most citizens believe that the War on Poverty has failed. The numbers are 77% overall, including 80% of Republicans, 72% of Democrats, and even 63% of those on welfare.[3]

Welfare thus fails all five of our tests of Legitimate Governance. There's no other way to say this: welfare needs to go!

Many people will be uneasy about doing away with welfare—why not improve the current system? Special interests who benefit from welfare will encourage that line of thinking. Despite this, welfare can *never* be an effective choice, because the incentives work against it.

How Can We Help?

Helping those in need is a worthy cause. But knowing *how* to help is an extraordinarily difficult problem, one that government is inept at solving. Further, welfare conflicts with other important government functions and opens up a cesspool of moral hazards and malincentives.

Society can help the poor in three main ways. In preferred order, they are: 1) Economic Growth, 2) Charity (private help), and 3) Welfare (government help).

Feedback and Incentives

Knowing how to help people can only be solved by ongoing trial and error. Doing that effectively requires two main elements. There needs to be feedback so that those providing help can know what those receiving it need. And there needs to be an incentive structure so that providers are motivated to offer what customers want.

Fundamentally, for-profit economic activity has feedback and incentives built in. Charity is lacking a lot of necessary feedback. Welfare has both missing feedback and malincentives. Perhaps the easiest way to understand the differences between the three is to ask: who is the customer?

In a for-profit market, vendors offer goods and services, and customers choose the products that they value the most. Vendors can only guess what customers want (though they are guided by their own experience as customers). If they get it right, customers will buy and in so doing, offer clear feedback about their preferences. Producers will in turn be incentivized to meet customer needs because there's no profit in selling unpopular stuff.

In any charitable situation, both feedback and incentives suffer a fundamental disconnect because the people paying are different from the people receiving.

For the donors, what are they buying for their money? Mostly, they are buying "feeling good about helping." That's fine, but it is not the same thing as helping.

For the customers, the recipients, what are they buying? Well, nothing, really, because they are not spending money (though they may spend time and effort to get aid.) They may like what they're offered, or they may not. But since it comes to them for close to free and with little choice, they are not buying the best product to meet their needs. They have limited ability to give market feedback through their choices.

For the charity workers, who are they serving? They are in the awkward situation of having two potentially conflicting sets of customers: donors with money, and recipients of charity.

None of the people involved—donors, workers, or recipients—acts out of ill will. Nonetheless, the incentives don't produce the feedback needed to give customers exactly what they need.

Despite the problems, charity does have built-in safeguards. Donors will stop giving if they can't see benefits. Charity workers will quit or stop volunteering if they don't feel useful. Ineffective charities naturally expire. For welfare, the feedback and incentives are similar to charity, only worse. As welfare programs get bigger, more agencies get involved, creating a chain of links between the persons paying (taxpayers), and the ultimate welfare recipients. Those chains might vary in complexity depending on how welfare is distributed via federal, state, and local programs and charities. It could get as complicated as:

Taxpayers → Feds → States → Municipality→ Charity → Recipients

Not only are there multiple links in the money flow chain, but each link is potentially arranged by politicians, overseen by bureaucrats, and manipulated by special interests. The net result is that nobody is in control. Recipients cannot give clear feedback to donors (taxpayers), and dozens of other players are involved, each with different masters and purposes.

Even if welfare recipients could give clear feedback about their needs, taxpayers cannot change anything. Taxpayers are forced to pay taxes no matter what their opinion about welfare, unlike charitable donors who can stop donating if they see no benefit.

Since administrators running welfare earn their living from welfare, they are content to leave things as-is. Politicians don't want to change things because that looks bad to voters. The net result is nothing changes! Ineffective welfare programs can and will drag on forever.

Resource Allocation

Another problem with both charity and welfare is that the lack of feedback makes resource allocation difficult. We only have so much money, so how do we best spend it?

In a market, buyers buy goods and services based on their budgets and their priorities. Individuals decide on an ongoing basis what to spend on food, housing, transport, and so on. They are always motivated to do what's best *for them.* Once they have enough of something they will stop buying that thing and buy something else they want instead.

In charitable situations, donors and charity workers may be able to at least ask individual recipients what they need and have the flexibility to change their offerings.

These mechanisms cannot work for welfare. Politicians and bureaucrats decide priorities for groups of people. They cannot know what each recipient needs, they can only guess. Yet there definitely are better and worse things to spend charitable or welfare dollars on.

Suppose that you meet a homeless person on the street about to die of starvation. If you give them a dollar to get a meal at a well-known burger chain, then you have spent a dollar to save a life. This is exceptional value for money.

Now suppose you meet a poor working person who has run out of money and won't get paid until tomorrow. They've been eating all week but will need to skip dinner this evening. You give them a dollar to get a meal. Your dollar is well spent, but it is not as well spent as the first dollar you gave to save a life.

Keep going down this chain of reasoning and you can start to see how we end up with 40 million US citizens claiming food stamps during an obesity epidemic! Something is seriously awry here. If someone is starving, then it is a good thing to help them. But are they starving? You can't know, only that person knows.

This is a systemic problem. The law of diminishing returns applies to all spending, including welfare. Yet welfare cuts off feedback about the effects of spending. No matter how well-designed or how well-intentioned a welfare program is, administrators cannot know what is needed. Only the individuals know.

The law of diminishing returns shows up clearly in the long-term data. In 1959 the poverty rate was about 22%. In 1964 the War on Poverty was declared, and spending ramped up. Initially, it had a big effect. By 1969 the poverty rate had fallen to about 12%. But by 2015, it had crept back up to 13.5% with welfare spending at 16 times greater than in 1965.[4] More welfare spending will not fix this.

Increasing Efficiency

A final reason to prefer for-profit service providers to charitable efforts is that the profit motive drives ever-increasing efficiency.

In a market, vendors are incentivized (by profit and competition) to keep improving their offerings to attract and keep customers. Customers are incentivized (by their desires and budget) to get the most stuff for the least amount of money. Suppliers and customers alike are incentivized towards continual improvement.

Charities and welfare do not have the same incentives. Charity leaders have been struggling with the issue of how to help for decades.[5] And even politicians will sometimes ask the right questions. Nonetheless, continuous improvement in charitable or welfare performance is difficult with no buying and therefore poor feedback.

Clear feedback is key to making any human activity more efficient, and that includes welfare and charity. For this reason, local charities are preferable to federal welfare schemes. The local charity can at least talk to charity recipients and have more flexibility to adjust to demand.

However, the best person to assess needs is the welfare recipient themselves. For this reason, cash payments to welfare recipients are better than directed programs, such as food stamps. If a recipient is well-fed today, they might be better off buying a warm coat, antibiotics, or gas to get to work. Only the recipients can decide their own priorities.

Malincentives

Along with poor economic incentives making welfare inefficient, welfare malincentives push everyone involved towards moral corruption. I am not saying that welfare *does* corrupt people, but the incentives are not aligned for positive outcomes:

- Welfare disincentivizes marriage.[6] When the War on Poverty began in 1964, about 36% of poor families with children were single-parent families. Today the figure is about 68%. Welfare should be neutral about marriage, and probably incentivize it. Welfare certainly shouldn't discourage marriage. And most citizens agree!

- Welfare disincentivizes employment and creates poverty traps.[7] This is madness. Welfare should be structured to encourage work.

- Welfare encourages political corruption in the form of spending welfare money to buy votes (vote for me, I am helping the poor, using taxpayer money to do it).

- Welfare incentivizes "us vs. them" thinking in the political arena, between taxpayers and welfare recipients, between rich and poor. Rather than *How can we all get ahead?* it incentivizes *How can I get mine?*

- Welfare puts government welfare workers at moral hazard. They are being paid to help the poor, but if they ever succeed, they will be punished because they will be out of a job. Welfare workers are therefore incentivized to maximize the number of people on welfare because that maximizes job security.

- Charitable activity is discouraged by government welfare activity because when a government tackles a problem that charities have been working on, charities move out and donors give less. (An effect known as "crowding out").

Manipulation Opportunities

When welfare is dished out it often comes with strings attached: food stamps to be spent only on specific foods, housing aid with restrictions on where you can live or types of housing, specified education courses, etc. This lack of choice is not random, it is the result of manipulation. Many private groups profit here such as:

- Agriculture, via food stamps and related programs supporting farmers and farmers' markets.

- Housing, via the HUD rent assistance programs.

- Medicine, via Medicaid, and other programs.

- Charities who administer aspects of welfare programs or receive grants from the government.
- Lawyers for welfare recipients.
- Grant writers consulting on getting government grants.

Fixing Welfare

If you agree with the Founders' vision, then government should not be involved in welfare at all. Welfare is a forced redistribution of wealth for which government has neither the moral authority nor the consent of the governed. It is rife with moral hazards, malincentives, unintended consequences, and special interest manipulation.

I believe welfare should end, but this may be taking things too far. So, instead, let's restructure things to encourage self-help and charity but leave welfare as a last resort. However, any change made must come in the form of a wholesale do-over. Piecemeal change won't work. Attempts to change or improve the current system will simply result in a massive and unwinnable fight about what to keep and what to let go. The only practical way to fix welfare is to start over.

To encourage self-help and charity, let's start by stimulating the economy. If we are all richer, then there will be less need for charity or welfare. The proposals in this book will simulate the economy by getting the government out of the way of citizens trying to innovate and do business.

Next, let's incentivize charity. Charity is superior to welfare. It also allows citizens to choose what charitable issues they think need addressing and to give accordingly, rather than the government choosing for them. Stimulating charitable giving will happen in three main ways:

- All charitable donations will be 100% tax deductible.
- All government-imposed fines and punitive damages will be distributed to charity, in proportion to what citizens give.
- PSAs can be used as a private charity. Citizens will be able to donate PSA funds to others in need, so long as they funds are used for allowable PSA spending or charitable spending.

Finally, we'll do away with the current system of welfare, but it will be allowable for a limited restarting of welfare, with severe restrictions.

At the federal level, the restriction is that the only welfare allowed will be cash payments payable to all real citizens without qualification. This provision makes Universal Basic Income (UBI) a possibility in the future. UBIs are an unknown factor (and problematic due to incentive problems), but let's allow for them in case they become relevant.

States will also be allowed to create welfare programs, but only if voters approve. State welfare programs will need to be designed to encourage recipients to get off welfare as quickly as possible, encourage job training, and encourage marriage. All welfare payments will be in cash only so that welfare recipients can decide what help they need for themselves. Cash payments will also cut out manipulation by directed welfare payments.

Future welfare spending (if any) will be kept in check by *Proposal 21—Taxation*, and *Proposal 25—Government Debt*. Together, these will severely restrict government income, spending, and debt.

As an aside, note that the incentive and feedback problems that charity and welfare suffer compared to for-profit market solutions are the same problems that socialist economies suffer compared to free market economies. Free markets are simply the best way yet discovered to lift everyone out of poverty and promote the common good.

Proposal 24—Money

Paper money has had the effect in your state that it will ever have, to ruin commerce, oppress the honest, and open the door to every species of fraud and injustice.
—George Washington, (letter to *J. Bowen 1787)*

A common historical pattern is that great empires fall because their money is corrupted. The US has been following the corruption script closely, abusing debt and the dollar to create inflation. Inflation is the great hidden tax, a massive and covert theft of resources from the people. Inflation is a destroyer of nations and civilizations.

Whenever the government has control of money—which historically, is almost always—then abuses will arise. The financial incentives are so strong that governments *always* abuse money eventually. Similar incentives also drive banks to manipulate the system for profit.

The proposals here aim to limit the worst abuses and address the incentives at play to lower the chances of future abuse.

Proposed Amendment: Money

1. Government shall have a duty of care to promote free markets and competition between currencies and currency equivalents.

2. Government may not own, operate, or control any banks.

3. No government or government-sponsored organization may increase the money supply.

4. Any currency issued by the US federal government shall be redeemable for gold upon demand.

5. State governments may issue currencies but shall have a duty of care that said currencies are backed by real assets and shall be redeemable for those assets upon demand.

6. Private entities may create and issue currencies. Said currencies shall not be regulated by any government except for requirements for auditing and transparency of operations.

7. Governments may not delegate their currency issuance to any private entity.

8. Citizens shall have the right to hold their money in any currency, crypto-currency, or currency equivalents such as precious metals.

9. Citizens may not be required to report or declare currency holdings, currency conversions, or movements of currency, unless by court order where there is probable cause of a felony.

10. Conversions between currencies, digital currencies, and currency equivalents shall not be taxable events.

11. Government may not create legal tender laws or otherwise place legal restrictions on citizens using any currency to trade or settle contracts.

12. Government may not fix exchange rates between currencies or current equivalents. All currency conversions shall be determined by market values on the relevant dates.

13. Fractional reserve banking shall be illegal.

14. *Transition.* Upon the passing of this amendment:
    a. There shall be public audits of the Federal Reserve Bank, all federal gold holdings, and total US dollars in circulation.
    b. All gold held by the Federal Reserve Bank shall be transferred to the control of the US Treasury.
    c. The US treasury shall take over responsibility for currency issuance and redemption for gold.
    d. All remaining functions of the Federal Reserve Bank shall be fully privatized, transferred to the US treasury, or halted.
    e. The above transition operations shall be completed within one year.
    f. All banking institutions operating on fractional reserves shall be required to increase their reserves to 100% within 10 years.

The US Dollar

Money, and the corruption of money, is one of the most complex topics addressed here, and one of the most manipulated. Politicians, bureaucrats, bankers, lenders, and spenders are all trying to manipulate the system to their advantage. It's easy to hide the manipulation with statistics and pretty graphs.

The abuse of money is one of the few places where, arguably, manipulation rises to the level of conspiracy. Big banks, though their proxy the Federal Reserve, are profiting in every way possible from the system.

The history of monetary manipulation is beyond the scope of this book. For an overview, I recommend *Dishonest Money*,[1] by Joseph Plumber as a starting point. For a deep dive into the function and meaning of money, start with the *What is Money*[2] podcast by Robert Breedlove.

The focus here will be on describing solutions. The aim of the proposal here (backed up by other proposals, especially *Proposal 25—Government Debt,* and *Proposal 26—Loans and Subsidies)* is to return the US to a sound money system by removing manipulation of the dollar.

Money and Morality

We need sound money. Debt, distorted interest rates, and inflation are undermining our economy and our country. We'll get into the specifics below. But let's start with the big picture.

We need to fix money because monetary policy directly affects public morality. Manipulation of money turns the economy into a network of distortions and lies. Everything in the economy is measured in prices. If you don't know what true prices are, because of distorted interest rates and inflation, then in a fundamental sense you cannot know what is true about anything in the economy. You cannot measure the value of anything because your unit of value—the dollar—keeps changing.

If you cannot trust money, what can you trust? *Chapter 2— Unsustainable Trends,* gave some statistics on the decline in citizens' trust in the government and each other over the last 50 years. Money, and the undermining of the value of money, is an integral part of that decline in trust.

Most of the trends described in this book go back over 150 years. But almost every one of them took a sharp turn for the worse around 1971 when the US came off the gold standard.[3] It's unlikely this is a coincidence.

There's another sense in which manipulation undermines public morals. One of the key insights of economics is that people respond to incentives. Bluntly: people tend to do what is most profitable.

If manipulation of the legal system is more profitable than honest competition in the marketplace, that incentivizes manipulation. If corruption is more profitable than honesty, that incentivizes corruption.

The direct manipulation of money is the most straightforward route to profits for manipulators. Banks profit from lending money and collecting interest. Banks are incentivized to lend as much money as possible whilst simultaneously lowering their risks through manipulation.

So, for example, fractional reserve banking (banks lending money they don't have) is legal. Deposit and mortgage insurance supposedly protect customers but in actuality protect banks. And the bankruptcy system has been rigged so that student loans cannot be discharged like normal loans.

Rather than prevent manipulation, governments (especially the feds) have colluded with the banks. Politicians and administrators alike are incentivized to spend and accumulate debt rather than maintain the integrity of the system. To fix this, there needs to be a change in the incentives working on both banks and on political actors.

Inflation

Inflation takes different forms and can be measured in various ways. For our purposes here though, the focus will be on monetary inflation— increases in the amount of money in the economy. Monetary inflation occurs through government printing of money and fractional reserve banking.

Inflation is perhaps the worst consequence of monetary manipulation. Inflation undermines the entire economy and the measurement of economic value in dollars. It is a hidden tax—a regressive tax that most affects the poor and those on fixed incomes such as Social Security.

In a normal, unmanipulated economy, there should be steady deflation. In other words, money should be steadily increasing in value. To explain this requires making a distinction between "value" and "price." Typically, the value of something is described by giving its price, stated in dollars or another currency. Nonetheless, value and price are different, and since both can change independently, measuring one in terms of the other is confusing.

To clarify this, let's invent a hypothetical Value Unit ($\tilde{V}$), which can be used to value the economy independently of dollars.

Now, suppose $100 trillion could buy all the stuff in the world, which we'll also value, as a starting point, at $\tilde{V}$100T. In other words, $1=$\tilde{V}$1. Stuff here means anything of economic value—anything that people are willing to pay for— be they goods or services.

Now, suppose a year goes by and the economy grows 10%—there is 10% more stuff and services. The total economic value is now $\tilde{V}$110T. Assuming the same number of dollars in the world, how much is a dollar worth now?

$$\$1 = \tilde{V}110T/\$100T = \tilde{V}1.1$$

In plain English, the value of a dollar has increased by 10%. More stuff, the same amount of dollars, therefore each dollar buys more stuff. Stuff costs less in dollars. This is deflation, and it is a good thing. It means your savings account, and your children's education accounts, buy more today than they did a year ago.

Deflation can be thought of as a byproduct of increasing productivity. Innovation, spread by free trade, makes us collectively more efficient. We can do more with less—less energy, less materials, and less money. This happens over and over. To take a recent example, the price of Li-Ion batteries has gone down 97% in the last 30 years.[4]

Now let's consider another scenario. Let's start at the same point ($1=$\tilde{V}$1), but this time there's no economic growth and the government prints $10T. What is a dollar worth now?

$$\$1 = \tilde{V}100T/\$110T = \tilde{V}0.91$$

Put simply, the value of a dollar has decreased by 9%. The same amount of stuff, more dollars, therefore each dollar buys less stuff. Stuff costs more in dollars. This is inflation. Inflation is marketed as positive. In reality, inflation is economically and morally damaging. Your savings, and your children's college funds, are worth less today than they were a year ago. Your money (technically, the value of your money) is being stolen from you.

If the value of a dollar goes down, where does the value go? In simple terms: the government is printing money that did not previously exist and spending it. Same amount of stuff, more dollars, therefore stuff costs more in dollars. But government (and banks) get to spend the new dollars first before prices start to rise.

In real life, the amounts of stuff and dollars are both fluctuating. Economic progress makes us richer over time (more stuff) but can ebb and flow and occasionally contract. Money supply can (in theory) decrease, but in practice never does. The headline inflation rate is a combination of:

- Economic growth, causing deflation.
- Increases in money supply, causing inflation.
- Manipulation of the figures hiding inflation.

Despite the complexities, the most important thing to keep in mind is that inflation is caused by increases in the amount of money. As the economist Milton Freedman put it: *inflation is always and forever a monetary phenomenon.* When the government controls the money, it is the government itself that is causing inflation.

Special interests will dispute this or confuse the issue and, to be fair, I'm describing the wood and not the trees. But the underlying truth remains: Inflation is always caused by an increase in the money supply.

Now, the money supply can increase independently of government action, depending on how money is organized. When money was measured in gold, for example, you could go out and mine gold and thus create more money. In the modern economy though, the amount of non-government caused inflation is negligible.

Until 1971 the US was (with wartime exceptions) on the Gold Standard. You could in theory take your dollars to the government and exchange them for gold. Nixon took us off the gold standard in 1971. Official cumulative inflation since then has been about 700%, so $1 in 1971 would be worth about 14 c today. If you measure inflation in terms of gold, gold's market price was about $45/ounce in 1971 and is about $1,950 in Jan 2023. That's an inflation of 4300%. Using this measure, one dollar in 1971 would be worth about 2.5 cents today.

All these figures are approximate because inflation is difficult to measure. The actual rate since 1971 is somewhere between these two measures of 700% and 4300% (though probably closer to the high end of that range). Even the official rates are lies because the feds keep messing with the calculators to keep apparent inflation down.[5] Even if you think your savings or Social Security are index-linked and supposedly safe from inflation, you are still steadily getting poorer.

Every penny you save for a rainy day, every dollar put into your pension or your children's education account is worth less when you come to spend it. No matter how you measure it, inflation since the US came off the gold standard has been rampant—and that's not a coincidence!

When questioned about inflation, a favored political ploy is to blame it on current events, such as war affecting the oil supply. This is to deliberately confuse monetary inflation (total money supply) and price fluctuations (of individual goods and services) due to supply and demand.

The confusion is so rampant that almost everyone uses the word "inflation" to describe "price increases." Things would be clearer if we all got in the habit of calling them "monetary inflation" and "price inflation" to distinguish them apart. This won't happen anytime soon because the government profits from blurring the distinction.

Even the government's official inflation figures are calculated by measuring the prices of a basket of commonly used goods. Price inflation is thus being used to measure monetary inflation when they are two different things. Any individual commodity—gasoline, housing, food, or whatever—will fluctuate in price. But individual price fluctuations are not general inflation, even though the same word is used for both.

If the money supply were fixed, then if something goes up in price due to supply or demand, something else must go down in price. However, it's not possible to predict what will go up or down due to the complexity of the marketplace (with a few exceptions, such as beachfront property where limited supply keeps prices rising).

Inflation is a hidden tax caused overwhelmingly by government money printing. It is also a major contributor to economic inequality, making the rich richer and the poor poorer. Suppose a poor person is working for a minimum wage. With inflation, each year their wages buy less. With deflation, even if nothing else changes, their wages buy more each year. Inflation concentrates wealth with the wealthy, deflation spreads wealth to everyone.

Restoring Sound Money

There's no single way to end monetary manipulation and with it end inflation. If there were, special interests would quickly subvert it. Fixing manipulation needs multiple actions, and multiple checks and balances.

Government's Role in Money

The government's role in the economy should be to protect free markets as part of protecting individual rights of freedom of contract and free trade. As that specifically relates to money, the proposals here:

- Give governments a duty of care to encourage a free market in currencies.

- Explicitly ban the feds from inflating the money supply.

- Allow the feds, states, or private entities to issue currencies as they see fit, but only allow governments to issue currencies that are backed by hard assets (such as gold).

- Remove all legal tender laws so that citizens can do business in any currency.

- Ban price fixing of currency exchange rates by government.

Separation of Bank and State

Whenever a government creates a central bank, the incentives are for them to accumulate power at the expense of other banks. The incentives are especially twisted in the US because the Federal Reserve is a weird private-public hybrid entity.

This legal ambiguity should not be allowed, so the provisions here will disallow government from creating, owning, or managing banks. We'll also disallow the government from delegating its money-issuing powers to private entities. Together these should effectively end the FR and prevent future versions from reoccurring.

Note also that the provisions in *Proposal 12—Legislation* will apply to banks—government will only be allowed to regulate large organizations. Small banks will be unregulated. It will be up to those small banks to convince customers they are trustworthy. It will be the free choice of citizens if they wish to be customers or not.

Citizen Rights to Do Business in Any Currency

US citizens already have the right to freedom of contact and the right to freedom of trade. Since those rights have been soundly abused by our governments, those rights are clarified and strengthened here to:

- Explicitly state that citizens have a right to hold currencies in any form—no future gold confiscations.

- Remove all taxes on currency conversions so citizens can switch currencies at will and without penalty.

- Remove all reporting requirements on currency holdings. Your money should stay private.

These rights, combined with bans on legal tender laws and price fixing by government, should mean that any manipulation of the US dollar by government would probably result in a wholesale switching by citizens to other currencies. It will also fully legalize competing currencies issued by state governments, foreign currencies, and cryptocurrencies.

May the best currencies win. I hope the US dollar is one of the winners, but the government will have to persuade us to use the dollar rather than force us. It will be up to citizens to choose whichever options they prefer. Citizens themselves will be part of the checks and balances against currency manipulation.

Making Bank Fraud Illegal

It is fraud when banks lend money they don't have, and it always has been. Fractional reserve banking is a cancer at the heart of our monetary system, and it's time to cut it out. The proposal makes it illegal.

Banning fractional reserve banking will remove most of the systemic risk from the banking system. Bank runs are not possible if banks have reserves on hand to pay all customers back the money they are contracted to pay.

Increasing Risk

Some risks should increase to correctly align incentives. Specifically, borrowing should be riskier. The proposal bans all government-sponsored or required insurance, such as deposit insurance issued though the FDIC.

Borrowing money is risky, lending money is risky. Risks should be clearly seen, discussed, and managed between the parties involved. If borrowers want to insure themselves, or if lenders want to require insurance, that's fine. But the government should have no part in lending or manipulating the lending market.

This is addressed further in *Proposal 26—Loans and Subsidies.*

Other Forms of Government Inflation

This chapter specifically addresses monetary inflation—the inflation of the money supply by government and crony banks. Note though that all government actions that impose costs on citizens are forms of inflation. Regulation, compliance, and reporting requirements all raise costs.

Proposal 25—Government Debt

We must not let our rulers load us with perpetual debt.
—Thomas Jefferson

America is swimming in a sea of debt, and we are in danger of drowning. The feds, with no legal restrictions to stop them, keep borrowing. Most states do have restrictions but have found ways around them by taking on unfunded obligations—monies they promise to pay in the future even though they have no funds to pay them. This is just debt by another name. The debts keep climbing with no end in sight. The federal General Accountability Office calls it "unsustainable."[1] This is deeply worrying for citizens, with polls showing over half the country thinking federal debt is a big problem.[2]

Despite declarations of concern, in practice politicians keep borrowing. They have no incentive to reverse direction, and money lenders have every incentive to manipulate politicians to keep at it. Our representatives need to be forced to be sensible before it's too late.

Proposed Amendment: Government Debt

1. Government has a duty of care to prudently manage its finances.

2. Governments may not accrue debt except for bonds with a term of at least 5 years, intended to fund specific projects. At least 2/3 of voters within that government's jurisdiction must approve the borrowing.

3. Repayment of principal and interest on bonds must come from current tax revenue. Government may not increase tax rates, introduce new taxes, or raise levies to pay off debt.

4. All future payments or promises to pay must be accounted for in current budgets. Government may not take on unfunded future obligations.

5. All debts and obligations of government-owned, subsidized, or sponsored organizations shall be included in any accounting of government debt.

6. Government budgets for a fiscal period may not exceed tax receipts from the previous period.

7. In any fiscal year in which a government has a surplus of tax receipts over the budget, the surplus shall be set aside in a savings account. Funds in this account may be spent on capital investment or for emergency spending. Spending from this account must be approved by a 2/3 majority of legislators.

8. If any legislature is unable to agree on where budget cuts should take place by their usual budget deadlines, then all spending cate-

gories controlled by that legislature shall have their budgets cut pro-rata, including all mandatory or entitlement spending.

9. *Transition*: upon the passing of this amendment:
   a. Every government shall make an accounting of all debts they currently owe. This debt shall be known as the Existing Debt.
   b. All governments shall pay off their Existing Debt, at a rate of at least 1% per annum. It shall be allowable to refinance Existing Debt, so long as the repayment schedule is kept.

Debt, Debt, And Yet More Debt

Official government debt was about $90 billion in 1900. As of March 2023, it was about $31.6 trillion. Expressed as debt per citizen, those figures are $1,185 in 1900, $94.560 in 2023. It's been growing on a steady exponential curve since 1900. It will exceed $120,000 by 2050 and be around $500,000 by 2100. (All those figures in inflation adjusted 2012 dollars).

Unofficially, our governments also owe:

- Agency debt (Fannie Mae, Freddie Mac, and others), about $7.4 trillion.

- Unfunded state liabilities (mostly pensions), about $3 trillion[3].

- Unfunded federal liabilities like Medicare and Social Security. Sums owed are unknowable but may be up to $127 trillion.[4]

The total comes to about $157 trillion owed by US governments. That's about $495,000 /citizen. Much of it is Social Security debt which needs to be paid off by taxpayers. Assuming about 121 million taxpayers, that's about $1.3 million/taxpayer today.

All these figures are estimates—no one has exact figures—but even halving these estimates would still leave us owing $250,000/citizen, or $650,000/taxpayer. Realistically though, it's likely these figures are underestimates, especially after the Covid disaster.

Do you have your share of that debt ready to pay back? Are your children ready to step up and pay their share? What if the debt is even bigger than the estimates?

You might also ask: why are these numbers not included in official debt figures? Whatever those silver-tongued devils in Congress say, the basic answer is fraud. If the government owes money, or is liable for payments, then that money is government debt. If a big corporation tried to hide debt on that scale, federal prosecutors would be hovering around them like vultures circling a dying cow.

How has the government managed to get away with this? In short, the government prints money, or creates digital credits which amount to the same thing. The government then lends that money to itself in complex ways via the fractional reserve systems (see *Proposal 24—Money.)*

It's easy to find experts who will argue that government debt is not a problem[5]. The economy will grow to cover the debt. Or a recent dip in government spending is the start of a new trend. Or since predictions of collapse have not happened yet, they will never happen.

Yet, no matter how expert the experts are, predictions are impossible. Spending projections are guesses, compounded by guesses about future economic growth, inflation, and expenditure. The more assumptions made, the more likely one or more of them is wrong.

My estimate of future spending which produced the numbers above (see *Chapter 2—Unsustainable Trends),* is also a guess, but it is at least a math-based guess. I am not an economist. I have no theories about growth, taxation, inflation, spending rates, or any of that. All I'm doing is basic spreadsheet math on a trend that's been in place for at least 120 years. My estimates are no more than a projection of the trend. And the trend is clear, even if the specific numbers are wrong. I hope my projections prove to be pessimistic. But I see little evidence that anything fundamental has changed that will affect the trend.

Another popular delusion about government debt is that it will never be a problem because the US government would never default. The US is a great country, but it is not immune from economic forces, or default.

Here's a partial list of government defaults[6] in the last 20 year (in Billions) Russia, 1998, $72.7B; Ukraine, 1998, $1.27B; Ecuador, 1999, $6.6B; Ukraine, 2000, $1.06B; Peru, 2000, $4.87B; Argentina, 2001, $82.26B; Uruguay, 2003, $5.7B; Dominican Republic, 2005, $1.62B; Ecuador, 2008, $3.2B; Venezuela, 2017, $65B; Lebanon, 2020, $1.2B.

Coming close to default in the last dozen years: Iceland, Hungary, Latvia, Russia (again), Ukraine (again), Argentina (again), and Greece.

The US has a big economy, which gives us leeway. The US also has enjoyed owning the world's reserve currency since WWII. Still, debts must eventually be repaid. Despite an overall excellent record, the US has technically defaulted a few times in its history, most recently in 1979[7]. And once again, in 2023, there was talk of default as Congress and Biden argued over the debt ceiling.[8]

If the US were unable to pay its debts, the economic consequences could be severe: inflation, hyper-inflation? Major devaluation of the dollar? Economic collapse? This has happened before: the great depression, hyperinflation in Germany (1920s), Zimbabwe (2000's), Venezuela (currently). The US is not immune from economic forces. And if the US went down in a major way most of the world would go down with it.

The states have a role here as well. What would happen if a big state defaulted on their debt? Remember the fuss back in 2016 when Puerto

Rico defaulted on its $70+ billion debt?[9] In 2018 California's debt was $495 billion, New York's $355 billion, Texas's $293 billion.[10] Default by a major state could have serious knock-on effects on the US economy, and with it the status of the dollar as the world's reserve currency.

Government Debt Is Different from Personal Debt

Government debt is debt. It needs to be repaid. If it is not repaid, then there will be unpleasant consequences. Given the size of the US debt, those consequences are likely to be extreme.

If you or I borrow money: we know we must pay it back *or else*. We are incentivized to be careful about how much is borrowed, and how we plan to repay it.

When governments borrow money though, *the politicians responsible for the borrowing are not personally responsible for paying it back*. They have little incentive to be careful about spending or repayment. They talk as if they worry, but in practice they always borrow more, leaving taxpayers (including your children) on the hook for repayment.

Debt is How Government Grows

Government has grown out of all proportion to the economy in the last century. The motivation for this—the why—has been special interest manipulation. The fuel for the growth—the how—has been debt. If a government has no money, then it has limited ways to get bigger.

Government should have a budget and should keep within that budget, the same as any citizen or corporation. Budgets force choices about the best use of resources and are a prudent financial and economic discipline, part of the system of checks and balances.

When governments instead keep borrowing, that fiscal discipline is removed. The result is the mountains of debt accumulated by US governments, and the risks of financial collapse, hyper-inflation, and chaos.

The growth of debt has occurred over decades—outside of crises like 2008 or Covid, you'd hardly notice it on a year-by-year basis. However, looking at long-term data, it's clear that something is out of whack. Over the last 50 years, the long-term inflation rate has averaged about 4.1% p.a.[11] In the same period, government spending om defense items (a republican favorite) has been growing at about 4.5% p.a. and on social items (a democratic favorite) at about 10% p.a.[12] Over 50 years, even small deviations from inflation compound. This is how we've accumulated such huge government spending and debts.

Earlier I offered the classic definition of economics as *the study of the use of scarce resources that have alternative uses*. The trend for government (especially the feds) is that anytime it runs out of money it borrows more. This is a moral hazard, because if government can easily borrow its way out of problems, resources are no longer "scarce."

Lowered scarcity means lowered incentives to be economical, less reason to consider if resources are being well spent. The result is ballooning government programs, over-budget projects, overpaid employees, over-generous pensions, and politicians ever incentivized to spend more.

While scarce resources are being spent on government programs, those same resources cannot be spent on alternative uses; uses which may be more productive. Money lenders are willing to lend to the government, often at low interest, because their money is "safe." In the long run though, it is neither safe nor well spent.

Another side effect of government debt is that it introduces a moral hazard with respect to inflation. Citizens would rather have low or no inflation, and stated public policy is to keep inflation low—the Federal Reserve has a goal to keep inflation at 2% or less.[13] But the feds owe trillions of dollars, and thus profit from inflation. Therefore, government is a moral hazard: claiming low inflation as a goal, profiting from high inflation. The hazard is extended when government encourages citizens to borrow, creating conflict between debtors and creditors. Debt fuels moral hazards. Public policy should not encourage debt.

Time to Reverse Direction: Start Paying Off Debt

Our politicians have failed to address the debt issue. Decades of evidence show that they never will. They are incentivized to keep borrowing and spending in their efforts to get reelected.

In 2019 the Republicans, the party of fiscal responsibility, passed a budget projected to increase debt by $1/trillion per year.[14] Coronavirus spending in 2020 ballooned the debt hugely again.[15] Whatever the economic arguments in favor of stimulus spending during a crisis, those debts are rarely repaid. Instead, they get rolled over.

If we citizens want fiscal responsibility, we must force it on our representatives. The proposals here will require:

- An exact accounting of *all* debt. No hiding it in obscure accounting rules, unfunded liabilities, or quasi-government entities.

- Debt repayment over the next 100 years. It's taken about 100 years to get in the current mess, and it will take time to reverse it. Let's at least start moving in the right direction.

- Balanced budgets from now on.

- Constraints on future borrowing. Future debt will need to be voter approved and paid for out of current income (no raising taxes to pay down debt).

- Budget surpluses must be saved and can only be spent on capital projects or crisis spending, approved by a super-majority of the legislature. Imagine if the feds had used savings to pay for Coronavirus stimulus checks, rather than having to borrow more.

Details will need to be worked out with the above. Nonetheless, the principles are clear, and would apply to your personal finances or to any corporate budget. It is common sense to have accurate accounts, to balance the books, pay down debt, and have a savings account for emergencies. Since defying common sense has no consequence on politicians, we instead need rules to enforce prudence.

Putting rules in place is one thing, but there's still no guarantee that politicians will follow them. Ideally, politicians who overspend should get fired, but it's difficult to find a simple way to do that. When or if I do, I'll add it to the proposals.

That said, the major motivator for politicians is getting reelected. Thus, term limits are one of the most important changes that could be made overall. See *Proposal 35—Term Limits.*

Another aim of the proposals here is to supply a default course of action for when politicians cannot agree. Experience shows that politicians rarely agree on cuts! Instead, they fight, posture, pass temporary budgets, and end up temporarily increasing borrowing, which somehow then becomes permanent borrowing.

The proposal short circuits this nonsense: If politicians can't agree, everything is cut pro-rata. If the budget requires a 2% cut, for example, and Congress can't agree on specifics, then every spending category takes a 2% cut. Individual departments who spend the money can take it from there.

How Will the Government Repay Its Debts?

No one knows how our governments can repay their debts, which is part of what makes it so frightening. The important thing right now is to change direction. The debt ceiling needs to be lowered, not raised.

It's taken a long time to accumulate the debt, so it makes sense to take a long time paying to down. At a rate of 1% a year the governments have 100 years to pay off their debts. But repayment must be the rule. Governments need to be forced, finally, to face the issue.

For any normal person, family, or organization, if you keep borrowing there comes a point where the bank says, "no more." What do you do then? You sit down, think about it, talk about it. You tighten your belt, find areas to economize, perhaps do without.

This is a healthy process of checks and balances for individuals, families, and organizations. But our governments have managed to evade this process, with horrible results. This proposal will ensure that government is subject to the same pressures as the rest of us. They should have a budget and keep to it, like everyone else.

The future is not predictable. Still, if we can curb government interference, then future economic growth should be similar to past growth. Paying off the debt over 100 years should be easily covered by economic expansion.

Debt reduction will cause disruption while governments choose where to make cuts. However, they will have time to prepare since it will take years to get a law or Constitutional amendment passed. Short-term belt tightening is preferable to a long-term financial crash.

Future Borrowing

The only borrowing allowed in future will be bonds with a minimum 5-year term and where 2/3 of voters authorize it. Repayments for that debt must be out of current tax revenue. No raising taxes to pay off debt!

Those are severe restrictions, and only the most important projects will get approved. If the feds wanted to borrow money, they would need permission from citizens via a nationwide referendum. That would be a big undertaking and won't happen easily. Only issues of national importance will be able to jump such a big barrier and get citizens' support. The feds will be forced to sort out their priorities and focus on those.

Note that, while debt is paid down, refinancing of existing debt will still be allowed. Refinancing to lower interest rates, where possible, is prudent debt management.

Short-Term Borrowing

Businesses and individuals often use overdraft facilities to manage their financial affairs and short-term cash flow. But when government does the same there's a moral hazard.

The problem is this: what would be the consequences if a government abused an overdraft? What would happen if a government did not pay back its short-term borrowing by the end of the fiscal year? What if a legislature voted to temporarily change the fiscal year end?

It's difficult to see how to enforce consequences if governments abuse short-term borrowing. Since governments always face moral hazards when borrowing money, they should be held to a high financial standard. The standard is this: no short-term borrowing. There will be a 5-year minimum term for any borrowing.

Where governments have seasonal expenditures and cash flow fluctuations, they should learn to deal with them like any other business or individual. They should budget accordingly so that they have funds on hand *before* that time of the year comes around.

Proposal 26—Loans and Subsidies

Government does not solve problems; it subsidizes them.
—Ronald Reagan

Government subsidies, loans and loan guarantees are hugely profitable for special interests who benefit from them. For the rest of us, they are expensive promotions of inequality and government complexity.

Any government interference in money lending is a moral hazard and should go. Government should never favor one citizen over another by subsidizing them or lending them money.

Proposed Amendment: Loans and Subsides

1. Government funds are intended for services that government offers to all citizens.

2. Government may not subsidize, grant, or give money to any specific group, industry, organization, or individual except as allowed for in the Constitution.

3. Government may not offer tax breaks, exceptions, or exemptions to any specific group, industry, organization, or individual.

4. Government may not loan money, subsidize loans, insure loans, or guarantee loans, nor sponsor organizations that do the same.

5. Government may not require private citizens and organizations to buy loan insurance.

6. Government may not buy holdings in existing corporations, nor require private third parties to do so.

7. *Transition:* Upon the passing of this amendment:
   a. Subsidies, tax breaks, and direct payments will end.
   b. Secured loans shall be honored in the terms existing.
   c. Unsecured loans shall be honored in the terms existing, except that they shall have a maximum life of ten years.
   d. Loan guarantees shall be honored in the terms existing, except that such guarantees shall expire after ten years.
   e. Government sponsored organizations issuing grants, loans, insuring, or guaranteeing loans shall be closed or privatized within two years.

Could You Lend Me A Dollar?

Governments are encouraging citizens to accumulate debt. They lend money directly. They manipulate borrowing and lending between private citizens via regulation, loan guarantees, insurance, and loan subsidies. They offer grants and tax breaks.

The government has constitutional authority *to coin Money, regulate the Value thereof, and of foreign Coin,* but there's no mention of lending money. Government lending fails the Test of Constitutional Authority.

Applying the test of Moral Authority: do I have the right to force my neighbor to subsidize a loan, guarantee a loan, or have him pay it off if something goes wrong? Can I offer special tax breaks to some and have my neighbor cover the shortfall in revenue? No, I do not have any of those rights. By extension, neither does the government. The government has no moral authority to be in the money lending business. Period!

Government lending also fails the Test of Purpose. You cannot have equal protection of individual rights when government takes money from some to lend to others. I am less free due to this action.

Despite failing most Tests of Legitimate Governance, our governments continue to meddle with money lending. This interference creates a cess-pool of moral hazard, cronyism, manipulation, and negative side effects such as boom-bust economic cycles.[1]

Flaws in government insurance of loans via the Federal Savings and Loan Insurance Corporation (FSLIC) was the main cause of the Savings and Loans crisis of the 1980s. The fallout is ongoing, nearly 40 years later, and may cost taxpayers in excess of $160 billion.[2] Encouraging homeownership for borrowers with poor credit was also a cause of the 2008 subprime mortgage crash.

Borrowing and lending money is risky. When the government makes borrowing easy, it hides risk and in so doing creates bigger systemic risks. People are incentivized to ignore risk. Debt makes individuals financially fragile[3] and makes the financial system unstable.

Fanny and Freddy

Congress has created several Government Sponsored Enterprises (GSEs) in the lending business. Among the best-known are Fannie Mae (created in 1938) and Freddie Mac (1968).

The stated idea was to increase homeownership by encouraging banks to lend to buyers. Fannie and Freddie buy mortgages from banks, lowering the risk to the banks, but also introducing moral hazards.

Firstly, it's not clear that GSEs are needed. If a GSE supplies a service customers want, then private businesses would be working to meet the demand. On the other hand, if the government has set up a GSE without market demand (citizens are not asking for it) then why is it needed at all, if not because of manipulation?

If a GSE enters the field as a new competitor, then GSEs tend to distort the market. GSEs have potential access to government money and legal advantages through regulation. And if anything goes wrong, taxpayers are liable. In 2008, that's what happened with Fanny and Freddy.[4]

Fannie and Freddy were set up to further the long-standing US policy of encouraging home ownership. But why should the US encourage home ownership? Individuals who want to own a house have every right to buy one as part of their *pursuit of happiness.* But why should the government sponsor them? Public policy should be neutral about where and how people live their lives, including their housing choices.

Public policy certainly shouldn't encourage people to buy things they can't afford. By offering close to 100% loans at low interest, and with little financial scrutiny, the government encouraged marginal buyers to buy houses. It may be a noble goal to help the poor buy houses, but it cannot be the government's goal. Government's job is to ensure *legal* equality, not to solve economic problems.

Indeed, is helping the poor to buy houses even a noble goal? Some argue that encouraging home ownership promotes the common good. But what evidence is there that home ownership makes for a stable country or a stronger economy?

In the US about 65% of us are homeowners.[5] Both Singapore and Cuba have ownership rates of about 90%, yet Singapore is wealthy, and Cuba is poor.[6] Germany and Switzerland, rich countries, have ownership rates of around 45-50%. In short, it's hard to see a direct link between ownership rates and overall economic success, or the stability of a country. The only real economic success story here is bank profits.

Perversely, encouraging home ownership often hurts the poor. If a poor person loses their job, their best choice may well be to move to find new work. If they own a house, moving is expensive. Selling a house typically costs 10% of the value,[7] and takes months. Renters might lose a month's rent or a security deposit but otherwise can move on quickly.

The moral hazards of government interfering with borrowing and spending are too great to allow the system to continue. So, let's end all government loans, grants, subsidies, loan insurance, and loan guarantees. If citizens want the services that the government is offering, then the market will find a way to meet that demand.

That said, it's not wise to shut down all government activity overnight. There exist millions of sponsored/guaranteed/insured loans, each of them an agreement between lenders, borrowers, and the government. These contacts should be honored.

Nonetheless there should be a stop to issuing new loans. Every agency or GSE involved in lending, loan guarantees, or loan support should be either closed or privatized within two years: Fannie and Freddie, the US Export-Import Bank, the Small Business Administration, the Farm Service Agency, the Fisheries Finance Program; VA Loans, Rural Housing Loans, Property Improvement Loans, Indian Loans and so on.

All government-related lenders should close or become private. No bailouts in the future if they get it wrong. Government should not be in the money lending business at all.

Student Loans

Government has encouraged student loans, and simultaneously restricted the supply of education (via accreditation) for decades. Add in a bunch of regulation,[8] and the result is rampant inflation in education costs,[9] high student debt, and the potential for a crash in the student loan market. Banks and universities are profiting mightily, but large-scale societal debt makes the country economically fragile and increases political anger.

Loan subsidies also add moral hazard to education choices.[10] In a normal market, lenders are incentivized to assess if borrowers are likely to repay their loans. Student loans should be easier to get for subjects with high employment prospects, and more expensive for subjects with low employment prospects.

When the government instead makes student loans easy and insures lenders against default by manipulating bankruptcy laws, it distorts incentives. Both students and lenders now have less incentive to ask if lending and borrowing is a good deal for both sides.

Individual students should be able to study anything they want to. But they should also question the value of what they plan to study. Correct pricing of student loans incentivizes them to ask questions about the benefits of study, or even if college is the right path.[11]

What needs to be done is to stop political meddling. Politicians won't stop meddling unless forced to, which the proposal here will do. Public policy should not encourage debt.

Subsidies etc.

The feds, states, cities, and counties are all offering subsidies, tax breaks, and grants. The feds are subsidizing farms, the oil industry, ethanol, exports, housing, and healthcare.[12] The States are competing to attract businesses through corporate tax breaks and subsidies.[13] And at the local level property tax breaks are common.[14]

The sums involved are small compared to welfare or defense, but the benefits are dubious at best. Some of the biggest recipients of subsidies are Boeing, Intel, Alcoa, General Motors, Ford, Chrysler, Shell, Nike, Goldman Sachs, and JP Morgan Chase. Do these businesses need government support? Does the government need to subsidize agriculture when there's an obesity epidemic in the US? Does the government need to subsidize oil companies when the US is close to oil independence due to fracking? Why is the government subsidizing turning corn into ethanol, making food expensive with no discernable effect on the US's energy needs?

No matter how justified a subsidy, tax break, cheap loan, or grant may appear, they all give legal and financial advantages to some citizens at the expense of the rest of us. They create legal inequality.

Subsidies involve manipulation of the economy for debatable social benefit, with scant evidence of success, and hidden side effects and downsides. Subsides are a moral hazard, open to manipulation. They should go.

You may personally support a particular subsidy. You may feel it benefits society, or perhaps you benefit personally. But the only fair way to end subsidies is to end all of them simultaneously. Let's be done with government manipulation of the economy.

Bailouts

As discussed in *Chapter 2—Unsustainable Trends*, Congress has spent billions of taxpayer dollars on bailouts, starting in modern times with the Penn Central Railroad in 1970, through the Savings and Loan Crisis of the 80s, the sub-prime loan crash of 2008, and now Coronavirus.

Without repeating the arguments made earlier, bailouts fueled by debt should end, especially corporate bailouts. If a stimulus to the economy is justified, it needs to be done in alignment with the government's primary role of protecting individual rights. The way to do this is to give all individual real citizens a check for the same amount. No bailouts for corporations, ever, under any circumstances.

Individual real citizen payouts would be the only form of welfare the federal government could engage in under *Proposal 23—Welfare*. Funds for those bailouts would need to be taken out of other government budget items, or perhaps from savings, if any, that might accumulate under the provisions of *Proposal 25—Government Debt*.

Encouraging Conflict

All government subsidies, loans, loan guarantees, grants, tax breaks, and a myriad of variants under other names, should be disallowed. Government attempts at social engineering, often in the name of promoting equality, result in legal inequality, and encourage conflict between citizens.

For example, take education loans again. Manipulation of the student loan market has generated huge profits for universities and banks. As a parent or student, is it unreasonable to ask why tuition costs have been rising at twice the rate of inflation?[15] Or why some colleges are non-profits sitting on massive endowment funds,[16] whilst other colleges flirt with bankruptcy?[17]

As a taxpayer, is unreasonable to ask why student loan providers (big banks) need taxpayer subsidies or special bankruptcy protection?

As a former student who worked hard to pay off your loans, is it unreasonable to ask why others should have their loans forgiven? Student loan forgiveness makes a mockery of those who played by the rules.[18] It encourages future generations to deliberately default on their obligations and complain about it in hopes of a government reprieve. Student loan forgiveness is, in short, immoral.

Other loans and subsidies incentivize similar conflicts between citizens. Why did banks get bailed out in 2008, and not mortgage holders? Why do some companies and industries get subsidies and not others? Why subsidize green energy—surely if it offered genuine value customers would willingly pay for it.

Regardless of which side you take in these debates, government policy is creating conflict. Government should not be lending money, nor should they be subsidizing any corporation, industry, or technology.

Government should not be deciding what are worthy goals for society. It is for each of us individually to decide on our own goals and ambitions in the pursuit of happiness.

Proposal 27—Monopoly

*Manufacturing and commercial monopolies owe their origin not to
a tendency imminent in a capitalist economy but to governmental
interventionist policy directed against free trade and laissez faire.*
—Ludwig von Mises

Everyone agrees that monopolies can be harmful. The US has antitrust
laws to keep monopolies in check and prevent abuse, but those laws have
been hijacked to become anticompetition laws. Antitrust laws need to be
rebalanced to protect customers rather than special interests.

There's also one monopoly that rarely gets attention: government.
Shouldn't citizens have protection against government monopoly abuse?

Proposed Amendment: Monopoly

1. Government has a duty of care to maximize competition and minimize monopoly abuse.

2. Monopoly shall be defined here as the exclusive possession or control of the supply of or trade in a commodity or service combined
   with the ability to legally enforce that exclusive possession.

3. Market dominance per se shall not be a crime. Only proven abuse
   of a monopoly position can be legislated or prosecuted.

4. Government may not enact laws that create a de jure or de facto
   monopoly of any service it offers.

5. Government may not create laws that protect, enhance, or promote
   any monopoly, nor create laws that prevent competition.

6. Antitrust legislation shall only apply to large corporations and the
   government itself.

7. Any legal action or enforcement activity by government under antitrust legislation, or any private lawsuit based on antitrust legislation, shall be known here as an antitrust action. Conditions for antitrust actions are:

   a. Antitrust actions may only occur where there is prima facie ev-
      idence that the defendant's actions have harmed consumers.

   b. Antitrust actions may not be premised on predictions of future
      behavior of customers or to prevent possible future harm.

   c. Antitrust actions may not be used to prevent harm to competi-
      tors.

   d. Lowering of consumer prices shall always be legal and shall not
      be prima facie evidence of monopoly abuse.

   e. Antitrust actions not brought to trial within one year of filing
      (excluding delays requested by defendants), shall be dismissed
      with prejudice.

8. Government may run or sponsor commercial service organizations, but government support must end after ten years.

9. Government may not act as a regulator to competitors of its own commercial services or sponsored organizations.

10. Where a government unit or large organization provides services to competitors, denial of service to competitors shall be illegal.

The Problems with Monopoly

Let's start by clarifying some terms. For our purposes here, monopoly breaks down into three types (with overlaps on occasion):

Competitive Monopoly: occurs when an organization is the biggest in the marketplace because it has grown to be the dominant player or where it is the first player in a new market. A competitive monopoly may have close to 100% of the market, but no legal barrier prevents competition. Microsoft, Google, Amazon, and Facebook are examples. They have competitors, but they are by far the biggest companies in their sector.

Natural Monopoly: occurs in circumstances where it's difficult to have multiple providers. For example, utilities: the expense and difficulty of digging up streets to lay water, sewer, and gas lines makes it unlikely that multiple companies would compete in a given location.

Legal Monopoly: occurs when a government grants someone an exclusive legal right to do something. In the US, outright legal monopolies are rare. But de facto monopolies abound through patents, business licenses, occupational licenses, certificate of need requirements, zoning laws, the Jones Act (only US ships can ply between US ports), and so on.

For further clarification, a *cartel* is where organizations conspire as a group to give themselves a monopoly position in a market.

If someone has a monopoly, the fear is that they could abuse their position to give poor service and inflated prices.

Monopoly was defined above as *the exclusive possession or control of the supply of or trade in a commodity or service combined with the ability to legally enforce that exclusive possession.* By that definition, competitive and natural monopolies are not problems. They lack *the ability to legally enforce that exclusive possession.* With competitive monopolies, customers always have the choice to shop elsewhere.

The real problem arises when special interests succeed in manipulation that gives them a legal advantage. It is *legal monopoly* that is the problem because now force is being used to deny citizens a free choice.

Take, for example, plumbers. In most jurisdictions, I must use a licensed plumber. If I use an unlicensed plumber, then both the plumber and I risk legal punishment. Licensed plumbers can legally *enforce their exclusive possession* of the plumbing trade.

This fails the Test of Purpose. The government is violating my rights to freedom of contract, free trade, and freedom to use my property as I see fit. It also fails the Test of Moral Authority. Do I have the right to dictate which plumbers my neighbor can use? No, I do not have that right, and neither does the government.

I'm in favor of plumbers who know what they are doing. If in doubt, I will ask to see qualifications or get references. But as a free citizen of a free country, I should be free to employ anyone I want as a plumber. My house, my plumbing, my choice.

Specific instances of legal monopoly—occupation licensing, permitting, certificates-of-need, requirements for unionized labor, patents, regulation requiring specific (patented) technologies, and denial-of-service—are addressed elsewhere. Here we'll specifically address antitrust laws, and then government monopoly.

Antitrust Laws

Antitrust laws, beginning with the 1890 Sherman Act,[1] are intended to prevent companies with a dominant market position from exploiting customers. Antitrust legislation started in the heyday of the "Robber Barons." Supposedly Andrew Carnegie (Steel), John D. Rockefeller (Oil), JPMorgan (Banks), and others—built huge industrial and financial empires and used their monopoly positions to abuse the public.

Take Rockefeller, creator of Standard Oil, and probably the richest American ever. Rockefeller was a reviled Robber Barron who so abused his monopoly position that by 1911 his company had to be broken up by the Feds to protect us.

Or did he? In essence, this story is a lie.[2] Rockefeller founded Standard Oil in 1870. Kerosene (the primary oil product at the time) sold for 27¢/gallon. By the late 1890s Standard Oil had close to 90% of the market, yet kerosene prices had steadily fallen to about 5.2¢/gallon. Along the way, Rockefeller invented or promoted gasoline, tar for roads, lubricating oils, and petroleum jelly. He also saved the whales: kerosene became so cheap that whale oil was no longer economic.

Who was harmed by this? Certainly not customers: they had ever cheaper and more plentiful kerosene to light and heat their homes, and new products to experiment with. No, the people harmed were Rockefeller's competitors. It was the competitors who successfully sold the Robber Baron myth and pushed for Standard Oil to be broken up.

Ironically, by the time Standard Oil was broken up in 1911, even the competitors were doing better. Standard Oil's market share peaked in the 1890s at around 90%, but by 1911 when it was broken up it had already shrunk to 64% as competitors got their acts together.

Right from its beginning, antitrust legislation has been abused to achieve the opposite of its intention. Legislators say they want to protect the public, but the real intent is to help uncompetitive special interests. Antitrust continues to hurt competition to this day.[3]

In 1915 when the Federal Trade Commission (FTC) was formed it was designed, as one legislator put it, to "check monopoly in the embryo."[4] This is a deeply flawed notion—the future cannot be predicted, and there's no knowing who the next monopoly *might* be.

Worse though, this approach is fundamentally backwards. To prevent monopoly, you should *encourage* monopolies-in-embryo. You want them to grow and take out the current competitive monopolies—and these newer smaller companies can only grow if customers like what they offer.

What's happening is that special interests benefit from suppressing possible monopoly-in-embryo companies. Those special interests are typically the existing monopolies. The policy supposedly designed to prevent monopoly encourages it!

Anti-trust laws have other problems, primarily that they are applied arbitrarily. Regulators have a huge amount of power to interfere with economic activity. In theory, they can prevent:

- Low or free prices (aka predatory pricing).
- Exclusive pricing (such as getting a discount if you buy in bulk).
- Bundling (selling one product with another, such as Microsoft selling Windows with Internet Explorer included).
- Distribution agreements (you can sell our widgets in Cleveland but not in Cincinnati).
- Exclusive dealing (you can sell Pepsi if you agree not to sell Coke).
- Minimum prices set by producers (you can sell our widgets if you agree not to sell them for less than $1,000).
- Technological lock-in (Apple decides what apps run on iPhones).
- Mergers of corporations that might leave too little competition in the market.
- Price cartels (companies agreeing to restrict supply and keep prices high).

Any of the practices above might be a problem, in theory. In practice they rarely are. On the contrary, customers often like and demand them.

Don't you like $2.99 apps on your phone (predatory pricing)? If you buy in bulk, don't you expect a discount (exclusive pricing)? Businesses like Costco are based on you buying cheap in bulk! Do you care if your phone comes with several bundled apps, like calendars, weather, note-taking, camera? No, you don't. You might even choose between an iPhone and an Android based on the pre-installed apps.

You'd be astonished if your new car didn't come bundled with wheels. You're probably annoyed when the optional extras you want on your car (heated seats, nice radio, towing package) are not bundled and cost more.

As for things like exclusive dealerships and minimum distributor prices, you may not like those things, but you can circumvent them. Ever heard of the internet? FedEx? If you live close to a state border, have you ever driven next door to buy something—either to get around a stupid rule or because it's cheaper?

In practice, regulators don't enforce all their antitrust powers. If they did, successful businesses could collapse. Non-enforcement though is effectively *arbitrary* enforcement. Regulators and judges make *subjective* decisions about what practices should be allowed and what should not.

For corporate mergers, regulators try to predict what *might* happen, often assuming that the merged companies *will* abuse customers. Regulators are acting with legal force, based on fears of an unknown future. The merged companies must prove something impossible to prove: their future behavior. This is an abuse of justice.

Even when unenforced, regulation dampens competition and innovation. Businesses are afraid that the regulators might come down on them. Or their competitors may try and sue them using antitrust legislation, rather than compete with them in the marketplace.

Competition Is Better Than Antitrust

Monopoly *can* be a problem, but it rarely *is* a problem. Big businesses *could* abuse commercial monopolies, and businesses *could* create cartels. They rarely *do* abuse customers because the incentives are against it. If a company exploits customers, competitors have an opportunity to steal them away by not exploiting them, and customers are motivated to move.

Likewise, if companies try to fix prices by creating a cartel, then the temptation is for one of them to profit by lowering prices and stealing customers from the others. As soon as that happens, the other cartel members are motivated to follow suit, and it all quickly collapses. Cartels rarely last long.[5]

These natural forces are always at play so long as there are no *legal* barriers to competition. No matter how big a market-share a company has, it will eventually be out-competed. Takedowns of big companies are accelerating. In the '50s the average lifespan of a company on the S&P500 was 60 years. Today it is 20 years and shrinking.[6] This is competition working as it should.

Meanwhile, antitrust laws are rife with problems and manipulation to the point where they often encourage or support monopoly abuse. The solution is obvious: repeal antitrust legislation and instead encourage competition. The proposal here, combined with others, would make antitrust unconstitutional as currently used:

- We'll ban government laws that promote monopoly, both in de jure or de facto manners. (This is a general catch-all proposal).

- Monopoly per se is not a crime, it is only abuse of monopoly that should be punished.

- Possible, potential, or speculative abuse cannot be a reason for anti-trust action. Only actual proven abuse will be prosecutable.

- Lowering prices is never evidence of monopoly abuse, and neither is harm to competitors.

- Antitrust prosecutions must come to trial within a year (excluding delays caused by the defense) or be dropped. Currently, antitrust actions can drag on for years, and the uncertainty is as big a problem as any monopoly abuse.

- *Proposal 17—Criminal Justice* provides that punitive fines are distributed to charity. This will remove any financial interest the government has in prosecuting.

- *Proposal 17* also stipulates that no defendant in any court case shall ever have to prove a negative. Prosecutors must prove actual abuse, rather than defendants having to disprove possible future abuse.

With the above provisions, most antitrust action will cease. Governments will still be able to prosecute monopoly abuse, but only if it is provable (past or current) abuse rather than possible (future) abuse.

This will not result in a torrent of abuse. Most notions of companies abusing us are nonsense! Unless they manipulate the law, companies can't force anyone to do anything. Companies get big and stay big by offering us stuff we want to buy—good services, products, and prices.

The only big business that does use force is the government, which makes us pay for expensive, inefficient, and manipulated services we often don't want. They get away with it because they have a monopoly on the use of force. It is this use of force that needs to be curbed.

Even if monopoly is potentially a problem, the nest way to minimize it is to maximize competition. Honest competition is the opposite of what most special interests want, so it's no surprise that curbing competition is the outcome of most manipulation. Public policy should instead encourage up-and-coming new competitors. Sooner or later, some of them will take down today's big commercial monopolies.

The winning up-and-comers will succeed by offering customers greater value and improved products and services. That will in turn encourage the big guys to up their game as well. Everyone wins and wins big, and the winners are chosen by citizens rather than bureaucrats.

Public policy doesn't even need to do anything specifically to encourage new companies. Government just needs to get out of the way and let smart, hard-working people try out new ideas, free from manipulation.

Let us citizens find solutions to our own problems. We'll know they are effective if other citizens spend their own money, voluntarily, on those solutions. Good solutions will become successful businesses. A few will grow so big that they will have, for a short while, a commercial monopoly.

Then someone will think of an even better solution, and a new business will grow to take out the current market leader. And so on, as it should be.

Government Monopoly

The biggest monopoly in the US today is the government. Any service that the government offers has the potential for monopoly abuse. because governments can wield legal power in addition to any competitive advantage they might obtain.

One potential problem area is private competition with what most people think of as legitimate government services. Most basic government services are also available in the marketplace. There are private roads (toll roads, bridges, subdivision roads), private police (security guards, private detectives), and private courts (arbitration). The government itself uses private military contractors. Even private legislatures exist in the form of condo boards and homeowners' associations.

Citizens should be free to use these services if they want, and normally they are. The proposal here makes sure this stays the case by banning governments from creating new de jure or de facto monopolies.

The only real concern is when private parties might use violence. Even here, violence is allowed under the right circumstances. Broadly, violence for defense is okay, violence to force other people to follow your wishes is not. State law, enforced by the courts, strives to keep this distinction clear. If you use violence and you step over the line, you'll be sued or prosecuted. Checks are in place.

Another area of concern is when a government offers what most people would think of as commercial services, especially when the government uses its legal powers to keep competitors down.

In some cases, a government forces the use of its service whilst allowing private services to run in parallel. For example, you must contribute to Social Security, but you may contribute to a private pension as well. In other cases, the government outright bans competition. Only the USPS can deliver regular 1st class mail, by law. Only the government can offer lotteries in most states.

Governments can also create de facto monopolies via sneaky regulation. You might not be required, for example, to hook your house up to city water and sewer. Yet your city bans new wells and septic tanks, so you have no other choice.

Occasionally a government is both service provider and regulator— perhaps offering a ferry service at the same time as overseeing private services. Even with no overt restrictions, the temptation is always there to create or interpret rules in such a way as to crimp the private operators.

Any time a government offers a commercial service, then a moral hazard is created. Government's primary role is the protection of individual rights, but when a government offers commercial services, it is now in competition with some of those individuals. The temptation to abuse government power for competitive advantage is enormous. Think of it this way: if you were playing football, and the referee played for the opposing team, wouldn't you question their impartiality?

The moral hazards could be avoided if governments did not offer commercial services, but a blanket ban would go too far. It's possible that sometimes government services are effective, or that no private parties are willing to risk starting a business.

So, let's allow government commerce, but with restrictions to minimize moral hazard. Let's stipulate that after the first ten years of operation, the government service will have to stand on its own feet financially. If a commercial organization cannot generate enough money from its operations to keep going, then something is wrong, and that organization should be allowed to wither and die. The same should apply to government-sponsored businesses.

As a further check, the rules will stop any government from giving its commercial operations a legal advantage. No laws restricting competition, and a ban on any government offering a service and simultaneously regulating the competition. These two rules won't be perfect, but together they should prevent most abuse and give competitors a way to sue government units that are acting in an anti-competitive manner.

Proposal 28—Intellectual Property

If I have seen further it is by standing on the shoulders of Giants.
—Isaac Newton

If I have not seen as far as others, it is because giants were standing on my shoulders.
—Hal Abelson

Intellectual property (IP) rights—patents, copyrights, and trademarks—are government-enforced legal monopolies.

Reasonable arguments can be made for giving IP some legal protection, but special interests have been steadily redefining the meaning of "reasonable" over the last decades, in particular how long protections should last.

It's time to correct the trends in IP and reassert the balance between the needs of the few and the interests of the many.

Proposed Amendment: Intellectual Property

1. Citizens have a right to profit from their intellectual property, but that right must be balanced with the needs of society to benefit from new ideas.

2. Patents, or any similar mechanism, shall be illegal.

3. Copyright shall last for the life of the author, or 50 years for a corporate copyright holder, from the date of first publication.

4. Copyright shall mean that 3rd parties may not directly copy or translate original works.

5. Fictitious characters, situations, and ideas within copyrighted works shall not be covered by copyright.

6. Up to 25% of any copyrighted work may be used or quoted in any derivative work.

7. Non-copyright holders may perform or read copyrighted material, without permission of the holder and without fees being due:
   a. At private events.
   b. At public events in venues holding less than 500 persons.
   c. In educational settings.

8. Copyright disputes are between the copyright holder and the violator. Third parties, publishers, and information service providers shall have no liability for copyright abuse and may not be required to act presumptively on behalf of copyright holders.

9. Trademarks are intended to uniquely identify a business or service.

10. Trademarks shall last only as long as the trademark holder continues to use the trademark in an active business.

11. Trademarks may be used in works of art, factual reporting, parody, and satire without the holder's permission, including as all or part of the title of a work.

12. Where trademarks include everyday language, that language per se may not be trademarked. It shall be considered a trademark only if combined with graphical or other contextual elements that give it a distinct quality beyond the text.

13. Trademarks may not be used as a proxy for copyright.

14. Trademark holders shall have no right to sue for breach of trademark. Only citizens who believe they have been defrauded by a trademark violation shall have a right to sue for fraud.

15. In any dispute about trademark infringements, courts must decide if a reasonable citizen would have confused the infringer with the trademark holder.

16. *Transition.* Upon the passing of this amendment:
    a. Existing patents will expire immediately.
    b. Copyrights outside of the new time limits for copyrights shall expire immediately.
    c. Intellectual property lawsuits extant under any of the old rules shall be dismissed.

Intellectual Property

IP is ideas. Ideas for inventions (patents), ideas for designs or works of art (copyright), and ideas for business branding (trademarks and service marks).

The Constitution gives Congress the power to *promote the progress of science and useful arts, by securing for limited times to authors and inventors the exclusive right to their respective writings and discoveries.*

In other words, the constitution authorizes government-created monopolies on behalf of special interests—legal and constitutionally authorized manipulation. This might be acceptable if the benefits of patents were overwhelming, but they are not. On the contrary, IP rights are antithetical to promoting the progress of science and useful arts. They need to be severely curbed.

We'll divide the discussion into the three main types of IP: patents, copyrights, and trademarks.

Patents

Patents are supposed to give inventors a short period of monopoly to profit from their ideas. In theory, this makes inventors more motivated to invent, and investors more likely to invest in producing the idea.

So, firstly, let's apply the Test of Efficacy: do patents *promote the progress of science and useful arts?*

Measuring innovation is tricky, so we'll leave the details to economists and jump straight to the conclusion: Patents result in *less* innovation.[1] Patents delay innovation, shut down competition, and slow growth.

A patent system, by its nature, assumes that the value of an invention lies inherently in the invention itself. In other words, if you invent a better widget, you profit from having a monopoly on that widget.

In real life though, widgets need to be manufactured, marketed, and sold. It's not only about how good the idea is—you have to produce a product that people want to buy. You must integrate your new ideas into a design, manufacture it efficiently, market and distribute it.

Ultimately, profit is only loosely related to the idea itself. *You must implement the idea to make money.* Financial rewards come from success in the market.

Without patent protection, the best course of action is to get the idea to market ASAP and reap profits from being there first. If the idea spawns a popular product, this rapid push to market is a win for inventors, investors, and consumers alike.

There's abundant evidence for innovation in fields where patents don't apply. The most successful industry over the last 30 years? Arguably, software, which in most cases could not be patented. In the words of Bill Gates: *If people had understood how patents would be granted when most of today's ideas were invented, and had taken out patents, the industry would be at a complete standstill today.*

Software is following the typical pattern of a new industry. A new technology appears. Dozens of new firms are born in a massive wave of innovation and competition. Customers benefit greatly, as do innovators who are successful *in the marketplace.*

Eventually, after years of fierce competition, a few large players emerge and consolidate their positions with patents. The patent protection happens *after* the innovation and is used to lock in monopoly profits *without further innovation.* Once patents appear on the scene innovation rapidly goes down. That's happening with software.[2]

There are other examples of commercial success without patent protection. Walmart, for example, has been one of the most successful retailers over the last 30 years. Their success is largely due to how they organize their supply chain.[3] Little of what they can be patented. They just do it better and keep improving faster than their rivals. Walmart wins and consumers win, without patents.

The empirical data is clear: patents damage innovation, the opposite of their stated intent. But what about the moral arguments?

It is wrong to steal things, and an important role of government is to protect citizens from theft. That's crystal clear when physical stuff is stolen. But when ideas are "stolen," things rapidly get murky.

The theft of ideas is not like the theft of physical stuff. If I steal your car, you no longer have a car. If I steal your idea, you still have the idea. We both have it!

It's also not clear how many ideas are genuinely new. Ideas flow from mind to mind. Humans have a huge pool of shared knowledge. People talk to each other, read each other's ideas, and bounce ideas off each other. Ideas are combined and produce new ideas. In a sense, ideas have sex with each other and keep producing new ideas.

Given this interchange, it is unclear how truly original any ideas are. And it's getting worse with the explosion of technology. The pool of knowledge is currently estimated to be doubling every year and accelerating.[4] The internet allows billions of people to access it. The sheer volume of information makes it increasingly difficult to say where an idea came from or who thought of it first.

Another reason to rethink patents is that production technology is making them obsolete.[5] New products come on the market faster than ever. Software can change overnight, but development times for physical products are getting shorter as well. As 3D printing matures, and as other production processes are created, the rate of change of physical stuff will accelerate. It will get cheaper to make, and cheaper to replace.

Physical stuff is becoming increasingly like software: most people prefer the latest version. Would you, for example, buy a five-year-old computer? Probably not, because today's computer is so much better. In short, do twenty-year patents make sense in a world where products are obsolete in five years?

Patent Law—A Special Interest Gold Mine

Evidence for the benefits of patents is scant, and the moral arguments against the theft of ideas are dubious. This is truer in the information age than it has ever been.

Meanwhile, patents have many downsides. Patent law is almost the definition of manipulation. It is private citizens (or corporations), using government force to stop economic competition.

Shutting down competition damages us as a society and has done so since the early days of patents. James Watt, inventor of the steam engine, may have delayed the industrial revolution by 30 years by getting a special patent on aspects of his engine from the British Parliament in 1775. What if you'd had today's technology 30 years ago? Without patents, the world might be decades, perhaps even a century ahead of where we are now.

Patents are also a monster of bureaucracy, with state and federal legislation, courts, and the administration of patent filing. Thousands of smart attorneys are working hard, filing patents, arguing about what's patentable, suing over infringements, negotiating licenses, and so on.

There's even manipulation from abroad! The US is a party to international agreements about IP. Whenever a change is made to US law, aligning it with international standards is part of the conversation. It's safe to assume that multinational corporations manipulate international law as effectively as they manipulate US law.

Like every government process subject to manipulation, abuse of the patent system steadily ramps up over time.[6] The earliest US patents in colonial days were 10 years, then 14 years (1790), 14 years + extension of 7 years (1836), 17 years (1861), and 20 years (1995). Notice a trend here?

Even though software was originally unpatentable, special interests have been working hard to change that. Software patents have exploded in volume over the last 30 years. Lawsuits have exploded with them. The number of defendants in software patents grew 129% between 2007 and 2011.[7] This is getting out of hand. New Zealand, for example, has banned software patents.[8]

Another recent problem is the "patent troll."[9] Trolls patent obscure things that probably shouldn't even be patentable, then sue others who violate the patent. They don't intend to manufacture anything, their profits come from lawsuits. If you're sued by a patent troll, it might cost millions to defend yourself. It's cheaper and easier to roll over and pay them, even if their claim is nonsense.

Overall, patents encourage corporations to compete in the courts and in manipulation of the legal system, to our collective detriment. Let's instead have them compete in the marketplace where profits accrue by benefiting customers.

Pharmaceuticals

Perhaps the strongest case for patents is pharmaceuticals. Potentially, when a new drug comes on the market, the first pill might cost a billion dollars, and the second pill costs one cent. Without patent protection, pharmaceutical companies would never invest money in new research.

This seems oh-so-plausible, and it should! Thousands of clever, eloquent attorneys and marketing experts have been paid hundreds of millions of dollars over decades to make this case, honing their arguments and finding exactly the right examples to back them up.

Nonetheless, this spin is questionable. The major expense is typically FDA approval. Safety is important (even if FDA regulation is problematic), but as far as the relationship between patents and innovation, FDA approval has little to do with the matter.

And the second pill does not really cost one cent, because costs are spread out over millions of pills. As for rivals copying the drug, in practice, the production of any drug is expensive, even if there's no research involved. It takes time and money to build factories and production lines and get a drug to market. Only larger companies can attempt it, and only if they see profit potential.

If a company invents a new drug without patent protection, it will still be first to market, it will still have brand name recognition, and it could still profit handsomely. This would be true even with a lengthy FDA approval process because competitors won't start producing copies until the original is approved, and until after the first company has proven the drug can be profitable.

Even with pharmaceuticals, the evidence is that patents lower innovation. Without patent protection, pharmaceutical companies tend to be more innovative and competitive. The proposal therefore is to end patents altogether.

Copyright

Copyright is the right to prevent other folks from copying things such as books, paintings, and music. Copyright started in the US with the copyright act of 1790, which gave authors a 14-year copyright, with the possibility of a 14-year extension.

Like patents, copyright times have steadily grown. Most recently the 1998 Copyright Extension Act extended copyright to the life of the author plus 70 years, or 75 years for a corporate copyright holder.

The 1998 act[10] is particularly galling on two fronts. Firstly, it extended copyright retrospectively in violation of the Constitution, even though there was a lawsuit about that which was lost.

Secondly, the official short title, right there in the text, is the Sonny Bono Copyright Extension Act. In other words, a special interest, Sonny Bono's family, is written right into law. Even that title was political theatre. The unofficial nickname of the act is the Mickey Mouse Protection Act. I'm sure you can guess the special interest involved.

Just like with patents, the data shows that copyright discourages innovation. For example, copyright is used to slow progress in software with arguments about the "look and feel" of software packages.[11]

In the arts, music is perhaps the most affected by copyright. Musicians learn to play by playing other people's music. Music evolves through variations of other people's music. In the modern age, with recording technology, there's even greater opportunity for copying, culminating with sampling—including snippets of old songs in new songs.[12]

As technology improves, copyright lawsuits in music have ramped up.[13] It's almost to the point where scales are deemed copyrightable. For non-musical folks, that's sort of like saying someone owns a copyright on the alphabet. This is madness.[14]

It's tempting to eliminate copyright like we eliminated patents, but care is needed. Patents are about ideas, while copyright is about the expression or form of ideas. Removing copyright protection entirely might produce immoral results in the age of digital copying.

Suppose JK Rowling came out with a new Harry Potter book. In a world without copyright, someone could download that book off Amazon, and "publish" a new version in 24 hours. This would steal sales from JK Rowling. This would be wrong. Some protection is needed.

The proposal here leaves copyright in place with severe restrictions. You would not be able to directly copy a work of art—books, music, or visual arts—nor directly translate it into foreign languages. Copyright would last for the life of the author or 50 years for a corporation.

Ideas within a copyrighted work though are like patents and should not be protected. So, if someone thought of a new line of novels based on the Harry Potter world—perhaps featuring Harry's long-lost cousin Little Jimmy Potter— that would be allowable. Such an innovation, if done well, might inspire a new generation of young readers, and benefit both society and JK Rowling as people go back to reread the originals. If done badly, it would sink without a trace.

In music, these provisions will prevent direct copies of the original recording, but samples and copying riffs and melodies will be fine. Music has always thrived on variations of a theme, and that should be encouraged. If someone created a great new work with a sample taken from a pop hit, that would benefit society but also benefit the first artist when people go back to listen again to the original.

The most important thing overall is to encourage artistic innovation rather than legal innovation. Let's remove the legal uncertainty that excessive copyright has produced. Public policy should instead encourage people to riff off each other's ideas: the more ideas the better.

Trademarks

Trademarks are intended to give businesses the ability to uniquely identify themselves. When you buy a Coke™, for example, you know exactly what you are getting. This helps cut down on fraud and encourages businesses to build and protect the reputation of their brand. However, the trademark system has been manipulated to produce some less desirable results.

Firstly, trademark laws empower special interests, rather than protect consumers. The law allows trademark holders to sue other people using their trademark and stop them, even if the trademark is used inadvertently. In theory, journalism, art, and satire are all exceptions. But even here the holder could sue and may win. Lawsuits are rare, but even the threat of lawsuits dampens creativity.

Secondly, trademark law empowers trademark trolls. These trolls register large numbers of words and phrases without ever intending to use them for a real business. Instead, they hope to legally extort other businesses who might want to use them. This growing problem is receiving congressional attention on how to curb it.[15]

Thirdly, trademark law is subject to drift as lawyers find innovative ways to pervert the original intent to help their clients. For example, titles of books have never been copyrightable, but lawyers have tried to get around this by claiming instead that titles are trademarks![16,17]

The point of trademarks is to protect the consumer. If a consumer feels they have been defrauded, they should have the right to sue. Beyond that, it's not clear how society benefits from trademark holders suing to stop the use of their trademark in situations they don't like.

If someone takes a no-name cola and sticks a Coke™ label on it, that's fraud. The proposal here will clarify that the consumer is the one with a right to sue, not the Coca-Cola Company.

As further protection against manipulation, Trademarks will need to be in commercial use. There will be a blanket ban on using trademarks as a proxy for copyright. And everyday language will not be allowable as a trademark unless accompanied by something that also makes it visually distinctive.

Proposal 29—Healthcare

It is amazing that people who think we cannot afford to pay for doctors, hospitals, and medication somehow think that we can afford to pay for doctors, hospitals, medication and a government bureaucracy to administer it.
　　　　　　　　　—Thomas Sowell, Knowledge and Decisions

Despite rumors to the contrary, the US healthcare system is among the best in the world for health outcomes and wait times[1].

On the other hand, the costs, the paperwork, and the bureaucracy are out of control. Obamacare, no matter how well-intentioned, is a monster of complexity and manipulation, shutting down competition, ensuring high costs, and forcing citizens to be customers of health insurers.

Government attempts to fix healthcare fail because they keep trying to prevent the main cure: making prices transparent and putting patients and providers back into a face-to-face negotiation about those prices.

Healthcare can't be fixed with a few tweaks because that's exactly where the problem has come from, decades of tweaks adding up to a mess. Time instead for a reset of the system.

Proposed Amendment: Healthcare

1. Government shall not interfere with or proscribe citizens' healthcare choices.

2. Parents shall be required to ensure that their children have health insurance up to the age of 18. Otherwise, government may not require any citizen or organization to provide health insurance, medical care, or coverage of medical costs for any other citizen.

3. It is for citizens to decide what medical insurance coverage they want. Government may not mandate any compulsory coverage or treatment options, nor mandate any conditions on medical insurance policies except that all policies:
   a. Must have a minimum deductible of $5,000/policy.
   b. Must have a minimum insured amount of $1,000,000.
   c. Must cover all accidents requiring hospitalization.
   d. Must cover all diseases and conditions with a 1% or greater chance of fatality or permanent disablement if untreated.
   e. May cover costs of diagnostic tests or preventative medicine below the deductible.

4. Treatments and pricing are a matter to be decided between provider and patient.

5. All citizen medical matters and medical records are private. Government may not require permitting or reporting of an individual

patient's medical status or procedures unless the patient has a disease that is both contagious and dangerous to the public at large.

6. Government may collect statistical population-level data on procedures performed.

7. Employers may only offer health insurance to employees as direct payments to an insurer of the employee's choice. Employer-paid insurance shall be a salary benefit taxable to employees.

8. Government may not mandate insurance as an employee benefit.

9. Government may pay medical costs for those in active military service and for ongoing costs of injuries received while on active military service.

10. Medical benefits for veterans and active military at the time of passing this amendment shall be honored under previous laws.

11. Medical benefits for persons entering the military after the passing of this proposal shall be subject to a $5,000 deductible, except for ongoing treatment for injuries received while in military service.

12. Charities and private citizens may voluntarily aid others with their medical bills.

13. Non-medical insurance may have a component for coverage of medical costs due to accidents below the $5,000 deductible.

14. Government may not run medical insurance schemes.

15. Hospitals may not use denial of admission privileges to stifle competition from smaller healthcare providers.

Healthcare—An Unhealthy System

There is a lot of discontent about healthcare in the US. Patients complain about prices. Doctors complain about paperwork. Everyone complains about insurance.

Pushed by special interests that profit greatly, government interferes extensively in healthcare. As a result, healthcare is a bloated bureaucratic monster, with costs rising much faster than general inflation.[2]

What justification does the government have to meddle in healthcare? The US Constitution says nothing specific about healthcare. Some state constitutions do give states a duty to provide for public health, though in practice this often conflicts with government's primary purpose of protecting individual rights.

Do I have any right to force my neighbor's healthcare choices? Force her to buy health insurance? Force her to use a certain doctor? Force her to eat healthy food, exercise, stop smoking? No, no, no, no. I have no right to do any of those things, and by extension, neither does the government. Use of government force in these areas fails the Test of Moral Authority.

Government attempts to force my health choices (mandatory insurance, taxes on cigarettes, bans on 32oz soft drinks, occupational licensing of providers) violate my fundamental rights to free trade, freedom of contract, and the freedom to use my own body as I see fit. Any interference with my rights, even if for my own good, fails the Test of Purpose.

Obamacare, despite protests, introduced health insurance mandates.[3] Lack of insurance could be due to over-expensive insurance. Or it could be a rational choice for some healthy people, in which case forced insurance fails the Test of Consent. About 16% of the population were uninsured before Obamacare, about 10% now.[4] If the goal was to get everyone insured, Obamacare failed The Test of Efficacy.

How to Fix Healthcare

Healthcare, like the general economy, is emergent: it evolves as new procedures, technologies and drugs are invented. It is not and cannot be planned, and there can be no single fix. However, incentives can be better aligned to improve health outcomes and value for money.

Fundamentally healthcare problems are supply side issues. There's a need for more of everything: providers and treatments. Government instead creates shortages. Educational bottlenecks create shortages of doctors and nurses. Occupational licensing requirements create shortages of staff and make staff movements difficult and expensive. Regulations slow the introduction of new drugs, medical equipment, and procedures.

Overall, health care is one of the most regulated industries in the country. As a result, costs have gone up far faster than general inflation. *Proposal 12—Legislation*, *Proposal 13—Regulation*, and *Proposal 15—Administrative Law* will fix most of this excessive regulation.

In the courts, doctors and hospitals are being assessed with punitive damages far beyond the costs of fixing mistakes. This results in doctors being over-cautious, ordering tests, scans, and second opinions whether needed or not. Everyone pays for this waste via insurance. *Proposal 18—Civil Justice* should fix these problems.

Another medical bottleneck is the patent system, which has slowed innovation in drugs and medical devices for decades. Society is on the brink of an explosion in medical technology with computing, biomedical devices, gene therapy and other promising technologies. *Proposal 28—Intellectual Property* will help unleash this progress so we can all reap the benefits.

Insurance

Problems in the healthcare market are mostly due to excessive regulation and legal issues stopping competition and innovation. Fix those, and everything will get cheaper. How it's paid for will become less of an issue. Insurance is thus the 3rd priority on the list of things to fix!

Debates about insurance typically focus on questions such as should it be compulsory, do insurance companies make too much money, or should there be a Medicare-for-all system? However, the really important issue with insurance is that it hides prices.

Of course, headline prices sometimes appear in the news, and they are often shockingly high. Many people assume that prices are only about profits, and that it is wrong to profit from someone who is ill. In this context, the prices look like gouging.

Prices are partially about profit, but that is only a small part of it. Fundamentally, *prices are information*. Prices inform both consumer and producer about where this service stands compared to other services. Prices enable the consumer to ask: is this worth it to me? Prices enable the producer to compare their costs to other producers.

Perversely (and despite occasional headline shockers) the current system does everything it can to hide prices. Employer insurance and healthcare systems such as Medicare and the VA all hide prices. Low or no deductible insurance schemes remove incentives to ask about prices.

Even if you wanted to know the cost of a procedure, it's often difficult to work out. Medical bills typically itemize things like "Provider Billed," "Member Discount," and "Amount Paid." Perhaps a co-pay, government cap or discount appears as well, other obscure items such as "facility costs," "recovery fees," and "offset fees." The final cost is hidden in an ocean of numbers and buzz words. This is billing transparency created by the Department of Obfuscation.

Hiding prices hides information. If you don't have accurate information, you can't have an efficient system. You cannot lower the price if you don't know what it is in the first place. People need to know prices. And to incentivize them to ask what the price is there needs to be a deductible.

The first thing a deductible would do is clear up confusion about billing. If I am sitting in my doctor's office and ask how much something will this cost, then she had better know. As a customer paying the deductible with my own money, I won't accept waffle as an answer.[5]

Next, a deductible encourages patients to keep costs in mind. Unless patients have a personal, direct stake in the costs of services, they will never ask the important questions. Is this worth it to me? Is it cheaper elsewhere? Is there an alternative?

For the providers (and a few patients) greater clarity about costs might incentivize them to look for other ways to provide services. The incentives would align to encourage new ideas, and ultimately cheaper, better healthcare.

Deductibles and clear pricing allow the carrot and stick psychology of competition to work as it should. Providers have the carrot of increasing business by lowering prices, or the stick of losing business if they get too expensive.

All these benefits of competition can only take place if prices are visible, and if customers can choose freely between services. Nobody spends other people's money as carefully as they spend their own money. Nobody spends money wisely if they don't know what they are spending. Forcing everyone to keep asking questions about costs and values will in the long run drive innovations, lower medical costs and improve outcomes.

So, the proposal here is that all insurance should have a deductible. The deductible should be priced so that most people can afford it, but big enough that it stings and gets people's attention. The figure proposed here is $5000.

Now, a safety net may still be needed for anyone who can't afford the deductible. The main proposal to help is Personal Savings Accounts (PSAs) described in *Proposal 22—Social Security.* Everyone will have tax advantaged incentives to save for emergencies, and those PSA funds can also be used for family, friends, or even neighbors if needed.

For families with kids, insurance policies with a family-wide deductible are allowed. For the average family of husband, wife, and 2.4 kids there'd be one overall $5,000 deductible.

As a last resort there is still charity. Charitable deductions will be fully tax deductible if you want to support charitable clinics, or if you need someone to support you in a medical emergency.

Insurance spreads the costs of unpredictable events over large numbers of people. Insurance is a good thing.

Insurance companies want to make profits, and that incentivizes them to keep an eye on costs. In this sense both insurers and customers (patients) want the same thing: cost effective healthcare.

Sometimes though, patient and insurer interests diverge. Only patients can decide if medical expenses are worth it *to them.* When insurers act as middlemen and negotiate prices with providers, patients get excluded. Your doctor argues why you needed a procedure; your insurer argues about why it won't pay, and you have little say in the matter.

Insurers acting as middlemen is another form of hiding prices from customers. To remove this hazard, costs should in principle be negotiated between patient and provider. Patients should make medical decisions with their doctors, including accounting for costs. Insurance comes later. If insurance companies want to argue about costs, they should argue with patients, because it is the patients who are most affected.

Now, insurers might have information about the market that customers can't easily access. If a procedure is twice as expensive in Chicago than it is in Miami, insurers will notice and investigate. No mandates are needed to minimize costs, they are already motivated to do just that! They will pass information along to patients and providers. Maybe it's worth flying a patient to the low-cost clinic.

How all this works in practice will evolve over time, negotiated out by patients, insurers, and providers, perhaps with the help of the courts if things go wrong. With prices negotiated between patients and doctors, and with a deductible in play, the incentives align to encourage greater cost effectiveness and patient choice.

Worrying About Prices

Many arguments about health insurance and costs revolve around the idea that people shouldn't have to worry about prices when making healthcare decisions. There's often an assumption that sick people are unable to make effective choices.

Am I alone in detecting a hint of condescension here? Personally, I don't believe my thinking shuts down when I'm ill, and I'd still consult with family and friends if I were unsure. I'm certain my wife would tell me if she thought I was making a stupid decision. She's willing to tell me I'm being stupid no matter what my state of health is! And I trust my wife way more than I trust any politician.

Now, there might be an emergency when I'm unable to think. If I'm hurt in a car wreck, then I want the EMTs to get me out of there and into the closest ER as soon as possible. I want the ER docs to operate if they think it will save my life, even if I am unconscious.

Emergency medicine is needed, and no one is negotiating prices during emergencies. That's a benefit of insurance. But most medical situations are not emergencies. I'll have time to consider options, consult other doctors, and get alternative price quotes.

Why is healthcare so expensive? Because the government makes it expensive. Time to stop them meddling. Let's restore the price system and allow it to inform everyone. Let's encourage the innovation and improvements that competition brings over time. Let the market work its magic.

Proposal 30—Children

The state must declare the child to be the most precious treasure of the people. As long as the government is perceived as working for the benefit of the children, the people will happily endure almost any curtailment of liberty and almost any deprivation.

—Adolf Hitler

In the name of protecting children, our government has introduced laws that curtail the freedoms of adults.

However, it is not the government's job to act as a parent! That's the actual parent's job. And the government has no moral authority to curb adult rights in the name of protecting children.

The biggest issues with respect to children are education, and single parent families. Both areas need a realignment of incentives to maximize benefits to children, and to society as a whole.

Proposed Amendment: Children

1. Responsibility for the care of children rests with their parents.

2. Government may not violate or restrict any adult's Constitutional rights for reasons of protecting children.

3. It is the responsibility of parents alone to protect their children from speech they consider inappropriate.

4. It is the responsibility of parents to ensure that their children are educated to become productive members of society.

5. Parents have the right to educate their children as they see fit. Government may enact safeguards to ensure schooling situations meet basic standards for reading, writing and mathematics.

6. Responsibility for the cost of educating children lies with the parents. State and local governments may subsidize the education of children from general tax funds as follows:
   a. Subsidies must be in the form of vouchers.
   b. Parents may use their vouchers to educate their children as they see fit.
   c. Voters in any jurisdiction offering vouchers shall vote on the amount of the voucher and any changes to that amount.

7. Government may not otherwise fund or subsidize education outside of a voucher system.

8. The costs of education vouchers shall come from general government tax revenue. There shall be no added taxes, levies, or payments required from any citizen to fund education.

9. Where parents choose to homeschool, the voucher shall be paid into a Personal Savings Account (PSA) where:
   a. The account shall be for the benefit of a named child.
   b. Funds in the account shall be used for educational expenses.
   c. A parent shall be named as trustee.
   d. Trustees and parents may not personally benefit from the account.
   e. Courts shall have the power to appoint alternate trustees in cases of abuse,
   f. Control of the account shall revert fully to the child at age 18 and for any normally allowed uses of a PSA.
10. The federal government shall have no role in education.
11. In divorce proceedings and custody disputes, both parents shall be assumed to have equal rights and responsibilities towards their children.
12. No parent may be denied access to their children unless they are a gross and proven danger to that child.
13. Children may not be separated from their parents nor removed from their homes except by court order after proven abuse or endangerment of those children.
14. Any woman who becomes pregnant through fraud or gross negligence shall have no legal claim of child support from the father.
15. No man shall have any legal duty to support any child that is not their child unless they agree to take on that responsibility in the full knowledge that the child is not theirs.
16. All parties involved in divorce proceedings and custody disputes shall have a right to demand paternity testing.

Not Our Children

What should we do as a society to protect, nurture, and educate our children? These questions are often debated publicly, but they are not answerable because they presuppose things that are not true.

Firstly, there is no "we." There's no way that 257 million adults can agree on collective decisions about the 53 million children in the US. Secondly, not everyone has children. According to the US Census, about 20% of citizens don't have children. Of those that do, for most older adults the kids are grown and no longer live at home. Thirdly, in what sense are the children "ours?" Do I have rights over my neighbor's children? Can I tell them what to do? What about the children in the next town over? In the next state?

So, when someone asks what "we" should do with "our" children, the question is close to nonsense. Literally, the question makes no sense.

What does make sense? How about this: the primary responsibility for the upbringing of children rests with the parents. Always, and forever: the primary responsibility for children rests with the parents.

Many non-parents have a general interest in education. You might think schools should prioritize STEM subjects, or teach logic, or teach whatever. It's also appropriate to take an interest in the welfare of your neighbor's kids as one of the responsible adults on the block. If I see kids trespassing, I'll ask them what they are doing. My neighbor's grandkids might wash my car to earn money for their school trip to DC.

Still, no amount of concern for education or good neighborliness gives me rights over other people's children. I have no right to tell my neighbor where or how to educate his kids. And my neighbor in turn has no right to prevent me doing things on my private property because it might upset his kids. And if I have no rights over my neighbor's kids, then neither does the government.

Dictating education choices to parents fails the Test of Moral Authority. Federal involvement in education fails the Test of Constitutional Authority. Censorship of broadcast TV to protect children fails the Test of Purpose.

Government interference in the upbringing of children violates freedoms for parents and non-parents alike. It also distorts incentives for almost everyone involved. If parents are relieved of their responsibilities by legislation, then they are being infantilized. Infantile parents in turn function as role models to their children.

When politicians dictate what's on TV, they behave like parents. If politicians are our parents, then we citizens are their children. Is that the correct balance of power?

There need to be some laws about children. Crimes against children should not be allowed, and sometimes the parents are the perpetrators. Nonetheless, day-to-day laws directed at children and child-raising should align moral responsibilities, practical issues, and incentives. The law should therefore start with the assumption that parents are fully responsible for their children and raising them to become mature adults.

Education

In 2019, the US spent about $750 billion on the 48 million kids in public schools.[1] There are ongoing arguments about quality, what should be on the curriculum, and the expense. There are no simple fixes, but the system can be arranged so incentives align to get it fixed.

The first issue is: who is responsible? Legislation is often badly worded to blur responsibility. Some state Constitutions require local authorities to provide free education. Education campaigners talk about children having a "right to an education."

Children should be educated, but giving children the right to an education can't work. If children have a right to education that takes liberty away from others (who have to pay for it).

Giving children a right to an education also creates a fundamental misalignment of responsibility. Children, until they mature, have no awareness of what rights are, no ability to argue for their rights, and no practical means to enforce them.

Assigning a right to the child creates a system where parents, governments and educators can argue for ever about who's in charge, because the primary beneficiary—the child—is clearly not in charge. To avoid this, let's reword the law to center responsibility where belongs. Children do not have a right to an education. Rather, parents have a responsibility to educate their children!

If education is seen as the responsibility of parents, it becomes clear who's in charge: the parents. Who loves the children the most? The parents. Who wants the children to succeed the most? The parents. Who, other than the children themselves, has the most to gain from the children succeeding? The parents.

So, if children are not learning, who's responsible for getting things back on track? The parents. If a school is failing to deliver results who will put pressure on it to change? The parents. And if that school won't change, who should have the power to move their children to a different school? Yes, the parents.

When you hear politicians speaking about "improving education for our children," doesn't it sound like the children belong to the government? It's as if the only issue in education to how well the government organizes the schools. But this ignores the parents. When the government acts *in loco parentis*, it robs real adults of their adult rights and responsibilities and the power to exercise them.

In principle, forcing citizens to pay for public education is a form of theft, and a violation of the Test of Purpose. In practice, I think this is a government service that almost everyone agrees with. The proposal here will allow state subsidized education, but also align incentives to produce the best results. That means vouchers.

Vouchers have been contentious in education circles for decades. Some powerful special interests are strongly against them. Teachers Unions, who represent teachers, don't want to give control to parents. Politicians, who want power, don't want to give control to parents. Education departments and schools, who are looking out for their own jobs, don't want to give control to parents. Educational "experts," who know better than parents what's best for children, don't want to cede any control to parents.

And yet, who should have control of their children's interests? The parents! Who should have primary responsibility for their children's education? The parents!

Politicians, educational experts, school administrators, unions, and individual teachers—everyone has their point of view. However, unless parents have true choices, and true control, arguments about education are self-serving for everyone else involved. Feel free to persuade parents that you have good ideas. Feel free to persuade parents to send their children to the local government school, or a charter school, or wherever. But it needs to be persuasion and not force.

Parents must have the final choice. Parents must have the ability to remove their children from any school and place them elsewhere if the school is not working.

The only effective way to keep schools correctly incentivized is to give parents the power to remove children *and education funds* from schools. So, again, that means vouchers.

Suppose you have a child, enrolled in our local government school, funded by a $5,000 a year voucher. As a tax paying parent in that jurisdiction this proposal will give you the right to take your child out of that school and enroll him or her in any other school, anywhere.

The voucher moves with the child. If you move your kid the new school gets $5000 extra, *the old one loses it*. It won't matter if the new school is a private school, a public school a few miles away, or even a school in the county, state, or country next door.

Vouchers can also be spent on homeschooling. About 5% of kids (and growing) were being homeschooled as of 2016.[2] The evidence is that homeschooled kids do well academically and socially, though some disagree.[3]

Currently, most US states have little or no financial support for homeschooling. However, if the state is allowed to subsidize education (an exception to the notion of legal equality for all), the exception should at least be as equal as possible. So, vouchers should be usable for homeschooling.

The proposed method is to create a Personal Savings Account for the child and pay the voucher into it. The parent acts as trustee, and the funds are spent on the child's education—textbooks, computers, online or college courses, education trips and so on.

Potential abuse could occur here: parents could take the money and spend it on themselves. That's unlikely, but let's stipulate that trustees and parents cannot personally profit from children's education accounts. And let's give courts the power to appoint alternate trustees in case of abuse.

Not all problems are solved by a voucher system. Any new school will have to accept your child, and if you send your child to a school 15 miles away, you'll need to work out how to get them there. But if that choice exists, vouchers will enable it. For the kid who wants out of a failing inner-city school, they have greater chances of finding an alternative if their vouchers are completely transferable.

Sometimes there won't be any decent schools within commuting distance. But even here, vouchers give parents power. They can use their financial leverage to demand changes and improve the schools they do have. If that doesn't work, they can fund new private schools, or start their own schools, or homeschool, or send their kids to a boarding school.

Will some new schools be failures? Will some schools close? Will some teachers lose their jobs? Yes, yes, yes! Any experiment will produce individual winners and losers, but in the long run we win collectively by allowing innovation. Unless you think the current system is perfect, then we need experimentation. Vouchers will enable that experimentation.

Vouchers correctly alight incentives to maximize the value we all get from education. Vouchers are in the best interests of the children, the parents, and ultimately of all taxpayers who subsidize schools.

The proposal here also gives state voters a say in how much education vouchers are worth. That opens the possibility that the voucher alone is not enough to completely cover a child's education costs. What then?

For parents who are struggling financially, there will still be charitable and religious schools available to many. As a further social safety net, tax-advantaged PSA funds are designed so that they can be spent on *anyone's* education. Grandparents, aunts and uncles, or family friends can contribute to a child's education through their PSAs. Financially strapped parents will still have options under this system.

Single Parent Families

The US has seen an enormous rise in the number of single-parent families over the last 50 years; primarily single mothers raising children alone. The results have been terrible for families, and especially for children raised in the absence of a father. It's difficult to untangle the reasons for this, but surely much of it is due to government policies that incentivize divorce and subsidize single parents. Policies such as:

- No-fault divorce.
- A welfare system that discourages two parent families.
- A war on drug takers that disproportionately punishes and removes men from families, especially African American men.
- A family court system biased in favor of women. Women almost always get custody and can make life difficult for fathers.
- Legislation that makes husbands responsible for illegitimate children or makes men responsible for children fathered by fraud.

The welfare system and the war on drug takers are addressed in other proposals. Legislative and court biases against men are addressed below. Collectively, the changes proposed should realign the incentives to increase the popularity of marriage. To be clear, it is not marriage that is important, so much as it is that children should, wherever possible, be raised by two parents in a stable long-term relationship.

Mothers and Fathers

First, let's address some legal issues related to how children arrive on planet earth.

Sometimes, women deliberately get pregnant through fraud.[4] If a woman wants to get pregnant, that's her choice. But if it's done through fraud, such as lying about being on birth control, she should not then expect the father to be legally liable for child support. Fraud is fraud, and no one should profit from fraud.

Another form of fraud is women becoming pregnant by men who are not their husbands, yet still expecting the husband to bear parental responsibility. If someone cheats on their spouse, that's a moral issue, but it should not be a legal issue. The law should not punish adultery, but neither should it indemnify adulterers from the consequences of their actions or punish innocent 3rd parties. Innocent husbands should not be forced into legal responsibility for other men's children.

To counter problems of fraud in pregnancy, the proposal here is that anyone involved in divorce proceedings have a right to paternity testing. This may already be the case in some jurisdictions, but it should be a blanket right. One function of the courts is, after all, to find the truth.

Another issue is negligent pregnancies. In the modern age, pregnancy is preventable, and therefore is a choice. If a woman neglects that choice, her negligence should not result in liability to the father. Yes, it takes two people to create a baby, and both parties bear some responsibility. But if she says to him "I'm on the pill" when she's skipped it for four days in a row and gets pregnant, why should he be liable? If fathers are *always* held legally responsible for maintenance costs of children, no matter what the mother did, then women are being indemnified for carelessness.

Individual men and women should negotiate their sexual interactions as they see fit, and it is no one else's business. It's especially none of the government's business, and certainly the law should not tip the scale in favor of supporting careless women.

Divorce

When marriages go wrong, there should be a legal escape hatch. However, it's often claimed that divorce courts are biased against men.[5] To be fair, I don't know if this is true or how to measure it. Nonetheless, a lot of men believe it and their belief may contribute to the decline in marriage rates.

Changing the divorce laws is not appropriate at a constitutional level. However, it should be a legal presumption that parents have 50/50 responsibility and authority over their kids.

And it should not be a legal presumption that husbands are responsible for their wives' illegitimate children. If men marry women who already have with kids and agree take on parental responsibilities, that's their choice. But the courts should not force this responsibility upon them.

Both the current policies, and the proposed fixes, will leave some children raised by single parents. It's impossible to prevent this happening. Perfection is not possible here, but the law should not make things worse. The corrections suggested here should rebalance things back to a neutral position of *equality under the law.*

Proposal 31—Immigration

Give me your tired, your poor,
Your huddled masses yearning to breathe free,
The wretched refuse of your teeming shore.
Send these, the homeless, tempest-tossed to me,
I lift my lamp beside the golden door!

—Emma Lazarus

For the last 30 years or so, congress has prioritized family immigration, and downplayed working immigrants. This is the wrong way round.

As a free citizen of a free country, you should be free to employ anyone you wish to employ, including non-citizens. Employing non-citizens is part of your rights to free trade and freedom of contract. Economically and socially, immigrants benefit society. And the US needs young people because our population is aging.

There should be safeguards to keep criminals out and to makes sure immigrants contribute rather than drain resources. But so long as those safeguards are met, the US should welcome new workers.

Proposed Amendment: Immigration

1. Government may not place restrictions on citizen's rights to employ non-citizens, other than the safeguards for public safety laid out below.

2. Non-citizens with a bona-fide job-offer from a US citizen or organization, or who have gained entry to a US post-secondary educational institution, shall be allowed to enter the country.

3. Government may refuse entry to non-citizens seeking to enter the country to who:
   a. Do not provide evidence of a job offer or educational placement.
   b. Have been convicted of a felony-level crime in any country.
   c. Have been convicted of violations of US immigration law.
   d. May pose a risk of disease contagion if admitted to the US.
   e. Are believed by US authorities to be a credible terrorist threat.

4. Any non-citizen in the US for any legal reason may work, create businesses or self-employment opportunities for themselves.

5. Upon termination of current employment or education, non-citizens shall have 100 days to find new employment or leave the US. Any income generating economic activity shall count as alternative employment.

6. Non-citizens working in the US shall be required to register for and pay US taxes.

7. Non-citizens residing in the US shall not be entitled to any government welfare assistance that has not been paid for by them.

8. Non-citizens married to US citizens or with US-born children shall have a right of residence in the US whilst any immigration processing takes place, provided that they are not a burden upon the state and have no felony convictions.

9. Congress shall create rules for processing entry and exit of non-citizens who enter for work or educational reasons. Processing shall be online, automated, and free of charge. Government must issue entry permission for non-citizens within 48 hours of application unless there are specific reasons to exclude them. Government must provide clear explanations for any refusal of entry.

10. Non-citizens in the country illegally may be deported immediately to their home country by court order.

11. Non-citizens refused entry or deported shall have a right of appeal at their own expense but must return to their country of origin whilst any appeal is in process. Courts may hear appeals from abroad by video conferencing at the court's discretion.

12. Immigration and immigrant status are matters for federal law alone.

13. Non-citizens in the US illegally at the time of passing of this amendment shall have amnesty for past immigration violations so long as they regularize their situation under the new rules within two years.

14. Any person who has committed immigration violations (including those granted general amnesty above) may be granted US resident alien status but may not be granted citizenship.

15. Non-citizens who entered the country illegally as accompanied minors shall be offered a path to citizenship under rules to be decided by Congress. Minors who entered illegally of their own volition shall be treated under the same rules as adult illegals.

16. Non-citizens shall be counted in any US census separately from citizens. Only citizen numbers shall be relevant in consideration of apportionment for any voting district for any US government.

Basic Immigration Facts

Let's start with some basic data. For legal immigrants in 2015: [1]

- 1,051,031 became legal residents in the US.
- About ½ were new arrivals, ½ were already here.
- 213,910 were children/grandchildren of US citizens.
- 104,892 were spouses/children/grandchildren of resident aliens.
- 465,068 were other relatives of citizens.

- 144,047 entered for work.
- 151,995 were refugees or asylum seekers.

These numbers are typical for the last decade or so. About 43 million total foreign-born people reside in the US as of 2016.[2] Your author is one of them: I was born in the UK.

Estimates for undocumented immigrants (as of 2015) are: [3]

- There are about 11-12 million of them.
- About 8 million of them are in the workforce.
- About 66% of them have been here 10 years or more.
- The largest group (about ½ of them) are Mexican.

The trends in illegal immigration rose steadily from about 1990, leveled off around 2005, and have been steady since then, +/- a million or so.

Crime rates among the undocumented are lower than for citizens. One estimate puts the incarceration rate at 1.53% for natives, 0.85% for illegal immigrants, and 0.47% for legal immigrants.[4] This makes sense: crime has a higher cost for immigrants (being sent home) than it does for citizens, and the highest cost is for legal immigrants.

On the negative side, immigrants use welfare a lot. In 2012, about 30% of citizens used some form of welfare, about 48% of legal immigrants, and about 62% of illegal immigrants.[5] For legal immigrants with children, welfare usage is as high as 72%.[6]

Maximize Benefits, Minimize Downsides

America is a nation of immigrants. We are all immigrants here, even the American Indians.[7]

Individual Americans hold a wide range of views about immigration, from an impractical "let 'em all in," to an equally impractical "keep 'em all out." Overall though most Americans see immigrants as a net benefit.[8]

Since the mid-1980s, US immigration law has emphasized family reunification. Whilst families are important, family reunification is the wrong emphasis. The priority should be economic immigration, people who came here to work.

If you believe in freedom as a guiding principle of our great country, then that freedom must apply to employers. Employment restrictions fail the Test of Moral Authority. Do I have the right to tell you who you can and cannot employ? No, I do not, and therefore neither does the government.

Arguments about immigrants taking our jobs are bunk because we do not have jobs that are ours. Jobs belong to those who offer them. Employers get to choose who will best do the job they want done, citizen or non-citizen. There's nothing else to argue about because it is *the employer's choice* to offer a job or not. No one else has any say in the matter.

Public policy should probably be neutral towards immigration in the big picture—neither encouraging nor discouraging it. Nonetheless, it should be easy for US employers to employ foreigners if they wish to do so. Allowing easy access for foreign employees does *promote the general welfare* in many ways:

- Immigrants do jobs that citizens don't want. Crops rot in the fields when immigrant labor is restricted,[9] and restaurants struggle to find summer staff.[10]

- Immigrants will work for lower pay: stuff gets done cheaper. It's a win for consumers, but also for the immigrants because their low ages are still better than they could get at home. Whilst working, they also gain skills and experience, improving their prospects.

- Competition from immigrants incentivizes citizens to get their act together. High school graduation rates go up when citizens are exposed to competition from immigrants.[11] Economic immigration, like free trade, keeps us honest.

- Working immigrants pay taxes, buy stuff, contribute to the general economy.

- Immigrants have started many successful firms, boosting the economy and employment.[12] Immigrants are about twice as likely as native born citizens to start new firms.[13]

- Immigrants add to our cultural diversity, food, arts and so on.[14]

So, public policy should facilitate economic immigration, but there should be safeguards in place to keep out criminals, terrorists, and spongers. The US can't have open borders and let random people in. That would be nuts. Would you invite random strangers to come have dinner at your house, and meet your kids?

The US border means something. There should be a wall, but primarily a legal wall. Let's arrange the incentives to maximize the chances of the US attracting good people and excluding bad people:

- Immigrants with a job offer *before* they enter the country should be admitted unless there is some other explicit reason to exclude them.

- The entry system should be quick, easy, and online; visas issued within 48 hours. Speed maximizes economic growth.

- US felony convictions, immigration violations and known foreign felony convictions can be attached to the foreigner's ID documents by the system, automatically excluding them.

- The system should be free to employer and employee. Fees would incentivize government to turn it into a profit center, and special interests will encourage fees as a barrier to entry.

- Reasons for refusal should be transparent. Employers don't want to hire immigrants with criminal records, immigrants won't want to commit crimes that will affect their immigration status.

- Easy come, easy go. The easier it is to enter legally then the easier it is for temporary workers to go home. Most immigrants want to go home when not working.

- Any non-citizen in the US legally should be able to work, start businesses and so on. Entrepreneurs should always be encouraged to maximize economic growth.

- Immigrants will have a duty to register for taxes. Failure to do so should be grounds to kick them out and keep them out.

- Courts will have powers to immediately deport immigration violators. This will be a choice for the courts, and why deport someone who is working, paying taxes, supporting a family etc.? But if the choice is between jailing someone or deporting them, it is less expensive *for US taxpayers* to send them home.

- Deportations will happen by court order and not by administrative action. Checks and balances are how things are done in the US.

- Deported immigrants will have a right of appeal, but they must exercise it from their home country and at their expense. Congress and the courts can work out the details.

- Any conviction for an immigration violation will be a prima facie reason to refuse an entry visa,

- The same overall process will apply to students. Public policy should encourage smart people to come and study in the US. After they are done, they can choose to stay and contribute here, or they can return home with goodwill toward the US.

Overall, it will be easier for foreign workers and students to come and go under these proposals. Immigrants will be incentivized to behave without heavy handed enforcement. Technology can automate the process, and only immigrants who get flagged by the system should need to visit US embassies or consulates.

Other than criminal background checks, the people deciding if immigrants can come are employers. Citizens who offer jobs to foreigners have skin in the game. They are putting money and their businesses on the line. They will only offer jobs to people who they think will contribute to their business and by extension, to the US economy.

The Undocumented

Why are there 11-12 million illegal immigrants in the US? Mainly it's because US citizens want cheap labor and services, and they can get them by employing illegal immigrants. Therefore, immigration laws do not have the consent of the governed. Millions of citizens are spending their hard-earned money to break immigration laws.

Another factor is that welfare incentivizes illegal immigration. Illegals are cheaper to employ when no Social Security or Medicare taxes are paid. Where illegals do pay welfare taxes, they are subsiding the system because they cannot claim benefits.

Making legal immigration easy and banning immigrants from collecting welfare will solve all these problems. There will be no incentives for illegal immigration other than for actual criminals, who can be sent home at once if caught.

What should be done about the large numbers of current illegals? On the one hand it would not be useful to throw them all out when most of them are working—that would hurt us all. On the other hand, continued large scale illegality is not healthy for the legal system or the country.

To resolve this, let's offer a general amnesty for past violations of immigration laws, so long as those involved legalize themselves under the new rules. Upon passing the amendment, illegals would have two years to come forward and get legal. If they are currently employed, then they have a right to work under the new rules. If they are a dependent of an employed non-citizen, then Congress will have to write rules about who can and cannot stay. In principle though, so long as they are not a burden on the state and are supported by a worker, they should be allowed to stay.

If they are currently unemployed, they will have 100 days to find employment, or leave. However—and this is important—they are welcome to come back next time they have a job offer. Easy come, easy go.

This would incentivize illegals to become legal. The upside (being here legally and able to travel home easily) is so much greater than the downside (immediate deportation if caught).

Felons, including those who continue to commit immigration violations, should go. If they hide and are caught, the new rules allow for immediate deportation. Persons deported will have rights of appeal, but those rights must be exercised at their own expense and from their home country. They will not be allowed to hang out in the US for years while the legal machine grinds through its motions. Collectively we'll be paying much less for detention centers!

There may be exceptions for genuine refugees whose lives are at risk if they are sent home, but that is not the case for most illegal immigrants.

One caveat here. If all current illegals became citizens, their votes could change the balance of power. This presents a moral hazard: it incentivizes politicians to pander to non-citizens who broke the law, rather than to focus on current citizens. To avoid this hazard, let's allow illegals who get legal to stay if they benefit the economy, but as resident aliens, not citizens.

Another unresolved immigration problem is Dreamers—people who were bought here illegally as children. Congress has dithered about this issue for years. Any decision Congress makes, of any sort, will piss somebody off. Rather than risk annoying potential voters and damaging their election prospects, members of Congress instead avoid making decisions!

In the face of Congress abdicating responsibility, presidents have tried to address the issue through executive actions. Obama tried to legalize Dreamers. Trump tried to reverse that. This can't be a permanent solution because any presidential order can be reversed by the next president.

If someone came here illegally as a minor, they had no choice about it, and they should not be punished for decisions their parents made. Further, most dreamers are indistinguishable from citizens. They grew up in the same neighborhoods and went to the same schools. Culturally, dreamers are Americans.

The proposal is to legalize dreamers. Congress can sort out the details, but let's end this perpetual inhumane limbo that dreamers live in.

One small grey area here is minors (teenagers) who came of their own volition, unaccompanied. These folks should be treated like adult illegals: they can stay so long as they legalize their position and are working.

Other Immigrants

Economic immigration is the most important issue that needs fixing here. However, let's briefly consider some other types of immigration.

Family Connections

About 75% of legal immigrants get here through family connections. This chain migration is a frequent complaint of those who would like less immigration.[15] Family connection immigrants should not be allowed to be a burden on society, but otherwise this is an issue for Congress to decide.

One small issue that does need addressing here is spouses and parents of US citizens. Under current law, these folks typically can immigrate but must leave the US while their paperwork is processed. Supposedly this discourages non-citizens from gaining citizenship through fake marriages.

Fake marriages are fraud and should be prosecuted. But requiring non-citizens to leave while paperwork is processed reverses the presumption of *innocent until proven guilty*. These are people married to citizens, and/or with citizen children. Since Americans believe in family, and in due process, the proposal will allow these to remain in the US with their families unless they are criminals or a burden on the state.

If economic migration gets easier, the incentives for fake marriages go down. To remain here legally, all an immigrant will need to do is keep working. There will be little incentive to commit fraud.

Students

Foreign students are a boon to US universities financially, add diversity to campus populations, and spread goodwill towards the US abroad. Foreign students should be encouraged.

Many foreign students already come to the US. The only change that's needed is to make it easier for them to work, both whilst studying and after they graduate. The changes proposed here will help that.

Refugees and Asylum Seekers

Refugees and asylum seekers are fleeing war and persecution in their home countries. They are not coming to the US for positive reasons, but rather to avoid their home country. If all was well at home, they would probably stay there.

Refugees may well be bitter and angry about being forced to leave home. They may not like the US, perhaps even harbor ill will towards US foreign policy and US culture. They may want to import their culture into the US rather than assimilate.

Despite these worries, refugees in practice are rarely troublemakers. Refugees are a small proportion of immigrants, and they go through an exhaustive process via the UN to get that status. In practice, the biggest problem facing refuges and their children is rising out of poverty.[16]

The US should be careful about taking in large numbers of refugees. No country can assimilate too many immigrants without causing social problems. Germany, for example, has created ghettos of Syrian refugees.[17]

The US already has a generous refugee policy, and historically has taken more refugees than any other country,[18] though Canada recently overtook us.[19] Probably, the US has the refugee flow about right, though there may be ways to improve the integration of refugees into the US and prevent ghettos.

If changes are needed, refugee policy should probably prioritize refugees with marketable job skills. That would boost both integration and the economy. However, there's no need to change laws about refugees at a constitutional level. Congress can continue to handle the details.

Checks and Balances

*[In government] the constant aim is to divide and arrange the
several offices in such a manner as that each may be a check on the
other.*

—James Madison

One way to think about special interest manipulation of the legal/political
system is from an evolutionary perspective.

The legal system can be thought of as an ecosystem in which special
interests act as parasites on the body politic. They ride on the back of government, harnessing its energy and power for their own ends.

For the most part these parasites just cause widespread inefficiency
and sub-par economic performance. Occasionally though they cause serious problems, perhaps the death of a competitive rival, sometimes more
extensive damage to the economy or citizen freedoms.

When a virus infects a human body, medical interventions try to slow
the spread, mitigate side effects, and repair damage. The proposals so far
have been in this vein, addressing problem areas that have been infected
and damaged by special interests, suggesting interventions to stop the in-
fection and heal past damage.

However, repairing past damage is not enough because special interests
evolve. Millions of clever people are maneuvering on behalf of special
interests, trying things out to gain advantage. Eventually they will find
loopholes in any legal system and exploit them.

So, this last section of the proposals aims to provide a general-purpose
boost to the immune system. The proposals are designed to enable the
body politic to fight off new infections (legal attacks) as they arise in future. The constitutional equivalent of an immune system is called checks
and balances.

Our system was designed right from the beginning to include checks and
balances, but they have become eroded over the last 240 years. It's time to
create some new ones and strengthen the old ones.

Proposal 32—Misuse of Force

Occupants of public offices love power and are prone to abuse it.
—George Washingon

The corrupt politician or bureaucrat applying pressure by threatening government attention is popular cliché in fiction. It's a cliché because it happens.
Government agents profiting from use of government force is probably illegal everywhere, but still it goes on. And as government grows the potential for abuse and moral hazard grows with it. It is time to strengthen our protections against this abuse.

Proposed Amendment: Misuse of Force

1. Government force shall be defined here as any government action or inaction, or threat thereof, that citizens consider to be coercive.

2. Government force may not be used to coerce citizens against their will, except as allowed for in the Constitution.

3. Government may not delegate any power of coercion to any non-government person or organization.

4. Government may not profit from law enforcement.

5. Government agents may not use or conspire to use government powers for personal or political gain.

6. Civil asset forfeitures or equivalents shall be illegal.

7. Fines, penalties, and seizures imposed by government upon citizens shall be donated to charity. No monies may be kept back for direct or indirect government costs nor 3rd party costs.

8. The distribution to charity shall be managed by each state's tax collection agency.

9. Any charity wishing to take part in that state's distribution system shall register annually, with registration including a statement of donations to that charity in that state in the previous financial year. Charites will be ineligible to register if they:
   a. Spend over 50% of their income on aid to government workers or their families.
   b. Are run by a government agency.
   c. Have been convicted of fraud within the last five years.

10. Government agencies imposing fines, penalties or seizures shall forward all monies received each month within that state to the state's tax collection agency.

11. The state tax collection agency shall total the sums collected and distribute them to the registered charities, prorating distributions in

278 | America: A Repair Manual

proportion to the amounts collected by the charities themselves in the previous financial year. Distributions shall be made quarterly, one month after each calendar quarter ends.

12. All agencies involved in this process shall be required to keep public records. There shall be a full ongoing accounting of monies collected and distributed on record.

My Way, or Else

Government officials have government powers at their disposal: inspections, audits, permitting, arrests, and imprisonment. Occasionally officials abuse their powers to coerce citizens for personal, financial, or political gain. Abuses happen from town hall to the Oval Office.

In 2018, a Mr. Lozeman won a Supreme Court case arguing that the City of Rivera Beach, Florida misused its powers to shut him up, in violation of his 1ˢᵗ Amendment rights.[1] The City had had him arrested for speaking at a public meeting.

The States are busy at it, with New York declared #1 in corruption by media sources.[2] In 2018 NY officials were convicted of taking bribes, rigging bids, lying on official filings, stealing FEMA funds, and getting jobs for relatives; among other things.[3]

At the federal level, a scandal occurred in 2013 when it emerged that the IRS had been auditing charities associated with the tea party. As of 2017 lawyers were still complaining about the IRS hiding information.[4] Historically, presidents have ordered audits as a political weapon.[5]

Some government actions are clearly coercive. If men in uniforms wave guns in your face, do what they tell you and save your objections for later. Often though, defining what constitutes misuse of government force can be problematic. Should cops always arrest lawbreakers, or is a warning sometimes appropriate? Are there rules that are open to interpretation? Could a charity be both disliked by the President and corrupt?

These and other gray areas are possible. However, everything related to government is in a long-term trend of ever greater complexity. The rules become more numerous, intrusive, and open to interpretation. The greys are getting greyer! To balance this, citizens need stronger protections.

The proposal here is for a constitutional duty on government and its employees never to misuse government force. That's probably the law already in most places, but let's reinforce it at a constitutional level: no misuse of government force for personal or government gain, ever.

Courts and juries will need to wrestle with the grey areas. But it is important that citizens (via courts) are the ones to decide where the lines are drawn, not government agents. We'll be giving citizens tools to do that in *Proposal 40—Protection of Rights.*

Profiteering

Governments are often profiting from law enforcement: collecting fines, punitive damages, and settlements from citizens who have (maybe) broken the law. The moral hazard is that if government makes money from law breakers, then government is incentivized to create more laws to break. More laws, and more crimes, certainly is the trend in the US.

Where government profits from fines and settlements, the government is incentivized to prosecute even if a case is legally dubious. In some cases (such as anti-trust cases), the settlements can be huge.[6] Innocent parties may agree to settle out-of-court rather than face years of legal uncertainty.

Civil Asset Forfeitures

Perhaps the worst contemporary abuse of force is civil asset forfeitures. Civil asset forfeiture is a legal process where law enforcement seizes property suspected of having been involved in a crime or being the profits of a crime, without charging the owner. The owner must then sue to get their property returned. They must prove their property is innocent!

Civil asset forfeiture laws started under British Maritime Law from the 1600s. The original problem was that if you came across a pirate on the high seas, there was no jurisdiction in which to prosecute the ship owner. The solution was to prosecute (seize) the ship itself. Today, if you're fighting a South America drug cartel, you can't prosecute them, so you prosecute (seize) their warehouse in the US instead.

Fighting crime is difficult when you cannot prosecute the criminals. Nonetheless, civil asset forfeiture is an awful solution. No matter how you justify it, civil asset forfeiture an end-run around *innocent until proven guilty*. This is government men with guns taking stuff by force.

Fueled by the War on Drugs and the War on Terror, law enforcement agencies have been ramping up seizures in recent decades. Not only is this considered legal, but the agencies who steal the stuff get to keep it. The goods are divided up between the feds and local police who have taken them, and they spend the money on shiny new toys: guns, armored vehicles, spiffy SWAT uniforms. They head off to conferences at fancy hotels where they discuss how to legally steal more stuff over food and drinks.[7]

The malincentives are appalling, the excuses get increasingly tenuous, and the scope of what's acceptable keeps expanding. The City of Chicago is now using civil asset forfeiture to seize badly parked cars, profiting mightily in the process.[8]

No matter how big a proponent of crime fighting you are, no matter how much you support law enforcement, this is corruption. This is armed para-military thugs stealing stuff. It violates everything that a law-abiding society should stand for: *innocent until proven guilty*, and due process. This should simply stop.

Stopping civil asset seizures will result in a few criminals living abroad getting away with crimes. And that's a price we pay for preserving justice itself. Civil asset seizures cross a line where the justice system is abusing freedom rather than preserving it.

Government Fines and Penalties

Are fines, penalties, and seizures of the proceeds of crime valid legal strategies? Do they act as a deterrent to criminals?

Maybe. If a court sees fit to impose any of those punishments, then so be it. But punishment should come *after* due legal process and a guilty decision in court. Citizens are *innocent until proven guilty.*

Additionally, to avoid conflicts of interest and moral hazards, it's important that neither the courts nor any part of government can keep money raised by fines or seized assets. Instead, let's give it to charity.

This will prevent distorted incentives within the justice system. Neither law enforcement officers, agencies, justice departments, or courts will profit from prosecuting crime. No profit from seizing assets, no profit from fines, no profits from civil or criminal penalties.

Removing money from the equation might refocus government agents on justice. Decisions about what crimes to prosecute, or even what is a crime, should be based on citizen priorities, not profits. We want a for-justice legal system, not a for-profit legal system.

This proposal reinforces *Proposal 15—Administrative Law* which bans administrative agencies from imposing fines and penalties. Punishment should be the prerogative of the courts alone. By giving money collected from fines to charity, there's no incentive for the administrative state to try an end-run around the ban on imposing fines. They will not profit from it!

Proposal 33—Open Government

A popular Government, without popular information, or the means of acquiring it, is but a Prologue to a Farce or a Tragedy; or, perhaps both. Knowledge will forever govern ignorance: And a people who mean to be their own Governors, must arm themselves with the power which knowledge gives.

—James Madison

How many secrets does a government need? Valid reasons exist for some secrets, for short periods. Yet the trend is for the feds, in particular, to create ever more secrets. The trend is out of control.

It's time to restrain government secrecy. Citizens need to know what is going on to root out special interest corruption. We can't fix problems we can't see clearly!

Proposed Amendment: Open Government

1. Government has a duty to be open and transparent in its operations.
2. All government internal reports and documents shall be available for public scrutiny within one year of creation unless:
   a. Classified as secret for national security reasons.
   b. Classified as work-product before legal proceedings.
3. All classified documents shall be declassified within ten years of their creation.
4. Government may not create secret courts or courts that sit in secret.
5. Citizens have a right to observe the proceedings of court sessions unless closed under the specific conditions defined here.
6. Judges may close specific court sessions to the public and temporarily classify the proceedings when public observation might:
   a. Prejudice the outcome of the case. If closed for this reason, the proceedings may be classified for up to one month after the end of the case.
   b. Prejudice National Security. If a closed for this reason, the proceedings may be classified for up to one year after the end of the case.
7. Where any classification takes place for National Security reasons, government may apply for an extension of the classification. A classification may be extended for up to ten years by majority agreement of a panel of three judges, none of whom sat on the original case. Only one such extension shall be allowed.
8. Citizens denied access to a classified document, whether an internal government or court proceeding, shall have a right to a judicial review of the classification. These reviews shall take place before a

panel of three US District Court judges. The presumption shall be that the document should be declassified unless the government affirmatively proves its justification for continued classification. A majority of the judges shall decide the issue.

9. Where government seeks a court order affecting third parties, including search and surveillance orders requiring the cooperation of third parties, those parties have the right to be represented in court, even if the court is closed for National Security reasons.

10. Third parties affected by court orders shall have a right of appeal. If time is of the essence an appeal will not stay execution of the order. However, if the appeal later succeeds, the fruits of that order may not be used as evidence in court cases related to the third party.

11. Court proceedings that are classified may not be cited as precedent.

12. Citizens have a right to observe the proceedings of legislatures.

Government Secrets

The government works for us citizens. We pay the government via taxes to do our bidding, and we want to know what it is doing in our name. We want to know what the laws are, how they are made, who influences them, and what our employees are up to. We want to know how decisions are made, and what our money is spent on. It's as simple as that.

The government, on the other hand, is under pressure to keep secrets. Some things need to be kept secret, at least for a while: national security issues, ongoing military actions, and police investigations among others. But there are also invalid reasons to keep secrets: unpopular spending, special interest favoritism, embarrassing mistakes, fraud, and theft.

For government agents, the temptation is to hide all secrets behind the same veil. It's too easy to pretend mistakes, fraud, and manipulation need to be kept secret for national security reasons.

The Information Security Oversight Office (ISOO) publishes an annual report summarizing the feds' classification activity.[1] (All numbers cited below are "documents per year ").

In recent times, classifications peaked in 2012 at 95 million (hidden in a sea of definitions of classification). That was up from 23 million in 2008. There were a mere 71 internal challenges to those 92 million classifications in 2011.

From 2012 to 2017 classifications appeared to decline steadily to 50 million. This decline was due to government employees finding a new way to classify things. The 2011 report shows "derivative classifications" rising from 20 million in 2006 to 90 million by 2011.[2] Derivative classifications are reworkings of already classified documents. In other words: no need to classify a new document, just pretend it's a new appendix to one that's already classified.

Those secrets are also expensive, costing about $8.6 billion in 2008, rising to about $18.4 billion by 2017. That's an annual inflation rate of 8%,[3] compared to general inflation of 1.5% in the same period. The 2017 ISOO report recommends making secrecy costs into a line item in government budgets!

How many secrets are really necessary for national security? How many are classified out of habit or to hide embarrassing facts? It's impossible to know because they are secret! However, officials with access to a lot of secret information have indicated that only about 10-25% of the documents genuinely need to be classified.[4] Arguably, keeping too many secrets makes us less secure.[5]

Opening the Vaults

There's probably no way to reliably check classifications of millions of individual documents. Nonetheless, the guidelines outlined here would cut down on the volume considerably and enable citizens (and journalists) to challenge classifications and improve access to government documents. Rules such as:

- All government documents should be made public within one year of creation unless classified.

- Classifications should only be allowable for national security reasons, or work-product before legal proceedings.

- All classifications will last for a maximum of 10 years. If something should stay secret for longer, then a review by 3rd party judges would be required.

- Citizens would have a right to request judicial review of classifications of individual documents.

Now, technologically, every computerized government document could be copied to a public database. That would not be helpful. Millions of government employees are firing emails at each other endlessly, mostly office chatter: "How do I?" "Where is?" etc.

Nonetheless, if a citizen wants to see a specific document, then they should have the right to do so. The mechanisms of judicial review suggested here would offer a means for that to happen if the administration resists handing over documents. Secrets cannot be left to administrators alone. Checks and balances are needed.

Citizen Privacy

Some government documents contain information about private citizens. *Proposal 6—Privacy* requires communications between government and citizens to be kept confidential. This proposal should not override the government's duties under Proposal 6.

In practice, this is a problem that has long been handled by redacting information from government documents released to the public. That will no doubt continue to be the case.

Secret Courts

In 1978 Congress passed the Foreign Intelligence Surveillance Act (FISA) creating the Foreign Intelligence Surveillance Court (FISC). The FISC holds proceedings in secret. The government applies to the court to do secret things, and only the government's side of the story is heard. Its reach and power have been described as close to that of the Supreme Court, [6] though it's difficult to know if this is true because the court's proceedings are secret.

The original intent of FISA and the FISC was the surveillance of foreign spies. That may be a reason for secrets. But blanket surveillance of US citizens? [7]

It also appears that the FISC rubber stamps surveillance applications. In 2016, for example, there were 1,457 government requests to the court to conduct electronic surveillance. The government withdrew one, and the court granted the rest.[8]

Another hazard of secret courts is that secret decisions may become precedents for the next secret decision. Over time a body of secret law builds up. The potential is there for someone to be prosecuted under secret law, with secret evidence, and no one else would know because it would be classified.

No matter the positive intent of the FISC, the moral dangers are too great. The FISC is an affront to open government, democracy, due process, and checks and balances. The FISC should be dismantled. Secret proceedings will still be allowable, but under strict conditions:

- Held in regular courts.

- De-classified after ten years.

- If third parties are materially affected, they should have a right of representation in that court and a right of appeal.

In short, a restoration of due process, checks and balances.

Proposal 34—Whistleblowers

*Often the best source of information about waste, fraud, and abuse
in government is an existing government employee committed to
public integrity and willing to speak out.*

—Barack Obama

The government should never break the law. But government is also so big
and complex that citizens may never find out when laws are broken.
The only people who might know are a few employees or contractors.
Those people need to speak up, but they may be afraid to do so. They may
lose their jobs or worse.

Congress has long recognized this problem and passed various whistleblower protection acts. Those acts have been corrupted by administrative
processes.

Proposed Amendment: Whistleblowers

1. Government has a duty to uphold the Constitution and the law.
2. Government agents have a duty to inform the public of any Constitutional or legal violations by the government. This duty shall override any other contractual or legal obligation of the agent.
3. In any prosecution of a government agent, where the agent believes
   they acted to fulfill their constitutional obligations, they may enter
   a "protecting the constitution" argument in their defense. Any such
   case must be held before a jury.
4. The jury shall be empowered and shall have the obligation to consider if the government violated the Constitution or any law. Government must release any information the jury demands to make
   their judgment.
5. If a jury has insufficient information to decide if government has
   violated the Constitution or the law, then the presumption shall be
   that the defendant acted in good faith.
6. Breaches of confidentiality between private citizens and non-
   government organizations fall under the jurisdiction of contract
   law.

Federal Whistleblower Protection

In 2013 Edward Snowden stole a large amount of information from the
National Security Administration (NSA) and fled the country. Partial releases of the information revealed that the NSA and other agencies were
collecting vast amounts of data about citizens, their phone calls, and computer usage.[1]

Snowden is controversial, a hero to some and a traitor to others. His activities were probably illegal. However, were they justified in the name of exposing government wrongdoing? Snowden made a moral judgment and acted based on that judgment. You would have to follow his chain of moral reasoning to decide if he was right or wrong.

To root out government corruption, Snowden and other whistleblowers need to be judged by a jury, and in public. These juries should be empowered to consider both the letter of the law and if the law itself is just. That's not happening, and the existing laws to protect whistleblowers have been corrupted. Whistleblowers often face administrative processes behind closed doors that are biased in favor of the government, or they might face criminal charges.[2] Whistleblowers fear losing their jobs or otherwise being punished for reporting government wrongdoing.[3]

It's not appropriate to specify details of whistleblower protection at a Constitutional level. These are potentially complex problems for Congress and other legislative bodies to sort out.

What is appropriate in the Constitution are principles. The principle here is simple: government employees should have a duty to inform the public of constitutional and legal violations by the government.

Arguably, government employees already have a moral duty to report wrongdoing, and sometimes a legal duty. But let's tilt the balance in favor of getting government lawbreaking reported. Let's *require* government employees (including contractors) to report constitutional and legal violations by the government. A constitutional duty to report wrongdoing should take precedent over any contractual agreement they have with the government.

If government employees must report lawbreaking, they will also need protection from persecution or prosecution. It's too easy for the government to silence employees through administrative processes or criminal prosecutions. When the government comes after you the deck is always stacked in their favor.

To balance things out, I propose giving whistleblowers a defense of "protecting the Constitution." If invoked, that defense must be argued in front of a jury. This will help prevent the government from hiding behind closed-door administrative processes.

If such a case goes to court, let's both require and empower the jury to consider the constitutional and legal issues. The jury will have the right to demand any information they see fit to judge the case.

Private Whistleblowers

If the government breaks the law, it does so in our name, on our behalf. We don't want that happening, so strong protections are needed for whistleblowers informing us about government violations. But what about private companies breaking the law?

In the last twenty years or so there has been a flood of legislation offering whistleblower protection to employees of private organizations. As of 2017, the Occupational Safety and Health Administration was overseeing about 22 whistleblower protection laws in areas ranging from workplace safety to financial reporting.[4]

This legislation leads us into murky territory. In principle, morally, law breaking should be reported. In practice, it is not so straightforward, especially when private employees are reporting about private companies.

Firstly, there's the question of what constitutes a crime. Everyone agrees about murder, theft, and fraud. But should regulatory violations be crimes? Many citizens already think regulation oversteps the bounds of government's authority, and often the individual rules are debatable.

Secondly, there's a short and slippery slope from protecting whistleblowers to requiring whistleblowing. Sooner or later a creative prosecutor will find a way to apply conspiracy laws to non-whistleblowers who could have acted. Conspiracy laws were discussed in *Proposal 17—Criminal Justice*. This is a variation of the same issue.

A third factor is privacy. *Proposal 6—Privacy* introduced a rule that citizens should never have to report on other citizens except by specific court order. Most people do not want to live in a world where neighbors are spying on each other.

Finally, there's the Test of Moral Authority. Do I have the right to tell you who you can employ and under what conditions? No, I do not have that right. By extension, neither does the government. If the government has no moral authority to dictate employment conditions, then it similarly has no right to protect those conditions.

Let Private Whistleblowing Be Private

What's the solution to these issues? Basically, keep it private. Private whistleblowing should be an issue for the conscience of individual citizens. If they feel something is a crime, and sufficiently important that they must report it, then they should report it. Then, and only then will law enforcement get involved.

Otherwise, whistleblowing is an issue for contract law. Employment contracts typically address issues about workplace confidentially, trade secrets and so on. Disputes between employer and employee, if they end up in court, are a matter for civil courts.

Will this produce a rash of corporations doing terrible things and hiding behind employee confidentiality contracts? Doubtful, because the incentives already work against corporate malfeasance.

Corporations profit from ongoing business with their customers. They are highly incentivized to protect their image as law-abiding citizens. The public relations and legal consequences can be severe if they are caught breaking the law.

Where corporations break the law, they should be prosecuted. But the long-term cure for corruption and law breaking is competition. Most citizens would prefer to work for or do business with reputable corporations. More competition means more choices. Bad actors will get squeezed out of the market.

Proposal 35—Term Limits

The security intended to the general liberty consists in the frequent election and in the rotation of the members of Congress.
—James Madison & Alexander Hamilton

Term limits (which the Founders called "rotation in office ") have a long history back to the Greeks and Romans. The Founders were aware of that history. Jefferson, Franklin, and Mason all wrote in favor of term limits and, where they could, enacted them in state legislatures. It is something of a puzzle that they were left out of the US Constitution.

It's time to correct this oversight and have term limits for all elected representatives. While we're at it, let's correct some related problems with career politicians.

Proposed Amendment: Term Limits

1. Representative as used in this amendment shall mean any person elected to government office by popular vote of citizens, or any person appointed in their stead.

2. All representatives shall have term limits on their length of office to be decided by each legislative body, but which may be no more than six years total in any position.

3. Representatives may not run for office unless running for reelection in their current office.

4. Representatives who resign from office may not run for another office until after the end of the term of the office they resigned from.

5. Persons convicted of a felony or of violating a citizen's Constitutional rights may not run for office for ten years after their conviction.

6. No person may run for more than one elective post at the same time.

7. Anyone who has held elected office, worked for an elected representative, or worked as a government employee or appointee, may not work as a paid lobbyist for a period of ten years after leaving office or their government job.

8. Any person found guilty of illegal lobbying shall be restricted from approaching any representative or their staff for a period of ten years. They shall further be required to make public all communications that they have had with any representative or their staff in the previous ten years, and this requirement shall override attorney-client or similar privileges.

9. Representatives who have had dealings with an illegal lobbyist shall be required to publicly disclose dealings they have had with that lobbyist, and to abstain on any vote of interest to the lobbyist.

How Long Is Too Long?

Term limits are needed to curb the abuses of power and other problems arising when legislators stay in power too long. The longer someone is in office, the more power they accumulate and the more they start to act as if they have a right to wield that power.

Long-term legislators become remote from everyday life, spending most of their time in the corridors of power rather than on main street. They become cozier with lobbyists the longer they know them. They find it difficult to admit mistakes that might affect their chances of reelection.

Term limits will limit the accumulation of power that comes with seniority and simultaneously limit the power of lobbyists because they will have to start over with each new representative. New representatives will have new ideas and perspectives and be less daunted by convention.

Term limits may lower the chances of malfeasance. Whilst in office representatives have power to hide their own wrongdoing, but that power diminishes after they leave office.

Term limits will also tend to focus representatives on what's important, rather than popularity and reelection. Politicians often have difficulty setting priorities because of special interest pressure. For campaigners, their issue is always the most important issue on any table, and they squeal loudly when ignored. Politicians will placate special interests to avoid adverse publicity that might damage their reelection prospects.

A final advantage of term limits is that last-term incumbents won't need to focus so much on fundraising. Some fundraising will still go on, but as a rule current representatives should prioritize today's issues, not filling their war chests for tomorrow's elections.

The basic proposal here is that *all* elected representatives, in all US governments, should have term limits.

At the federal level, while the President is currently limited to two 4-year terms, Senators and Representatives have no limits. Average completed time-in-office for most members of congress is currently around 10 years, but some leaders currently have been serving 20 years or more.[1]

About 15 states have term limits as of late 2020.[2] In another six states voters approved term limits, but their votes were nullified. Supposedly this was for technical reasons, nothing to do with the perverse incentives of representatives who voted to nullify citizen wishes!

Data for every county and municipality is difficult to collect, but it seems that only about 10% of cities nationwide have term limits for majors.[3] Among major cities, most do have limits with the notable exception of Chicago.[4]

The maximum any elected representative can serve is set here at 6 years. This will dovetail with existing election cycles. Almost all legislators are elected on 2-, 4-, or 6-year terms depending on the jurisdiction. Legislators can iron out the details within the framework.

This will effectively create one-term presidents, governors, majors, senators, and other representatives at all levels of government. It will end most reelection campaigning. *It will end the cult of personality in politics.* Perhaps instead we can focus on effective government.

Term limits come with a new set of moral hazards.

Firstly, representatives coming to the end of their term don't fear losing an election and may be tempted to act in ways that benefit them or their friends. Take, for example, presidential pardons. There's a place for clemency, but also potential for abuse. Was someone pardoned to correct a miscarriage of justice, or because they are the friend of a friend?

The proposals on equality of law and on rent seeking clarify that using a government post for personal gain is unconstitutional. Such cases may be difficult to prove in court. Nonetheless, if the outcry about a situation is great enough, and with a mechanism to prosecute, departing representatives will feel pressured to behave.

Another possible problem with term limits is inexperienced legislators passing bad legislation. However, there's no evidence of good legislation being passed today. Even defining "good" legislation is a problem, especially when manipulation is going on.

As for the argument that we needed experienced legislators, we might ask what exactly legislators are experienced at. Arguably, it is fundraising for reelection! Let's improve legislation by improving the legislative process, as outlined in *Proposal 12—Legislation*, rather than improving legislators. Rather than depend on good people, let's design good systems.

A final possible problem with term limits is that senior civil servants become de facto power centers.[5] Perhaps the best example in US political history is J Edgar Hoover's 47-year tenure as head of the FBI.

Civil servants accumulate power in any political system. Congress has acted to combat these problems. Current FBI directors, for example, are appointed for 10-year terms. Often new presidents or governors can appoint new heads of agencies, which is an opportunity for house cleaning. *Proposal 36—Government Employment* will strengthen the powers of legislators to remove civil servants as an added check.

Career Politicians

Even with term limits, an individual could still spend their entire working life in politics. They could move from one political job to another—intern to advisor to staffer to representative to senator to president to lobbyist.

As a citizen, a politician has a right to the *pursuit of happiness,* as they see fit. From a public policy perspective though, career politicians create some hazards. Too much time in politics and they become detached from ordinary life. They live in a political bubble with other political people, where the real world rarely intrudes. How can anyone represent the average citizen when they have no experience of being one?

A related problem is that when someone jumps from one political job to another, they risk not paying attention to the current job whilst focused on the next one. How effective was Governor Bush whilst on the campaign trail to become president? How effective was Senator Obama whilst on the campaign trail to become president?

Laws vary by state, but sometimes representatives can hold one post whilst campaigning for a different post. Yet they are being paid to do their current jobs, not to be out canvassing for the next one.

These problems can be solved with a few simple rules: No running for multiple offices at a time. No running for elective office while you are in office (except for a second term in the same office).

To stop possible end-runs around this last rule, let's also stipulate that if you hold an elective office, you cannot quit early to run for something else. Elected officials can still quit if they are no longer willing or able to do their jobs. But they won't be able to run for a new office during the period of their original term.

Since most of the country is on a two-year election cycle matching up with the federal election cycle, most representatives will have to spend a minimum of two years out of office between posts.

Another problem with career politicians is the moral hazard of former politicians becoming lobbyists after they leave office. Insiders can use their connections and knowledge of the system for personal gain, for themselves and their clients. In Washington this is known as the revolving door problem: departing politicians leave through a revolving door, go around 180 degrees, and come straight back in as lobbyists.

Term limits would help with the revolving door problem because even if departing politicians came straight back, they would find new people in place rather than old friends. Even so, let's ban the revolving door after someone leaves office. Enforcement may be difficult, but if the ban is clear, then the courts can shine a light into the grey areas.

This ban is designed to create negative consequences for both lobbyists and representatives if they are caught. Both sides of the lobbying transaction will face incentives to keep it legal.

None of the above proposals will stop determined individuals from spending a lifetime in politics. There will still be people who hold several elected offices. But they will be forced to take breaks between offices. They will have to take regular walks down main street and come into contact with real people and real life. And we'll all be better off for it.

Proposal 36—Government Employment

Millions of Americans who work hard & play by the rules every day deserve a government and a financial system that does the same.

—Barrack Obama

Perhaps there was a time when government employment was a genuine public service staffed by overworked and underpaid workers. However, over decades, government employment has morphed into overpaid jobs for life and pensions so generous that unfunded pension schemes are in danger of bankrupting many states and municipalities.

Something is out of alignment here, and it is time to rebalance it.

Proposed Amendment: Government Employment

Note: As throughout the proposals here, *agent* refers to anyone who is employed directly or indirectly by government: employees, contractors, and employees of government sponsored organizations.

1. Managers of government agencies shall have a duty of care to ensure maximum efficiency in their agency's operations and to employ minimum numbers of staff to fulfil their objectives.

2. Managers of government agencies shall have a duty of care to ensure that government jobs are awarded to those best qualified to do the job.

3. Previous or current government employment may not be a hiring criteria per se when hiring for a position.

4. No government agent shall have any right of tenure.

5. Persons who have served in the military may not work in law enforcement for five years after the end of their military service.

6. Legislatures may release any agent from their administration's employment with a 2/3 super majority vote.

7. Government may not create private benefits programs for government agents. Benefits programs offered to agents must be purchased in the open market.

8. Government agents shall take an oath to uphold the Constitution.

9. Government agents shall have a duty to protect citizens' constitutional rights from encroachment by other agents.

10. Defending a citizen's constitutional rights shall be a valid prima facie defense in any lawsuit, civil or criminal, involving one government vs. another government or their agents.

11. Government agents acting to defend a citizen's constitutional rights, who are disciplined under any administrative process for ac-

tions they have taken, shall have the right of appeal to a court of law where it shall be for a jury to decide the merits of the case.

12. Government agents shall have a duty to report other agents who violate the Constitution or the constitutional rights of citizens.

13. Failure to uphold the Constitution or any lesser law shall be a prima facie fireable offense for government agents.

Special Workers

Bureau of Economic Analysis figures (2015) show that federal civilian employees earn about 78% more than private sector employees for equivalent jobs.[1] State and local employees earn about 24% more than private sector wages. Benefits are generous and working conditions are good.

In a free market, on average, people get paid the value they return to the economy. If federal workers are paid 78% more than private workers, that would imply they are 78% more valuable to the economy. This seems unlikely. Unless you can find evidence that federal workers are more productive than private workers—approaching twice as productive—it's more likely that federal workers are over-paid.

Lest you think that salaries are not a fair comparison, jobs can also be compared in other ways, such as rates of firings, layoffs, and quitting. The results are similar: government workers are overpaid.[2]

This is not about specific jobs or any individual worker. Many government employees are dedicated and hardworking. Some may even be underpaid. But on average, something is out of alignment between government and private salaries, and this needs to be corrected.

A powerful special interest—government employees (or their unions)—have manipulated the system to give themselves systematic advantage. They get away with it because government workers are not subject to market discipline.

There's a natural tendency for us humans to think we're special. It's easy to think you're the best employee ever, deserving the best pay and benefits. This is the way of the world, and it applies equally to government and private employees.

In the commercial world, market forces act to keep things in check. If your pay and benefits get too far out of alignment with the market, you'll eventually lose your job to someone who does it better or cheaper. This market discipline ensures that everyone working in a for-profit enterprise must keep an eye on the bottom line and must keep customers happy. Otherwise, they are out of work.

Government employees are not subject to the same market forces and are relatively immune from the need to keep customers happy. Customers pay for government services indirectly, and by force. It's difficult to fire government workers, even if they underperform. Some even have tenure.

As a result, over time, abuse has gradually crept into government employment practices. The people being abused are you and I, the taxpayers, who are overpaying our employees.

Correcting Incentives

Fixing these problems requires aligning incentives correctly. That's difficult to do, but the proposals here will produce a quasi-market discipline.

To start with, managers of government units should have a duty of care to ensure that they carry out their operations with maximum efficiency, and minimum staff. That should already be the case, but in practice government agencies prioritize expansion over efficiency.

When hiring staff, managers should have a duty to employ the people best qualified to do the job. As part of that, earlier government employment should not be a hiring criterion. Programs like Veterans' Preference[3] should go. Employees should be chosen for their likely ability to do the next job, and not their past government service. Unless their previous government employment gives them relevant experience, it should be of no bearing on employment decisions.

Next, no government employee should have tenure, ever—both formal tenure and quasi-tenure such as prioritizing former government employees. Taxes should never be used to pay someone who can never be fired.

Removing tenure will free managers to fire unproductive employees. As a backstop—if administrators do not act—legislators will have the power to remove any employee of that administration by a supermajority.

These measures are not perfect, but together they will put government workers on notice: they are expected to perform or be out. Changes to the tax code described in *Proposal 21—Taxation* and a ban on debt accumulation described in *Proposal 25—Government Debt* will further incentivize governments to focus on budgets and efficiency. Over time, government is likely to scale back to essential services only.

Are these changes unfair to government employees? It will certainly be a change, but once in place, anyone thinking of applying for a government job would know this was the way things were done. If they don't want to live with it, they don't need to take the job! This will be a government equivalent of market discipline: underperform and you are out.

Note that unions representing government workers have been working for decades to keep their members employed, no matter what. They will continue to work on behalf of their members, as they should. Nonetheless, these measures will tip the balance back towards government employers who answer to taxpayers, first and foremost.

Proposal 19—Law Enforcement discussed how to counter the problem of police forces becoming increasingly militarized. An added counterbalance proposed here is to bar ex-military from employment in law-enforcement for a period of five years after their military service ends.

The military takes young men and women, fresh out of high school, and trains them to fight. It then puts them in situations where civilian insurgents are trying to kill them. Of necessity soldiers will start to see all civilians as a potential threat.

That might work on the streets of Iraq or Syria, but it does not work in America. US civilians rarely kill or bomb police officers. It's unhelpful for police officers to see civilians as dangerous enemies or encourage an "us and them" attitude.

Law enforcement is a popular career choice for ex-military personnel, and many of them successfully transition back to normal life and work effectively as police officers. Nonetheless, military training and police training are not the same. We'll have a more mature and civilized law enforcement force if officers have to spend time as adult civilians living normal lives in the US. A five-year gap between military and law-enforcement careers would help ensure that.

Another abuse that needs fixing is government pensions. *Proposal 2—Legal Equality* will end legal advantages offered to government employees, including pension schemes. To reinforce this, the proposal here is that government pensions should be the same as private pensions. Government should either buy pension plans from the private market (like corporations) or contribute to employees' individual PSAs as described in *Proposal 22—Social Security.*

The Primary Duty of Government Employees

If the primary responsibility of government is the protection of individual rights, then, implicitly, government employees have that same duty. The proposals here are designed to reinforce that duty. Government employees have an individual duty to protect citizen rights, and a duty to prevent other employees from abusing those rights.

If that then puts them in conflict with other employees, or with their own managers, they may need protection themselves. The proposal is that if they are subject to administrative punishment because of actions they have taken to protect citizen rights, then they should have a right of appeal to a court and a citizen jury who can decide the merits of the matter.

Proposal 37—Campaign Finance

In 2004, over $2.1 billion was spent lobbying Congress. That amounts to over $4.8 million per Member of Congress.
—Barack Obama

Is big money corrupting our political process? Do the rich buy elections? About 80% of Americans think so,[1] and voters for both major parties agree. Time to fix this.

Proposed Amendment: Campaign Finance

1. Political contributions shall be defined here as financial or in-kind contributions or gifts to any political person or organization, including persons running for office, or campaigns for a change in the law or public policy.

2. Real citizens may make political contributions in any amount. They shall have a duty of care to publicly declare all contributions of more than $10,000.

3. Recipients of political contributions shall publish an annual accounting of contributions received and spent, including sources.

4. Congress shall establish a national database, standards, and mechanisms for the reporting of political contributions by both donors and recipients.

5. Anyone found guilty of accepting illegal political contributions shall be barred from working for government or running for public office for a period of ten years.

6. Non-citizens may not make political contributions.

7. Organizations may not make political contributions with the exception of political organizations defined in the tax amendment. Monies given to political organizations shall be considered political contributions subject to the rules outlined here.

8. Organizations may not donate to charity with the exceptions of:
   a. Donations for good works in communities where they operate.
   b. For humanitarian aid in times of disaster.

Buying politics

Lots of money is spent on politics. For the right people, investing in manipulation is highly profitable, so they want to invest more. Things are likely to get worse as special interests get ever better at manipulation.

Politically, campaign finance appears to be a divisive left/right issue. Typically, the Right supports less restricted giving as a protection of free speech, and the Left thinks that big money corrupts politics. Behind the rhetoric all politicians want money for their campaign funds. Both main political parties get huge amounts of money, and over time in roughly similar amounts.[2]

As a result, Congress argues about campaign finance, but rarely does anything.[3] Only every 20-30 years does enough pressure build to get a reform act passed, such as the 1971 Federal Election Campaign Act, and the 2002 Bipartisan Campaign Reform Act.

The Supreme Court has weighed in as well. The 2010 *Citizens United*[4] case decided that corporations were citizens who could give as much campaign money as they liked. The 2014 *McCutcheon* case overturned aggregate contribution limits.

Citizens are much less divided than their representatives. One 2015 poll found 4/5 of Americans think money plays too much of a role in US politics, and 2/3 think that the wealthy have too much influence on politics.

Republican and democratic voters alike want restrictions on political donations and fuller disclosure of money sources and spending. This is not a partisan issue; it is a politician vs. citizen issue.

I should point out, in the spirit of fairness, that a few economists believe money in politics is not as big a problem as it is made out to be. By some measures political spending has gone down.[5] However, it's difficult to get clarity on these issues because politicians and special interests alike are incentivized to lie about how much is contributed and what influence it has. Politicians can also easily rationalize their decisions, i.e.: "I voted on principle, it's just a coincidence that my donors liked my vote."

No Longer for Sale

Campaign finance presents a clear conflict of interest between citizens and elected representatives. Citizens want less money in politics, representatives want more. A constitutional amendment is the best way to put restrictions on representatives that they have no incentive to put on themselves. But what should that amendment say?

Arguments about campaign finance boil down to two main issues. On the one hand, most citizens think money is corrupting our political system, buying politicians, and buying legislation. On the other hand, the Supreme Court has decided that spending money is a free speech issue, so that curbing spending is tantamount to curbing freedom of speech.

Both sides have a point, to a degree. So, here's a solution: allow individual spending on politics, ban organizational spending.

Individuals, real people, should be allowed to spend money as they see fit. Spending money is a form of expressing your opinion, as in "put your money where your mouth is."

Citizens also favor political transparency. So, let's create a rule that if anyone spends over $10,000 p.a., they will be required to declare it publicly. Citizens should know who is paying our politicians. And to help our rich citizens have their free speech rights heard loud and clear, let's require Congress to create a public database of political contributions. Let's see clearly who is spending money on what.

Money spent on politics should also not be subsidized. No tax breaks, no calling it charity or a business expense. Spend as much money you want on politics, but the rest of us shouldn't have to subsidize you.

By contrast, organizations should not be allowed to spend money on politics. Period. Organizations are not people, and they don't vote.

This would curb organizations from buying special favors. It would also resolve a moral hazard for the organizations themselves. When leaders spend organizational money on politics, they are spending other people's money. Those other people might not agree with them.

For example, unions traditionally give to democratic politicians. Many union members are democrats, but not all, so when a union spends money to elect democrats it is often using republicans' money to do it. If a big company gives to the republicans, many owners (shareholders) are republicans, but not all, so now democrats' money is being spent to elect republicans.

Many union members and shareholders alike could care less about politics, yet their money is still being spent. There are also many non-citizen union members and non-citizen shareholders. So now foreigners' money is being spent on US politics, which should not be allowed.

Let's simply stop all spending on behalf of other people—union members or corporate shareholders. Let those citizens spend their own money as they see fit.

There will be one exception allowed here, which is for organizations that are specifically "political organizations" as defined in the tax code. Political parties, and campaign raising organizations and pressure groups might fall under these categories.

Many of these groups are best organized as formal groups or corporations, so we will allow that. However, this is not an end run around the transparency and contribution rules outlined here. The finances of political organizations will be public. And contributions to political organization will be considered to be political contributions subject to the rules here.

Consequences of Illegal Contributions

Despite the rules outlined here, special interests will still be motivated to buy favors, and politicians will still be tempted to accept illegal money.

So, as an added check, let's enforce consequences on anyone caught handling illegal money. For the politicians, the consequence would be to ban them from running for office or holding any government post for a period of ten years. For the special interests, their guy will be out of office and less able to deliver the favors they wanted to buy. For all parties, there will be reputational damage and possible corruption charges.

Note that there might be a small downside here of politicians forced to resign mid-term, and the hassle and expense of an additional election. This is unlikely to happen often and would be a small price to pay for cleaning up corruption.

It's unlikely that money can be entirely removed from politics. However, that influence can be severely curbed with greater transparency, and meaningful consequences for rule-breakers. Let's take those basic common-sense steps.

Proposal 38—Interaction Between Governments

The powers of government should be so divided and balanced among several bodies of magistracy, as that no one could transcend their legal limits, without being effectually checked and restrained by the others.

—Thomas Jefferson

The US was designed as a federal republic with multiple layers of checks and balances. As part of this, local, state, and federal governments were meant to have different responsibilities to balance each other out.

Over time, the higher-level governments have slowly accumulated power to themselves at the expense of more local governments. It is time for a rebalancing.

Proposed Amendment: Interaction Between Governments

1. US governmental responsibilities must be exercised at the most local level of government applicable to the issue at concern.

2. No government may violate its constitutional obligations via agreement with any other domestic or foreign government.

3. No lower government shall have a legal obligation to cooperate with higher government action they believe to be unconstitutional.

4. In legal disputes about the constitutionality of legislation that a higher government has passed, the higher government must demonstrate they have a constitutional right to impose that legislation before a jury of citizens of the lower government.

5. No lower government shall have a legal obligation to cooperate with higher government legislation that imposes unfunded costs greater than 1% of the lower government's annual budget.

6. Citizens in any jurisdiction shall have the right to vote on any legislation. A majority vote against any locally passed legislation shall void the legislation. A majority vote against any higher government legislation shall suspend enforcement by local authorities.

7. If 2/3 of the counties in a state vote not to enforce state laws under article 6 above, the state laws shall be repealed. If 2/3 of states vote not to enforce federal laws under article 6 above, the federal laws shall be repealed.

8. State governments shall have the right to remove any government responsibility from federal authority if a 2/3 majority of states vote to do so. The process shall be as follows:

    a. A responsibility must be clearly defined by the participating states, along with a list of pertinent federal statutes and federal agencies managing that responsibility.

b. Each participating state legislature must pass a bill authorizing removal of that responsibility from federal government control.

c. Once such a bill is passed by 2/3 of state legislatures, then the federal government shall have no further authority or control of that responsibility. It shall be an issue for state control alone.

d. States that did not take part or did not vote for that bill will be obliged to take responsibility for that area of authority.

e. After responsibility has moved to the States, federal employees involved in that responsibility shall be released from federal employment.

9. No higher government may mandate funds transfers from lower governments to the higher government.

10. At least 50% of any lower government's spending on any local project must be paid out of local funds.

11. Where a possible felony crime is reported within a government unit or government sponsored organization, investigation must be overseen by law enforcement agents not employed by that unit or organization.

Who's in Charge Around Here?

Ever since it was created, the federal government has been growing at the expense of the states:

- The civil war established that states could not leave the union, so that threats to leave no longer had teeth to keep the feds in check.

- Federal regulation grew quickly after the civil war with the Interstate Commerce Act (1878) and the Sherman Act (1890), and later the New Deal (1930's) and Civil Rights Acts (1960s).

- The 16th Amendment (1913) ratified a federal income tax which in turn financed federal growth from then on.

- The 17th Amendment (1913) caused federal senators to be elected directly by citizens rather than state legislatures. This disconnected the federal government from caring about states' rights.

- Numerous 20th century wars fueled federal growth: WW1, WWII, Korea, Vietnam,

- Wars on Citizens helped, especially the war on alcohol drinkers (prohibition), and the war on drug takers.

- The creation of the Federal Reserve (1913) and leaving the gold standard (1971) massively fueled and enabled federal manipulation of the dollar, ballooning federal debt, and inflation.

The country has gone too far in the direction of federal power, and the states have in recent years started to push back more, with the Supreme

Court becoming the arbitrator of the balance between state and federal power.[1] Large cities have long agitated against state and federal law, and debates about the balance of power between counties and states frequently occur in the media.[2]

Citizen opinions on the balance of fed/state/local powers are difficult to pin down precisely. However, Gallup conducts regular polls about the "size and power of the federal government."[3] In February 2018 only 34% of citizens reported they were "satisfied" or "somewhat satisfied." Satisfaction peaked after 9/11 at about 60%, but for most of the last decade has been under 40%. Republican voters tend to be in support of states' rights, but so are a sizable minority of democrats.

Politically though, no mechanism exists for citizens to give clear feedback about the size of government overall, or the relative sizes of federal, state, and local governments.

In a market economy firms prosper according to how well they meet the needs of their customers compared to their competitors. Government has no direct equivalent. Politicians make promises, but there's no necessary connection between your vote and what politicians do in practice. And all governments have their own incentives to keep growing.

What's needed are feedback mechanisms giving citizens meaningful input about the size of our governments and the distribution of power between them. Citizens can (over time) right-size their governments.

As a starting point, *Proposal 21—Taxation* splits tax revenue in equal thirds: federal, state, and local. Currently the feds collect most of the taxes, but they give much of it back via welfare and grants, making it almost impossible to say who spends what. A clear three-way split right from the start keeps each level of government about equal.

Then, let's introduce rules to protect lower governments from manipulation by higher governments, starting with a ban on unfunded mandates—situations where a higher government requires a lower government to do something but won't pay for it. Let's also disallow higher governments from mandating payments from lower governments. Lower government can choose to buy services from a higher government, but the higher government should not be able to force services on the lower.

Next, let's provide a mechanism for voters to nullify legislation imposed on them—a constitutional challenge of a higher law. If voters agree a law is unconstitutional, then enforcement is suspended locally, and higher government will have been given notice the law does not have the consent of the governed.

If enough lower jurisdictions do this, then the higher-level law is repealed. This might be a long process since 2/3 of counties would need to vote on a state law, and 2/3 of states would need to vote on a federal law.

Nonetheless, we'd have a clear democratic path to nullification. Voters could vote away laws they don't like.

Finally, let's give state legislatures a mechanism to formally remove responsibilities from the feds. If, for example, 2/3 of states decided that the feds should not have a role in healthcare, then the feds would be required to repeal federal legislation and close federal agencies dealing with healthcare. Control would be devolved, permanently, to the states. This could be more nuanced: states could for example vote to get the feds out of health insurance but leave the CDC.

This provision would empower the 10th Amendment: *The powers not delegated to the United States by the Constitution, nor prohibited by it to the States, are reserved to the States respectively, or to the people.* States would have a mechanism to affirmatively *prohibit* federal powers.

Empowering local governments may give new teeth to an old problem: the local petty tyrant. Sometimes a local leader can exercise power for their own benefit at the expense of citizens. Sometimes local laws can violate individual rights. For example, where dry counties forbid the sale of alcohol, curbing citizen rights to free trade.

Local government overreach is a problem, but less so than excessive state and federal power. Local government tyranny has several factors keeping it in check:

- Local laws are enacted by people with local knowledge. They can create solutions better tailored to local problems.

- Local leaders live with you. They must look you in the eye when you ask them why they made a decision.

- Local law enforcement lives with you. They will be reluctant to enforce unpopular laws on their neighbors.

- Local leaders have less power and are subject to higher government oversight.

If local government becomes too big a problem, then as a last resort you can always leave town, or even leave your state. That's not ideal, but at least it's an option.

By contrast, it is difficult to leave the US if you disagree with federal policy. You'd have to find somewhere you can go—a foreign place, with foreign customs, laws, and languages. You'd be cut off from friends and family. And the IRS could keep chasing you unless you go through a complicated and expensive process to renounce your citizenship.

Overall, local tyranny is a lesser problem than federal tyranny. Additionally, the proposals here will strengthen citizens' rights in the face of any government misuse of power, local, state, or federal.

Proposal 39—Rent Seeking

Oft 'tis seen, the wicked prize itself buys out the law."
—Shakespeare, Hamlet

What recourse do citizens have when someone else manages to get the system rigged in some way? Legislation, once passed, is difficult to repeal. It's difficult to sue because the new law is the law, even if it is blatantly unfair or discriminatory.

What's needed is a higher-level mechanism, a constitutional right, which can be used to counter manipulation of lesser laws.

Proposed Amendment: Rent Seeking

1. Rent Seeking is defined here as manipulation of the legal system to produce systematic competitive advantage to some person(s) over others. It shall include all laws, regulations, or judicial decisions that favor any persons by offering them legal advantage or putting legal restrictions on competition.

2. Rent Seeking shall be a Tort under civil law in cases where the economic gain to beneficiary(s) of the rent seeking is more than $100,000 for a county/municipal law, more than $1,000,000 for a state law, or more than $10,000,000 for a federal law.

3. This amendment is intended to address laws that provide ongoing systemic legal advantage to some person(s). It may not be used to dispute awards of government contracts, provided that such contracts were awarded by an open and fair bidding process.

4. Cases brought under this provision shall be held in the lowest practicable level of court and decided by a jury. The jury shall be explicitly required and empowered to consider if the law at issue offers systemic legal advantage to one party over other citizens.

5. If the plaintiff wins the suit, the law at issue shall be declared unconstitutional and void. If appeals are lodged, the law shall remain suspended until appeals are exhausted.

6. Jurys may award damages against defendants found guilty in an amount equal to the economic loss to the plaintiff(s).

Rent Seeking

Rent seeking is a term used by economists to describe situations where someone tries to profit by having the legal system rigged in their favor, rather than by competing in the market. It's a confusing term,[1] but we're stuck with it!

Suppose that Company A invents a pollution control device for autos. They bribe a few legislators and get legislation passed requiring vehicles to have this device installed. Let's call it the "Clean Auto Act."

Now suppose Company B has a different but equally effective pollution control device. They could try selling their device, but since autos are required by law to use Company A's device, Company B must persuade auto makers to install two similar devices on the same car.

Company B is stuck, not because they have an inferior product, but because the law effectively prevents them marketing it. They have been out-competed legally rather than in the marketplace. This is rent seeking.

Rent seeking takes many forms, but often shows up as legal rules that favor one technology over another; rules making it difficult for new companies to start in a field, or legal monopolies. To counteract rent seeking, this proposal introduces a constitutional rule that allows plaintiffs to sue those who have managed to get the law written in their favor.

When that lawsuit happens, the jury in our example above would have to address questions like: is this Clean Auto Act constitutional? Does this act give Company A an unfair systematic legal advantage? It's for the jury to decide, a jury of citizens not seeking reelection.

A right to sue for rent seeking would be a powerful tool for citizens to push back against manipulation, leveling the playing field in favor of equal laws. However, safeguards are needed to prevent frivolous lawsuits.

Firstly, no matter what any legislation says, there's always someone who feels they lost out. Legal costs are a natural barrier on lawsuits, and in practice, most plaintiffs will be economic rivals of the defendant, who have the most at stake financially. Even so, the proposal puts financial limits on rent seeking suits to ensure they are only used in economically important cases.

Secondly, this is a tool to root out systemic manipulation, and not a way for disgruntled losers to sue happy winners. Government often hands out contracts to private parties as part of its everyday business. Only one bidder can win, the rest must lose. If the bidding process were unfair, then losers would have the right to sue over that. But this is not rent seeking unless there was evidence of systematic legal bias.

There will still be regulation. Auto pollution (the example used here), is a textbook case of a mass action effect externality: one car makes no difference, but 274 million US vehicles produce a lot of greenhouse gases. Pollution is a case where regulation can help. This proposal is about *how* the regulation is written to avoid manipulation. Regulations should specify results (grams of pollutants/engine power) rather than methods (use XYZ technology, patent held by Special Interest, Inc).

Proposal 40—Protection of Rights

*People shouldn't be afraid of their government. Governments
should be afraid of their people.*

—Alan Moore, V for Vandetta

What can you do if the government abuses your constitutional rights? In
theory you can sue the government, but the government itself makes the
rules. Suing the government is a big deal, and expensive. For the average
citizen suing is rarely practical.

Perhaps there's another way, or an additional way. What if you could
sue individual government agents for abuse of your constitutional rights,
and if you won, they would be fired?

Proposed Amendment: Protection of Rights

1. No government agent may violate the Constitution, break any lesser law, or order any subordinate to do the same.

2. Citizens shall have the right to sue any agent for breach of their
   Constitutional rights, or for ordering another to breach their rights.
   The plaintiffs in such a suit must have had personal contact with
   the defendant or their immediate subordinates.

3. Prosecutors may charge agents for breach of a citizen's Constitutional rights in criminal court. Prosecutors may press charges
   against any government agent acting within their jurisdiction.
   Higher level governments may not hold harmless agents who act
   unconstitutionally in a lower government's jurisdiction.

4. Government may not provide legal or financial support to any
   agent accused of violating a citizen's constitutional rights in any
   civil or criminal prosecution.

5. All lawsuits and prosecutions about a breach of constitutional
   rights shall be held in the lowest level of court practicable and in
   front of a jury.

6. Jurys considering such a lawsuit or prosecution shall be explicitly
   empowered to consider if the agent's actions were a breach of the
   Constitution.

7. Where an agent is accused of violating a citizen's Constitutional
   rights, the following shall not be valid defenses:
   a. Acting under the provision of a lesser law.
   b. Acting under the provision of an international treaty.
   c. Following the orders of a superior.
   d. Ignorance of the Constitution or any other law.

8. A guilty verdict must be found by 2/3 of the jurors for conviction.

9. Agents found guilty shall be terminated from their government post and banned for a period of ten years from holding any government office, employment, or contract. Terminated agents may not receive any financial compensation upon termination. No other punishment shall be required by law, but citizens retain the right to sue for damages as part of their original suit or separately.

10. Agents shall have a right to appeal any court's decisions. However, where an agent has been found guilty of a violation of a citizen's Constitutional rights their ban on government employment shall take effect immediately and may only be removed by another jury. The agent shall not be compensated for the period between the original court's decision and any overturn.

11. It shall be a violation of a citizen's constitutional rights for any agent or agency to interfere with their right to sue for breach of constitutional rights or harass them for having sued.

It's Not a Right Unless It's Enforceable!

The government is big and powerful. But it cannot do anything to you directly because it is not a person. The government works through its agents: employees, appointees, representatives, and contractors.

If you go up against the government, you are a flea trying to take on an elephant. You are a minor irritation, likely to get trodden on and crushed. But if you could take on an individual agent, now it's closer to a fair fight.

The proposal here gives citizens a right to sue any government agent they have contact with, or that agent's immediate superior, for a Breach of their Constitutional Rights. If found guilty the agent will be terminated from government employment. This will provide citizens with direct push back against individual agents who violate their rights, and indirectly against the government that employs those agents.

Suppose a law is passed that many citizens consider to be unconstitutional. There would be a rash of lawsuits against individual agents trying to enforce that law. Citizens would have a direct method to push back against unconstitutional laws. It would be a balancing check on the powers of government, as well as feedback to legislators.

Agents will know that they could be sued for abuse of a citizen's rights, then they would be incentivized to think! They cannot blindly follow orders without consequences: they must consider if a law or their orders break the Constitution. The agents themselves become part of the checks and balances. Agents will rightly fear losing their jobs if they abuse citizens' rights.

Over time, there would be less abuse of the Constitution by individual agents, and less abuse of the Constitution by the government itself. It will have difficulty enforcing unconstitutional laws through its agents.

For this to work arguments such as "I was following orders" or "I was obeying the law" cannot be allowed as a defense in court. Government agents swear to uphold the Constitution. They should be presumed to know the Constitution because, duh, they swore to uphold it. That knowledge would include knowing that these excuses are invalid.

The proposal also bars government from supporting agents accused of violating a citizen's constitutional rights. Agents should not be allowed to hide behind government legal and financial firepower. They should be, metaphorically, naked in front of citizen courts. Fear of the legal costs is part of that nakedness.

Practically speaking, these lawsuits need not be long, drawn out or expensive affairs. The issues will usually be straight forward: did the agent breach a citizen's rights, or not? A jury should decide, because that's the most important part of the process, but otherwise lawsuits should be kept to the simplest and cheapest levels of court.

Additionally, government employees will often have legal help as a benefit of union membership. Private legal help is fine, so long as the government cannot shield its own employees from citizens.

If citizens can sue government agents for violating their rights, then some agents will be found guilty.

Many citizens feel that violating the Constitution is a serious matter, and an agent who violates rights should be hung, drawn, and quartered, and have their remaining parts dragged through the streets by horses as a public display of their evil wrongdoing! Or, at the very least, long jail sentences would remind agents that citizen rights are paramount.

I propose a different solution. If a government agent violates the Constitution, they should be fired. If punishments are too harsh, citizens will be reluctant to sue, prosecutors will be reluctant to prosecute, and juries will be reluctant to convict.

Firing will solve most problems without over-the-top and expensive punishment. Suppose there's a local cop who is a bully and steps over the line too often. Your community might not want him as a cop, but it would be unfair to send him to jail for twenty years. And sending him to jail might cost more than his salary. This makes no sense. Better to fire him as unfit to uphold the Constitution.

Potential Problems

One potential problem here is that law enforcement officers, prosecutors and judges could face harassment suits from vengeful criminals.

In practice this is unlikely to be an issue. Most citizens will give officers of the justice system a little leeway, recognizing that they do difficult jobs, and that criminals may want to harm them. Also, the bar for conviction in all these cases is set at a 2/3 majority—there will need to be clear evidence of an abuse to reach that bar.

Another potential problem is that Breach of Constitutional Rights cases might result in miscarriages of justice, just as any court case might reach the wrong result. However, miscarriages here have relatively low consequences—defendants face unemployment, not incarceration.

Nonetheless, as is just, appeals should be allowed by defendants found guilty. However, the deck should still be stacked against government agents to incentivize them to be fierce protectors of the Constitution. As part of that stacking, whilst there must be an appeals process, that process cannot allow one government employee (a judge) to veto citizen's decisions about other government employees. So, if a jury decides someone should be fired, only another jury will be able to reverse that decision.

Finally, citizens cannot be allowed to sue any government agent anywhere for perceived breaches of the Constitution. That would cause legal chaos. To keep things reasonable, citizens will only be allowed to sue agents they have had personal contact with, or that agent's immediate boss if they think the boss ordered a violation of their rights. This would be a personal right to sue when your personal constitutional rights have been violated.

Government prosecutors though will have wider standing to prosecute anyone within their jurisdiction. If a federal agent does something illegal in your county, the county attorney will have authority to prosecute them.

Now, in theory, a county prosecutor could already do that. In practice, the states and feds can protect their agents by removing them physically or claiming preemption of jurisdiction under a higher law. Therefore, to give this proposal teeth, those things will be specifically banned. Local prosecutors will have a blanket right to sue any government agent for constitutional breaches on their turf. Feds and states will not be able to exercise a higher-than-mighty right to stop local prosecutors doing their jobs.

Part 3—Implementation

Between the idea
And the reality
Between the motion
And the act
Falls the Shadow

—T.S. Elliot, The Hollow Men

So far in this book I've laid out a set of proposals to get us out of our political mess, free us from special interest manipulation, and reverse the long-term trends causing today's problems. All that's needed to do now is have Congress pass a set of constitutional amendments, and we're done. Right?

Well, not so fast! That would be wonderful, but it's unlikely to be so easy. Political and social change can happen but is usually a multistep process.

This part of the book covers two topics:

- The *Transition Problem.* Sometimes you can't simply switch off the old way of doing things and switch on the new. People have made life-long plans and taken life-long actions based on the old ways. Transitions need to be managed carefully to avoid undue hardship.

- A *Call to Action*—some suggested first steps towards ending special interest manipulation.

Chapter 6—The Transition Problem

Those who make peaceful revolution impossible will make violent revolution inevitable.

—John F Kennedy

For the political and legal system to change, citizens must support the changes. Ultimately, they will need to vote for change, or for legislators who will support change, and they will only do so if they believe change is in their best interests.

The willingness of Americans to support change will depend in large part on how those changes are made. So, in this chapter I'd like to discuss *The Transition Problem:* how can the transition to a new system be made with minimum disruption and maximum fairness?

Many people are distressed at the direction our country is going in and feel things are declining. Simultaneously, almost everyone gains something from the status quo and is effectively part of a special interest. People will need to be persuaded that change is in their interests, and that any change is not unduly harsh. Part of the conversation needs to be about how fast things change.

Overnight change—just end the old system and start with the new—is arguably the fairest way to do things. It would ensure we sacrifice our special benefits equally. But it may be too harsh for many to stomach.

When government has been pursuing policies for decades, an abrupt stop will cause hardship—people have been acting based on the current system. To minimize disruption, it may be necessary to take things a little slower. Nonetheless it's important that the timetable is laid out clearly, in advance, and is fixed. No political fiddling after the event. People need to know what will happen and when so that they can plan.

So, for example, some welfare reformers believe welfare should just end, be stopped dead. If that were to happen, most recipients would probably find ways to cope. Nonetheless, an excessively sharp cut-off might seem too harsh for many, and that could result in citizens agreeing in principle that welfare should end but voting in practice to keep it to avoid too much hardship on the poor.

A transition period (I'm suggesting 10 months) would give welfare beneficiaries time to plan, charities time to organize, and so on. Individuals might feel called to start new charities, organize church groups, or approach neighbors and ask if they could help. Everyone would have time to organize and get ready, and citizens might therefore feel better about supporting reform.

Another important issue with a wholesale transition is that it must be seen to apply to everyone equally and on the same timetable.

If you were a welfare recipient, would you be willing to give up your benefits today for a promise that middle class voters will give up their mortgage interest deductions next year? If you were an electrician, would you be willing to have your licensing requirements eliminated today, on the promise that we'll get to plumbers tomorrow? If your industry is protected by tariffs, would you be willing to give them up while your rivals are receiving subsidized loans?

None of the above options will work. No one believes that if they give up their benefits today, others might follow tomorrow. The incentives are such that no one *should* trust anything other than a wholesale reset. The only fair way to end special interest benefits is if everyone—citizens, unions, corporations, charities, and government units alike—gives up their benefits simultaneously.

Transition Strategies

In making a major change to the system as proposed in this book, it's probably not possible to eliminate fear entirely, but transition strategies should try to minimize it. Here are some suggestions on how to do that:

- **Restoration of Individual Basic Rights:** any government action suppressing individual rights should end immediately. Courts and legislatures can sort out details within the new framework.

- **Government Debt:** it has taken the best part of 100 years to get to the current debt levels. Let's take 100 years to pay it down. Debt can't be eliminated today, or anytime soon, but let's at least reverse the trend.

- **Government Loans**: stop issuing new loans. Have old loans paid off within ten years. Ten years is plenty of time for the borrowers to either pay off the loan or find private alternatives.

- **Government Debt Guarantees:** implicit guarantees need to end immediately (such as the implicit agreement that the feds will bail out Wall Street if there's a crash). There never was any legal guarantee here! Explicit guarantees should expire within ten years. Plenty of time for everyone to find alternatives if needed.

- **Welfare:** federal welfare programs should taper down. Benefits will decrease from 100% to 0% over ten months, i.e.: 100% benefit the first month, 90% the second, and so on. State welfare programs will be allowable but will need to be organized.

- **Taxes:** there's no easy way to transition from one tax system to another without winners and losers, so the new system will just start at the beginning of the next tax year i.e.: 1st January. Everyone will have about a year to plan for the changeover.

- **Personal Welfare:** PSAs should become legal at once. People will have an extra tax-advantaged way to save in the year leading up to the tax system transition.

- **Social Security:** should remain for those who are already retired. Those who have invested in Social Security but are still working will have the choice to move funds to a PSA and opt-out. There will be no new entrants to Social Security—it will wither away over the next 40-50 years as beneficiaries die off.

- **Regulation:** will only apply to large corporations, so no immediate change for them. For small businesses, formal regulation will disappear overnight. They can continue with them voluntarily if they see value in doing so.

- **Government Workers:** workers released from government employment due to the proposals will get laid off on the same sliding scale as welfare recipients. I.e.: 1st month full salary, 2nd month 90%, 3rd 80%, and so on.

- **Simplification of Legislation**: will take years of reviewing and rewriting. However, the most recent legislation tends to be the most complex, so there should be rapid simplification of the legal system over the first decade of this process.

- **Justice Reforms**: the changes in the rules governing both civil and criminal justice should be implemented immediately, but it will take time for courts to settle into their new formats. If the Supreme Court has more than nine judges sitting at the time of implementation, then excess judges should be released on a last-in-first-out basis.

- **Civil War on Drug Takers**: this should end at once. Anyone incarcerated for non-violent drug crimes should be released as fast as the system can process them.

- **Term Limits**: should be implemented immediately but staggered over the first decade so that future elections result in a balanced mix of new and reelected representatives. The longest-standing incumbents should be the first to go.

The Moral Hazard of Incomplete Transition

During any transition, there may be times when both old and new systems are running side by side. This is often done deliberately to provide special interest benefits.

For example, suppose Congress decides a tax scheme should be illegal, they might change the tax code to close the loophole. But often they create an exception: if you are already using that tax scheme you are "grandfathered" and allowed to continue using it.

There's an element of fairness here. You arranged your affairs based on an understanding of the tax law. If the law changes, is it fair that a legal deal made in good faith suddenly becomes illegal?

On the downside, grandfathering also has moral hazards because it is a form of legalized inequality, one law for grandfathers, and a different law for everyone else. The legal system is now more complex. Special interests will also deliberately exploit grandfathering using older laws.

In general, grandfathering should be avoided to minimize the moral hazards. This can be done in two primary ways:

1. A transition period that ends. For example, a year to move into a new tax system with a new tax code. No grandfathering, no carrying forward of old law into the new system. A fresh start for everyone on an even legal playing field. This is the ideal.

2. Allow the old system to remain but incentivize the new system. For example, PSAs are tax-advantaged, flexible, easy to set up and use, and highly protected from lawsuits. Social Security will remain legal for those already in it, but you'll have an option to rollover into PSAs if you wish. Social Security will fade away.

Despite the suggestions above, there will almost certainly be unforeseen consequences to the proposals, and unforeseen transition issues. The courts and legislatures may need to intervene to ease some of the problems.

In the big picture though, the proposals here will free citizens to find their own solutions. Citizens can and will step up, deal with problems arising in their own lives, and do their best to help their neighbors as needed.

Chapter 7—A Call for Action

*Start a huge, foolish project, like Noah…it makes absolutely no
difference what people think of you.*

— Rumi

We live in contentious times. The arguments are heated, partisan, and extreme. Everyone wants change, but nothing fundamental changes.

If you accept the central premise of this book, then it's easy to see that
things will continue to get worse. The incentives favor more of the same:
more manipulation, more corruption, more arguments. Manipulation gets
ever more profitable. It's increasingly dangerous not to manipulate when
your competitors are working hard to take you out legally. Politicians, paid
by special interests and with their own career interests, have little incentive to change anything. No government employee wants to lose their job,
even if they would also like to shrink government.

Citizens also are often incentivized to support manipulation. Decades
of political rhetoric have focused on the wrong solutions to the wrong
problems: immigration, trade policy, gun control, the 1%, sexism, racism,
and so on. The worse it gets, the more afraid people get, and the more they
want to cling to simplistic explanations and solutions.

Meanwhile, the longer things continue as they are, the bigger the problems become and the more traumatic the corrections. If you are afraid of
the national debt now, how will you be feeling in ten years? If you agree
there's too much regulation now, how will you feel after another 10 years
of rule-making?

This book offers a set of suggestions for how we could get out of our current political mess, free ourselves from manipulation, and reverse long-
term trends that have caused today's problems.

I won't go into the ins and outs of how the constitution gets changed—
that's beyond the scope of this book. However, realistically, let's
acknowledge that getting a *Bill of Protections* passed would be a long up-
hill battle. The forces against change are strong.

Nonetheless, starting progress in the direction of a *Bill of Protections*
is still a worthwhile endeavor. Even if constitutional amendments never
get enacted, gains can still be made by getting the ideas implemented on a
smaller scale. So, if you agree with the central premises of this book, there
follows a short list of action steps to start taking.

Political Discussions

In every political debate you get into, be it with friends, family, at city
hall, online, or when speaking to politicos: apply the Tests of Legitimate
Governance. Whenever a government solution to a problem is proposed,
ask if it passes the Tests of Legitimate Governance.

We'd have far fewer rules made if politicians and administrators honestly asked themselves if they had the moral or constitutional authority to act, or if what they were proposing was in alignment with the purpose of government. To get there, questions like the Tests of Legitimate Governance need to be asked often, and answers need to be demanded.

Do not expect changing the mindsets of political actors to be easy. Activists have strongly held beliefs, both about the correct course of action and their right to implement their solutions. All politicians are skilled in not answering questions, deflecting criticism, and ignoring facts.

Nonetheless, keep asking the right questions, and in time, things may change. Even small changes towards less meddling would be welcome,

As part of spreading the word, please consider recommending or giving copies of this book to friends, family, or anyone you think might find it interesting or valuable. Even if you don't agree with everything I have to say, it might at least help us to get away from the entrenched arguments, political clichés, and partisan positions.

Vote Against the Incumbent

How can citizens ever hope for change if we keep voting the same people back into office? Yet voting is the one place where citizens have a say in what legislators we get.

In a typical US presidential election about 55-60% of eligible voters vote. About 40% vote in a typical midterm election.[1] Frankly, I sympathize with those who don't vote, I have been a non-voter most of my life. An individual vote counts for little, so what's the point?

Nonetheless, in many elections, a relatively small proportion of non-voters could swing the results from one candidate to another. So, I have recently started voting. My strategy, which I urge you to adopt, is:

1. Vote (especially if you currently don't vote).

2. Always vote against the incumbent.

Now, I appreciate that lifelong voters for one party or the other might have difficulty voting for the other side. Personally, though, I can't see much practical difference between them. Their excuses may be different, but both parties keep overstepping their bounds, regulating, and growing ever bigger government.

Nonetheless, if you can't vote against your usual party, you can still partially implement this strategy by always voting against the incumbent in your party's primaries.

The Libertarian Party

I'm not a member of any political party, but I'd put myself broadly in the libertarian camp. Many of my proposals will probably sit comfortably with most libertarians.

If ever a libertarian government got voted in, then perhaps laws approximating my proposals might get implemented. However, I don't have any dogmatic attachment to the libertarian party, or to voting libertarian, and I don't recommend it as a blanket strategy for two reasons:

1. It's more important to get rid of the incumbents first, regardless of party.

2. Absent structural (systemic) change, libertarian politicians will end up being under the same pressures are the current republicans and democrats. They are likely to end up behaving in the same ways.

The American political system has gravitated towards a two-party system from the beginning. The names of those parties, and their positions, have changed over time, but two main parties are a feature.

The chances of the libertarians gaining power are slim, but there's still a benefit to voting for them. If enough citizens vote libertarian, then both the main parties will start to move in a libertarian direction to try and capture those voters. If the main parties gave individual freedom even a slightly higher priority, we'd start to see an improvement in the political and economic life of our nation.

If libertarians started gaining real traction in national elections, then I'd probably change my strategy and vote for them more often. However, even a majority libertarian government could not solve our problems. Fundamental changes are needed in the system—preferably at a constitutional level—otherwise, the incentives would remain the same for libertarians as for all politicians.

The forces on politicians are so strong that if the system was unchanged other than substituting libertarians for democrats and republicans, then over time we'd end up with corrupt libertarians instead of corrupt democrats and republicans. The special interests are still there, still motivated to try and rig the system. In the long run, finding the right people to run the system won't help. We need to fix the system itself.

I believe the priority is removing our current politicians, which is why I am suggesting that you always vote against the incumbent. However, if the incumbent has such a huge lead that they are unlikely to be unseated, or if the second choice is so awful that you can't in good conscience vote for them, please consider voting libertarian.

Activism

The trend of recent decades is increasingly to assume that all problems are solvable by political means. Protests and campaigns for change are often seen as synonymous with change. Protestors sometimes garner more prestige than than problem solvers.

If you see something happening that you disagree with, then please speak up. If you have an idea about how to improve things, advertise it far and wide. If you think you have better ideas than I do, please publish them. Write your own book, start a blog, and get your ideas out.

However, political campaigns are not real change. Talk is not action. Protest is not progress. Virtue signaling is not virtuous. Actual results are, in the real world, more important than intentions.

Personally, I think research on green energy is more important than campaigns for Green New Deals. Elon Musk and other engineers are likely to do a better job of greening the planet than Congress.[2]

Perhaps I am a cynic. Or maybe, like many of my fellow citizens, I have been driven to despair. No matter how keen you are on politics, do you really think, in your heart of hearts, that any individual politician can fundamentally change things for the better?

Practical Steps

What if, instead of asking: *who is the great leader who will save us all*, you instead asked yourself: *what can I do to improve the world?*

It doesn't have to be a big thing. Maybe swap out your old light bulbs for LEDs. Insulate your loft. Practice reading, writing, and arithmetic with your kids so they have usable skills when they graduate high school. Go plant a tree or dig a vegetable bed. Get involved in a local charity or donate $10 to a worthy cause. Invite your evil Republican/Democrat neighbor over for coffee and talk to them. Maybe go for a walk instead of getting angry at the news!

You can go bigger if you want. If you're a woman who thinks men discriminate against you in business, start your own company and outcompete them.[3] If you think capitalism is evil, start a co-op. If you think state education sucks, start a private school. If you see an unaddressed problem, start a business or charity to tackle it.

What can you do to improve the world, today? Whatever it is, large or small, just start today.

Appendix 1—Lies, Damn Lies and Statistics

There are three kinds of lies: lies, damned lies, and statistics.
—Unknown, popularized by Mark Twain

Chapter 2—Unsustainable Trends had several graphs illustrating secular trends in our current political economy: government spending, volumes of legislation, and so on.

Dates Chosen

For the date ranges illustrated, I started in 1950 because it is the modern post-WWII era. However, for many of the topics illustrated, particularly government finances, data goes back to 1900, sometimes earlier. If you plot the data from 1900, it makes little significant difference to the trends.

I graphed 50 years into the future because most readers can probably relate and may live another 50 years. For the sake of completeness, the text gives a wider range. Figures run from 1900 (where I have the data) and extrapolate forward to 2100, an easy-to-remember reference point.

Creation of Trend Lines

The graphs were created using an Excel spreadsheet trendline (growth) function, choosing the trendline with the highest R^2 value as the best fit.[1] That turns out to be most often an exponential curve.

If I were trying to ascribe causation, then I'd need to justify my choice of curve more rigorously. However, I am merely trying to illustrate trends that have been in place for at least 120 years and project them loosely into the future. I am not making predictions.

Data Sources and Accuracy

The data used to create these graphs comes from US government data, often collated via private sources as described below.

You cannot assume 100% accuracy in any of the data sets. Statisticians do their best, but collecting country-wide data is beset with practical difficulties. Federal data collectors often rely on state, local, and sometimes private sources. It takes a long time to collect, collate and check. Data is typically published with a lag of a couple of years.

For most of the financial data used here, the last actual reported figures are for 2018 (approximately). I have used estimated data for the years 2019-2022 from my data sources below, which will be close but subject to final revisions. After 2022 everything is a trend line extrapolation.

Inflation

Inflation makes comparing spending across time problematic. In theory, inflation is the total increase in the amount of money in the economy. In practice, inflation is estimated by choosing a basket of goods representing what people typically buy and recording their prices over time. However, many goods in common use today (phones, computers etc.) are recent inventions. And things that did exist in the past (say, a loaf of bread), may not have had the same ingredients or importance in day-to-day life. All this makes calculating inflation complex and manipulatable.

For our purposes here, I have used official government figures. I'll leave the rest to the economists to debate.[2] However, due to the practical difficulties, inflation estimates are subject to frequent correction, especially in the first few years after publication.

To be safe, I have therefore chosen to quote financial data in 2012 dollars, even though this book was published in 2023. It's close enough to today that when I say something costs $10 in 2012 dollars, you'll have a gut feel for what that means. 2012 dollars were also used by most of my data sources as of 2020/2021.

Overall inflation in the 2012-2020 period is likely to be in the range of 11-12%.[3] Inflation has also spiked sharply since 2020, but it will take some time to get accurate figures.

Secular Trends

I want to emphasize that minor data discrepancies, like minor ticks up or down in a long-term series of data, are not especially relevant. The trends shown here are clear, and they are all *long-term (secular) trends*.

Special interests will try to persuade you otherwise, and you can always find holes in government data if you look hard enough. Special interests are skilled at finding small errors or apparent discrepancies and making a big deal out of them. Don't be fooled!

Government spending and debt, for example, have been rising exponentially for the last 120 years with only a few minor downturns (often after major wars). The trend is clear, and clearly not sustainable.

Data Sources

Government Spending: www.usgovernmentspending.com. The website owner, Mr. Christopher Chantrill, does an excellent job of collating and presenting large volumes of government data, along with detailed explanations of data sources.

GDP Data: www.MeasuringWorth.com. This website also has clear explanations of the difficulties of measuring GDP and inflation.

Population Data: US census data reports at www.census.gov. The Census Bureau also projects population out to 2060 and I used their figures for projections to then. Beyond that point, I used UN projections taken from www.population.un.org. Where they overlap (until 2060) UN data and US census data projections are quite similar.

Regulation: Page counts are taken directly from the federal register at wwwfederalregister.gov.

Bailouts: ProPublica's *History of US Government Bailouts,* www.propublica.org

Data collected from the above sources was converted to 2012 dollars where relevant. Any holes in the historical data were filled by extrapolation between known points on either side of the hole. (Little was needed post 1950.)

Though I've done my best, any transcription and data manipulation errors are mine alone. If you think I have a gross error in my data or graphing, please let me know. I'll be embarrassed if I've made errors, but I might also be relieved if things are not as bad as the data show.

Appendix 2—Definitions and Assumptions

The following definitions and assumptions will apply to the proposed amendments.

- *Citizen*: any person, group of persons, artificial persons, corporations, or any type of organization who are not the government. Unless otherwise specified it will include US citizens, resident aliens, and foreign persons subject to US law.

- *Government*: the government in its broadest sense including all law, legislation, regulation, and court decisions, all legislators, representatives, political appointees, government employees, and government contractors. It will apply to all levels of government, federal, state, county, municipal, territorial, etc. It includes anyone who represents or works for any US government in any role.

- *Government agency*: or *agency:* any discrete agency, bureau, department, authority, sub-authority, or other division of government.

- *Government agent*: or *agent:* anyone who represents or works for the government in any capacity, including contractors and persons working for government-sponsored organizations.

- Unless otherwise specified, *Citizen* includes government agents when acting in a private capacity, but not when acting in their governmental capacity.

- *Representative*: anyone who is elected by citizens to an elective office in government.

- All monetary sums that are applied in the proposals will be indexed to the consumer price index (CPI), which shall be calculated to accurately convey the rate of inflation in the economy. The same CPI shall be used for dealings with citizens, tax and benefit calculations, forecasts, and other processes.

- All monetary sums cited in the amendments shall be recalculated as of 1st January each year based on the CPI for the previous calendar year. The results of the calculations must be officially announced by the 1$^{st \, of}$ February each year at the latest but shall apply retrospectively from the 1st of January of the same year.

- *Adult*: natural persons 18 years of age or older.

- *Parent:* person(s) who have legal responsibility for a child.

- *Violent crime*: crimes involving violence against persons or their property, including actual bodily harm, theft, property damage, and threats of force or coercion.

- *Non-violent crime*: any other crime.

- *Organization*: any grouping of persons; corporations, partnerships, unions, or other artificial persons.

- *Large organization*: corporations listed on public stock exchanges, private organizations employing over 1000 full-time employees or an aggregate equivalent thereof, privately owned organizations with sales of over 100 million dollars, charities with an endowment of over 100 million dollars, and any other organization having more than 10,000 members who pay dues or fees to be a member.

- *Full-time employee*: anyone who works an average of 30 hours or more a week for an organization.

- For related organizations and where at least 50% of the ownership is held in common, the number of employees will be aggregated for purposes of determining if those organizations fall under the definition of large organization given above.

- All constitutional restrictions applied to large organizations shall also apply to the government unless otherwise specified.

- *Transition*. Unless otherwise stated, upon passing of these amendments:

  o Any law, legislation, regulation, ordinance, court precedent, or other government rule that contradicts or is in violation of a new provision of the Constitution shall be void.

  o Any government agency regulating an activity that becomes unregulated shall be disbanded and its employees shall be released from government service within 100 days.

  o Any law enforcement agency enforcing any activity that becomes legal shall be disbanded and its employees shall be released from government service within 100 days.

  o All employees released from government employment due to these amendments shall be paid for ten months following their release. In the first month they shall receive 100% of their final monthly salary, in the second 90%, and so on until the tenth month when they receive 10% and thereafter no further salary.

  o Unless otherwise specified, recipients of government welfare who lose that benefit due to these amendments shall have their benefit continued for ten months following the end of the benefits program. In the first month they shall receive 100% of their final benefit, in the second 90%, and so on until the tenth month when they receive 10% and thereafter no further benefit.

  o All government programs ended, transferred, or privatized due to these amendments must have that action completed within one year of passing the amendment.

Appendix 3—Coronavirus

Power, like a desolating pestilence, pollutes whatever it touches.
—Percy Bysshe Shelley

The Coronavirus pandemic has perhaps been the economic and political event of our lifetimes. Like everyone, I watched things unfold with, to say the least, mixed feelings about the Covid-induced turmoil, ugly politics, and riots.

America: A Repair Manual is not about Coronavirus. However, the political response to the virus is entirely consistent with the themes of this book. The virus accelerated political corruption to a new low.

Special interests—politicians, health departments, media, academics, experts, and businesses—all had their part to play, pushing governments large and small into violations of citizen rights. With the virus as an excuse, governments routinely violated individual rights: freedom of association, freedom of movement, freedom to use private property (business closures), and freedom of contract.

A secondary role of government (public health) was used to justify violations of the primary role (protection of individual rights), resulting in absurd political logic. Effectively, the government shut the country down to save the country. It took away freedom to preserve freedom.

These government actions fail the Test of Moral Authority. Do I have the right to lock my neighbor in her home to protect my family from her? Sure, if she's a zombie out to bite me and turn me. But for a flu-like virus, infectious, but not that dangerous? I don't have the right to lock my neighbor up in this instance, and neither does the government.

At every level of government, constitutional abuses occurred. Mayors, Governors, and Directors of health departments all issued orders shutting down citizen rights, *acting as dictators*. And with little evidence of any health benefits, and many adverse consequences[1]

Their abuses have accelerated many long-term negative political trends: centralizing control, mandating instead of persuading, ongoing misinformation from governments and experts, impoverishing people through economic shutdowns, and damaging the prospects of children by shutting down the education system. And as the system breaks down, civil disobedience ramps up.

How it might have been?

We can't know how Coronavirus might have been received in a less manipulated world but allow me to speculate based on *what if the suggestions made here had already been implemented.* You can refer to the specific sections for discussion of each issue:

- Dialing back excessive regulation would make us all much richer. We'd all have had a much bigger financial buffer—even the poor and the infirm—and have been able to afford more health care or to take time off work.

- Without patents, the world would probably be decades ahead in technological progress. Perhaps there might have been a ready-to-go vaccine for Coronavirus the day it arrived. Perhaps medical science would have already cured many of the comorbidities that made coronavirus fatal—hypertension, diabetes, and heart disease.[2]

- Other technologies might have made life easier, even if there were no medical solutions. What if everyone had 3D printers to make their own masks? What if everyone had almost immediate home delivery of anything? How much will video conferencing technology improve in the next 20 years?

- If executive orders were taken off the table, governments would have needed to persuade us rather than order us to do things. *Persuasion offers immunity from special interest manipulation,* of all sorts: political, medical, financial.

- If government borrowing was curbed, there would be less spending on special interest schemes to "save us" and less temptation to push economic problems into the future.

- Welfare might be unnecessary if everyone was richer, but if needed the government might have had emergency funds ready to go. The only form of welfare would be individual checks to real citizens, and the only question would be how much. The answer is $ per citizen = $in rainy day fund/number of citizens.

- Banning subsidies would cut out corporate loans and welfare as well as the political infighting about who gets what. No need for 5,500-page legislative bills to divide up the pork.[3]

- Maybe AI would have advanced to the point where it could sort facts from fiction. AIs might prove to be less biased than human media sources.

Removing government interference, in the long run, will leave us better able to deal with any future pandemic. And if decisions reverted to citizens rather than "decision makers" there would be much less political infighting of all sorts, fewer arguments, and less anger. There'd be a chance to restore public civility.

Acknowledgments

Writing a book is a huge undertaking, to say the least. The ideas discussed here started with notes I was making nearly twenty years ago! It's been a long process of focusing and shaping those ideas into the results you are reading today. Of course, I've not spent all that time writing: research, life, work, and house renovations have all made writing a part-time effort! The book has also changed focus over the years as my understanding of the issues increased, causing rewrites.

Along the way, I have had help from many sources. First and foremost, I would like to thank my wife, Ellie Harold, for putting up with me in all that time! We don't always see eye to eye on politics, and she'd certainly like to see me spend my spare time writing poetry or playing guitar, rather than wrestling with politics. Nonetheless, she has lovingly supported me throughout.

My reviewers, Steve Bocckino, Paul Lutton, Bob Tarkington, Chris May, and Ellie Harold have been immensely helpful. Even when they disagreed with my views, they still gave me valuable feedback and helped me to structure the book. Some irrelevant stuff got thrown out, some important parts were added, and arguments were strengthened. This book is much improved by their input, and I thank them all.

And finally, I would like to thank my teachers of economics, especially Russ Roberts (Stanford University's Hoover Institute) and Don Boudreaux (George Mason University).

I have not met these gentlemen in person, but I have been listening for over a decade to EconTalk podcasts hosted by Russ Roberts (www.econtalk.org) and reading Café Hayek blogs posted by Don Boudreaux (www.cafehayek.com). I highly recommend both of those sources to anyone interested in economics and the political economy.

Through these outlets, I have been exposed to literally dozens of fine thinkers in economics, politics, law, and related fields. Among those who spring first to mind are Mike Munger (Duke University), Richard Epstein (New York University), Thomas Sowell (Hoover Institute), the late Milton Friedman (University of Chicago), Deirdre McCloskey (University of Illinois at Chicago)., and Tyler Cowen (George Mason University and www.MarginalRevolution.com).

I am not a formal student of these fine professors, and any mistakes and misunderstandings I have of their teachings are mine alone.

References

For sake of compactness, I omitted the subtitles of articles and books, shortened long titles, and removed the www of website addresses. Since websites are frequently reorganized, I have only cited the top-level website address. I have not bothered to reference anything you can look up on Wikipedia.

Introduction
[1] Many positive world statistics can be seen at gapminder.org
[2] Matt Ridley, *The Rational Optimist*, Harper Colins, 2010, mattriddley.co.uk
[3] Xiao-Peng Song et al, *Global land change from 1982 to 2016*, Nature International Journal of Science, Aug 2019, nature.com
[4] Andrew McAfee, *More from Less*, Scribner, 2019, andrewmcafee.org
[5] Tim Worstall, *The Average American Today Is 90 Times Richer Than The Average Historical Human Being*, Forbes Magazine, Jan 2016, forbes.com
[6] Stephen Pinker, *Enlightenment Now*, Penguin Books, 2019, stevenpinker.com
[7] Mark Perry, *Yes, the US middle class is shrinking*, American Enterprise Institute, Jan 2018, aei.org
[8] *President Obama: College Students Shouldn't Be Coddled*, Foundation for Individual Rights in Education, Sep 2015, thefire.org
[9] Jennifer Elias, *Google employees weighed free speech concerns before the 2016 elections*, CNBC Aug 2019, cnbc.com
[10] Gallup conducts regular congressional approval polls, gallup.com
[11] John Anderer, *Vexed Voters*, Study Finds, Dec 2019, studyfinds.org
[12] Ben Shapiro, *The Right Side of History*, Harper Collins, 2019

Chapter1—Special Interest Manipulation
[1] Bruce Yandle, *Bootleggers and Baptists*, Regulation, May/June 1983, cato.org
[2] Timothy P. Carney, *How Hatch Forced Microsoft to Play K-Street's Game*, Washington Examiner, Jun 2012, washingtonexaminer.com
[3] John W Dawson and John J Seater, *Federal Regulation and Aggregate Economic Growth*, Journal of Economic Growth, Jan 2013, ncsu.edu
[4] *Moral Hazard* has technical meanings in insurance & economics related to *perverse incentives*. I am using the term more broadly and with explicit moral implications.

Chapter 2—Unsustainable Trends
[1] Jesse Nankin & Krista Kjellman Schmidt, *History of US Government Bailouts*, ProPublica, Apr 2009, propublica.org
[2] *Covid-19 Spending*, usaspending.gov
[3] Megan Henny, *Coronavirus stimulus deal includes rewards for special interest groups*, Fox Business News, Mar 2020, foxbusiness.com
[4] Stephen Gandel, *Coronavirus pandemic to cost Americans $16 trillion*, CBS Money Watch, Oct 2020, cbsnews.com
[5] *Regulatory Impact on Small Business*, US Chamber of Commerce Foundation, Mar 2017, uschamber.com
[6] Mary Kate Hopkins, *Donald Trump's regulation cuts are having an effect*, Financial Times, May 2019, ft.com
[7] *Public Trust in Government*, Pew Research, 1958-2017, pewresearch.org
[8] Rebecca Riffkin, *Big Government Still Named as Biggest Threat to U.S.*, Gallup Polls, Dec 2015, gallup.com
[9] Art Swift, *Americans' Views on Government Regulation Remain Steady*, Gallup Polls, Oct 2017, gallup.com
[10] Art Swift, *Majority in U.S. Say Federal Government Has Too Much Power*, Gallup Polls, Oct 2017, gallup.com
[11] James Sweet, *Faith in America and institutions is collapsing*, Washington Examiner, Jul 2022, washingtonexaminer.com

[12] Lydia Saad, *Perceived Need for Third Major Party Remains High in U.S.* Gallup Polls, Sep 2017, gallup.com

[13] Dana Blanton, *Fox News Poll: Voters want government to leave them alone as midterm elections near,* Fox News, Aug 2014, foxnews.com

[14] Josh Morgan, *The Decline of Trust in the United States*, Medium, May 2014, medium.com

[15] Max Fisher & Amanda Taub, *How Venezuela went from the richest economy in South America to the brink of financial ruin*, The Independent, May 2017, independent.co.uk

Chapter 3—Thinking About Solutions
[1] *The Hidden Tribes of America*, More In Common, Oct 2018, hiddentribes.us

Chapter 4—The Proper Role of Government
[1] Martin Cothran, *The Classical Education of the Founding Fathers*, Memoria Press, Apr 2017, memoriapress.com

[2] Ben Shapiro, *The Right Side of History,* 2019, Harper Collins

[3] *Preambles to state constitutions*, Ballotpedia, ballotpedia.org

[4] John Locke, *Second Treatise of Government*, 1689, gutenberg.org

[5] Thomas Jefferson to Spencer Roane, *The Writings of Thomas Jefferson*, Memorial Edition 1903-04, Vol. 15, P328

[6] John Locke, *An Essay Concerning the True Original, Extent and End of Civil Government,* 1689.

Chapter 5—Promoting the General Welfare
[1] Data from *New Maddison Project Database and World Bank*, 2017, Our World In Data, ourworldindata.org

[2] For a more detailed discussion: *The Top 20 Untruths of COVID with Nick Hudson*, What is Money Podcast, whatismoneypodcast.om

Proposal 1—Adulthood
[1] Camile Paglia, *The Drinking Age Is Past Its Prime,* Time Magazine, Apr 2014, time.com

[2] *Safe Driver Apprenticeship Pilot Program*, Federal Motor Carrier Safety Administration, fmca.dot.gov.

[3] Andrew Cohen, *Libertarianism and Parental Licensing*, Bleeding Heart Libertarians, Jul 2014, bleedingheartlibertarians.com

[4] Murry N Rothbard, *For a New Liberty*, Mises Institute, 1973, mises.org

[5] Amanda Morris, *Britney Spears's Case Calls Attention to Wider Questions on Guardianship*, New York Times, Jul 2021, nytimes.com

Proposal 2—Legal Equality
[1] *End Qualified Immunity,* Institute for Justice, ij.org

[2] *5 Tax Breaks for Veterans*, TurboTax, Jun 2022, turbotax.intuit.com

Proposal 3—Free Speech
[1] Wesley Pruden, *Spooked by the power of words, words, words*, Washington Times, Apr 2017, washingtontimes.com

[2] *Cambridge University Just Delivered A Clear Victory For Free Speech*, The Federalist, Dec 2020, thefedearalist.com

[3] Michael Poliakoff, *In Defense of the Chicago Principles,* Inside Higher Ed, Dec 2018, insidehighered.com

[4] Thomas B. Edsall, *Have Trump's Lies Wrecked Free Speech?* New York Times, Jan 2021, nytimes.com

[5] *State of the First Amendment Survey 2019*, Freedom Forum Institute, freedomforuminstitute.org

[6] *The State of Free Speech and Tolerance in America*, Cato Institute, Oct 2017, cato.org

[7] David L. Hudson Jr., *Libel and Slander,* First Amendment Encyclopedia, mtsu.edu

[8] Hailey Marting, *On the Hook: Jury's Hefty Defamation Award Against Alex Jones*, University of Cincinnati Law Review Vol. 91, Feb 2023, uclawreview.org

[9] Hannah Denham, *These are the platforms that have banned Trump and his allies,* Washington Post, Jan 2021, washingtonpost.com

Proposal 4—Freedom of Contract
[1] *Fifty Years of Research on the Minimum Wage,* Joint Economic Committee Republicans, Feb 1995, jec.senate.gov
[2] Mark Wilson, *The Negative Effects of Minimum Wage Laws,* Cato Institute, Jun 2012, cato.org
[3] Drew DeSilver, *Who Makes Minimum Wage,* Pew Research, Sep 2014, pewresearch.org
[4] Chris Calton, *The Racist History of Minimum Wage Laws,* Mises Institute, 2017, mises.org
[5] Thomas Sowell, *Basic Economics,* Basic Books, 2014 (5th Ed).
[6] Occupational Licensing: A Framework for Policy Makers, The White House, Jul 2015, obamawhitehouse.archives.gov
[7] Mitchel C Rothholz, *The role of community pharmacies/pharmacists in vaccine delivery in the United States,* presentation to the CDC, Jul 2013. pharmacist.com
[8] Jake Rossen, *Fathers Are Right to Fear Family Court,* Fatherly, Jan 2018, fatherly.com
[9] Jennifer Bennett Shinall, *Settling in the Shadow of Sex,* Cardozo Law Review, 2019, cardozolawreview.com
[10] Micheal Levenson, *Price Gouging Complaints Surge Amid Coronavirus Pandemic,* New York Times, Mar 2020, nytimes.com
[11] *Price Gouging Laws by State,* findlaw.com

Proposal 5—Free Trade
[1] Bradley Jones, *Americans are generally positive about free trade agreements,* Pew Research, May 2018, pewresearch.org
[2] Brian Blank, *Executive Incentives, Import Restrictions, and Competition,* Mercatus Center, George Mason University, Nov 2019, mercatus.org
[3] Annie Lowrey, *The Limits of 'Made in America' Economics,* The Atlantic, Jul 2017, theatlantic.com
[4] *Export Controlled or Sanctioned Countries, Entities and Persons,* Stanford University, doresearch.stanford.edu
[5] *How gas price controls sparked '70s shortages,* The Washington Times. May 2006, washingtontimes.com
[6] *Invasive Species,* US Fish and Wildlife Service, fws.gov

Proposal 6—Privacy
[1] Brooke Auxier et al, *Americans and Privacy,* Pew Research, Nov 2019, pewresearch.org
[2] Cady v. Dombrowski, 413 U.S. 433 (1973), supremecourt.gov
[3] *Community Caretaking Function,* Alert Training Guide, 2002, AELE Law Enforcement Legal Center, aele.org
[4] A.W. Geiger, *How Americans have viewed government surveillance and privacy since Snowden leaks,* Pew Research, June 2018. PewResearch.org
[5] Michael Isikoff, *NSA program stopped no terror attacks,* NBC News, Dec 2014, nbcnews.com
[6] Kim Zetter, *Personal privacy is only one of the costs of NSA surveillance,* Wired Magazine, Jul 2014, wired.com

Proposal 7—Sex
[1] Debora L Rhote, *Why is adultery still a crime*? LA Times, May 2016, latimes.com
[2] *Prostitution Statistics,* Havocscope Global, havocscope.com
[3] Maggie McNeill, *Lies, damned lies and sex work statistics,* Washington Post, Mar 2014, washingtonpost.com
[4] *Should Prostitution Be Legalized?* Marist Poll, May 2016, maristpoll.marist.edu
[5] Devin Bowen, *The Impact of Legalizing Prostitution on Violent Crime,* Mercatus Center, George Mason University, May 2013, mercatus.org
[6] Tim Worstall, *Legal Prostitution and Sex Trafficking,* Forbes Magazine, Jun 2013, forbes.com

[7] Robin McKie, *Onset of puberty in girls has fallen by five years since 1920*, The Guardian, Oct 2012, theguardian.com

[8] *Trends in the Prevalence of Sexual Behaviors*, CDC National Youth Risk Behavior Survey 1991—2007, 2007, cdc.gov

[9] Meredith Cohen, *No Child Left Behind Bars*, Journal of Law and Policy, 2009, brooklynworks.brooklaw.edu

[10] Amanda Y. Agan, *Sex Offender Registries*, Journal of Law and Economics, 2011 54(1), journals.uchicago.edu

[11] Debora Jacobs, *Why Sex Offender Laws Do More Harm Than Good*, ACLU (New Jersey), 2016, aclu-nj.org

[12] Tim Cushing, *Another Cop Treats Sexting Teens Like Child Pornographers*, TechDirt Podcast, Feb 2016, techdirt.com

[13] Chanakya Sethi, *The Ridiculous Laws That Put People on the Sex Offender List*, Slate Magazine, Aug 2014, slate.com

[14] David R. Francis, *Megan's Law Hits Local Property Prices*, Jun 2006, National Bureau of Economic Research, nber.org

[15] Jonathan H. Adler, *Court voids state sex offender registry for imposing unconstitutionally retroactive punishment*, Washington Post, Aug 2016, washingtonpost.com

[16] Douglas Hanks, *Tent camp of homeless sex offenders near Hialeah 'has got to close,' county says*, Miami Herald, Aug 2017, miamiherald.com

[17] Jane Gallop, *Feminist Accused of Sexual Harassment*, Duke University Press, May 1998, dukeupress.edu

[18] Kate Wheeling, *Are Student Athletes More Likely to Commit Sexual Assault?*, Pacific Standard Magazine, Jun 2017, psmag.com

[19] Due Process, thefire.org

[20] *Harvard Law Faculty Members Blast New Sexual Harassment Policy*, Foundation for Individual Rights in Education, Oct 2015, thefire.org

[21] Ashe Schlow, *5 problems with California's 'affirmative consent' bill*, Washington Examiner, Aug 2014, washingtonexaminer.com

[22] Benjamin Rachlin, *Who to Believe*, The New Republic, newrepublic.com

Proposal 8—Drugs

[1] *Rates of Drug Use and Sales, by Race; Rates of Drug Related Criminal Justice Measures, by Race*, The Hamilton Project, hamiltonproject.org

Proposal 9—Guns

[1] District of Columbia v. Heller, 554 U.S. 570 (2008), supremecourt.gov

[2] Bigfoot Gun Belts, *A Brief History of Concealed Carry Laws*, Medium Magazine, Apr 2016, medium.com

[3] Kim Parker et al, *America's Complex Relationship with Guns*, Pew Research, Jun 2018. pewresearch.org

[4] Salena Zito, *The Second Amendment Sanctuary Movement Isn't Going Away*, Wall Street Journal, Jan 2020, wsj.com

[5] D'Vera Cohn et al, *Gun Homicide Rate Down 49% Since 1993 Peak*, Pew Research, May 2013, pewresearch.org

[6] Max Roser, *Homicides*, Our World in Data, ourworldindata.org

[7] John R Lott, *More Guns, Less Crime: Understanding Crime and Gun Control Laws*, 2000, University of Chicago Press, CrimeResearch.org

[8] *Annual Report 2018*, Small Arms Survey, May 2019, smallarmssurvey.org

[9] Kevin O'Brien, *Total US Firearms*, Weapons Man Blog, weaponsman.louserounds.com

[10] *Firearms Commerce in the US, Annual Statistical Update 2018*, Bureau of Alcohol, Tobacco, Firearms and Explosives, atf.gov

[11] Andy Greenberg, *Someone (Mostly) 3-D Printed a Working Semi-Automatic Gun*, Wired Magazine, Feb 2016, wired.com

[12] Delvin Brown, *It's not just toilet paper: People line up to buy guns, ammo over coronavirus concerns*, USA Today, Mar 2020, usatoday.com

[13] Daniel Nass, *How Many Guns Did Americans Buy Last Month?* The Trace, Aug 2020, thetrace.org

[14] Andrea Cipriano, *Gun Sales Spike Across the U.S. Following Capitol Riots,* The Crime Report, Jan 2020, thecrimereport.org

[15] *Illicit Firearms in Australia,* Australian Criminal Intelligence Commission, 2016, acic.gov.au

[16] J.D. Tuccille, *Noncompliance Kneecaps New Zealand's Gun Control Scheme,* Reason Magazine, Jul 2019, reason.com

Proposal 10—Abortion

[1] *Abortion,* Gallup Polls, gallup.org

[2] Laurie Shrage, *Is Forced Fatherhood Fair?* New York Times, Jun 2013, nytimes.com

[3] Richard Faussetjan, *Law on Ultrasounds Reignites Abortion Battle in North Carolina,* New York Times, Jan 2010, nytimes.com

[4] Alexandra DeSanctis, *Democrats Overplay Their Hand on Abortion.* The Atlantic, Feb 2019, theatlantic.com

Proposal 11—Discrimination

[1] Monica Potts, *Most Americans Wanted The Supreme Court To End Affirmative Action — Kind Of,* Five Thirty Eight (ABC News), Jun 2023, fivethirtyeight.com

[2] *Jim Crow Laws and Racial Segregation,* Virginia Commonwealth University Libraries, Social Welfare History Project, socialwelfare.library.vcu.edu

[3] Glenn Kessler, *Here are the facts behind that '79 cent' pay gap factoid,* Washington Post, Apr 2016, washingtonpost.com

[4] Roger Clegg, *The Supreme Court's Bad 'Disparate Impact' Decision,* National Review, Jun 2015, nationalreview.com

[5] Thomas Sowell, *Discrimination and Disparities,* Basic Books, Mar 2019

[6] *FAQs about Private Schools,* Council for American Private Education, capenet.org

[7] *College & University - Statistics & Facts,* Statista, statista.com

Proposal 12—Legislation

[1] J.W. Hampton, Jr. & Co. v. United States (1928), 276 U.S. 394, supremecourt.gov

[2] USC can be found at uscode.house.gov. This count done as of 3/10/23.

[3] Reader Aids: Federal Register & CFR Statistics, federalregister.gov

[4] For example: EC Klatt, *How much is too much reading for medical students?* US National Library of Medicine, Sep 2011, ncbi.nlm.nih.gov

[5] *Speed Reading Facts,* ExecuRead, secure.execuread.com

[6] US Report are at supremecourt.gov. Total volumes estimated based on 3-4 volumes/ year.

[7] Harvey Silverglate, *Three Felonies A Day,* Encounter Books, 2011

[8] McLaughlin et al, *Dodd-Frank Is One of the Biggest Regulatory Events Ever,* Mercatus Center, Aug 2017, mercatus.org

[9] Nathan Dean and Ben Elliott, *Dodd-Frank's state of play,* Bloomberg Intelligence, Sep 2016, bloomberg.com

[10] Zach Wolf, *The Senate voted on a tax bill pretty much nobody had read,* CNN, Dec 2017, cnn.com

[11] Grace Shao et al, *China accuses US of 'sinister intentions' after Trump signs bills supporting Hong Kong protesters,* CNBC, Nov 2019. cnbc.com

[12] Jon Strauss, *Nonpayment of Taxes: When Ignorance of the Law Is an Excuse,* Akron Law Review, Winter/Spring 1992, uakron.edu

Proposal 13—Regulation

[1] Paul Strassel, (former IRS Agent), Wall Street Journal, 1980, wsj.com

[2] Reader Aids: Federal Register & CFR Statistics, federalregister.gov

[3] Gerald O'Driscoll, *The Gulf Spill, the Financial Crisis and Government Failure,* Wall Street Journal, Jun 2010, wsj.com

Proposal 14—Executive Orders
[1] Joy Wang, *How accessible are executive orders in each of the 50 states?* Sunlight Foundation, Jul 2014, sunlightfoundation.com
[2] federalregister.gov
[3] How Laws Are Made, usa.gov
[4] Ben Kesslen, *New York City to close schools; bars, restaurants around U.S. ordered closed over coronavirus,* NBC News, Mar 2020, nbcnews.com
[5] Associated Press, *Washington state orders all restaurants and bars to close over coronavirus,* New York Post, Mar 2020, nypost.com
[6] Nick Corasaniti and Patricia Mazzei, *Louisiana Postpones April Primary as 4 More States Prepare to Vote on Tuesday,* New York Times, Mar 2020, nytimes.com

Proposal 15—Administrative Law
[1] Philip Hamburger, *Is Administrative Law Unlawful?* University of Chicago Press, 2014
[2] For example: Laura Kipnis, *My Title IX Inquisition,* The Chronical Review 2010, laurakipnis.com
[3] Mace Yampolsky, *No more implied consent in Nevada,* Las Vegas Tribune, Oct 2014, lasvegastribune.net

Proposal 16—Judicial Review
[1] Debs v. United States, 249 U.S. 211 (1919), Supreme Court, supremecourt.gov
[2] Astead W. Herndon & Maggie Astor, *Ruth Bader Ginsburg's Death Revives Talk of Court Packing,* New York Times, Sep 2020, nytimes.com
[3] Adam Kazda, *Why Supreme Court Nominations Have Become So Political,* Pursuit, Sep 2018, ourpursuit.com
[4] Sarah Turberville & Anthony Marcum, *Those 5-to-4 decisions on the Supreme Court? 9 to 0 is far more common,* Washington Post, Jun 2018, washingtonpost.com
[5] Rachel Shelden, *The Supreme Court used to be openly political,* Washington Post, Sep 2020, washingtonpost.com
[6] Dan Merica, *Bill Clinton says he made mass incarceration issue worse,* CNN, Jul 2015, cnn.com

Proposal 17—Criminal Justice
[1] *Facts About Prisons and People in Prison,* The Sentencing Project, sentencingproject.org
[2] Gary Fields & John R. Emshwiller, *Many Failed Efforts to Count Nation's Federal Criminal Laws,* Wall Street Journal, Jul 2011, wsj.com
[3] Devah Pager & Bruce Western, *Investigating Prisoner Reentry: The impact of conviction status on the employment prospects of young men,* The National Reentry Resource Center, Oct 2009, csgjusticecenter.org
[4] Kim Zetter, *FBI File on Steve Jobs Notes Use of LSD, Dishonesty,* Wired Magazine, Sep 2012, wired.com
[5] *History of the Death Penalty,* Death Penalty Information Center, deathpenaltyinfo.org
[6] *Death Penalty,* Gallup Polls, gallup.org
[7] *Death penalty in 2018,* Amnesty International, amnesty.org
[8] *Death Penalty Cost,* Amnesty USA, amnesty.org
[9] April M Short, *In America, Innocent Until Proven Guilty?* Truth Out, Dec 2014, truthout.org
[10] F.E.Devine, *Commercial Bail Bonding, A Comparison of Common Law Alternatives,* Praeger, 1991
[11] Harvey Silvergate, *Three Felonies A Day,* Encounter Books, 2011
[12] Philip Locke, *Prosecutors, Charge Stacking, and Plea Deals,* Wrongful Convictions Blog, Jun 2015, wrongfulconvictionsblog.org
[13] Tim Lynch, *The Devil's Bargain: How Plea Agreements, Never Contemplated by the Framers, Undermine Justice,* Reason, Jul 2011, cato.org
[14] Philip E Johnson, *The Unnecessary Crime of Conspiracy,* California Law Review, Volume 6 Issue 5, Sep1973, scholarship.law.berkeley.edu

[15] The 2018 documentary film *The Sentence* gives a harrowing example of how this can sometimes play out, thesentencedoc.com

[16]"*Girlfriend Problem* " *Harms Women and Children* ALCU, Jun 2005, aclu.org

[17] Tiernyy Sneed, Texas' 6-week abortion ban lets private citizens sue in an unprecedented legal approach, Sep 2021, CNN, cnn.com

[18] Peter Green, *Teacher Anti-CRT Bills Coast To Coast: A State By State Guide*, Feb 2022, forbes.com

[19] *Report of the Sentencing Project to the UN Human Rights Committee Regarding Racial Disparities in the United States Criminal Justice System,* The Sentencing Project, Aug 2013, sentencingproject.org

[20] Mathew Cella & Alan Neuhauser, *Race and Homicide in America, by the Numbers,* US News and World Report, Sep 2016, usnews.com

[21] Radley Balko, *There's overwhelming evidence that the criminal-justice system is racist,* Washington Post, washingtonpost.com

[22] David Arnold et al, *Racial Bias in Bail Decisions,* Quarterly Journal of Economics, Vol 133, Issue 4, Nov 2018, academic.oup.com

[23] *Mental Health by the Numbers*, National Alliance on Mental Illness, nami.org

Proposal 18—Civil Justice

[1] American Tort Reform Association, atra.org

[2] Joanne Doroshow Interview by Ryan Watson, *A voice against tort "reform,"* Trial Magazine, American Association for Justice, May 2017, justice.org

[3]*History of Tort Reform,* US Chamber of Commerce Institute for Legal Reform, institutefor-legalreform.com

[4] GC Christie, *Current Trends in the American Law of Punitive Damages,* Anglo American Law Review, 1991, journals.sagepub.com

[5] John Y. Gotanda, *Punitive Damages: A Comparative Analysis*, Villanova University, 2003, digitalcommons.law.villanova.edu

[6] Victor E Schwartz et al, *Deep Pocket Jurisprudence*, Oklahoma Law Review, Vol. 70, # 2, 2018. digitalcommons.law.ou.edu

Proposal 19—Law Enforcement

[1] *History - Broad Range of Authority*, US Marshals Service, usmarshals.gov

[2] Micheal N Ingrisano, Jr, *The First Officers of the United States Customs Service,* US Customs and Boarder Patrol, cbp.gov

[3] *The Scope and Mission of Federal Law Enforcement*, FederalLawEnforcement.org

[4] *Preparing for a Job in Federal Law Enforcement*, FederalLawEnforcement.org

[5] Tom Jackman, *Study finds police officers arrested 1,100 times per year, or 3 per day, nationwide,* Washington Post, Jun 2016, washingtonpost.com

[6] Jonathan Blanks, *Let's Talk about Respect: Chicago Police Officers Continue to Fail the Communities They Are Sworn to Serve,* Justice Today, Nov 2017, cato.org

[7] Radley Balko, *Rise of the Warrior Cop*, Public Affairs, 2013

[8] Radley Balko, *Shedding light on the use of SWAT team*, Washington Post, Feb 2014, washingtonpost.com

[9] *Wilson v. Arkansas, 514 U.S. 927 (1995)*, supremecourt.gov

[10] Dara Linddara, *Cops do 20,000 no-knock raids a year*, Vox, May 2015, vox.com

[11] Sean Piccoli, *No-Knock Raids Statistics,* Newsmax, Jun 2015, newsmax.com

Proposal 20—Defense

[1] Jim Talent, *A Constitutional Basis for Defense*, Heritage Foundation, Jun 2010, heritage.org

[2] William H. Wrist et al., *The Role of Public Health in the Prevention of War,* American Journal of Public Health, Jun 2014, ajph.aphapublications.org

[3] usgovermentspending.com

[4] Bryan Bender and Jeremy Herb, *War budget might be permanent 'slush fund',* Politico, Mar 2015, politico.com

[5] *Overseas Contingency Operations: The Pentagon Slush Fund*, National Priorities Project, nationalpriorites.org

[6] Leo Shane III, *Price tag of the 'war on terror' will top $6 trillion soon*, Military Times, Nov 2019, militarytimes.com

[7] By Kevin Baron, *Do Americans Really Want to End 'Forever Wars?'*, Defense One Policy, Sep 2019, defenseone.com

[8] Frank Newport, *Americans Remain Divided on Military Spending*, Gallup, Feb 2014, gallup.org

[9] David Mark, *Did Obama buck Congress on Libya?* Politico, Mar 2011, politico.com

[10] Jennifer Bendery, *If Trump Bombs Syria, He'll Be Doing It Without Congress' Authorization*, Huffington Post, Apr 2018, huffingtonpost.com

[11] *What about the National Guard?* endmilitarism.org

[12] Kavan Peterson, *Governors Lose in Power Struggle Over National Guard*, American City and Country, Jan 2007, americancityandcounty.com

[13] Jay Cost, *On War Matters, Where Is Congress?*, National Review, Apr 2018, nationalreview.com

Government and Economy

[1] *Price changes in consumer goods and services in the United States*, Our World In Data, ourworldindadta.org. Based on Bureau of Labor Statistics, bls.gov. Original concept by Mark J Perry, American Enterprise Institute, aei.org

Proposal 21—Taxation

[1] The TAS is part of the IRS, taxpayeradvocate.irs.gov

[2] Thompson-Reuters offers a similar publication, "US Tax Reporter." Both companies offer weekly & daily updates as well as tax database products.

[3] George Skelton, *Sacramento wants to tax soda, tires, guns, water, pain pills, lawyers, car batteries*, LA Times, Apr 2019, latimes.com

[4] Jamie Young, *Really weird and crazy U.S. state taxes and deductions*, CBS News, Mar 2016, cbsnews.com

[5] Janine Perri, *25 Most Ridiculous Taxes of All Time*, Wealth Fit, 2019, wealthfit.com

[6] Samuel Stebbins and Evan Comem, *How much do you need to make to be in the top 1% in every state?* USA Today, Jul 2020, usatoday.com

[7] Kimberly Amadeo, *U.S. Federal Budget Breakdown*, The Balance, Oct 2020, thebalance.com

[8] Roberton C. Williams, *New Estimates of How Many Households Pay No Federal Income Tax*, Oct 2015, taxpolicycenter.org

[9] Julia Kagan and Chris B Murphy, *Double Irish With a Dutch Sandwich*, Investopedia, Apr 2019, investopedia.com

[10] Robert Frank, *In Maryland, Higher Taxes Chase Out Rich*, CNBC, Jul 2012, cnbc.com

[11] Fair Tax, fairtax.org

[12] Flat Tax, hoover.org

[13] Thomas Sowell, *Basic Economics, 5th edition*, esp. Chapter 19, Government Finances.

Proposal 22—Social Security

[1] Bob Greenslade, *Is Social Security Constitutional?*, Tenth Amendment Center, Aug 2010, tenthamendmentcenter.com

[2] findlaw.com

[3] Richard B. McKenzie & Dwight R. Lee, *Security in Old Age—And We Mean Old Age*, Wall Street Journal, Jun 1998, wsj.com

[4] Organizational Structure of the Social Security Administration, Social Security Administration, ssa.gov

Proposal 23—Welfare

[1] *Welfare Opinion: Public Opinion Polls on Welfare and Poverty*, Federal Safety Net, federalsafetynet.com

[2] *Poll: Vast Majority Support Four Simple Fixes to Welfare System*, Heritage Foundation, Dec 2017, heritage.org

[3] Michael D Tanner, *The Poor Want More Opportunity, Not More Entitlement Spending*, Cato Institute, Jun 2019, cato.org

[4] Baruti Libre Kafele, *Welfare by Government Contradicts Welfare*, Foundation for Economic Education, Nov 2016, fee.org

[5] Robert D Lupton, *Toxic Charity*, Harper One, 2012

[6] Robert Rector, *How Welfare Undermines Marriage and What to Do About It*, Heritage Foundation, Nov 2014, heritage.org

[7] Michael D. Tanner and Charles Hughes, *Work versus Welfare Trade-Off: 2013*, Cato Institute, Aug 2013, cato.org

Proposal 24—Money

[1] Joseph Plumber, *Dishonest Money: Financing the Road to Ruin*, BookSurge Publishing, Dec 2009.

[2] Robert Breedlove, *What is Money*, podcast. In particular the first 9 episodes with Micheal Saylor, also available as a book: *What is Money: The Saylor Series*, Jul 2022

[3] WTF Happened in 1971, wtfhappenedin1971.com

[4] Hannah Richie, The price of lithium-ion batteries has declined by 97% since 1991, Our World In Data, Jun 2021, ourworldindata.org.

[5] See commentary on inflation at shadowstats.com

Proposal 25—Government Debt

[1] *FY 2019 and FY 2018 Consolidated Financial Statements of the U.S. Government*, U.S. Government Accountability Office, Feb 2020, gao.gov

[2] *Views of the major problems facing the country*, Pew Research, Dec 2019, pewresearch.org

[3] Joshua Rauh, *Unfunded Pension Debts of U.S. States Still Exceed $3 Trillion*, Forbes Magazine, Aug 2015, forbes.com

[4] Vance Ginn, *You Think the Deficit Is Bad?* Forbes Magazine, Jan 2014, forbes.com

[5] For example: Paul Krugman, *The debt crisis was invented to attack Social Security, Medicare*, Penn Live Jul 2014, pennlive.com

[6] Dave Manuel, *Which Countries Have Most Recently Defaulted on Their Sovereign Debt Obligations?* Feb 2010, davemanuel.com

[7] Daniel Kurt, *Why and When Do Countries Default?* Investopedia, Oct 2014, investopedia.com

[8] Andrea Shalal and David Lawder, Treasury confirms U.S. default as early as June 1 without debt ceiling hike , Reuters, May 2023, reuters.com

[9] Heather Long, *Puerto Rico makes historic default*, CNN Business, Jul 2016, cnn.com

[10] *State and local government debt outstanding in the United States in 2018, by state*, Statista, statista.com

[11] *Inflation Calculator*, Smart Asset, smartasset.com

[12] Antony Davies & James R. Harrigan, *Why Does Government Keep Expanding?* Foundation for Economic Education, Feb 2018, fee.org

[13] Board of Governors of the Federal Reserve System, *What are the Federal Reserve's objectives in conducting monetary policy?* Federal Reserve FAQs, federalreserve.gov

[14] Jeanne Sahady, *Why Trump's budget proposal is too optimistic on deficit*, CNN, February 2018, cnn.com

[15] Jeff Stein & Andrew Van Dam, *U.S. budget deficit breached $3.1 trillion in 2020*, Washington Post, Oct 2020, washingtonpost.com

Proposal 26—Loans and Subsidies

[1] Mike Maharrey, *The Fed's Endless Boom-Bust Cycle*, Mises Institute, Jun 2019, mises.org

[2] Bert Ely, *Savings and Loan Crisis*, Library of Economics and Liberty, econlib.org

[3] Nassim Nicholas Taleb, *Antifragile*, Random House, January 2014

[4] Kimberly Amadeo, What Was the Fannie Mae and Freddie Mac Bailout? Feb 2022, thebalance.com

[5] *Home Ownership Rates*, Trading Economics, tradingeconomics.com

[6] *Countries with the Highest Home Ownership Rates*, World Atlas, worldatlas.com

[7] Bridget Seilick, *How much it costs to sell a house*, Jun 2018, bankrate.com

[8] Jon Marcus, *The $150 million question—what does federal regulation really cost colleges?* Hechinger Report, Jul 2015, hechingerreport.org

[9] Steve Odland, *Tuition Inflation, College Costs Out Of Control*, Forbes Magazine, Mar 2012, forbes.com

[10] Liz Peak, *How Gov't Student Loans Ruined College Education*, Fiscal Times, Jun 2013, thefiscaltimes.com

[11] *Is College Education Worth It?* procon.org

[12] Kimberly Amadeo, *Government Subsidies*, The Balance, Mar 2018, thebalance.com

[13] Niraj Chokshi, *The United States of subsidies*, Washington Post, Mar 2015, washingtonpost.com

[14] Kasia Tarczynska, *Show Us the Local Subsidies*, Good Jobs First, Mar 2017, goodjobsfirst.org

[15] *Tuition Inflation*, FinAid, finaid.org

[16] James A Barham, *The 100 Richest Universities*, The Best Schools, Sep 2019, thebestschools.org

[17] Jessica Dickler, *Will pandemic force your college to go bankrupt*, CNBC, May 2020, cnbc.com

[18] Steve Forbes, *Student loan debt forgiveness would 'make a mockery' of those who already paid*, Fox News, Nov 2020, foxnews.com

Proposal 27—Monopoly

[1] FTC Fact Sheet: Antitrust Laws: A Brief History, ftc.gov

[2] Donald J Boudreaux & Burton W Folsom, *Microsoft and Standard Oil*, The Anti-Trust Bulletin, Fall 1999, cafehayek.com

[3] Ryan Young, Clyde Wayne Crews, *The Case against Antitrust Law*, Competitive Enterprise Institute, Apr 2019, cei.org

[4] Brian Fung, *The FTC was built 100 years ago to fight monopolists*, Washington Post, Sep 2014, washingtonpost.com

[5] *Why Commodity Cartels Break Apart*, Winton Group Longer View, Aug 2019, winton.com

[6] Michael Sheetz, *Technology killing off corporate America*, CNBC News, Aug 2018, cnbc.com

Proposal 28—Intellectual Property

[1] Michele Boldrin & David K. Levine, *Against Intellectual Monopoly*, 2005, dklevine.com

[2] Eric Goldman, *The Problems With Software Patents*, Forbes Magazine, Nov 2012, forbes.com

[3] *Walmart's successful supply chain management*, Trade Gecko, Oct 2018, tradegecko.com

[4] David Russell Schilling, *Knowledge Doubling Every 12 Months*, Industry Tap into News, Apr 2013, industrytap.com

[5] Vivek Wadhwa, *Do patents harm innovation?* World Economic Forum Annual Meeting, Mar 2015, weforum.org

[6] Charles Duan & Daniel Nazer, *Patents are out of control, and they're hurting innovation*, Learn Liberty, Mar 2017, learnliberty.org

[7] *Assessing Factors That Affect Patent Infringement Litigation Could Help Improve Patent Quality*, Government Accountability Office, Aug 2018, gao.gov

[8] Timothy B Lee, *New Zealand just abolished software patents*, Washington Post, Aug 2013, washingtonpost.com

[9] Nick Skillhorn, *How the Current Patent System Actually Hurts Inventors*, Inc. Magazine, Aug 2015, inc.com

[10] Public law 105-298, 112 Stat. 2827, govinfo.gov

[11] *Protect Your Freedom---Fight ``Look and Feel''*, League for Programming Freedom Newsletter, emerson.emory.edu

[12] *Digital Music Sampling* NPR Talk of the Nation, Jan 2011, npr.org

[13] Mike Masnick, *How Years Of Copyright Maximalism Is Now Killing Pop Music*, Tech Dirt, Jan 2020, techdirt.com

[14] Amy X Wang, *How Music Copyright Lawsuits Are Scaring Away New Hits*, Rolling Stone, Jan 2020, rollingstone.com

[15] Mary Boney Denison, *Counterfeits and Cluttering*, Statement to US House Subcommittees, Jun 2019, docs.house.gov
[16] Corynne McSherry, *You Didn't Ask For it*, Electronic Frontier Foundation, May 2013, eff.org
[17] Mary LaFrance, *A Material World: Using Trademark Law to Override Copyright*, MI Telecommunications and Technology Law Review, Vol 21, Issue 1, 2014. *repository.law.umich.edu*

Proposal 29—Healthcare
[1] Scott W Adams, *In Excellent Health,* Hoover Institution Press, 2012
[2] Rahah Kamal et al, *How has U.S. spending on healthcare changed over time?* Health System Tracker, Dec 2020, healthsystemtracker.org
[3] *The Debate Over Mandatory Health Insurance,* Talk of the Nation, NPR, Sep 2009, npr.org
[4] RA Cohen, *Long-term Trends in Health Insurance: Estimates from the National Health Interview Survey, United States, 1968–2017,* Jul 2018, cdc.gov
[5] An example of healthcare done right: *Surgery Center of Oklahoma*, surgerycenterok.com

Proposal 30—Children
[1] Erika Chen, *U.S. Spending on Public Schools in 2019 Highest Since 2008*, May 2021, uscensus.gov
[2] Brian D. Ray, *Homeschool Fast Facts*, National Home Education Research Institute, Jan 2019, nheri.org
[3] Kate Barrington, *What are the Benefits of Public School Over Homeschooling?* Public School Review, Mar 2017, publicschoolreview.com
[4] Charley Lanyon, *Derrick Rose Testifies That the NBA Teaches Players to Get Rid of Their Used Condoms*, New York Magazine, Oct 2016, nymag.com
[5] Jake Rossen, *Fathers Are Right to Fear Family Court,* Fatherly, Jan 2018, fatherly.com

Proposal 31—Immigration
[1] *2015 Yearbook of Immigration Statistics*, Office of Immigration Statistics, Dec 2016, dhs.gov
[2] *Place of birth for the foreign-born population in the United States*, US Census Bureau, 2016, factfinder.census.org
[3] Jens Manuel Krogstad et al, *5 facts about illegal immigration in the U.S.* Pew Research, April 2017, pewresearch.org
[4] Michelangelo Landgrave and Alex Nowrasteh, *Criminal Immigrants*, Cato Institute, Mar 2017, cato.obrg
[5] Steven A. Camarota, *Welfare Use by Legal and Illegal Immigrant Households,* Center for Immigration Studies, Sep 2015, cis.org
[6] Steven A. Camarota, *Heavy Welfare Use by Legal Immigrants,* Center for Immigration Studies, Sep 2015, cis.org
[7] Catharine Paddock, *Native American Ancestors Came from Asia In Three Migrations,* Medical News Today, Jul 2012, medicalnewstoday.com
[8] Bradley Jones, *Majority of Americans continue to say immigrants strengthen the U.S.*, Pew Research Fact Tank, Jan 2019, pewresearch.org
[9] Benjamin Powell, *The Law of Unintended Consequences*, Forbes Magazine, May 2012. forbes.com.
[10] Ruth Simon, *Summer Is Here. Where Are All the Workers?* Wall Street Journal, May 2018, wsj.com
[11] Jennifer Hunt, *The Impact of Immigration on the Educational Attainment of Natives*, National Bureau of Economic Research, Working Paper No. 18047, May 2012, nber.org
[12] Stuart Anderson, *55% Of America's Billion-Dollar Startups Have an Immigrant Founder*, Forbes Magazine, Oct 2018, forbes.com
[13] Arnobio Morelix et al, *2017 Index Kauffman Index of Startup Activity*, Ewing Marion Kauffman Foundation, indicators.kauffman.org
[14] Charles Hirschman, *The Contributions of Immigrants to American Culture*, US National Library of Medicine, Summer 2013, ncbi.nlm.nih.gov

[15] *End Chain Migration*, Numbers USA, numbersusa.com
[16] Alexia Fernández Campbell, *America's Real Refugee Problem*, The Atlantic, Oct 2015, theatlantic.com
[17] Philip Oltermann, *Sanctuary or ghetto?* The Guardian, Apr 2016, theguardian.com
[18] Jie Zong and Jeanne Batalova, *Refugees and Asylees in the United States*, Migration Policy Institute, Jun 2017, migrationpolicy.org
[19] Douglas Todd, *Canada vs U.S. on immigration*, Vancouver Sun, Jun 2019, vancouversun.com

Proposal 32—Misuse of Force

[1] Glenn Garvin, *He's a Marine, a renegade, a vanquisher of corrupt pols.* Miami Herald, Jan 2018, miamiherald.com
[2] Alan Greenblat, *Congratulations, New York, You're #1 in Corruption*, Politico Magazine, May 2015, politico.com
[3] Jon Campbell, *New York corruption scandals: Here's who has been convicted in 2018*, Democrat and Chronical, Jul 2018, democratandchronicle.com
[4] Doug McKelway, *IRS releases list of groups targeted in scandal*, Fox News, Jun 2016, foxnews.com
[5] Gail Russell Chaddock, *Playing the IRS card,*, Christian Science Monitor, May 2013, csmonitor.com
[6] Nat Berman, *The 10 Largest Antitrust Fines in History*, Money Inc, 2016, moneyinc.com
[7] Robert O'Harrow Jr, Steven Rich and Shelly Tan, *Asset seizures fuel police spending*, Washington Post, October 2014, washingtonpost.com
[8] C.J. Ciaramella, *Chicago Is Trying to Pay Down Its Debt by Impounding Innocent People's Cars*, Reason, Apr 2018, reason.com

Proposal 33—Open Government

[1] *Information Security Oversight Office's (ISOO) Report for Fiscal Year 2017*, National Archives and Records Administration, June 2017, archives.gov
[2] *Information Security Oversight Office's (ISOO) Report for Fiscal Year 2011*, National Archives and Records Administration, May 2012, archives.gov
[3] *Return on Investment Calculator*, calculator.net
[4] James Gibney, *The U.S. Has Way Too Many Secrets*, Bloomberg Opinion, Dec 2017, bloomberg.com
[5] *Examining the Costs of Overclassification on Transparency and Security*, Hearing of Committee on Oversight and Government Reform, Dec 2016, house.gov
[6] Eric Lichtblau, *In Secret, Court Vastly Broadens Powers of N.S.A.*, New York Times, Jul 2013, nytimes.com
[7] Glenn Greenwald, *NSA collecting phone records of millions of Verizon customers daily*, The Guardian, Dec 2015, theguardian.com
[8] Holly Yan, *What is the FISA court, and why is it so secretive?* CNN, Mar 2017, cnn.com

Proposal 34—Whistleblowers

[1] *Edward Snowden Fast Facts*, CNN Library, cnn.com
[2] Shanna & Tom Devine et al, *Whistleblower Witch Hunts: The Smokescreen Syndrome*, Government Accountability Project, 2010, whistleblower.org
[3] Mieke Eoyang, *Protect Intelligence Whistleblowers*, Democracy Journal, 2016, democracyjournal.org
[4] *Whistleblower Statutes Desk Aid*, Occupational Safety and Health Administration, 2017, whistleblowers.gov

Proposal 35—Term Limits

[1] US Term Limits, termlimits.com
[2] *State legislatures with term limits*, Ballot Pedia, ballotpedia.org
[3] *Cities 101—Major's Term*, Oct 2016, National League of Cities, nlc.org
[4] Stacey Selleck, *Chicago Mayoral Candidates Propose Term Limits on Mayor as Part of Ethics Package*, US Term Limits, Jan 2019, termlimits.com

[5] The British TV shows *Yes, Minister* and *Yes, Prime Minister* are comedic takes on a serious problem.

Proposal 36—Government Employment
[1] Chris Edwards, *Federal Government Pay Exceeds Most Industries,* Cato Institute, Oct 2015, cato.org
[2] Chris Edwars, *Federal Pay Outpaces Private-Sector Pay,* Cato Institute, May 2006, cato.org
[3] Veterans' Preference, fedshirevets.gov

Proposal 37—Campaign Finance
[1] Nicolas Cofessore & Megan Thee-Brenanjune, *Poll Shows Americans Favor an Overhaul of Campaign Financing,* New York Times, Jun 2015, nytimes.com
[2] *Learning Center*, opensecrets.org.
[3] Kate Pickert, *Campaign Financing: A Brief History,* Time Magazine, Jun 2008, time.com
[4] Citizens United v. Federal Election Commission, 558 U.S. 310 (2010)
[5] Tyler Cowen, *Why is there so little money in politics?* Marginal Revolution, Feb 2012, marginalrevolution.com

Proposal 38—Interaction Between Governments
[1] Scott Gaylord, *States Need More Control Over the Federal Government,* New York Times, July 2013, nytimes.com
[2] For example: Lise Bang-Jensen, *Balance of Power Between New York State and Local Governments has Shifted,* New York State Bar Association, Apr 2016, nysba.org
[3] Andrew Dugan, *U.S. Satisfaction With the Government Remains Low*, Gallup Polls, Feb 2018, gallup.org

Proposal 39—Rent Seeking
[1] David R. Henderson, *Rent Seeking,* The Concise Encyclopedia of Economics, Library of Economics and Liberty, econlib.org

Chapter 7—A Call for Action
[1] *Voter Turnout In the United States*, Fair Vote Organization, fairvote.org
[2] *From Energy To Transport To Healthcare, Here Are 8 Industries Being Disrupted By Elon Musk And His Companies,* CB Insights, cbinsights.com
[3] Mary Fernandez, *Tara Gentile, Sophia Amoruso and More Women Entrepreneurs Share How They Got Started,* 2018, creativelive.com

Appendix 1—Lies, Dam Lies and Statistics
[1] *Coefficient of Determination*, wikipedia.org
[2] The difficulties of measuring inflation are discussed at measuringworth.com
[3] You can estimate inflation rates at usinflationcalculator.com

Appendix 3—Coronavirus
[1] PANDA (pandemic data), panda.org
[2] Madalina Gabriela Barbu1, et al. *The Impact of SARS-CoV-2 on the Most Common Comorbidities*, Frontiers in Medicine, Sep 2020, frontiersin.org
[3] Douglas Ernst, *Tulsi Gabbard rips 'slap in the face' COVID-19 relief bill,* Washington Times, Dec 2020, washingtontimes.com

About The Author

Roo Davison was born in his grandmother's house in the suburbs of London, England in 1961 and raised on small farms near Guildford, southwest of London.

For as long as he can remember, Roo has been curious about systems and problem-solving. Early days found him wading in the stream in his red Wellington boots, building dams, and discovering the forces at play in his endeavors. When his parents' marriage broke down and his mother took charge of the farm, it fell to Roo to figure out how to fix the tractor and other machinery.

This interest in "how things work" was later translated into a degree in engineering from the University of Leicester, followed by a master's degree in computer science from Imperial College, University of London.

After university, Roo lived in London, working as a computer programmer, primarily focused on creating management information systems for British Telecom. Over time he also developed an interest in management training and spent a lot of time in personal development courses. This path eventually took him to America to study with Dr. Richard Moss, a teacher of Radical Aliveness.

Whilst studying with Dr. Moss, Roo met his wife-to-be, Ellie. They trans-Atlantic dated for a couple of years, and then in 1998, Roo navigated the immigration system to move to Atlanta. GA. In 2005 he became a citizen of the United States.

In 2010, Roo and Ellie moved to Frankfort, MI, a small town on the shores of Lake Michigan. For the first three years of their time in Frankfort, they lived in a very small apartment on Main Street while Roo devoted himself to renovating their 1895 Victorian house—a total down-to-the-studs renovation, so that (behind the Victorian trim) it now has all modern systems.

Today, Roo partners with his wife Ellie in their art business which they run out of their home. He plays guitar, practices Brazilian Jiu Jitsu, writes poetry, and kayaks year-round—rain, shine, or snow!

Roo is available for talks and interviews.

Email: inquiries@RooDavison.com.

Or via his website www.RooDavison.com

If You Found This Book Valuable

Please recommend it to family, friends, or anyone else who might gain something from reading it. Suggest it to your book club, or discuss it in online forums.

If you bought the book on Amazon, please leave a review. Amazon has become (by far) the biggest market for books on the planet. Reviews help to make the book visible to Amazon buyers. The more people who read the book, the more the ideas in it can circulate, and the greater the chance we have of getting some real changes made.

If you bought elsewhere, please leave feedback there. All feedback (positive or negative) is much appreciated.

Thank you!

www.ingramcontent.com/pod-product-compliance
Lightning Source LLC
Chambersburg PA
CBHW060834280326

41934CB00007B/782